Christianity in Oceania

Editorial Team

Editors
Kenneth R. Ross
Katalina Tahaafe-Williams
Todd M. Johnson

Associate Editor
Albert W. Hickman

Managing Editor
Nadia Andrilenas

Editorial Advisory Board
Tamsyn Kereopa
Nāsili Vaka'uta
Jenny Te Paa Daniel
Rusiate Tuidrakulu
Aisake Casimira
Graham Joseph Hill
Upolu Lumā Vaai

Demographic Profile
Editor: Gina A. Zurlo
Data Analyst: Peter F. Crossing
Layout and Design: Justin Long
Cartography: Bryan Nicholson

EDINBURGH COMPANIONS TO GLOBAL CHRISTIANITY

Christianity in Oceania

Edited by

Kenneth R. Ross, Katalina Tahaafe-Williams and Todd M. Johnson

EDINBURGH
University Press

Edinburgh University Press is one of the leading university presses in the UK. We publish academic books and journals in our selected subject areas across the humanities and social sciences, combining cutting-edge scholarship with high editorial and production values to produce academic works of lasting importance. For more information visit our website: edinburghuniversitypress.com

Edinburgh University Press Ltd
The Tun – Holyrood Road
12 (2f) Jackson's Entry
Edinburgh EH8 8PJ

Typeset in Palatino and Myriad
by R. J. Footring Ltd, Derby, UK, and
printed and bound in Poland by Hussar Books

A CIP record for this book is available from the British Library

ISBN 978 1 4744 8007 9 (hardback)
ISBN 978 1 4744 8010 9 (webready PDF)
ISBN 978 1 4744 8009 3 (epub)

Contents

Series Preface

While a number of compendia have recently been produced on the study of worldwide Christianity, the distinctive quality of this series arises from its examination of global Christianity through a combination of reliable demographic information and original interpretative essays by Indigenous scholars and practitioners. This approach was successfully pioneered by the *Atlas of Global Christianity 1910–2010*, published by Edinburgh University Press on the occasion of the centenary of the epoch-making Edinburgh 1910 World Missionary Conference.

Using the same methodology, the Edinburgh Companions to Global Christianity take the analysis to a deeper level of detail and explore the context of the twenty-first century. The series considers the presence of Christianity on a continent-by-continent basis worldwide. Covering every country in the world, it maps patterns of growth and/or decline and examines current trends. The aim of the series is to comprehensively map worldwide Christianity and to describe it in its entirety. Country-specific studies are offered, all the major Christian traditions are analysed and current regional and continental trends are examined.

Each volume is devoted to a continent or sub-continent, following the United Nations classifications. Through a combination of maps, tables, charts and graphs, each of the successive volumes presents a comprehensive demographic analysis of Christianity in the relevant area. Commentary and interpretation are provided by essays on key topics, each written by an expert in the field, normally an Indigenous scholar. By the use of these various tools each volume provides an accurate, objective and incisive analysis of the presence of Christian faith in the relevant area.

The volumes (published and projected) in the series are:

1. Christianity in Sub-Saharan Africa (published 2017)
2. Christianity in North Africa and West Asia (published 2018)
3. Christianity in South and Central Asia (published 2019)
4. Christianity in East and Southeast Asia (published 2020)
5. Christianity in Oceania
6. Christianity in Latin America and the Caribbean
7. Christianity in North America
8. Christianity in Western and Northern Europe

9. Christianity in Eastern and Southern Europe
10. Compact Atlas of Global Christianity

As series editors, we rely heavily on the regional expertise of the dedicated third editor who joins us for each volume. Furthermore, each volume has its own editorial advisory board, made up of senior scholars with authoritative knowledge of the field in question. We work together to define the essay topics for the volume, arrange for compilation of the required demographic data, recruit the authors of the essays and edit their work. Statistical and demographic information is drawn from the highly regarded *World Christian Database* maintained by the Center for the Study of Global Christianity at Gordon-Conwell Theological Seminary (South Hamilton, MA, USA) and published by Brill. For each volume, at team of 35–40 authors is recruited to write the essays, and it is ultimately upon their scholarship and commitment that we depend in order to create an original and authoritative work of reference.

Each volume in the series will be, we hope, a significant book in its own right and a contribution to the study of Christianity in the region in question. At the same time, each is a constituent part of a greater whole – the 10-volume series, which aims to provide a comprehensive analysis of global Christianity that will be groundbreaking in its demographic quality and analytical range. Our hope is that the Companions will be of service to anyone seeking a fuller understanding of the worldwide presence of the Christian faith.

Kenneth R. Ross and Todd M. Johnson
Series Editors

Volume Preface

The geography of Oceania, dominated by the vast expanse of the Pacific, is very different from that of any other region in the world. Apart from Australia, New Zealand and Papua New Guinea, the nations are made up of small islands separated by long distances. Nevertheless, there is a shared culture among Pacific Island communities that sets them apart from the larger and more Westernised countries of Australia and New Zealand. In many respects, the region presents a study in contrasts. This applies also to the internal dynamics of Australia and New Zealand as they accommodate the very different perspectives of their 'first peoples' and 'second peoples'. Though the total population of the entire region is less than that of a single large country elsewhere, the variety of geography and history that shapes their experience ensures that there is much that invites analysis.

The diversity extends to the forms of Christianity that have found expression in the region. The character of Christianity in many of the islands is marked by the particular missionary tradition to which it owes its origins. Inward migration has added further variety, particularly in Australia and New Zealand. Meanwhile, Pentecostal and Charismatic movements, often spawned within the region, are transforming the Christian landscape today. This is a volume therefore that takes account of the distinctive characteristics of very different contexts, communities and churches while at the same time being sensitive to a certain commonality that makes it possible to consider Oceania as a whole.

Differences come to the fore when considering issues of faith and culture. With their orientation to the Western world, Australia and New Zealand have been heavily affected by secularising trends, with all the questions that these raise for church and faith. By contrast, the prevailing culture of the Pacific Islands is one in which all of life is understood within a religious framework. A sharp question in the context of the Islands is whether missionary Christianity was too narrowly defined to accommodate the all-embracing spirituality that defines the heritage of many Pacific communities. While the different contexts might seem to be worlds apart, the 'first peoples' of Australia and New Zealand are now bringing their moral and spiritual vision to challenge the direction being taken by the 'second peoples'. This discussion is further enriched by migrants who have come from the Pacific Islands and from a variety of Asian contexts to make their home in New Zealand or Australia. Very different outlooks, including contrasting perspectives on what faith is all about, add to the fascination of this volume.

Equally, there are experiences and concerns that are held in common throughout the vast region. Few are untouched by the experience of migration. People have been on the move across the Pacific from time immemorial. For many of the smaller islands, in recent times outward migration has been a major feature as economic opportunity has drawn many of their people to Australia, New Zealand or even beyond. In some cases, only a minority of the population remains on the island and there are questions about future viability. In New Zealand and Australia, meanwhile, where the large majority of the population are descended from immigrants, recent waves of immigration are creating a much more plural and diverse society. The situation is far from static and faith identity is often a defining feature of the migrant experience, which forms a recurrent theme in this book.

Despite the geographical isolation that is common to much of the region, the experience of globalisation is a major factor shaping personal, communal, national and ecclesial life. While this offers opportunities, it also applies pressures in a variety of ways that call for exploration as they impact the expression of Christianity in the region. A related issue is climate change, which raises particularly acute concerns in Oceania. Most of the countries of the region have played a minimal role in the industrial activity that causes climate change, yet they are among those most immediately exposed to its effects. With their geography making them vulnerable to rising sea levels and an increased incidence of tropical storms, the islands of Oceania are united by a common threat. The question of what this means for Christian witness is another thread that runs through the book.

In pursuit of understanding, the volume offers four angles of analysis. The first is demographic, using the methodology of the highly successful *Atlas of Global Christianity* (Edinburgh University Press, 2009) to present reliable statistical information in an attractive, user-friendly format. Maps and charts depict the status of Christianity regionally and in terms of the principal church traditions. In this region almost all countries have been majority Christian since the nineteenth century, but inward migration has brought increasing religious diversity and, particularly in Australia and New Zealand, growing numbers profess a secular worldview. At the same time, new movements of Christian faith are changing the religious landscape. These trends are tracked in the demographic analysis.

The second angle of analysis is at the country level. Account is taken of the presence and influence of Christianity in each of the 23 countries of Oceania. Scholars who are either indigenous or have long experience of the region have contributed interpretative essays that offer a 'critical insider' perspective on the way in which Christianity is finding expression in their context. Larger countries are the subject of a dedicated essay, while some of the smaller island nations have been grouped together according to geographical proximity and affinity.

Thirdly, Christianity in Oceania is considered in terms of its principal ecclesial forms or traditions. Five types of church are considered: Orthodox, Catholic, Protestant, Independent and Anglican. In addition, the Evangelical and Pentecostal/Charismatic movements, which cut across ecclesial affiliation, are examined. In each case, an author who is identified with the tradition in question again brings a 'critical insider' perspective to the analysis. A special feature of this volume is that it also includes an essay on the Pacific Conference of Churches, recognising the ecumenical expression of church life in the Pacific Islands.

Fourthly, selected themes are considered. Eight of these run right through the entire Edinburgh Companions series: faith and culture, worship and spirituality, theology, social and political context, mission and evangelism, gender, religious freedom, and inter-religious relations. A further three have been selected by the editorial board specifically for this volume on account of their salience in the context of Oceania: integrity of creation, Indigenous spirituality, and migration and diaspora. Each of these themes is examined on a region-wide basis, deepening our understanding of features that are definitive for Christianity in this part of the world. We are indebted to Michael Hahn, graduate student at Gordon-Conwell Theological Seminary, for his editorial assistance in the preparation of these essays.

As is evident from the short bibliography offered at the end of each essay, this book rests on the body of scholarship that has illumined our understanding of Christianity in Oceania. While many fine books have been written about particular aspects of Christianity in the Pacific context, rather few attempt to comprehend the whole. Ian Breward's *A History of the Churches of Australasia* (Oxford: Oxford University Press, 2001) is a valuable reference work but with no coverage of the twenty-first century on which the present book is focused. Another major study is Manfred Ernst's *Globalization and the Re-shaping of Christianity in the Pacific* (Suva: Pacific Islands Theological College, 2006), which offers a valuable perspective but lacks the comprehensive coverage that is offered in this volume. John Garrett's three volumes – *To Live Among the Stars, Footsteps in the Sea* and *Where Nets Were Cast* (Geneva: WCC; and Suva: University of South Pacific, 1982, 1992, 1997) – remain classic works but have now become dated, whereas the present book concentrates on current issues.

While resting on the preceding scholarship, this volume breaks new ground through its reliable demographic analysis, its contemporary focus, the Indigenous authorship of its essays and the originality of the analyses. The essay authors employ a variety of disciplinary approaches – historical, theological, sociological, missiological, anthropological – as appropriate to their topics. Taken together, the volume offers a deeply textured and highly nuanced account of Christianity in Oceania, one that will reward the attention of any who wish to deepen their knowledge of this subject.

Kenneth R. Ross
Katalina Tahaafe-Williams
Todd M. Johnson

August 2020

Contributors

Faafetai Aiavā is an ordained pastor of the Congregational Christian Church in Sāmoa, currently serving as Head of the Department for Theology and Ethics at the Pacific Theological College, Fiji. He teaches across the fields of theological hermeneutics and contextual theology, with a special focus on ecology, the Trinity, and gospel and culture.
Mission and Evangelism

Tau'alofa Anga'aelangi was raised in the Free Wesleyan Church of Tonga and ordained as a deacon in the Uniting Church in Australia. She is currently a tertiary chaplain with Charles Sturt University. Her interests are in contextual theology, Christianity in Oceania and postcolonial Bible translations.
Worship and Spirituality

Cliff Bird is an ordained minister in the United Church in the Solomon Islands and a renowned Pacific theologian. He spent many years serving in ecumenical institutions and organisations in Oceania and beyond. He is volunteer Advisor to the United Church in the Solomon Islands and founder and principal consultant/researcher of YUMI Go Globol Consultants.
Integrity of Creation

Aisake Casimira is originally from Hau, No'atau, Rotuma, in the Republic of Fiji, and is the current Director of the Institute for Mission and Research, based at the Pacific Theological College, in Suva, Fiji, where he and his family reside.
Social and Political Context

Nathalie Cawidrone is the holder of a research master's in theology from the Faculty of Protestant Theology of Montpellier and is Professor of Church History at the Center for Pastoral and Theological Training of the Protestant Church of Kanaky New Caledonia, Bethany.
New Caledonia, Wallis and Futuna Islands

Doru Costache is Senior Lecturer in Patristic Studies at St Cyril's Coptic Orthodox Theological College and a faculty member of Sydney College of Divinity's Graduate Research School. A Romanian Orthodox protopresbyter, he is the founding Director of the Australian Institute for Orthodox Christian

Studies and a co-author of *Dreams, Virtue and Divine Knowledge in Early Christian Egypt* (Cambridge University Press, 2019).
Orthodox

Richard A. Davis received his PhD from the University of Edinburgh in political theology. Originally from Aotearoa New Zealand, he is Senior Lecturer in Theology and Ethics at the Pacific Theological College in the Fiji Islands.
French Polynesia

Andrew Dutney is Professor of Theology at Flinders University, Principal of the Uniting College for Leadership and Theology, and past President of the Uniting Church in Australia. He was born on Bidjara country and lives on Kuarna land.
Australia

Rocío Figueroa is a Peruvian theologian, Lecturer in Systematic Theology at Catholic Theological College in Auckland, New Zealand, and External Researcher at the Centre for Theology and Public Issues at Otago University. Her research has focused on theological and pastoral responses for survivors of church-related sexual abuse. Her current interests are the relationship between faith and culture and a theological response to a secular society.
Catholics

Teatu Fusi is Elder Church Minister for the Tuvalu Church Overseas Mission in New Zealand. He graduated from Malua Theological College, Sāmoa, in 1990, was ordained as a Tuvalu church minister in 1991 and received his bachelor of divinity in 2005. He has served with the Tuvalu Church in Nauru Island and in Wellington.
Tuvalu and Tokelau

Philip Gibbs is a Divine Word missionary serving as Deputy President of Divine Word University in Papua New Guinea. He holds a doctorate in theology from the Gregorian University, Rome, and has published numerous articles on socio-cultural issues in Papua New Guinea and other parts of the Pacific region.
Catholics

Francis X. Hezel, a Jesuit priest, is pastoral vicar of a parish on Guam. Formerly the Director of Micronesian Seminar, he is the author of several historical works on Micronesia.
Guam, Micronesia (Federated States of), Marshall Islands, Northern Mariana Islands, Palau

Graham Joseph Hill is interim Principal and Director of Research of Stirling Theological College, the University of Divinity in Melbourne. An ordained Baptist pastor, he is the author of 10 books and writes on missions, theology and world Christianity at www.grahamjosephhill.com.
Protestants

Kevin Hovey is an ordained minister of the Australian Christian Churches. After 31 years as Assemblies of God missionaries in Papua New Guinea he and his wife have more recently served in missions leadership or training roles. He is currently Senior Lecturer and Head of the Department of Pastoral and Cross Cultural Ministry at Alphacrucis College in Sydney, Australia.
Pentecostals/Charismatics

Darrell Jackson is Director of Research at Whitley College, University of Divinity, Melbourne. An ordained British Baptist pastor and missiologist, he now lives with his US-born wife and their two children in New South Wales, Australia.
Theology

Todd M. Johnson is the Eva B. and Paul E. Toms Distinguished Professor of Mission and Global Christianity and Co-Director of the Center for the Study of Global Christianity at Gordon-Conwell Theological Seminary in South Hamilton, Massachusetts, USA. His most recent book is the *World Christian Encyclopedia*, 3rd edition (Edinburgh University Press, 2019). He also serves as a Series Editor for the Edinburgh Companions to Global Christianity (Edinburgh University Press).
Methodology and Sources of Christian and Religious Affiliation

Cruz Karauti-Fox is a priest of the Anglican Church in Aotearoa New Zealand, and Polynesia. A young man of Māori, Cook Island, Tahitian and European decent, Fr Cruz currently serves as the Missioner of Waikato for Te Hui Amorangi o Te Manawa o Te Wheke, an Indigenous diocese of the province.
Indigenous Spirituality

Victoria Kavafolau is Lecturer in Theology and Ethics, Sia'atoutai Theological College, Tonga. She is Representative for the Free Wesleyan Church of Tonga on Gender Equality.
Gender

Elizabeth Krishna is a lay consecrated virgin in the Catholic Church. She graduated in Women's Peacebuilding and Leadership at Eastern Mennonite University, Virginia, USA, and engages in inter-religious and inter-ethnic peace-building and reconciliation work.
Inter-religious Relations

Stuart Lange is Senior Research Fellow (and former Vice Principal) of Laidlaw College and the author of *A Rising Tide: Evangelical Christianity in New Zealand, 1930–65* (Otago University Press, 2013).
Evangelicals

Brian Macdonald-Milne is an Anglican priest who worked for many years for the Anglican Church of Melanesia in the western Pacific, for the Solomon Islands Christian Association and for the Pacific Conference of Churches. He is now Honorary Archivist of the Melanesian Mission UK. He is author of the forthcoming *Seeking Peace in the Pacific: The Story of Conflict and Christianity in the Central Solomon Islands*.
Solomon Islands

Tessa Mackenzie has lived in Fiji since January 1961. She is a lay minister in the Anglican Church and has been a member of Interfaith Search since 1988.
Inter-religious Relations

Nga Mataio is Secretary General of the Cook Islands Christian Church (CICC), a post he has held since 2005. He is a retired senior public servant and editor of the quarterly *Cook Islands Christian Church Newsletter* and several CICC publications, including the Prayer Book, Manual (English and Māori), Karere and Pure Epetoma.
Cook Islands and Niue

Feleterika Nokise is minister of Pacific Islanders Presbyterian Church in Wellington, New Zealand. From 2002 to 2018 he was Principal of the Pacific Theological College in Suva, Fiji, where he also served as Professor of Ecumenism.
Pacific Conference of Churches

Marc Pohue is a PhD student in theology at the Pacific Theological College, Suva, Fiji. He is an Indigenous Māòhi Nui and an ordained minister of the Māòhi Protestant Church.
French Polynesia

Randall Prior is an associate teacher/researcher with Pilgrim Theological College in the University of Divinity in Melbourne, Australia. His involvement in Vanuatu spans more than 30 years. He is one of the founders of the Vanuatu Gospel and Culture Movement.
Vanuatu

Brenda Reed is a member of the Aiga Urban Ministry of All Saints Anglican Church, Sāmoa. She is an ordained non-stipendiary priest and has served in the Diocese of Polynesia as Coordinator for the Moana Children's Ministry and Chaplain of All Saints Anglican School, Apia.
Anglicans

Tanya Riches is a Senior Lecturer at Hillsong College, Sydney. She is the author of *Worship and Social Engagement in Urban Aboriginal-Led Australian Pentecostal Congregations: (Re)imaging Identity in the Spirit* (Brill, 2019) and is on the editorial board of the journal *Pneuma*.
Worship and Spirituality

Kenneth R. Ross is Professor of Theology at Zomba Theological College, Malawi, and Associate Minister of Bemvu Parish, Church of Central Africa Presbyterian. His most recent book, co-edited with Wapulumuka O. Mulwafu, is *Politics, Christianity and Society in Malawi* (Mzuni Press, 2020). He serves as a series editor for the Edinburgh Companions to Global Christianity (Edinburgh University Press).
Independents

Jacqueline Ryle is a social anthropologist who has researched the relations between Christianity, tradition and politics in Fiji and Oceania since the early 1990s, conducting extensive fieldwork in rural and urban contexts in different denominations; and on inter-faith dialogue. She is Senior Lecturer in Sociology at the University of the South Pacific with a research focus that includes ritual, prayer, religion, environment and climate change, and religion and gender-based violence.
Religious Freedom

Soama Tafia is a retired ordained minister of the Kiribati Uniting Church. He was Lecturer in Theology and Biblical Studies 1983–90 and Dean of Studies and Lecturer in History 2015–18 at Tangintebu Theological College. He also served the Pacific Conference of Churches 1997–8 and 1999–2005 and was Programme Secretary of Tuvalu Church 2007–15.
Kiribati and Nauru

Solo Tafokitau is Minister of the Word of Penieli Uniting Church, Sydney, Australia.
Tonga

Katalina Tahaafe-Williams is an Oceanian theologian educated in Australia and the United Kingdom. She has had extensive involvement in the world church and ecumenical movement and has strong interests in theological education, worship and liturgy, mission and discipleship, and social responsibility and justice.
Christianity in Oceania; The Future of Christianity in Oceania

Fetaomi Tapu-Qiliho is Academic Director, Sāmoa programme of the School for International Training (SIT), and a layperson of the Anglican Church of the Diocese of Polynesia in the Parish of All Saints, Apia, Sāmoa.
Sāmoa and American Sāmoa

Geoffrey Troughton is Senior Lecturer in Religious Studies at Victoria University of Wellington and author of *New Zealand Jesus: Social and Religious Transformations of an Image, 1890–1940* (Peter Lang, 2011). His work on Christianity in New Zealand includes two edited volumes: *Saints and Stirrers: Christianity, Conflict and Peacemaking in New Zealand, 1814–1945* (Victoria University Press, 2017) and (with Philip Fountain) *Pursuing Peace in Godzone: Christianity and the Peace Tradition in New Zealand* (Victoria University Press, 2018).
New Zealand

Rusiate Tuidrakulu is General Secretary of the South Pacific Association of Theological Schools, based in Suva, Fiji Islands. He is an ordained minister of the Methodist Church in Fiji and a contributor and board member of the *Pacific Journal of Theology*.
Fiji

Jack Urame is Head Bishop of the Evangelical Lutheran Church of Papua New Guinea. An ordained pastor, he has researched and published on various social and theological issues in Papua New Guinea and Melanesia.
Papua New Guinea

Upolu Lumā Vaai is Professor of Theology and Ethics and Principal of the Pacific Theological College in Fiji. He is an ordained minister of the Methodist Church in Sāmoa and lead editor of *Relational Hermeneutics: Decolonising the Mindset and the Pacific Itulagi* and of *The Relational Self: Decolonising Personhood in the Pacific* (USP & PTC, 2017).
Faith and Culture

Nāsili Vaka'uta is Principal and Ranston Lecturer in Biblical Studies, Trinity Methodist Theological College, Auckland, New Zealand. He is the author of *Reading Ezra 9–10 Tu'a-wise: Rethinking Biblical Interpretation in Oceania* (SBL, 2011), editor of *Talanoa Rhythms: Voices from Oceania* (Massey University, 2011) and co-editor of *Bible and Art, Perspectives from Oceania* (Bloomsbury, 2017). He has also published many journal articles and book chapters.
Theology

Andrew Williams is a minister of the Uniting Church in Australia. As well as serving local congregations he was for eight years the Executive Secretary for Personnel and Training in the Council for World Mission and for six years the General Secretary of the New South Wales/ACT Synod of the Uniting Church in Australia.
Migration and Diaspora

Gina A. Zurlo is Co-director of the Center for the Study of Global Christianity at Gordon-Conwell Theological Seminary (South Hamilton, Massachusetts, USA). She is co-author of the *World Christian Encyclopedia*, 3rd edition (Edinburgh University Press, 2019) and co-editor of the *World Christian Database* (Brill).

A Demographic Profile of Christianity in Oceania; Methodology and Sources of Christian and Religious Affiliation

Introduction

A Demographic Profile of Christianity in Oceania

Gina A. Zurlo

Majority Religion by Province, 2020

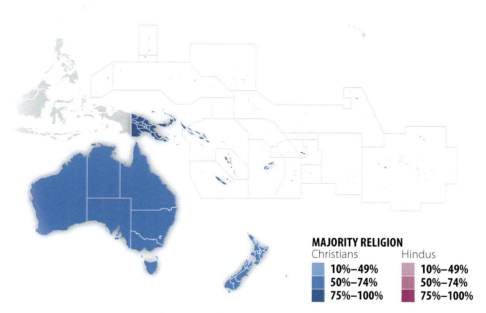

MAJORITY RELIGION

Christians		Hindus	
10%–49%		10%–49%	
50%–74%		50%–74%	
75%–100%		75%–100%	

Oceania is a unique region, home to three large countries (Australia, New Zealand and Papua New Guinea) plus many small island nations. The region was 77% Christian in 1900, dropping to 65% by 2020. Other religions have increased in the same period, mainly the result of Asian immigration to Australia. Buddhists, Muslims and Hindus in Oceania now number at least 800,000 each.

Religions in Oceania, 1970 and 2020

Religion	1970		2020	
	Adherents	%	Adherents	%
Christians	18,250,000	92.6	27,606,000	65.1
Agnostics	658,000	3.3	8,826,000	20.8
Atheists	215,000	1.1	1,895,000	4.5
Buddhists	16,600	0.1	1,016,000	2.4
Muslims	70,900	0.4	917,000	2.2
Hindus	218,000	1.1	826,000	1.9
Other	289,650	1.5	1,298,100	3.1
Total	19,718,000	100.0	42,384,000	100.0

Source: Todd M. Johnson and Gina A. Zurlo (eds), *World Christian Database* (Leiden/Boston: Brill), accessed January 2020. Figures do not add to 100% due to rounding.

Christianity in Oceania, 1970–2020

Christians by Country, 2020
28 Million Christians, 65.1% of Population

% Christian	
—	3%
—	10%
—	50%
—	75%

The proportion of Christians in Oceania changed dramatically over the twentieth century, dropping from 93% in 1970 to 65% in 2020. This overall trend, however, masks significant changes within its regions. Melanesia experienced a profound transformation: in 1900 the region was only 15% Christian, whereas in 2020 it was over 92% Christian. In particular, Papua New Guinea has seen tremendous change over the century, moving from majority traditional religions to Christianity (now 95% Christian, though many tend to combine traditional Indigenous beliefs with Christian faith). Micronesia also has seen an increase in Christian adherence since 1900, from 76% to 93%. Australia/New Zealand has fallen from almost 97% Christian to 54% Christian. The region was divided between the United States, France, Germany (until the First World War) and the British Empire during the twentieth century, all majority-Christian nations whose religious practices left an impact on the developing region.

Christians by country, 2020

Country	% Christian
American Sāmoa	99.0
Australia	54.1
Cook Islands	96.1
Fiji	64.6
French Polynesia	93.7
Guam	93.6
Kiribati	96.9
Marshall Islands	94.1
Micronesia (Federated States of)	94.5
Nauru	74.2
New Caledonia	84.8
New Zealand	54.2
Niue	96.6
Northern Mariana Islands	77.9
Palau	91.6
Papua New Guinea	95.2
Sāmoa	98.8
Solomon Islands	95.0
Tokelau	94.5
Tonga	95.7
Tuvalu	94.8
Vanuatu	93.5
Wallis and Futuna Islands	97.0

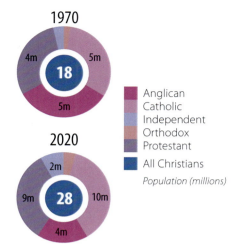

1970

2020

Anglican
Catholic
Independent
Orthodox
Protestant

All Christians

Population (millions)

Major Christian traditions, 1970 and 2020
Christianity in Oceania has increased in diversity over the last 50 years with the growth of Independent traditions, such as the Church of Jesus Christ of Latter-day Saints. Catholics doubled in size by 2020 and are followed in size by Protestants, together making up more than two-thirds of all Christians in the region.

Christians, 1970–2020
The percentage share of Christians in Oceania peaked around 1970 and has been since in gradual decline, dropping from 93% to 65% in 2020. Countries with the most significant decline are Australia (93% to 54% Christian) and New Zealand (95% to 54%).

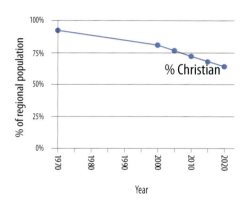

% Christian

Religious affiliation, 1970 and 2020
Oceania became more religiously diverse over the course of the twentieth century, largely due to the arrival of millions of Muslims, Hindus, Sikhs and Buddhists into Australia and New Zealand. The region has a significant population of non-religious, consisting of both White Australians and New Zealanders and also a large Han Chinese presence.

1970	2020	
92.6%	65.1%	Christians
3.3%	20.8%	Agnostics
1.1%	4.5%	Atheists
0.1%	2.4%	Buddhists
0.4%	2.2%	Muslims
1.1%	1.9%	Hindus
0.8%	1.0%	Ethnic religionists

% of regional population

Note: For Oceania, traditions will not add up to total Christians in each region because of double affiliation and the unaffiliated. Only the religions over 1% in 2020 are identified.

Major Christian Traditions, 1970 and 2020

Christians

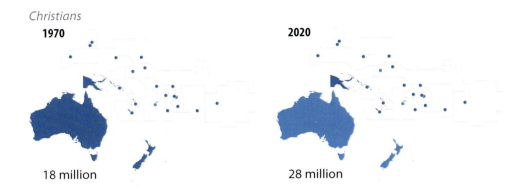

1970

2020

18 million

28 million

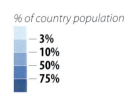

% of country population

— **3%**
— **10%**
— **50%**
— **75%**

Overall, Oceania was largely Christianised by 1970. Christianity has declined as a proportion of the population since then, though some countries did see an increase between 1970 and 2020, such as Fiji (61% to 65%). The largest Christian populations are found in Australia (14 million), Papua New Guinea (8 million), New Zealand (3 million) and Fiji (570,000).

Anglicans

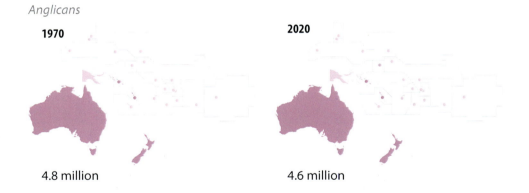

1970

2020

4.8 million

4.6 million

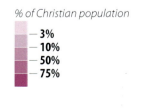

% of Christian population

— **3%**
— **10%**
— **50%**
— **75%**

Anglicans in Oceania are the historic majority due to British colonial presence since the late eighteenth century but have been eclipsed by Protestants as of 2020. However, Anglicans declined as a proportion of all Christians from 1970 to 2020, from 26% to 17%. The highest percentages of Anglicans (among all Christians) are found in the Solomon Islands (33%), Australia (25%), New Zealand (23%) and Vanuatu (13%).

Catholics

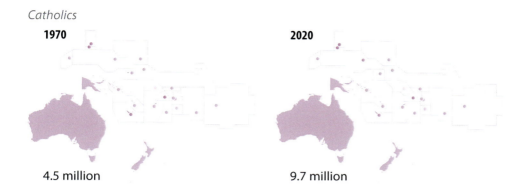

1970

4.5 million

2020

9.7 million

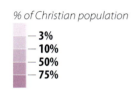

% of Christian population

— 3%
— 10%
— 50%
— 75%

The number of Catholics has declined slightly in proportional terms (23.1% in 1970 to 22.9% in 2020) but doubled in absolute terms, from 4.5 million to 9.7 million. Between 1970 and 2020 the proportion of Catholics among Christians grew substantially in some countries, such as the Federated States of Micronesia (35% to 64%) and Australia (25% to 43%). In other countries it dropped, such as New Caledonia (77% to 59%) and Tonga (17% to 14%).

Independents

1970

542,000

2020

2.1 million

% of Christian population

— 3%
— 10%
— 50%
— 75%

Independent Christianity grew the second fastest (after Pentecostals/Charismatics, with overlap between the two) regionally between 1970 and 2020, averaging over 2.7% per year. Yet only 8% of all Christians in the region are Independents, due mainly to the historic influence of Catholics and Protestants in Australia and New Zealand. The Church of Jesus Christ of Latter-day Saints increased significantly over the period, for example in Sāmoa and Tonga.

Major Christian Traditions, 1970 and 2020

Orthodox

1970   **2020**

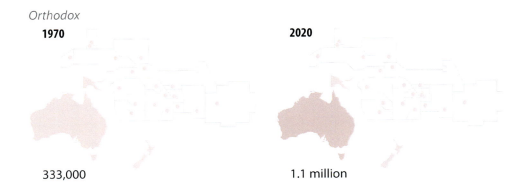

333,000   1.1 million

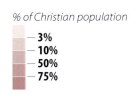

% of Christian population
- **3%**
- **10%**
- **50%**
- **75%**

Orthodox Christianity is a minority tradition in Oceania, with around 1 million members in the region. Australia and New Zealand are the only countries with any indication of a robust Orthodox community (8% and 0.6% of all Christians, respectively), largely due to immigration.

Protestants

1970   **2020**

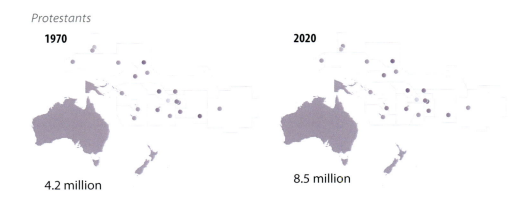

4.2 million   8.5 million

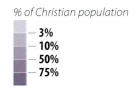

% of Christian population
- **3%**
- **10%**
- **50%**
- **75%**

Protestantism grew to 8.5 million adherents by 2020, up from 4 million in 1970. Protestants make up half of all Christians in both Micronesia (49%) and Polynesia (50%). The largest Protestant denomination in Melanesia is the Evangelical Lutheran Church of Papua New Guinea (950,000 members); in Polynesia, the largest is the Maohi Protestant Church in French Polynesia (95,000 members).

Movements within Christianity, 1970 and 2020

Evangelicals

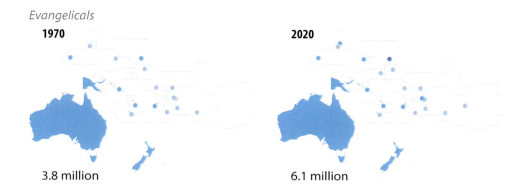

1970

2020

3.8 million

6.1 million

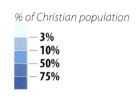

% of Christian population

— **3%**
— **10%**
— **50%**
— **75%**

The number of Evangelicals grew by more than 2 million in Oceania, mainly in the small island countries. The percentage of Evangelicals declined in Australia/New Zealand and rose in Melanesia, Micronesia and Polynesia. The Marshall Islands has the highest Evangelical percentage (71% of all Christians).

Pentecostals/Charismatics

1970

2020

289,000

4.5 million

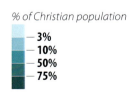

% of Christian population

— **3%**
— **10%**
— **50%**
— **75%**

Pentecostal/Charismatic Christianity was the fastest-growing tradition in Oceania from 1970 to 2020 and now represents 16% of the region's Christian population (up from nearly 2% in 1970). Christians are more than 40% Pentecostal/Charismatic in the Marshall Islands (75%), Vanuatu (40%) and American Sāmoa (43%).

Christianity in Australia/New Zealand, 1970–2020

Christians by Country, 2020
16.4 Million Christians, 54.1% of Population

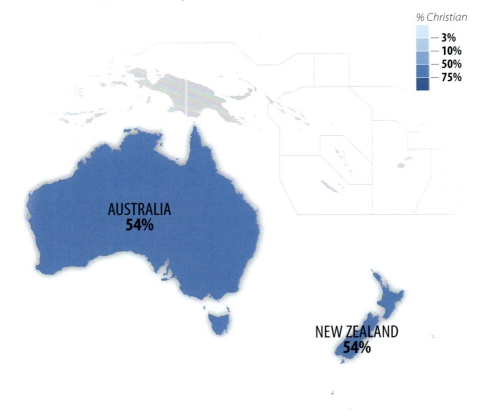

The four largest denominations depict the diversity that exists in Christianity in Australia: Catholic, Anglican, Uniting Church in Australia (Protestant) and Greek Orthodox. Together they represent almost 70% of the nation's Christians. Until 1950, Australian Christianity tended to reproduce the denominational pattern of the British Isles, although more cosmopolitan in membership. Since 1950, with immigration from all parts of Europe, and then Asia, Africa, Pacific Islands and the Americas, the country's diversity has increased rapidly. Coptic Orthodox have grown rapidly over recent years, reflecting contemporary immigrant patterns. Anglicans remain the largest tradition in New Zealand, although they have been in steady decline over the twentieth and twenty-first centuries. Although most of Australia's Aboriginal and New Zealand's Maori populations are Christian, the churches in each of these countries are still grappling with issues related to historical forced assimilation, land and lack of Indigenous rights.

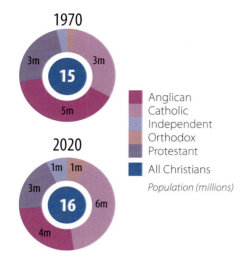

1970

3m   3m

15

5m

2020

1m 1m

3m

16   6m

4m

Anglican
Catholic
Independent
Orthodox
Protestant

All Christians

Population (millions)

Major Christian traditions, 1970 and 2020
In 2020, Christianity in Australia/New Zealand was largely Catholic (39% of all Christians) and Anglican (25% of all Christians). Orthodox had the fastest growth rate between 1970 and 2020, averaging nearly 2.5% per year, though Independents also experienced a high growth rate, nearly 2%.

Christians, 1970–2020
Christianity in Australia/New Zealand is in proportional decline, dropping from 93% in 1970 to 54% in 2020. Australia declined from 93% to 54%, while New Zealand declined from 95% to 54%. Both countries are experiencing rapid secularisation and decreased influence of Christianity in public life.

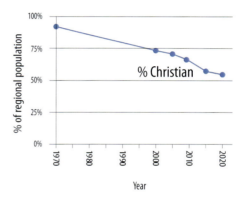

% Christian

1970	2020	
93.4%	54.1%	Christians
4.1%	28.8%	Agnostics
1.4%	6.2%	Atheists
0.1%	3.3%	Buddhists
0.2%	2.8%	Muslims
0.1%	1.9%	Hindus
0.1%	0.6%	Sikhs

1970   2020
% of regional population

Religious affiliation, 1970 and 2020
Atheists' and agnostics' share increased dramatically because of the large number of people leaving Christianity. From 1970 to 2020, the non-religious increased from a combined 5.5% in 1970 to 35% in 2020. Gains were also made by Buddhists (to 988,000 in 2020) and Muslims (to 846,000).

Christianity in Melanesia, 1970–2020

Christians by Country, 2020
10.1 Million Christians, 92.3% of Population

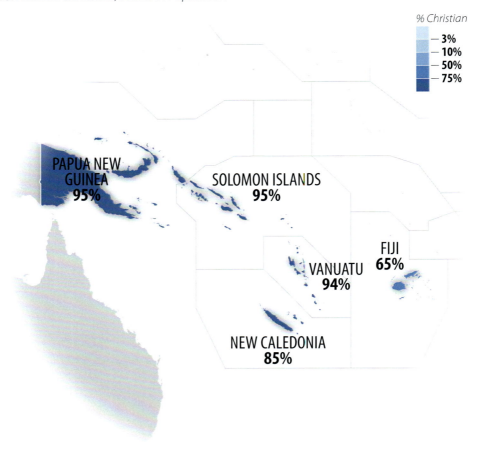

% Christian
— 3%
— 10%
— 50%
— 75%

PAPUA NEW GUINEA
95%

SOLOMON ISLANDS
95%

FIJI
65%

VANUATU
94%

NEW CALEDONIA
85%

Christianity arrived in each of the five countries of Melanesia during the nineteenth century, but many missionaries were murdered or died from tropical diseases. Christianity continues to grow in Melanesia and over the last 50 years increased from 88% to 92% of the population. Papua New Guinea experienced one of the most dramatic changes in religious affiliation over the twentieth century, rising from just 4% Christian in 1900 to 95% Christian in 2000. Many Indigenous churches have emerged in the region and churches also have actively embraced the development of Indigenous theology and leadership. Church leaders in some areas, like the Solomon Islands, work with village chiefs to reconcile Christian beliefs and practices with traditional beliefs and practices. Indigenous missionary-sending is on the rise as more Christians are equipped with tools and resources to specifically minister to people on nearby remote islands.

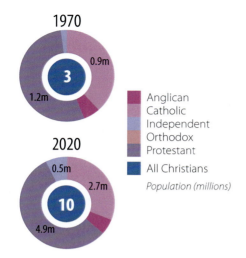

1970

0.9m
3
1.2m

2020

0.5m
2.7m
10
4.9m

- Anglican
- Catholic
- Independent
- Orthodox
- Protestant
- All Christians

Population (millions)

Major Christian traditions, 1970 and 2020
In 2020, Christianity in Melanesia was largely Protestant (49% of all Christians) and Catholic (27% of all Christians). Large Protestant churches include Evangelical Lutherans, United Church and Assemblies of God in Papua New Guinea, as well as the Methodist Church in Fiji.

Christians, 1970–2020
Christianity in Melanesia increased from 88% of the population in 1970 to 92% in 2020, an average of almost 2.5% growth per year. The Solomon Islands experienced the fastest growth, at 2.9% per year; Papua New Guinea has the highest concentration of Christians, at 95%.

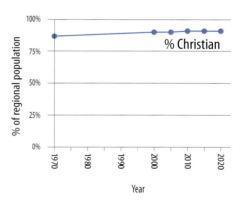

% Christian

Year

	1970	2020	
Christians	87.6%	92.3%	
Ethnic religionists	4.0%	2.7%	
Hindus	6.2%	2.3%	
Agnostics	0.3%	0.9%	
Bahá'ís	0.3%	0.8%	
Muslims	1.3%	0.6%	

1970   2020
% of regional population

Religious affiliation, 1970 and 2020
The religious makeup of Melanesia has changed little over the last 50 years. The share of Ethnic religionists, Muslims and Hindus has decreased with the proportional rise of Christianity. Vanuatu has the highest percentage of traditional religionists, at 4%, followed by the Solomon Islands and Papua New Guinea, both 3%.

Christianity in Micronesia, 1970–2020

Christians by Country, 2020
501,000 Christians, 92.5% of Population

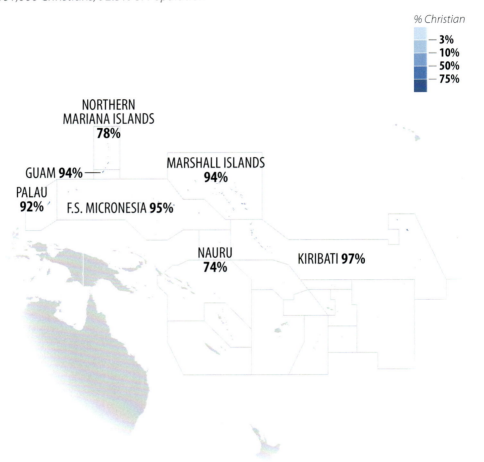

% Christian
— **3%**
— **10%**
— **50%**
— **75%**

NORTHERN
MARIANA ISLANDS
78%

MARSHALL ISLANDS
94%

GUAM **94%**

PALAU
92%

F.S. MICRONESIA **95%**

NAURU
74%

KIRIBATI **97%**

Each of the seven island nations of Micronesia is very small. The largest by population is Guam, a territory of the United States, with 169,000 inhabitants, and the smallest is Nauru, with 11,200. Christianity arrived in each country during various centuries, including via Western Christian explorers in the Marshall Islands in 1529; Spanish troops in Palau in 1710; and Protestant missionaries from Kiribati arriving in Nauru in 1887. Colonial authorities suppressed Indigenous expressions of Christianity throughout the region; despite this, every country is majority Christian today. This region faces the particular challenge of rising sea levels due to climate change. Kiribati, for example, lies only two metres (six feet) above sea level. Entire villages could be obliterated by powerful storm surges in the near future. Many churches are advocating for the development of new eco-theologies for survival.

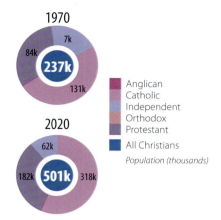

1970

Anglican
Catholic
Independent
Orthodox
Protestant
All Christians

Population (thousands)

2020

Major Christian traditions, 1970 and 2020
In 2020, Christianity in Micronesia was majority Catholic, with Catholics the largest denomination in four of the seven countries (Guam, Micronesia, Kiribati, Northern Mariana Islands). Protestants make up the largest denomination in the Marshall Islands (Assemblies of God). Independent Christianity has grown slightly, mostly due to the Church of Jesus Christ of Latter-day Saints.

Christians, 1970–2020
As a proportion of the population, Christians in Micronesia have decreased slightly over the last 50 years, from 96% to 93%. However, Pentecostal/Charismatic Christianity has experienced tremendous growth over that period, increasing from 3% to 15%. Evangelicals have also grown, from 8% to 15% of the population.

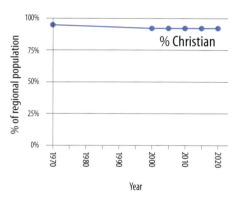

Religious affiliation, 1970 and 2020
The religious makeup of Micronesia has changed little over the last 50 years. Bahá'ís increased from 2,600 to 8,700 and have the largest presence in Kiribati (though still fewer than 3,000 people). Buddhists have the largest population on the Northern Mariana Islands (5,700).

1970	2020	
95.6%	92.5%	Christians
0.1%	1.8%	Buddhists
1.1%	1.6%	Bahá'ís
0.5%	1.4%	Agnostics
0.6%	1.2%	Chinese folk-religionists
2.1%	0.8%	Ethnic religionists

1970   2020
% of regional population

Christianity in Polynesia, 1970–2020

Christians by Country, 2020
673,000 Christians, 95.9% of Population

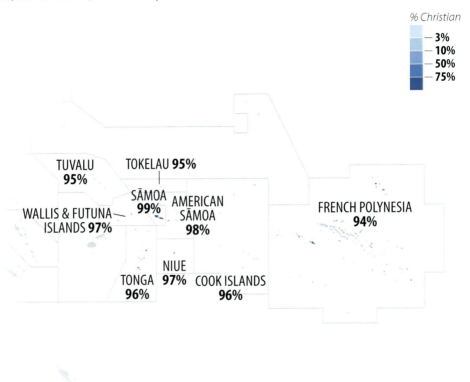

Polynesia is home to nine island nations and covers over 800,000 square miles (1.2 million km²). French Polynesia is the largest country, with 291,000 people; the smallest is Tokelau, with only 1,400 people. This region is home to some of the highest percentages of Christians in the world, with each country between 94% (French Polynesia, Tokelau) and 98% (American Sāmoa) Christian. Many of these countries received Christianity via missionaries from other islands in Oceania. Christian diversity is limited, given how small the populations are. Tokelau, for example, is largely Congregationalist (50% of the population) and Catholic (44%). The region is also home to one of world's only two countries where the Church of Jesus Christ of Latter-day Saints makes up the majority, Tonga (60% Latter-day Saint). Climate change is a major issue for churches throughout the region. New eco-theologies are being developed that encourage Christians to think about the link between climate change and church reform.

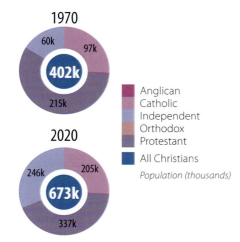

1970

60k

97k

402k

215k

2020

246k

205k

673k

337k

Anglican
Catholic
Independent
Orthodox
Protestant

All Christians

Population (thousands)

Major Christian traditions, 1970 and 2020
Christianity in Polynesia is majority Protestant, with comparable populations of Catholics and Independents. The largest Protestant denominations in the region are the Māòhi Protestant Church (French Polynesia), Congregational Christian Church (Sāmoa) and Free Wesleyan Church (Tonga). Catholics are the largest denomination in French Polynesia and the Wallis and Futuna Islands.

Christians, 1970–2020
Christianity's share of the population is declining in Polynesia, but only slightly, from 98% in 1970 to 96% in 2020. This does, however, represent an increase of 271,000 Christians over the 50-year period.

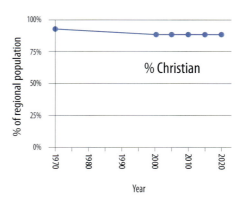

% Christian

Religious affiliation, 1970 and 2020
The religious and non-religious makeup of Polynesia changed little over the last 50 years. Christianity remains largely the same, with only a slight increase in the agnostic population due to general secularisation. Bahá'ís have increased slightly, but the largest population is still fewer than 4,000, in Tonga.

98.1%	95.9%	Christians
0.6%	2.4%	Agnostics
0.9%	0.9%	Bahá'ís
1970	**2020**	

% of regional population

Future of Christianity in Oceania, 2020–2050

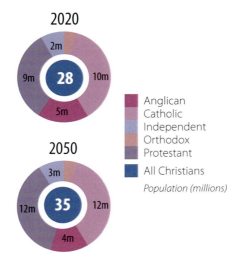

2020

2m
9m   28   10m
5m

2050

3m
12m   35   12m
4m

Anglican
Catholic
Independent
Orthodox
Protestant

All Christians

Population (millions)

Major Christian traditions, 2020 and 2050
Looking forward, Pentecostal/Charis-matic Christians – many of whom are Independent – are likely to increase their share of Oceania's Christian popu-lation in 2050. Catholics and Protestants are projected to have nearly an equal share of Christians.

Christians, 2020–2050
By 2050, Christians will likely number 35 million in the region, 61% of the pop-ulation. The demographic weight of Australia and New Zealand drives this decline. The islands in Micronesia and Polynesia are also experiencing decline, but not nearly at the same rate.

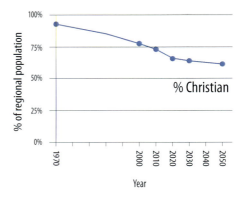

% Christian

		Christians
65.1%	60.5%	Christians
20.8%	23.3%	Agnostics
4.5%	5.9%	Atheists
2.4%	2.6%	Buddhists
2.2%	2.5%	Muslims
1.9%	2.0%	Hindus
1.0%	0.9%	Ethnic religionists

2020   2050
% of regional population

Religious affiliation, 2020 and 2050
The proportion of Christians is pro-jected to decline due to gains by the non-religious (both atheists and ag-nostics combined). Muslims, Hindus and Buddhists are likely to continue increasing due to immigration and higher-than-average birth rates.

Christianity in Oceania

Katalina Tahaafe-Williams

When scholars and demographers paint the global Christian landscape of the past 50 years as a demographic shift from the global North to the global South, the regions of Africa, Asia and Latin America might loom large in their imagination of the global South, but not necessarily Oceania. The geographical remoteness, the tyranny of distance and the unimaginable vastness associated with the region can often translate into a kind of metaphysical remoteness in the human imagination. Mapping the development of Christianity in a region that covers the whole Pacific Ocean – also known as the 'liquid continent' – is a challenge many demographers would recognise. The area is so vast that the land mass of five continents can fit quite easily into it. It comprises approximately 30,000 islands with many different dialects, languages and cultures grouped into Melanesia (Greek *melas*, black; *nesos*, islands), Micronesia (Greek *mikros*, small) and Polynesia (Greek *poly*, many). French explorer Jules-Sébastien-César Dumont d'Urville drew on the earlier work of historian Charles de Brosses to coin these terms of classification for the Pacific Islands and its peoples based on physiological, cultural and language differences. Though numerous, the islands are mostly small, and the populations are relatively scattered, with high numbers concentrated in the bigger islands of Papua New Guinea, New Zealand and the island continent of Australia. Indeed, Oceania is a region of vast dimensions, but its population is relatively modest compared to its three sister regions in the global South of Africa, Asia and Latin America.

The expansion and demographic shift in Christianity from the northern to the southern hemisphere might be indisputable, but what does that mean for Oceania? It is true that Europe can no longer claim to be the 'Faith', and the notion of the 'Christian West' is now fundamentally disputed. But what are the implications of that reality for Oceania, when Christian history and identity are so bound up with European, and later American, imperial expansion? Oceania is a region in which over 90% of the population of the Pacific Islands, outside of the more secular contexts of New Zealand and Australia, is Christian. It is a region in which – with the exception of Fiji, where the descendants of Indian indentured labourers brought by the British to work on sugarcane plantations maintain their

Hindu and Muslim religious identities – religious diversity is quite recent and concentrated mostly in New Zealand and Australia due to immigration. What is the significance of this global shift in Christian identity for the majority of Pacific Islanders, for whom Christianity is the only religion they have ever known? What does it mean for the historic mainline Pacific Island churches that have taken for granted the privilege of being the dominant religious presence in their respective nations? These are just some of the realities that encapsulate the development of Christianity in Oceania which the writers in this volume of the Edinburgh Companions to Global Christianity analyse, interpret and present in the essays that follow.

This introduction is not a summary of the essays that compose the volume but an attempt to outline pertinent factors pointing to significant trends in Oceanian Christianity. It is often said that the Oceania region is a microcosm of the trends and changes seen in global Christianity. If this is true, then we are seeing some phenomenal growth in newer Christian movements, including the Pentecostal-Charismatic, Evangelical and Independent groups, while there is a marked decline in historic mainline churches, particularly the Protestants. The exceptions seen in the cases of the Roman Catholics and the Anglicans, where there are signs of stability and even modest growth, are likely due to their capacity to retain Charismatically inclined adherents within their ecclesial bounds. The unprecedented growth in the newer Pentecostal-Charismatic forms of Christianity is attributed to a mixture of greater adaptability to modern globalising processes and a certain level of proselytising in historical mainline church neighbourhoods. Though the two types of church in the region do not usually interact or collaborate with each other, both are indispensable to the continuing existence and presence of Christianity in Oceania. Both types of church have contributed significantly to the cross-fertilisation of Christian innovations and missions across the Tasman Sea and throughout the Pacific Islands.

New Zealand and Australia are rapidly becoming the secularising centres in Oceania, to the extent that one can accurately point to secularist and materialist influences as chief rivals of Christianity not only within their national boundaries but in the wider region as well. Some insights into the dynamics of the relationship between the two 'big islands' and their smaller counterparts are valuable since the issues that these highlight mirror and reflect significant developments in Christianity in Oceania.

It is fair to describe Australia and New Zealand as two offspring of Oceania with split personalities. Geographically they are southern, but culturally, socio-economically and politically they are northern. New Zealand and Australia are colonised/invaded territories initially settled by emigrants from Britain during its imperial age who then formed independent, autonomously governed countries – while decimating, displacing and marginalising the Indigenous populations in the process. (It should be noted that colonised territories yet to gain independence from their Euro-American rulers remain in the region, such as Māòhi Nui – also known as French Polynesia – which is still under French rule.) Indeed, New Zealand and Australia stand out in the region for several reasons: the majority of their populations are of white European origin, socio-economically they are 'developed' rather than 'developing', they are settler societies with Indigenous minority populations, they are secular liberal democratic capitalist societies – in short, the very model of a 'Western' society.

This split personality or dual identity of Oceania's 'big islands' can be confusing and complicates the relationships between and among Oceania island siblings and churches. The close links between the two nations and the former British colonial power are quite strong on various levels, and some of those links are visible in the essays of this volume (the scholarly consensus that Australian and New Zealand theologies are extensions of British European theologies, for one). Even in the earliest missions, Australia was a base for British missionary activities in the region. In fact, some of the mission churches in the Pacific Islands, such as the Methodists, were still under Australian administrative oversight until the latter half of the twentieth century.

In terms of church partnership and cooperation within the region, the complex dynamics in these relationships are often exposed in light of the paradox of the so-called shift in global Christianity to the south – where the majority of Christians are located – even as the money and resources continue to be controlled by the northern Christian minority. Not only are the churches in Australia and New Zealand ranked alongside the European and North American mission funders and donors, they also oversee strong theological education institutions in the region that are critical for equipping the next generation of Oceania's Christian leaders.

As major funders of mission projects in Oceania, the Australian and New Zealand historical mainline churches, with their more liberal approaches to theology and biblical hermeneutics, are often in the tricky situation of seeking to maintain respectful and mutual relationships with their Pacific Island partners while being confronted with pushback on matters of theological differences (such as issues of human sexuality). Such negotiations are further exacerbated by challenges related to structural dependency that have developed in the Pacific churches over the years. Maintaining theological positions and commitment to social justice and radical politics are constant negotiations in the region. Nevertheless, the contribution of missions and the churches they established to various

French Polynesia

Richard A. Davis and Marc Pohue

French Polynesia is the name given to the French 'overseas country' of the south-eastern Pacific that encompasses 118 atolls and islands within five archipelagos (the Society Islands, composed of the Windward Islands and the Leeward Islands; the Tuamotu Archipelago; the Gambier Islands; the Marquesas Islands; and the Austral Islands). Tahiti, an island within the Society Islands, houses the capital, Papeete, and is the most populous island, with more than half of the country's population of 291,000. Tahitians are people living on the island of Tahiti, while the name taken by the Indigenous occupants of French Polynesia is Māòhi. They call the country Māòhi Nui.

The Missionary Period

French Polynesia has several firsts in Pacific mission history. The first Protestant mission to French Polynesia and the South Pacific was initiated by the London Missionary Society (LMS). They sailed on the *Duff* from England, arriving in Tahiti on Sunday 5 March 1797. This day is now an annual holiday called Missionary Day (Arrivée de l'Évangile). The conversion of King Pōmare II through the work of the LMS and his subsequent baptism on 16 May 1819 gave the church a major boost as it spread from Tahiti to other islands. From both necessity and missiological strategy, the LMS later used new converts from French Polynesia in missions to other nations, including the Cook Islands, Fiji, Hawaii, Tonga, Sāmoa and Papua New Guinea. From 1863, the Protestant Church fell under the direction of the Société des Missions Évangéliques de Paris (SMEP, or Paris Evangelical Missionary Society). This forced a shift from the congregationalism of the LMS to the presbyterian-synodal model of the SMEP. From 1884 the Protestant Church was, by decree of the French regime, an established one. The aim of establishment was to eliminate the influence of the English missionaries; it also encouraged local Protestants to engage in political activities to entrench their advantage. With *laïcité* being made French law in 1905, however, it was just a matter of time before this impacted the churches in French colonies. In 1927 the government stopped all financial support for the churches and halted control of church activities.

Catholics may have arrived first in French Polynesia in the seventeenth-century expedition of Pedro Fernandez de Quirós. They then had a failed Tahiti mission that began in 1774 and lasted only about a year. The Catholic mission got underway on a firm basis in 1834, with the mission of the Picpus Fathers. The Catholics formed strongholds in the Tuamotu, Gambier and Marquesas island groups, where they remain strong. When, in 1836, they tried to expand into Tahiti, the Protestant Queen Pōmare IV chased the Catholics out. They returned to Tahiti in 1838 with a French military accompaniment, which led to the islands becoming a French protectorate in 1842. This intervention precipitated the French-Tahitian War (1844–7), ending with the defeat of the Tahitians. These conflicts between the Indigenous Protestants and the invading French Catholics helped to fuse in the minds of the people the close connection between France and Catholicism, and to some scholars this explains the later dominant position of the Protestants in French Polynesia. Nevertheless, a Catholic cathedral was built in Papeete in 1860.

Other faiths also date from the nineteenth century. Missionaries from the Church of Jesus Christ of Latter-day Saints (LDS) arrived on 30 April 1844 on the island of Tubuai in the Austral Islands. This mission, sent by Joseph Smith himself, included Addison Pratt and was its first foreign-language mission. The LDS was forced out of the islands in 1852 but returned in 1892. Meanwhile, in 1873 missionaries from the Reorganized Church of Jesus Christ of Latter-day Saints arrived and began work. They eventually became known locally as the 'Sanitos'. These two branches of the LDS movement continue today. Being of American, rather than of French, origin, joining the LDS or Sanitos provided an avenue for Māòhi to express anti-French resentments. The Seventh-day Adventists (called locally *petenia*, after their origin in Pitcairn) arrived in Tahiti in 1890.

The mid-twentieth century saw increased diversity of religious groups, with the arrivals of the Jehovah's Witness (1956/7), the Bahá'í Faith (1958),

Christianity in French Polynesia, 1970 and 2020

Tradition	1970		2020		Average annual growth rate (%), 1970–2020
	Population	%	Population	%	
Christians	106,000	96.1%	272,000	93.7%	1.9%
Independents	9,700	8.8%	51,800	17.8%	3.4%
Protestants	47,000	42.5%	104,000	35.8%	1.6%
Catholics	36,000	32.5%	120,000	41.3%	2.4%
Evangelicals	2,300	2.1%	8,900	3.1%	2.7%
Pentecostals/Charismatics	1,100	1.0%	27,000	9.3%	6.7%
Total population	**110,000**	**100.0%**	**291,000**	**100.0%**	**2.0%**

Source: Todd M. Johnson and Gina A. Zurlo (eds), *World Christian Database* (Leiden/Boston: Brill), accessed January 2020.

Pentecostals (from 1962) and various splinter churches from the mainstream Evangelical Church of French Polynesia. Yet the religious landscape remains dominated by the two biggest churches, the Protestant and the Catholic, which both experienced radical change from the mid-1960s, with the era of decolonisation and the effects of the Second Vatican Council.

The Protestant Church

On 1 September 1963 the Protestant church became autonomous as the Evangelical Church of French Polynesia (Eglise Protestante de Polynésie Française). In 2004 it changed its name to the Etärëtia Porotetani Māòhi (EPM, or Māòhi Protestant Church). The EPM is a self-supporting church, which depends entirely on its members' annual collection, with the funds utilised for internal activities as well as for the larger community and global missions.

The majority of EPM members are Indigenous Māòhi. Other members include descendants of both French immigrants and Chinese people who migrated to Tahiti in 1865 to work on cotton, coffee and sugar cane plantations. Indigenous members comprise the majority in EPM parishes, with the exception of the French parish Bethel and the Chinese parish Jourdain, both located in Papeete. The EPM assembles annually in order to make decisions in relation to: its internal issues; social, political, ecological, health and economic issues affecting Māòhi Nui; and the regional and global ecumenical church missions.

Besides its internal spiritual and community concerns, the EPM also has commitments to the national and the global community and claims to undertake a prophetic role of vigilant guardian over the society of Māòhi Nui. As such, in 2017 the EPM, through the World Council of Churches, took action to seek justice with regard to health issues caused by the French nuclear tests in French Polynesia. Radioactivity still threatens the health of many Māòhi and Europeans in French Polynesia.

After being the largest church in French Polynesia for many years, the EPM is now in second place to the Catholic Church. This has been a recent development, as membership numbers have gradually declined in percentage terms over the last 60 years. In the 1962 census about 54% of the population identified with the EPM. By 1971 the number was about half the population, falling again by 1992 to 44%. By 2000, its membership was 38%, falling to 36% by 2020. While such percentages can be read as an indication that the Protestant Church was declining from 1962 to 2020, it should be noted that with steady population growth over the same period the church has grown in absolute numbers from about 45,000 members in 1962 to 104,000 in 2020. Over recent years the membership numbers have been relatively stable.

The Catholic Church

The Catholic Church began to indigenise in the 1950s, with a local translation of the Psalms and the ordination of a second priest of Indigenous Polynesian descent, Michel-Gaspard Coppenrath (1954). Like the EPM, the Catholic Church has seen dramatic changes since the 1960s. The Second Vatican Council (1962–5) encouraged vernacular expressions of worship and respect of local cultures. As a result, Mass was no longer said in Latin and the first local Chinese priest, Lucien Law, was ordained in 1964.

Through the increased openness of the Catholic Church to Chinese culture, many in the Chinese community joined the Church. This was helped by the creation of the Chinese high school in Papeete, primarily allocated to Chinese students, thus offering chances to large numbers of Chinese people to integrate into the Catholic Church of French Polynesia. In contrast to the Protestant Church, the Catholic Church never set out to become the church of the Māòhi people. As a multicultural Christian community, the Catholic Church promotes the integration of French, Chinese and Māòhi languages and cultures.

From the late 1970s into the 1980s, the Catholic Church benefited greatly from a Charismatic revival that swept the islands. This movement saw the launch of the prayer group from the Canadian sisters of Our Lady of Angels, the healing masses performed by the priest Fr Tardif, and the opening of the Tiberiade spiritual retreat centre. This centre also attracts numerous people from various other churches, including the EPM and Seventh-day Adventists. The Charismatic movement remains influential and established within the Catholic Church today.

The Catholic Church in French Polynesia is now the largest church, having displayed gradual growth over many decades. At the beginning of the twentieth century, Catholics numbered less than one-fifth of the population, nearly a quarter by 1950 and more than 25% by 1960. A decade later, in 1970, they were nearly a third of the population. This growth has continued into the twenty-first century. In 2000, Catholics exceeded 40% and were starting to overtake the EPM. By 2020 they had eclipsed the EPM, with over 120,000 adherents, representing more than 41% of the population. The membership is mostly Māòhi, alongside the Chinese community and a minority of Europeans.

The Churches and Politics

Modern politics in French Polynesia is dominated by two issues, French nuclear testing and the movement for independence. Churches, especially the EPM, have been very active on these issues. In general, the Catholic Church is perceived to be more supportive of French positions, while the EPM has been more activist in opposing testing and French imperialism.

When Algeria won its independence from France, the French, wishing to remain a nuclear power, had to find another location to test nuclear weapons. Following the example of the British and Americans, they chose small, relatively powerless Pacific Islands as testing sites. In 1963 the Centre d'Expérimentation du Pacifique (CEP) was established to conduct the tests. Between 1966 and 1996 France conducted 193 atmospheric and underground nuclear tests at the remote atolls of Mururoa and Fangataufa. The period brought much money into French Polynesia, but at the cost of increased foreign control and long-term environmental harm.

While international pressure led to the cessation of testing in 1996, locally the churches were split over the tests. It would be incorrect to say that the French-leaning Catholic Church was in support and the Protestants were against, but one would be justified in gaining that impression from the literature. Locally it was the EPM that led the opposition to the tests. Support soon came from other churches and ecumenical bodies across the region.

From 2001 the Protestant Church supported the formation and work of the Mururoa e Tatou, the association of workers on Mururoa and Fanga-taufa, which seeks justice for these former workers who suffer poor health due to the effects of radiation exposure. Ongoing church activism exists around the environmental and health effects of the nuclear waste and the regional issue of transporting nuclear waste through Pacific waters.

French nuclear tests could have taken place, and their full effects been hidden from scrutiny, only because of the ongoing colonisation of French Polynesia. For this reason, and the desire for self-government, the churches have been active on the issues of decolonisation and self-determination for French Polynesia. With the support of the Commission of the Churches on International Affairs of the World Council of Churches, in collaboration with the Pacific Conference of Churches (PCC) and the EPM, in 2013 French Polynesia was reinstated to the United Nations' list of Non-Self-Governing Territories (Resolution 67/265). But not all residents of French Polynesia value moves toward independence. The French-leaning politicians are keen to point out that the majority of residents support links to France. The official French position seeks to have the 2013 resolution reversed. Meanwhile, the EPM and PCC are continuing their activism toward full self-determination for Māòhi Nui.

The Catholic and EPM churches find more common ground in response to domestic issues, as was seen in the dockers' strike in October 1987. After social tensions erupted into the strike and a spate of arson attacks in Papeete, the churches worked together mediating the restoration of peace between the unions and the government. The divisive nature of politics in French Polynesia, especially over church–state relations, has impacted the churches. Especially within the EPM, religion and politics have not always mixed well, with the political affiliations of deacons causing divisions within the Church. This resulted in the 1995 EPM synod decision that deacons interested in a political role must choose between their church office or their political position. As a result, many deacons resigned.

Cultural Developments in Spirituality and Liturgy

The growing independence and inculturation of the mainline churches since the 1960s has manifested itself in practical ways. The developments in spirituality and liturgy in the EPM have to be understood as coming from the deep Māòhi spiritual beliefs regarding the natural world (including the human community), as well as in the belief of the Māòhi in the spirits of the ancestors, land, ocean and sky. This spirituality takes as its starting point the Māòhi worldview, which portrays the whole cosmos, encompassing every creature and living thing (also including water, rocks and air) as one big *ôpü* (household). This worldview forms the principal force that underpins the Indigenous theology of the EPM, from the time of the establishment of Christian missions by the LMS.

Modern influences on developments in spirituality and liturgy within the EPM can be traced to the 1980s and the work of local theologians and cultural revivers Henri Hiro and Turo Raapoto. Their cultural renewal, together with the Māòhi worldview of the created world as one big *ôpü*, gave rise to numerous Indigenous expressions of Christianity. These theological, liturgical and practical affirmations within the EPM included the Church's use of the Māòhi language as its primary language in liturgy and other activities, thereby relegating the French language and colonial presence. In addition, the reintroduction of the Māòhi traditional cultural hymns (*tärava, rüàu, rärï*) that were banned by the missionaries, the introduction of the conch shell and the cultural drums (*pahu*) into the worship of the Church, and the use of the local percussions (*töère*) and folkloric dances (*ôteà, àparima*) in the activities of the Church, all demonstrate the Māòhi people's unique manner of worshipping and celebrating God's all-embracing love. Furthermore, the readjustment of the clerical clothing from the typical European vest or coat and necktie to the Māòhi-designed shirts to officiate the liturgy displays the Church's theological liturgical expression of bearing the Māòhi social, cultural, communal and Christian lifestyle in worship and in the celebration of the sacraments.

Finally, some EPM churches have adopted the use of local elements for Holy Communion, such as taro, breadfruit or coconut flesh in the place of bread, and coconut juice in the place of wine. This innovation, which began in the EPM churches of Afareaitu (Mooreà) and Mataiva and Tikehau (Tuamotu Islands) in 1991, was justified by Indigenous theological inculturation, specifically a position that highlights God's love for all things in creation. However, not all church members agreed with this change to tradition. In 1999, the EPM church of Papetoai split over these issues, with some members leaving the EPM to join other Protestants in Independent churches under the Confederation of Reformed Churches.

New Religious Movements and Ecumenism

As the previous sections show, the modern French Polynesian religious landscape was never homogeneous, even if some islands or island groups were predominantly Catholic or Protestant. Sociological studies show that the period since the 1950s and 1960s has seen a growing diversity of religious groups, yet perhaps not to the extent seen in other Pacific countries. The largest churches remain the Catholic Church and EPM, with the next largest and oldest religious group being the LDS.

From its early beginning, the LDS developed slowly, but it was given new impetus in the 1950s, when more missionaries, now with greater freedom, were allowed to operate. In part, the success of the movement can be linked to the number of local missionaries (a majority since about the late 1980s), even if the church centralises leadership in Utah, USA. The highest growth rate of any new religious group has been with the Jehovah's Witnesses. Their missionary work originated in the mid-1950s, with the first congregation forming in 1959 in Papeete. From having 132 Tahitian adherents in the 1962 census, they now number around 6,000 nationwide.

Since gaining autonomy, the Protestant Church has been very active in global and regional ecumenical cooperation, joining the World Council of Churches, the Pacific Conference of Churches and the Communauté Evangélique d'Action Apostolique (CEVAA). In 2016 the Church became a member church of the Council for World Mission, the successor of the LMS. The return of the Revd François Pihaatae to Tahiti after completing his tenure as General Secretary of the Pacific Conference of Churches in Fiji gives the churches the benefit of his ecumenical energy and activist experience. However, there is the risk here, as elsewhere in the Pacific, of a gulf existing between the leadership and the grassroots in their understanding of ecumenism. The Catholic Church cooperates regionally through the Episcopal Conference of the Pacific, known as CEPAC (Conferentia Episcopalis Pacifici).

Apart from international and regional ecumenical initiatives, there are also positive signs locally. In 1985 the churches established the Ecumenical Association of Churches to deal with national social issues, such as substance abuse and family planning. An Ecumenical Committee for Non-government Schools was set up to represent the interests of religious schools. Less institutional forms of ecumenism, such as participation in the World Week of Prayer by both Protestants and Catholics, have also enjoyed success. This local cooperation is seen on various islands, where community affiliations trump denominalisation in bringing people together for joint celebrations and worship. There is, however, no national council of churches in French Polynesia. Nor is there any organisation uniting the churches of Franconesia, the Francophone countries of the Pacific.

Conclusion

French Polynesia remains a solidly Christian Pacific nation. The main two churches still dominate the religious landscape and there is little likelihood of this changing in the near future, although interesting developments might be ahead if the Catholics continue to grow and the EPM continues its decrease. The prospects for individual churches, however, will also vary according to the public acceptance of their political agendas and to the acceptance of efforts to contextualise liturgy and other church practices.

Bibliography

Ernst, Manfred, *Winds of Change: Rapidly Growing Religious Groups in the Pacific Islands* (Suva: Pacific Conference of Churches, 1994).

Fer, Yannick and Gwendoline Malogne-Fer, 'French Polynesia', in Manfred Ernst (ed.), *Globalization and the Re-shaping of Christianity in the Pacific Islands* (Suva: Pacific Theological College, 2006), 649–83.

Garrett, John, *To Live Among the Stars* (1982); *Footsteps in the Sea* (1992); *Where the Nets Were Cast* (1997) (all Suva: Institute of Pacific Studies; Geneva: World Council of Churches).

Malogne-Fer, Gwendoline, 'A Dispute at the Lord's Supper: Theology and Culture in the Māʻohi Protestant Church (French Polynesia)', in Fiona Magowan and Carolyn Schwarz (eds), *Christianity, Conflict, and Renewal in Australia and the Pacific* (Boston: Brill, 2016), 35–58.

Tauira, Marama Gaston, 'Ecumenism in French Polynesia: A Maohi Understanding that Springs from the Fenua', in Manfred Ernst and Lydia Johnson (eds), *Navigating Troubled Waters: The Ecumenical Movement in the Pacific Islands since the 1980s* (Suva: Pacific Theological College, 2017), 97–131.

Cook Islands and Niue

Nga Mataio

The Cook Islands – named after the famous English explorer Captain James Cook – comprise 15 small tropical atolls and volcanic islands totalling just 94 square kilometres, surrounded by its Exclusive Economic Zone area of 2 million square kilometres of the South Pacific Ocean. The total resident population is about 18,000, with over 60,000 Cook Islanders living in New Zealand or Australia. Cook Islanders are part of the Polynesian race and speak both Cook Islands Māori and English.

The Revd John Williams of the London Missionary Society (LMS) introduced Christianity to the Cook Islands, landing on Aitutaki on 26 October 1821 after first establishing himself in nearby Tahiti in 1797. It took 40 years to reach all 15 islands of the country, Palmerston Island being the last. From just the one church almost 200 years ago, the country now has six mainline churches and seven newly established ones.

Early Developments and Growth

The LMS Cook Islands branch was administered from London until 1968, when management was localised and the name changed to the Cook Islands Christian Church (CICC). The church played a prominent role in the early expansion of Christianity in the Pacific; from 1872 to 1975, it sent over 200 of its own missionaries to evangelise Papua New Guinea, New Caledonia, Sāmoa and Vanuatu. Despite new denominations arriving in the twentieth century, over half of the population are members of the CICC. There are currently 23 established branches on all islands in the Cook Islands, 20 in New Zealand and 22 in Australia, served by ordained ministers. Takamoa Theological College – the only theological training institute in the country, and also one of the oldest in the Pacific Islands, having been established in 1839 – is based at Takamoa, Rarotonga, where the CICC's head office is also located.

Seventh-day Adventists (SDA) arrived in 1891, the Cook Islands Mission being part of the New Zealand and Pacific Union Conference. It has four branches on Rarotonga, where its head office is also located, and a number of branches on some of the outer islands.

The Roman Catholic Church arrived in 1894 and a prefecture was established in 1922. It was elevated to the Vicariate Apostolic of Cook Islands in

1948 and to the Diocese of Rarotonga in 1966. The Diocese of Rarotonga is now a suffragan of the Archdiocese of Suva in Fiji. Catholics run Saint Joseph's School and Nukutere College on Rarotonga. The cathedral church is St Joseph's Cathedral in Avarua, the main town. There are three other branches on Rarotonga and a few on some of the outer islands.

Assemblies of God mission work began from New Zealand in the early 1960s and was formally established as a church in the Cook Islands in 1975. It has four branches on Rarotonga and three of the outer islands. The Apostolic Church of the Cook Islands was established in 1988 on Rarotonga. It was founded by Theophilus Augustus Ernest Price, an American evangelist and pastor, under the auspices of the Pentecostal Assemblies of the World, Inc. It quickly spread to the outer islands of Aitutaki, Atiu and Mangaia. Its head office is on Rarotonga, where it also has one branch.

The Cook Islands was first visited by a missionary of the Church of Jesus Christ of Latter-day Saints (LDS), Elder Noah Rogers, in May and June of 1845. On 23 May 1899, Daniel C. Miller in Tahiti sent Elders Osborne J. P. Widtsoe and Marvin W. Davis to Avarua, Rarotonga, to begin missionary work. Missionary efforts ended in November 1903 without any conversions but recommenced in May 1942 under member Fritz Bunge-Kruger, a baker who settled briefly on the Cook Islands along with his wife and family. By 1946 there were almost 40 LDS followers. Today, the church has three branches on Rarotonga, where its head office is also based, and branches on Aitutaki and Mangaia.

Churches that have arrived or been established since the turn of the millennium include Holy Spirit Revival, Cornerstone, Celebration on the Rock, Rarotonga Community, New Life, New Hope and a branch of the Fiji Methodists. Apart from the Methodists, these new churches have drawn the majority of their members from the CICC.

Christianity in the Cook Islands, 1970 and 2020

Tradition	1970 Population	%	2020 Population	%	Average annual growth rate (%), 1970–2020
Christians	21,300	99.3%	16,800	96.1%	−0.5%
Anglicans	100	0.5%	90	0.5%	−0.2%
Independents	1,300	6.0%	3,000	17.1%	1.7%
Protestants	16,100	75.4%	10,700	61.1%	−0.8%
Catholics	2,300	10.6%	4,900	28.0%	1.6%
Evangelicals	740	3.5%	1,100	6.3%	0.8%
Pentecostals/Charismatics	130	0.6%	3,000	17.1%	6.5%
Total population	**21,400**	**100.0%**	**17,500**	**100.0%**	**−0.4%**

Source: Todd M. Johnson and Gina A. Zurlo (eds), *World Christian Database* (Leiden/Boston: Brill), accessed January 2020.

Significant Occasions

Apart from the arrival times of the different church denominations, the main events commemorated annually include the following:

- National Gospel Day – 26 October. This is a public holiday, also referred to as Nuku Day. All CICC branches, joined by members of other denominations, put up biblical dramas and displays for the occasion.
- Individual island gospel days. Apart from the national event mentioned above, each island also commemorates the gospel's arrival on their respective islands with their own set programmes.
- Constitution celebrations – the last week of July, culminating on 4 August, Constitution Day. The church plays an important role in the religious components of the week-long event on both Rarotonga and the outer islands.
- Thanksgiving services. These are organised by the Religious Advisory Council to coincide with the commencement of the official cyclone season, which begins in November and ends in March.
- ANZAC Day service – 25 April. This is another event for which the church plays a major role in the commencement and closing of the day's programme.
- House of Ariki Day – 6 July. The church conducts a service of worship as part of the programme for the country's traditional leaders.

In the government sector, religious observance is part and parcel of almost all official functions conducted at all levels: national, local and agency.

Migrant Churches

Partly as a result of the expansion of the Rarotonga International Airport in the early 1970s, and given that Cook Islanders travel on New Zealand passports, migration increased significantly, to the extent that 20 CICC branches were established in New Zealand, the first one in 1975, and another 22 established in Australia, the first one in 1992. New but yet-to-be commissioned branches are still being established in the latter two countries, the main destinations of migrant Cook Islanders. Those migrating from other mainline churches (Catholics, SDA, Assemblies of God, LDS) did not have to establish new branches in these countries but rather joined the branches closest to where they settled.

The eleventh general assembly of the Pacific Conference of Churches (PCC) was held in Auckland in October–November 2018, partly to recognise the movement of Pacific Islanders from different denominations to settle in New Zealand. The theme chosen for the occasion, Psalm 137: 4, aptly fitted the well managed event, which was hosted by the migrant churches themselves, the main ones being the Methodist churches of Fiji,

Sāmoa and Tonga; the Anglican Church of Melanesia (Solomon Islands and Vanuatu); the Congregational Christian Church in Sāmoa; and the CICC.

Spirituality and Liturgy

Sunday observance is a way of life and all residents, as well as visitors, give it their full respect. Different denominations run their own regular and special worship programmes throughout the week, which culminates on Sunday. While essential services across the nation (telecommunications, health, law and order) continue on Sundays, there are no organised sports, shops are closed most of the day, and there is no fishing or work in the plantations. The country's laws prohibit the sale of alcohol on Sundays and other restrictive processes are put in place for Sunday observance. The Sabbath observance by the SDA on Saturday has many fewer restrictions compared to the Sunday observance.

Theological Education

Takamoa Theological College, the only theological training institution in the Cook Islands, comes under the CICC. Established in 1839, it offers undergraduate-level qualifications in biblical studies. After four years of full-time study, students get a certificate or diploma, depending on how well they perform. In recent years, exceptional students have been granted a bachelor's degree, and those who wish to do postgraduate studies tend to go to Fiji, New Zealand or Australia. Most Takamoa graduates are posted in the CICC's parishes in the Cook Islands, New Zealand and Australia. Formal theological education for students in other church denominations is undertaken overseas, mainly in Fiji, New Zealand and Australia.

While Takamoa does not offer formal lay training, several short-term training programmes are conducted by various church departments throughout the year on a range of biblical topics and their applications today. Ministers also conduct regular Bible classes in their parishes as part of their job description and according to the needs of members.

Ecumenism at Work

In 1975, the government enacted the Religious Organisations Restrictions Act, confirming the following as the initial members under the Act: Cook Islands Christian Church, Roman Catholic Church, Seventh-day Adventist Church and Church of Jesus Christ of Latter-day Saints. Added to the list in the 1980s were the Apostolic Church and the Assemblies of God. Under the Act, a management body called the Religious Advisory Council was established to manage ecumenical affairs – for example the two annual thanksgiving services that the leaders of the six churches jointly conduct.

National Influence

The influence of religion on the social, cultural and political spectrums of the nation is significant, in that major events in any of these three categories are started with a prayer and close with a prayer. In most cases, because the CICC is the main denomination, its members – be they ministers or elders in the gathering – are accorded the responsibility of conducting the prayers. Other mainline church personnel can also be allocated the tasks, depending on the venue and purpose of the event.

Although this has been the practice for many generations, some present-day organisers are not requiring the devotions to be conducted, especially at smaller events. The pace of things today, modern lifestyles and processes that require things to be done promptly and punctually are largely responsible. This leads some to discontinue the practice of prayer, which is perceived to be old-fashioned and unnecessarily time-consuming.

What the Future Holds

Plans are already underway to commemorate the two hundredth anniversary of the arrival of Christianity in the country. Since 2014, the CICC's Bicentennial Celebrations Unit (BCU) has been organising, behind the scenes, the programme for the national event that will be held where it all started, at Aitutaki, in October 2021. Smaller bicentennial celebrations are already being planned thereafter for each of the outer islands.

There is no doubt that the Cook Islands is a relatively religious country, where Christianity across the board thrives. Indeed, this is something it has in common with such neighbouring countries as Tonga, the two Sāmoas, Niue, the Solomon Islands, Vanuatu, Fiji, Tuvalu and French Polynesia. But challenges to the status quo have already taken place and will no doubt continue into the future: new denominations arriving or being established, non-Christian religious groups gathering momentum, even cult-like groups finding their way into the country. This means the mainline churches might have to adapt and restructure to meet the new challenges.

Niue

Niue is a coral atoll in the South Pacific, some 1,500 miles from New Zealand. It is one of the world's largest coral islands, with a population of 1,600. Niue was made a British protectorate in 1900 and placed under New Zealand's control in 1901, which made it easier to have contact with the outside world. Today, Niue is a self-governing territory in free association with New Zealand, which is responsible for external affairs. Niueans are citizens of New Zealand and enjoy all basic human rights and civil liberties. Since the 1960s Niue has seen a steady decline in its population, with most emigrating to find employment in New Zealand, where more than 24,000 Niueans now live.

The first attempt to introduce Christianity to Niue was made in 1830, by the pioneering missionary John Williams of the London Missionary Society (LMS). Though this initial effort was unsuccessful, the LMS continued to make periodic visits to the island. In 1846 Nukai Peniamina, a Niuean trained as a teacher in an LMS school in Sāmoa, returned home and was followed three years later by a Sāmoan named Paulo, who was instrumental in establishing the church in Niue. There was no resident European missionary until 1861. The early LMS influence was decisive, and Niueans still consider themselves predominantly Congregationalists. The church remained under the LMS until 1970, when it became independent and took the name Ekalesia Niue. Today it is officially recognised as the Ekalesia Kerisiano Niue (Congregational Christian Church of Niue) and represents some 75% of the total population. The Federation of Christian Women plays an active role in the life of the church and also includes women from other denominations. A branch of the church was planted in Auckland, New Zealand, in 1996 to minister to the large migrant community of Niueans there.

The Church of Jesus Christ of Latter-day Saints (LDS) is the second-largest denomination on the island. The LDS was introduced by Fritz Bunge-Kruger in 1952, and 65 were baptised in the first year of ministry. Sionemologa Tagavaitau was the first Niuean missionary. Although initially met with opposition, Latter-day Saints are now found throughout the island and some hold positions in the government. Jehovah's Witnesses and the New Apostolic Church are also present in small numbers. Fr Herman Joseph Therriault, the first permanent Catholic missionary to Niue, arrived in 1955. Today the small Catholic community is served by a Marist priest at Alofi and, since 1957, has been part of the Catholic Diocese of Tonga.

Christianity in Niue, 1970 and 2020

Tradition	1970		2020		Average annual growth rate (%), 1970–2020
	Population	%	Population	%	
Christians	5,100	99.9%	1,600	96.6%	−2.3%
Anglicans	30	0.6%	40	2.5%	0.6%
Independents	380	7.4%	460	27.9%	0.4%
Protestants	3,800	73.2%	860	52.7%	−2.9%
Catholics	220	4.3%	150	9.2%	−0.8%
Evangelicals	220	4.3%	50	3.1%	−2.9%
Pentecostals/Charismatics	0	0.0%	200	12.3%	6.2%
Total population	**5,100**	**100.0%**	**1,600**	**100.0%**	**−2.3%**

Source: Todd M. Johnson and Gina A. Zurlo (eds), *World Christian Database* (Leiden/Boston: Brill), accessed January 2020.

Today Niue is almost entirely Christian, though many Christians are still influenced by traditional Polynesian religion, even if only minimally. For example, Western medicine is available at the hospital in Alofi but herbalists and traditional healers (*taulaatua*) are also frequently visited. The Niue National Council of Churches consists of five religious groups: the Niue Christian Church, the Catholic Church, the Apostolic Church on the Rock, the Christian Outreach Centre and the Seventh-day Adventist Church (observer status).

Current concerns of the Christian community in Niue include climate change and the related issues of economic decline and unemployment. These have resulted in a very high rate of outward migration, with most of the population having moved to New Zealand during the past few decades. Since 1988 the Niue Christian Church has had a presence in New Zealand, ministering to its migrant members and engaging with the New Zealand government to try to find constructive ways to stem the flow of migration.

Bibliography

Ernst, Manfred and Lydia Johnson (eds), *Navigating Troubled Waters: The Ecumenical Movement in the Pacific Islands since the 1980s* (Suva: Pacific Theological College, 2017).

Goodman, Robert Maurice, *Niue of Polynesia: Savage Island's First Latter-day Saint Missionaries* (Powhatan, VA: Brookstone, 2002).

Jackson, Hawea Albert Reed, *Relationship Between the Church and State and Church and Culture: Changes and Development of the Ekalesia Niue Church. Before and After Independence, 1970* (Saarbrücken: Lambert Academic Publishing, 2010).

Paea, Afele and Birth Wilma Lisimoni-Togahai, *Ko e maama kua kikila ki Niue nukututaha* [*The Dawning of the Gospel on Niue*] (Niue: Nevat Press, 2010).

Rere, Taira, *The Gospel Comes to Rarotonga* (Rarotonga: publisher unknown, 1980).

This chapter has been helpfully informed by the entry on Niue in Todd M. Johnson and Gina A. Zurlo, *World Christian Encyclopedia*, 3rd edition (Edinburgh: Edinburgh University Press, 2019), 596–7.

Tonga

Solo Tafokitau

The Kingdom of Tonga is a Polynesian island state comprising an archipelago of 169 islands, 36 of which are inhabited. It lies to the south of Sāmoa and covers 800 kilometres in a north–south line. The majority of the population live on Tongatapu, the largest island. Tonga was never colonised, though from 1900 to 1970 it was under British protection through a Treaty of Friendship that made Britain responsible for its foreign affairs. Today it is a constitutional monarchy, with the king highly respected but, following constitutional reforms in the early twenty-first century, no longer involved in day-to-day government. More Tongans are living overseas than in their own homeland, with Australia, New Zealand and the USA all having large Tongan communities, whose remittances play a significant role in the island economy. Christianity plays a central role in national life, with the Free Wesleyan Church of Tonga closely related to the royal family and Sabbath observance enshrined in the constitution.

The Coming of Christianity

The Christian faith, first introduced by Tahitian Wesleyan missionaries, began to spread during the 1820s through the work of Pita Vi, a local evangelist in the Ha'apai group of islands in central Tonga. Despite lacking any deep knowledge of the Bible and missionary work, Pita Vi was a source of spiritual inspiration for many. He opened the way for his people to read and write. With the support of King Tāufa'āhau I, Vi started a school at Lifuka and reported to the British missionaries on Tongatapu (who had arrived in 1826) that Tāufa'āhau had commanded his people to learn to read and write and destroyed the objects of their traditional religion, and the houses in which they were kept.

Methodist missionary John Thomas arrived at Ha'apai on 30 January 1830 to find wide support for the new religion, through the work of Vi and the great influence of the king. The turning point of the mission in Ha'apai was when King Tāufa'āhau almost died from being poisoned by those who opposed his acceptance of the new faith. After Thomas and Vi prayed with the Christian group throughout the night, the king recovered. Tāufa'āhau took the name of the English King George III (Sioasi in Tongan) at his baptism on 7 August 1831. Thomas subsequently recorded the occasion in large and bold handwriting: 'George Taufa'ahau, King in Lifuka'. Tāufa'āhau later became a local preacher and together with his wife, Sālote Lupepau'u, became a Methodist class leader, assisting their people to grow in spiritual life.

Soon after his baptism, King George and Pita Vi decided to begin mission work in the Vava'u group of islands. The way had been prepared by an island chief, Aleamotu'a, who advised the local ruler, Fīnau 'Ulukalala III, to accept Christianity. Pita Vi preached the Christian message before King George at the first public Christian worship service at Vava'u on their first Sunday. The following day, King George and Fīnau attacked the old religion by burning and destroying the gods and their houses, and the sacred objects of worship. The final establishment of Christianity at Vava'u was sealed by the baptism of Fīnau 'Ulukalala with his new name Zephaniah, along with eight of his children.

Through the influence of Methodist missionary Peter Turner, the emerging Christian community in Vava'u was distinguished by a fervent desire for religious revival. This resulted in the outbreak of a revival movement in the village of 'Utui in Vava'u on 23 July 1834, which led to widespread acceptance of the new faith. Soon the whole of Tonga embraced Methodist Christianity, with its emphasis on John Wesley's doctrine of sanctification and holiness and on helping the less fortunate.

The effects of the religious revival divided the country. Those who were against the new faith felt that their traditional privileges were being undermined and that their status and position in society and the community were being threatened. They therefore took strong action against the new movement, chasing Christians from their homes, burning down churches, imprisoning those who accepted Christianity and stripping some of them of their titles – for example Tu'ivakanō, the chief of Nukunuku village.

Aleamotu'a appealed to King George for help. King George arrived in Tongatapu on 1 January 1837 with his warriors from Ha'apai and Vava'u,

Christianity in Tonga, 1970 and 2020

Tradition	1970		2020		Average annual growth rate (%), 1970–2020
	Population	%	Population	%	
Christians	83,200	98.7%	106,000	95.7%	0.5%
Anglicans	800	0.9%	1,800	1.6%	1.6%
Independents	26,200	31.0%	84,500	76.1%	2.4%
Protestants	38,700	45.9%	43,800	39.4%	0.2%
Catholics	14,300	17.0%	14,400	13.0%	0.0%
Evangelicals	6,700	7.9%	8,500	7.7%	0.5%
Pentecostals/Charismatics	4,300	5.0%	14,100	12.7%	2.4%
Total population	**84,400**	**100.0%**	**111,000**	**100.0%**	**0.6%**

Source: Todd M. Johnson and Gina A. Zurlo (eds), *World Christian Database* (Leiden/Boston: Brill), accessed January 2020.

who carried both club and Bible to engage the 'powers of darkness' and to destroy the 'heathen fortresses'. They burned down the sacred places of traditional religion, destroying the 'heathen gods' and objects of worship. Three hundred men, women and children were killed. After these wars, Tonga experienced a time of peace while King George consolidated his political position. His partnership with many chiefs in Tongatapu and Christian followers consolidated the bonds between himself, the people and Christianity in Tonga. Meanwhile, the effect of the revival was tremendous growth in church membership. The new faith spread to the whole of Ha'apai, Vava'u, the Niuas and the greater part of Tongatapu.

Christian Diversity

Today, Christianity in Tonga is marked by diversity of expression. The historical influence of Methodism is still evident, particularly through the place given to the Free Wesleyan Church of Tonga, which was formed with royal approval in 1885. Its leader, Jabez Bunting Watkin, was born in Tonga and was identified with Ha'apai, the original home of the king. The church functioned as the church of the monarch and people and became an integral part of the Tongan social system.

The origins of the Free Wesleyan Church lie in tensions that developed between Methodist missionary John Thomas and King George. These came to a head when the chairman of the Methodist Society at Ha'apai in 1862 dismissed from the Society all the chiefs and people who had practised the custom of presenting gifts of food and domestic goods to King George at the funeral of his son. The king took this as an insult and decided to resign all his positions in the Society, and the queen did the same. They felt that the Methodist mission lacked understanding of their cultural and traditional life and was also failing to help the people economically. Large sums of money were sent from Tonga every year to the mission fund in Sydney, particularly during the latter half of the 1860s and the 1870s. Believing that this money could have been used to improve conditions within Tonga, the king and his chiefs thought that it was time for Tonga to have its own independent church. Accordingly, in 1873 King George sent a letter to the Methodist Conference in Sydney asking that the mission district in Tonga be made an independent church. The request was refused, on the advice of the Mission Board, on the ground that Tonga was not yet ready for independence. This refusal led to the establishment of the Free Wesleyan Church of Tonga in 1885, which was joined by the king and most of the chiefs. Conflict between the two factions of Wesleyanism continued for several generations, and even today the rift has not been fully healed.

In 1924, Queen Sālote, as head of the Free Church — and likely influenced by her marriage to a Wesleyan high chief — attempted to reunite the Free Church with the Wesleyan mission. However, the president of the Free Church of Tonga, Jabez Watkin, opposed the measure and, after his dismissal by the queen, started the Free Church of Tonga (FCT) with a minority group of 1,234 members. The majority, 16,848 members, joined the new established Free Wesleyan Church of Tonga (FWC), which was from that time the dominant church in Tonga.

The king is still the titular head of the FWC. He confirms the election of Church presidents and has the right to appoint a new one if the incumbent cannot fulfil his duties. The position of ordained ministers (*faifekau*) is still prestigious and comparable to the rank of a minor chief, while the power and authority of the Church's president is even more extensive.

The Church of Tonga, founded in 1919, is a second very traditional independent church in Tonga. Though it is marked by some influence of the Methodist tradition, its character is more that of an autonomous local church. Its similarities to the FCT include its constitution, dress, and order and style of services, as well as its administrative structure. The Revd Dr Tevita Feke Mafi, who became director of its Youth Department during the 1980s, was the first and only theologian of the Church with a doctor of divinity degree from the USA. Dr Mafi started his theological training at the Free Wesleyans' Sia'atoutai Theological College. He then moved on to study at the Pacific Theological College and graduated with a bachelor of divinity. Currently, 20 ordained ministers of the Church have completed formal theological training.

The Free Constitutional Church (FCC) regards itself as representing the true tradition of the Free Church from 1885. It emerged out of conflicts that occurred within the FCT in 1930, 1939 and 1959–61. Issues caused by amendments to the original constitution and a perceived misuse of power, money and the assets of the FCT in New Zealand finally led to the establishment of the new church in 1979. The highest decision-making body is the annual general conference, which appoints the president and ordains and appoints ministers. The FCC and the FCT have not allowed their ministers to undertake further education and have particularly discouraged theological and Christian education. According to the 2016 Tonga national census, membership in the FCC of Tonga had declined from 1,200 in 1992 to 957 in a period of 24 years.

The Church of Jesus Christ of Latter-day Saints (LDS), sometimes described as the Mormons, sent 19 travelling preachers to Ha'apai in the 1890s. Until 1916 it was a branch of the mission in Sāmoa, but the pace quickened under two successive mission presidents, Willard L. Smith and Mark V. Coombs. Rumours and allegations about the morals of the Latter-day Saints were rife concerning polygamy (which they officially suspended in 1890, but part of the Mormon sacred scriptures). Attempts were made within the Tongan parliament to exclude LDS missionaries. However, as they were Americans it was thought they could be used for international leverage. The Mormon Excluding Law was passed by the Tongan legislature in June 1922 but was repealed in 1924. Resumption of the LDS mission in Tonga was assured. Since then the church has grown rapidly and Tonga has become the country with the highest proportion of LDS members in the world.

The stronghold of the Roman Catholic Church on Tongatapu was at Mu'a, the village of the Tuí Tonga line of sacred chiefs, who possessed priestly power under the old religion. As a minority religion, Tongan Catholicism has had a difficult history, particularly on account of the hostility it faced from the Methodists. There can be no doubt that the Roman Catholic priests contributed to the bad relationship between the two missions by trying to counter Protestant and British influence in the islands. Yet the fact remains that the Wesleyan missionaries spent too much time and energy fighting Roman Catholicism. To be consistent with their Protestant principles, the Wesleyan missionaries presented the priests as 'instruments of the Devil'; their teachings were described as a pack of lies and their form of worship denounced as idolatrous. Part of the incentive for the translation of the Bible and instruction in literacy was its perceived value in combating Catholicism. Nevertheless, the Catholic Church gradually established itself and is organised today as the Diocese of Tonga.

The Assemblies of God (AOG) was established by overseas missionaries from America, Fiji, India and New Zealand, who arrived in Tonga in 1966 with a well planned evangelistic outreach programme. It became the fastest-growing religious group in Tonga, with an annual growth rate of as much as 20%. Small worshipping communities were established in the islands, especially Ha'apai and Vava'u. To this day, the AOG is not a member of the Tonga National Council of Churches, but it is a member of the interdenominational committee of Pentecostals and Charismatics, which is more popular because its membership has a far wider range than the ecumenical body. According to the 2016 Tonga national census, the AOG membership had grown to 2,347 in all parts of Tonga in the space of 24 years.

The evangelistic goal of Jehovah's Witnesses in Tonga is to convert new members and to translate their books into the Tongan language. The church was finally established in 1970 in Nuku'alofa. Jehovah's Witnesses first attempted to spread the message in Tonga during the second quarter of the twentieth century, when a returned Tongan sailor was approached to translate a booklet he had read titled *Where Are the Dead?* Due to opposition, it was difficult for Jehovah's Witnesses to grow in number: in 1992 the organisation had 120 members. According to the Tonga national census of 2016, the Jehovah's Witnesses membership had risen to 385.

The Salvation Army came to Tonga in 1986 through the invitation of King Tāufa'āhau IV, who was impressed by its outreach to society, evangelistic approach, non-political orientation and popular brass bands. In 1992, it had 150 members, with a single building at Sopu. It has reached out to many people through its programmes on youth, women and agricultural projects, which rely heavily on financial support from 'mother churches' overseas.

The presence of the Seventh-day Adventist church goes back to the close of the nineteenth century, when Edward Hilliard and Edwin Butz were welcomed by King George I and started their small colony of *papālangi* (non-islanders) on the beach. A second start by George G. Stewart and his wife Grace in 1912 was more promising. By then Adventism was adapting itself better to the needs of the islands through the location of its base for Oceania in Australia and New Zealand by their founding mother, Ellen G. White, during her years in Australia. With the use of the Tongan language the SDA school drew more pupils under Maggie Ferguson at Nuku'alofa. A great disaster faced the mission when the Spanish influenza in 1918 caused the death of Adventist missionary Pearl Tolhurst and severely undermined the work that had begun. By then the small mission could see that the only way forward would lie in further developing its schools.

The small Anglican flock presented a further combination of foreign forces. The Anglican Church concluded a treaty of protection with a threatened and somewhat reluctant King George II in 1900 and again in 1905. Shirley Baker and Alfred Willis formed the Siasi 'o Vika, the Church of Queen Victoria. As Willis settled among the Tongans, he brought connections with the colonial Anglican minority in Fiji – and with the Bishop of London, under whose general jurisdiction he served as a missionary of the Society for the Propagation of the Gospel. All these manoeuvres were suspected of being promoted by *papālangi*, in contrast to the home-grown and autonomous Methodist Free Church.

By 1992, three Evangelical-Fundamentalist organisations had offices and staff in Tonga: World Vision, which started in 1983; Youth With A Mission, dating from 1984; and Campus Crusade for Christ, established in 1987. All of these organisations experienced hostile attitudes from the mainline churches, while only a few, like the Free Wesleyan Church, Church of Tonga, Anglican Church, and the fundamentalist Gospel Chapels (Brethren), worked together with them.

The Tonga National Council of Churches (TNCC) was founded by members of the Free Wesleyan Church, Roman Catholic Church and Anglican Church in 1973. The Church of Tonga later joined but withdrew after five years due to conflict within the church. The Free Constitutional Church of Tonga was later admitted to full membership. Today the TNCC represents slightly more than half the population, compared with over 70% in 1976.

Future Prospects

Since the turn of the millennium, the number of Christian adherents in Tonga has grown. According to statistical data recorded by Manfred Ernst, in 1992 there were a total of 91,068 Christians in Tonga. Over the next 24 years, this number increased by 7,657 to reach a total of 98,725 according to the Tonga 2016 census of population and housing.

In 1992, it was recorded that Tonga's population was 93,500. By 2016, the total population had increased to 100,651. This growth of the population created new members and a rise in adherents being baptised into the churches. Therefore, the rise of the population over the last two decades has played a role in the growth and development of Christian adherents in the twenty-first century as it provides an opportunity for different denominations to introduce and establish more members in their congregations.

New denominations that did not exist in the twentieth century include the Mo'ui Fo'ou 'ia Kalaisi (New Life in Christ) and the Constitutional Church of Tonga. The addition of these denominations is a result of the split in churches, and has produced a decrease in the number of members of pre-existing denominations. However, it also provides an opportunity to increase the number of Christian adherents in Tonga through the attraction of new members.

The most influential denomination in Tonga today is the Free Wesleyan Church of Tonga, with 35,082 members. Since 1992, its membership has increased by 1,082. The denomination that has had the most significant growth since the end of the twentieth century is the Latter-day Saints, with an increase in membership of 4,473 between 1992 and 2016. Most Christian denominations have seen an increase in their number of members. The reasons for this growth are many, including changes to the style and the method of worship in the different denominations. Such changes have opened a door for a whole new community of adherents in different age groups and sectors of society. There is also a trend of members leaving the five existing churches of Wesleyan Methodist origins in order to join such churches as the Latter-day Saints, Seventh-day Adventists and Assemblies of God. The future is likely to be shaped by the ways in which Tongans navigate the relationship between Christian teaching and their traditional customs and culture.

Bibliography

Ernst, Manfred, *Winds of Change: Rapidly Growing Religious Groups in the Pacific Islands* (Suva: Pacific Conference of Churches, 1994).

Latu, Paula Onoafe, 'Fakaongo and Tau'ataina: The Influences of the Tongan Traditional Religion, the European Civilization and Wesleyan Teachings on the Formation of Tongan Religious Identities', MPhil thesis, Massey University, 2014.

Lātūkefu, Sione, *Church and State in Tonga: The Wesleyan Methodist Missionaries and Political Development, 1822–1875* (Honolulu: University Press of Hawaii, 1974).

Tonga Statistics Department, *Tonga 2016 Census of Population and Housing, Volume 1: Basic Tables and Administrative Report* (Nuku'alofa, 2017).

Vaipulu, Sioeli F., 'Towards an 'otualogy: Revisiting and Rethinking the Doctrine of God in Tonga', PhD thesis, Charles Sturt University, 2013.

Sāmoa and American Sāmoa

Fetaomi Tapu-Qiliho

Sāmoa gained its independence from New Zealand in 1962 and was known as Western Sāmoa until 1997. American Sāmoa is an unincorporated territory of the USA and lies to the east of Sāmoa. Both island groups belong to the Sāmoan archipelago and have had the same journey with Christianity.

It was in the late eighteenth and early nineteenth centuries that Sāmoans encountered Europeans and, hence, Christianity. By the 1820s, Europeans who had arrived in big ships were present in Sāmoa. Sailors and beachcombers began to speak with Sāmoans about Christianity. Prior to the arrival of Christianity, Sāmoans already had an Indigenous religion in which the supernatural was significant and in which sustainable relationships with the environment and kin were central, complete with its own story of creation validating their place and space in the universe. According to legend, Nafanua, a goddess, prophesied that a new religion would come by way of the sea. It was not until after 1828, with the arrival of missionaries who were formally trained in theology, that missionary work started to gain momentum.

The introduction of Christianity revolutionised Sāmoan culture as some of its basic tenets and biblical teachings, together with the views of English missionaries, created discord and challenged the authority of chiefs, the place of women, and traditional customs, practices and structures. Missionaries abolished many practices and beliefs in Sāmoan society that were deemed un-Christian and also advocated retention of some practices such as tattooing. Sāmoans likewise incorporated aspects of Christian values and beliefs that were similar to their own into their traditional structures. By the mid-nineteenth century, Christianity was truly Sāmoanised. Lalomilo Kamu poignantly captures this when he states in *The Sāmoan Culture and the Christian Gospel* that 'it is impossible to speak of the history of Sāmoa without referring to the history of Christianity in Sāmoa'.

John Williams, a missionary of the London Missionary Society (LMS), pioneered the advance of Christianity in Sāmoa from 1830 and established a Congregational denomination (today the Ekālēsia Fa'apotopotoga Kerisiano I Sāmoa, or EFKS). It remains to this day the church with the biggest following in Sāmoa. The Methodist Church soon followed in 1835 through the mission work of Peter Turner, who was a part of the Wesleyan Methodist Mission Society. In 1845, the Catholic Church also entered the Sāmoan islands, through the missionary work of two Marist priests, Fr Foudaire and Fr Violette. All three Christian denominations have a huge presence in both Sāmoa and American Sāmoa today and have remained the most influential traditional mainline churches.

Growth of Christianity

Sāmoa has a population of 200,000 and American Sāmoa's 2017 *Statistical Yearbook* indicates that there are 60,300 people in residence on those islands. In both places, more than 90% of the people state that they belong to the Christian faith. Of this Christian population, Protestants form the largest number. There is also a significant Roman Catholic presence in both places. In both American Sāmoa and Sāmoa, the EFKS is the largest Christian denomination. Despite this, there is also an indication that their numbers have decreased. This can also be said of the other two mainline

Christianity in Sāmoa, 1970 and 2020

Tradition	1970 Population	%	2020 Population	%	Average annual growth rate (%), 1970–2020
Christians	141,000	98.7%	198,000	98.8%	0.7%
Anglicans	350	0.2%	340	0.2%	−0.1%
Independents	20,200	14.1%	84,000	42.0%	2.9%
Protestants	82,500	57.6%	125,000	62.5%	0.8%
Catholics	29,800	20.8%	38,000	19.0%	0.5%
Evangelicals	9,000	6.3%	26,700	13.3%	2.2%
Pentecostals/Charismatics	3,900	2.7%	29,500	14.7%	4.1%
Total population	**143,000**	**100.0%**	**200,000**	**100.0%**	**0.7%**

Source: Todd M. Johnson and Gina A. Zurlo (eds), *World Christian Database* (Leiden/Boston: Brill), accessed January 2020.

Christianity in American Sāmoa, 1970 and 2020

Tradition	1970 Population	%	2020 Population	%	Average annual growth rate (%), 1970–2020
Christians	27,000	99.0%	54,400	97.5%	1.4%
Anglicans	100	0.4%	60	0.1%	−1.0%
Independents	2,600	9.6%	21,500	38.5%	4.3%
Protestants	18,500	67.8%	41,900	75.1%	1.6%
Catholics	5,000	18.3%	16,000	28.7%	2.4%
Evangelicals	2,500	9.1%	15,400	27.6%	3.7%
Pentecostals/Charismatics	1,600	5.8%	23,500	42.1%	5.5%
Total population	**27,300**	**100.0%**	**55,800**	**100.0%**	**1.4%**

Source: Todd M. Johnson and Gina A. Zurlo (eds), *World Christian Database* (Leiden/Boston: Brill), accessed January 2020.

churches that were responsible for the initial Christian movement into Sāmoa. In both places, despite the high membership numbers of the mainline churches, movement to newer faith denominations is evident.

Pentecostalism in the form of the Assemblies of God church became an expression of Christianity in Sāmoa from the 1960s onward. It quickly gained momentum after its initial setup in American Sāmoa and today boasts a growth evidenced by the many congregations they have in both Sāmoas. In the 1970s and 1980s, Youth for Christ (YFC) established an informal ministry. It was popular with young, educated people of the urban area in Apia. Its tent revival approach popularised the message of Christianity with a more youthful population. YFC gained accept- ance and became trendy as it preached against mainstream churches. It was common for sermons to berate practices in the mainline churches such as monetary obligations and giving as being exploitative of people, diverting their personal resources for the benefit of the churches. In the same manner, mainline churches' disapproval of the Pentecostal move- ment's lack of theology, 'prosperity gospel' focus and economically driven approaches and cult-like leadership were made known. As the Pentecos- tal movement has formalised and has given rise to the establishment of a plethora of smaller Pentecostal churches, leading personalities of the YFC movement such as Revd Viliamu Mafo'e have become prominent figures in the Pentecostal movement. He has a following of 5.5% of Sāmoa's Christian population and is the leader of a growing Pentecostal community popularly known as the Worship Centre.

The contraction in numbers of mainline church adherents can be attrib- uted to the increasing presence of Charismatic and Pentecostal churches and other groups such as the Church of Jesus Christ of Latter-day Saints (Mormons) and Seventh-day Adventists. Mormons first arrived in the Sāmoa archipelago by way of American Sāmoa in 1888. In 1889 they officially began their mission work in what is today known as Sāmoa on the island of Upolu. The Church of Jesus Christ of Latter-day Saints has grown exponentially in Sāmoa and has surpassed the Methodist Church in numbers to become the third-largest denomination. Increased proselytism through its missionaries and lucrative opportunities for upward mobility through access to education in the USA has resulted in the successful con- version of members of the traditional mainline churches to the Church of Jesus Christ of Latter-day Saints.

Another reason for a shift in emphasis from the traditional mainline churches to newer Pentecostal churches has been the desire for freedom from the conservativism associated with mainline Christianity. As the mainline churches became established, Christianity was expressed through and endorsed by the *fa'asāmoa* (the Sāmoan way of life) and traditional

Sāmoan structures of governance, namely that of the *matai* (chiefs), were incorporated into the life of Sāmoan Christianity. The increased movement of people away from mainline churches to other Christian denominations is because of the pressure of financial commitments and the stringent structures of the *matai* system that govern mainline churches. It is also said that one is able to acquire status and positions of responsibility more readily in the Pentecostal churches than in mainline churches due to the latter's insistence on the importance of the *matai* as a model for apt lay church leadership.

As in the 1970s and 1980s, a generational shift is also evident today in the movement of people towards Pentecostal churches as the young are drawn to the contemporary Evangelical approaches associated with Pentecostalism. Tele-evangelism-style worship modelled on the likes of Benny Hinn have resulted in Pentecostal churches' accusations of the 'lack of spirit' in mainstream traditional Sāmoan Christianity. Mainline churches and their traditional hymn singing and styles of worship are considered less desirable as Sāmoans opt for a more Charismatic spirituality that is free-style and influenced by American-styled Pentecostalism. There is a perception that everyone is equal in the Pentecostal movement – hence the tendency to opt for it as a more valid expression of Christianity in Sāmoa today as it inculcates a personal relationship with Christ.

Very few Sāmoans convert to other faiths, except the small number who have converted to the Bahá'í faith. Muslims are also present in both Sāmoas and account for 0.1% of the total population. Aside from Daniel Stanley of Sāmoa, who converted to Islam with his family, and a few Sāmoan women who have married Muslim men, conversion to Islam has been rare. The Jehovah's Witnesses faith is also present in both Sāmoas, where it has small followings. Small numbers of Hindus, Buddhists, Muslims and Jews, mostly expatriates and businesspeople, also live in both places. The Confucius Institute at the National University of Sāmoa fosters interest in Chinese language and culture. Interfaith relations are cordial, and there have not been any interfaith conflicts. Tolerance for other faiths by the Christian churches in Sāmoa is visible to a large degree, although interfaith worship is very rare.

Churches and Ministry

Theological colleges have been a huge part of the Christian presence in both Sāmoa and American Sāmoa and are institutions that Sāmoans hold in very high regard. The Congregationalists established Malua Theological College in Leulumoega in 1844. The Methodists started Piula in the village of Lufilufi in 1868 after an initial training college was started in 1859 in Savai'i. Kanana Fou Theological College was established in

American Sāmoa in 1983 after a conflict in 1980 that resulted in American Sāmoa withdrawing from the EFKS in Sāmoa and forming the Ekalesia Fa'apotopotoga Kerisiano I Amerika Sāmoa (EFKAS; Congregational Christian Church of American Sāmoa). The Roman Catholic Archdiocese of Sāmoa has a theological college in Moamoa that is dedicated to the training of catechists and deacons for local ministry.

All theological institutions continue to play an essential role in the furthering of mission in both Sāmoas. Indigenous Sāmoan theologies that encourage the use of Sāmoan cultural motifs, values and knowledge systems are a major focus of theological education today. The curriculum in all theological institutions is determined by the various churches, but there is also a focus in the development of resources for ministry in Sāmoa and the Pacific today. The emphasis on theological education that highlights stewardship of creation and that responds to climate change, climate justice and environmental issues is a priority.

Today, many Sāmoans reside outside of the country due to emigration following the Second World War to capitalise on employment opportunities made available because of labour shortages in Pacific Rim countries such as New Zealand, Australia and the USA. The chain migration of Sāmoans outward was the beginning of a huge diasporic community. As American Sāmoa is an unincorporated territory of the USA, many American Sāmoans have made their permanent homes on the mainland and in Hawai'i. Clergy trained in these home-grown theological institutions are instrumental in the mission to diasporic Sāmoans who desire to maintain ties with the homeland and adhere to a Sāmoan-oriented Christianity in their new homes away from the motherland.

Ecumenism is officially expressed in both Sāmoas through the existence of their separate national councils of churches. Through these bodies, support for ecumenical events at the national level is galvanised and organised. Leaders of the national councils of churches have been vocal at the national level about various issues pertaining to the Christian faith and its views on society. Such issues include the elimination of violence and domestic violence, eradication of poverty and the recent measles outbreak in Sāmoa. In addition to these official national bodies, the EFKS, EFKAS, Methodists, Anglicans and Roman Catholics have longstanding ecumenical relations with other mainline Christian churches throughout the region through their association with regional ecumenical bodies. Leaders of the churches in Sāmoa have been at the forefront of Pacific ecumenism. The late Revds Oka Fau'olo, Vavae Toma and Faigāmē Tago'ilelagi of the EFKS; the late Cardinal Pio Taofinu'u, who was the first Polynesian Roman Catholic bishop; and the late Revds Sione Tamali'i and Fa'ato'ese Auva'a of the Methodist Church were avid supporters of Pacific efforts to unite the Christian movement and were instrumental in Sāmoa's contribution to ecumenism.

Through formal links established in the 1960s with the formation of the Pacific Conference of Churches and the Pacific Theological College, Sāmoan mainline churches have participated in regional ecumenism. This partnership has spanned a period of nearly 60 years and has been responsive to and advocated for various socio-economic, environmental and political issues of concern throughout the Pacific region. The theological colleges of the mainline churches in Sāmoa have also participated since the late 1960s in ecumenism through the South Pacific Association of Theological Schools (SPATS). However, it can be said that women's groups are the most successful drivers of ecumenism throughout the Sāmoan archipelago as they regularly share in grassroots approaches to ecumenical ministry through prayer and worship.

Critics of ecumenism in Sāmoa have suggested that it has focused only on visible unity at the clerical level and not on a genuine desire to inculcate an ecumenical spirituality as expression of Christianity in Sāmoa. Contrary to this, there has been a vibrant ecumenical tradition of worship in Sāmoa between the Apia Protestant congregation, the Anglican Church and the English-speaking congregation of the Roman Catholic Cathedral. It has existed for more than 40 years and is evidence of ecumenical relationships that work well in Sāmoa. The Roman Catholic Church in both Sāmoas owns and operates institutions for the care of the elderly. Despite the ownership being particular to a denomination, it can be said that through these institutions of care, the Sāmoan churches' witness as an ecumenical body is alive and well. As gerontocracy and spirituality are core values of the *fa'asāmoa*, all Sāmoan churches converge in these spaces through mission to provide for the needs and care of the elderly in various ways.

Mission has continued to be an integral part of the Sāmoan Christian journey since the late eighteenth century, when Sāmoan converts were prominent members of mission teams to other parts of the Pacific on mission ships. More recent examples of international missionary service include the late Revd Dr Peniamina Vai, who served as a missionary in Kingston, Jamaica, and Revd Nuuausala Siaosi (now of the Apia Protestant Church) who served in Chad, both through the auspices of the Council for World Mission in the 1980s.

In Sāmoa today, mission schools that began with the missionaries continue. The mainline churches, the Church of Jesus Christ of Latter-day Saints and, more recently, some Pentecostal churches are all involved in successful provision of education. Many primary, secondary and vocational schools in Sāmoa are owned and run by various churches.

Gospel and Cultural Change

Christianity has had a huge impact on culture and change in Sāmoa. The central role of Christian churches in Sāmoa is evident in their influence over the social, political and economic life of Sāmoan people and society. Sāmoa is today an independent nation whose motto is 'Sāmoa is founded on God' ('Fa'avae i le Atua Sāmoa'). Through a constitutional amendment bill unanimously passed by the government in 2016, Sāmoa declared Christianity to be its official state religion. This was a controversial move that sparked much discussion about the necessity for it, given the country's diverse nature. Despite this and the change that ensued, the religious freedoms of all citizens are guaranteed through the constitution.

A recent event that highlighted the immense influence the church has in Sāmoa was the taxation of church ministers by the Sāmoan government. When Sāmoan villages decided to accept Christianity, they built churches and houses for their pastors and were responsible for their upkeep through food and support. Despite the decision of other churches to pay income taxes for their ministers, the EFKS stood firmly convinced that church ministers should not be taxed for *alofa* (monetary gifts) that they are given by the congregations. This practice, it argued, was foundational to the church in Sāmoa and was an expression of contextual theologies relating to giving. The stand-off between the EFKS and the government resulted in a court ruling in August 2019 to dismiss all charges relating to the non-payment of income taxes of EFKS ministers, due to insufficient evidence.

Today, Christianity is an integral part of the *fa'asāmoa* and has influenced Sāmoan society and traditional structures in such a profound way that it is difficult to imagine a Sāmoa without its presence. The physical presence of Christianity throughout Sāmoa is such that one cannot help but notice its centrality in the lives of Sāmoans. Large church structures and places of worship beautify the countryside, prayers are offered at every function of either a secular or a religious nature, church bells ring in the early hours of the morning throughout the week to signify worship, and families gather in the evenings for dedicated family vespers. On Sundays it is normal practice that congregants bring gifts of food and money for clergy and their families. The life of service of those who hold authority in the church is deeply embedded in the Sāmoan psyche and informs reciprocal relationships that are important in daily Sāmoan life. Sāmoans are deeply committed to their Christian faith, and this is evident in their support for the activities of the various churches to which they belong.

Indigenous Sāmoan spirituality – which valued the importance of harmonious relationships with kin, environment and the supernatural – has also informed a Christian Sāmoan spirituality that Sāmoans enjoy as their Christian heritage today. The enculturation process associated with universal Catholicism has developed liturgical practices that utilise Indigenous knowledge systems and validate them as the purview of Sāmoan Christianity.

Sāmoan culture is rich with the performing arts and music. The traditional mainline churches have had a huge influence on music in Sāmoa. Choral music and its beauty bear traces of the traditional tunes of the European missionaries that influenced them but are uniquely Sāmoan in their rhythms and traditional melodies. Contextualised lyrics referencing the environment and God in creation are an important part of Sāmoan spirituality. The Pentecostal movement in Sāmoa has contributed immensely to the music in Sāmoa. Worship music that invokes a personal spiritual journey has increasingly become a part of Sāmoan spirituality. It is not unusual to watch a televised national talent quest in which contestants sing Christian music as part of their repertoire.

Today in Sāmoa, Christianity is alive and well and is uniquely Sāmoan in its expressions and manifestations, bearing little resemblance to the Christianity introduced by missionaries from Europe. Christianity is deeply entrenched in the *fa'asāmoa*, gives meaning to a Sāmoan worldview and is a source of identity for all Sāmoans.

Bibliography

Ernst, Manfred (ed.), *Globalization and the Re-shaping of Christianity in the Pacific Islands* (Suva: Pacific Theological College, 2006).

Kamu, Lalomilo, *The Sāmoan Culture and the Christian Gospel* (Apia: Donna Lou Kamu, 1996).

Meleisea, Malama, *Lagaga: A Short History of Western Sāmoa* (Suva: University of the South Pacific, 1987).

Tomlinson, Matt, *God Is Sāmoan: Dialogues between Culture and Theology in the Pacific*, Pacific Islands Monograph Series (Honolulu: University of Hawaii Press, 2020).

Vaai, Upolu Lumā and Aisake Casimira (eds), *The Relational Self: Decolonising Personhood in the Pacific* (Suva: University of the South Pacific Press, 2017).

Tuvalu and Tokelau

Teatu Fusi

Tuvalu has always been understood by the Tuvaluans as a gift from the gods. The ancestors knew and believed that the gods created the islands of Tuvalu for the people of Tuvalu to treasure forever. They believed that the gods were part of creation and always involved in the lives of the people. *Tuvalu* means a cluster of eight, or eight (*valu*) standing together (*tu*). The reference is to the eight islands of Nanumea, Nanumaga, Niutao, Nui, Vaitupu, Nukufetau, Funafuti and Nukulaelae, which – together with a ninth island, Niulakita – make up the modern-day country of Tuvalu. The earliest known written reference to Tuvalu was by the London Mission-ary Society missionaries in their newspaper *Sulu Sāmoa*. Niulakita, the smallest and most southerly of the nine islands, is administratively part of Niutao and is not regarded from that point of view as a separate island.

The previous name of the country was the Ellice Islands. This name was chosen by Captain Arent de Peyster, an American who was in command of the British brigantine *Rebecca* when he discovered the islands in May 1819. He named them after Edward Ellice, the Member of Parliament for Coventry who owned the *Rebecca*. The change of name from Ellice Islands to Tuvalu took place on 1 October 1975, when the country was separated from what was then the Gilbert and Ellice Islands Colony.

The islands of Tuvalu are a spectacular formation of coral atolls. They are geologically very young, with most of the islands poorly developed, and infertile, with sandy or gravel coralline soils. The islands are of sediment, produced by the forces of the sea, and firmed reefs. The highest point of land stands no more than four metres above sea level, and they have a combined land area of 25.9 square kilometres, with a population, according to the December 2004 census, of 10,326. The islands suffer from severe flooding from waves washing inland during the cyclone seasons.

The Coming of Christianity

It was in the early nineteenth century that the people of Tuvalu first became aware of Christianity as they came into contact with European traders and beachcombers who visited and settled on some islands in Tuvalu. Gradually the Tuvalu people became anxious to receive and learn more about Christianity. It is reported that an elderly lady on Nukulaelae

Island, known as Kafoa, prophesied the coming of Christianity, with the words, 'Something is coming from beyond the horizon. When it comes it is good for you to listen to it and take it to your heart. But as for these superstitions and worship of idols and magic, we do not know what will happen to them.'

Christian missionary work began on the island of Nukulaelae on 10 May 1861 with the arrival of Elekana, a Congregationalist deacon, from Manihiki in the Cook Islands. Elekana, along with his son Tavita and four other men, named Tuitolu, Parana, Ninoko and Larilari, were washed ashore on Matamotu, an islet off Nukulaelae, after their ship was struck by a storm and they had drifted at sea for eight weeks.

When they came ashore, Elekana saw that there was a need to teach Christianity to the people. He was successful in attracting the attention of the people, and they began to learn about the Christian message. He could see that the people were desperate to learn more about the Word of God but required someone suitably trained in order to receive the ministry for which they longed. He therefore planned to train for the holy ministry by attending Malua Theological College in Sāmoa. Before he left, he tore some pages from his Cook Islands Bible and gave the pages to those whom he thought would continue the missionary work. On his way to Sāmoa, he stopped on Funafuti, where his teaching was well received.

When Elekana reached Sāmoa he reported to the London Missionary Society the need for missionaries on Tuvalu. After Elekana completed his training, he was appointed with two other teachers, Matatia and Ioane, to start the work. Together, under the leadership of the Revd A. W. Murray, they sailed to Tuvalu.

They visited five islands, and Murray was greatly surprised to see that people on Nukulaelae totally renounced their traditional form of worship and were eager to receive a missionary to teach them about Christianity. Murray was touched by their repeated requests, so he agreed to leave

Christianity in Tuvalu, 1970 and 2020

Tradition	1970		2020		Average annual growth rate (%), 1970–2020
	Population	%	Population	%	
Christians	7,200	98.6%	10,900	94.8%	0.8%
Independents	24	0.3%	920	8.0%	7.6%
Protestants	7,100	96.9%	9,600	83.9%	0.6%
Catholics	100	1.4%	100	0.9%	0.0%
Evangelicals	290	4.0%	580	5.0%	1.4%
Pentecostals/Charismatics	7	0.1%	1,900	16.5%	11.7%
Total population	**7,300**	**100.0%**	**11,500**	**100.0%**	**0.9%**

Source: Todd M. Johnson and Gina A. Zurlo (eds), *World Christian Database* (Leiden/Boston: Brill), accessed January 2020.

Ioane to be their teacher. Similar developments occurred throughout the islands of Tuvalu.

By 1878, Christianity was well established in Tuvalu through the work of the London Missionary Society, which deployed teachers on every island. Tuvalu was treated as a district of the church in Sāmoa. It was administered from the London Missionary Society station in Sāmoa but directed on the ground by the Sāmoan pastors. The people were trained spiritually but at the same time were influenced by Sāmoan culture and traditions. The Tuvalu people learned how to read the Sāmoan Bible fluently and even how to sing the Sāmoan hymns harmoniously. Worship was conducted in the Sāmoan language, and the Sāmoan way of life was also practised by the Tuvaluans. The Sāmoan teachers, working under the London Missionary Society, established a mission school on Vaitupu in order to educate the local people. The successful candidates were sent to Sāmoa to be trained as pastors at Malua Theological College.

As the number of Tuvaluan graduates from the College increased, a proposal was made at the 1952 general assembly in Sāmoa to hand over the mission work in Tuvalu to the Tuvalu teachers, allowing the Sāmoan teachers to be repatriated. However, this proposal was not accepted until 1958, when the first permanent missionary of the London Missionary Society arrived to assist and organise the Church of Tuvalu.

The Revd Brian Ranford was appointed to be the first president of the Tuvalu Church during its 1959 general assembly, where it was agreed to write a letter to thank the London Missionary Society in Sāmoa for the prolonged nourishment and great care it had given in teaching and Christianising the people of Tuvalu. In 1968, the first draft of the constitution of the Church of Tuvalu was approved. The London Missionary Society also agreed that Tuvalu should have a translation of the Bible into its own language. Ranford was given responsibility to arrange for this.

In 1969, leadership of the Church of Tuvalu was completely handed over to the Tuvalu teachers. The Tuvalu Bible was on the way, with the New Testament completed in 1977. Later, the Old Testament was also finished and the two were combined so that the complete Tuvalu Bible could be published in 1987. Now, the Tuvalu Church, known as the Ekalesia Kelisiano Tuvalu, is administered by Tuvalu trained ministers with the support of its members and congregations.

Continuing Value of Traditional Religion

The seed of the Christian gospel is deeply rooted in the hearts and lives of the people of Tuvalu, but this does not mean that there is no continuing influence of their traditional beliefs. From time immemorial, there was always a divine conception in the culture of the Tuvaluans, which was deeply rooted in their worship life and the respect they had for their gods. The coming of foreign missionaries, both Europeans and Pacific Islanders, displaced that divine sensibility in the culture of the people, which included respect for the environment – sea and land. The environment in this sense was part of the people's culture and religion.

Though Christianity was welcomed by the people, something of the old cultural-religious *mana* (divine power) had gone missing from the lives of the people. There might have been a theological problem in the abstract teachings of the missionaries about Jesus Christ and God which somehow gave the wrong impression that God lives in heaven, 'out there', and can be reached only through prayers. This understanding puts God outside of creation and outside of the private lives of the people as well as their culture. With the old religion, the people felt the presence of their gods all the time in their environment and in all aspects of their everyday lives. Such beliefs were too quickly dismissed as heathenism. It must be acknowledged that there were life-denying aspects of the traditional culture that were best abandoned. But there were also many life-affirming beliefs and practices that could have been useful in cultivating the care needed for the environment and people today.

A strong feature of Tuvaluan belief, prior to the coming of Christianity, was a creation myth that has much resonance with the biblical creation myth recounted in the Book of Genesis. The missionaries introduced the heavenly God into the faith of the people, but the Tuvaluans always believed in earthly gods, which were with and around them. Something significant was therefore missing in the new beliefs of the people: the belief that the divine was always with them. A theological challenge is how this aspect of traditional faith can be integrated into Christian belief in God as the Creator of all things.

Church Life in Tuvalu Today

The Tuvalu Christian Church (Ekalesia Kelisiano Tuvalu) is the predominant religion in Tuvalu today. It is estimated that 91% of Tuvalu's population belong to it. Some 3% are members of the Seventh-day Adventist Church, and another 3% belong to the Brethren Church, while 3% adhere to the Bahá'í Faith. There is also a very small number of Roman Catholics. The Ekalesia Kelisiano Tuvalu, which is the country's state church, officiates at important national events and festivals.

The Tuvalu Christian Church has an extensive mission overseas. There has been remarkable growth in its churches in New Zealand, Australia, Hawaii, the Marshall Islands and Fiji. However, the constant drift of people from Tuvalu to these countries does not mean that they always retain their loyalty to their mother church.

The Tuvalu Christian Church has also made links with the outside world through engagement with partner churches and Christian organisations. It collaborates in mission and sharing of resources in order to cultivate a strong spirit of advocacy on matters of faith, justice and peace. This allows it to engage with economic, political and ecological issues causing globalisation, terrorism, climate change and rising sea levels, which have devastated the earth and humanity.

Tuvalu's constitution allows its citizens to practise the religion of their choice. Citizens are also allowed to convert to another religion by their own will. Forced conversions or discrimination on the basis of religion are not permitted. Religious education is not offered in Tuvalu's schools. Some cases of religious discrimination have occurred in Tuvalu but have been dealt with through the country's legal system. The government of Tuvalu generally respects its citizens' rights and freedoms regarding religion as outlined in the constitution. The act of proselytising is allowed in Tuvalu as long as it does not violate the freedom of others to convert at their own will.

Island Life in a Globalised World

The fast-changing world of the twenty-first century, with the world economy controlled by international organisations dominated by the affluent countries, makes an impact on the Pacific as well. The increase of technological development, production and consumption, and accessibility of transportation have allowed the powerful nations to create one world market that determines the wealth of nations. People of the Pacific today can travel to and from the outside world in a matter of hours. The recruitment of islanders to regional and international schemes has closed down the remoteness of earlier history. These movements contribute greatly to behavioural change in Pacific societies. Above all, the threat of climate change and rising sea levels directly affects the people of Tuvalu, who live on low-lying atolls. Already they are exposed to constant droughts and cyclones. These are some of the challenges to the mission of the Church in Tuvalu in our contemporary context.

Regional secular institutions such the South Pacific Community have recognised the value of church mission in countering violence against women and children in the Pacific. Faith-based organisations were called upon to take immediate action to support the implementation of legislation to protect the family and children. Churches have expressed concern about the government's bill on the eradication of corporal punishment as a form of discipline of students. This could lead to a situation where, if the principal of a school disciplines a student with corporal punishment, the government would terminate the principal's appointment of service.

Though geographically remote, Tuvaluan Christians are deeply aware of the calling they share with those who follow Christ in every part of the world. At a time when global issues call for global action, they are alert to the need to play their part in advancing the one mission of Jesus Christ in today's world.

Tokelau

Tokelau, previously known as the Union Islands, is a dependent territory of New Zealand, located to the north of Sāmoa and to the east of Tuvalu. It comprises the three coral atolls of Atafu, Nukunonu and Fakaofa, with a combined land area of just 10 square kilometres. Since most of the land is less than 2 metres above sea level, the islands are vulnerable to tropical storms and rising sea levels resulting from climate change. The ancestors of the Indigenous Polynesian population are thought to have settled on the islands around 1,000 years ago. The first European visitors arrived in the late eighteenth century, and British rule was established in 1877. New Zealand took responsibility for the administration of the islands from 1926 and Tokelau became formally part of New Zealand in 1949. Two referenda have been held on the question of independence for Tokelau, in 2006 and 2007. On both occasions the people voted in favour of retaining the status quo. According to the 2016 census, the total population is 1,499, of whom the vast majority speak Tokelauan as their first language. Many Tokelauans live in New Zealand, and their remittances play an important part in the economy of the islands. With fishing as the main industry, it has the smallest economy of any country in the world and depends heavily on budget support from New Zealand. It is the first nation to run entirely on renewable energy through its extensive use of solar power.

The population of Tokelau has a very high rate of adherence to Christianity. In the 2006 census everyone who answered the religion question gave one of the Christian denominations as their religion. This

Christianity in Tokelau, 1970 and 2020

Tradition	1970		2020		Average annual growth rate (%), 1970–2020
	Population	%	Population	%	
Christians	1,600	96.3%	1,300	94.5%	−0.4%
Independents	0	0.0%	20	1.5%	6.2%
Protestants	1,000	63.4%	800	59.0%	−0.5%
Catholics	400	24.7%	500	36.8%	0.4%
Evangelicals	56	3.5%	80	5.9%	0.7%
Pentecostals/Charismatics	0	0.0%	65	4.8%	3.8%
Total population	**1,600**	**100.0%**	**1,400**	**100.0%**	**−0.4%**

Source: Todd M. Johnson and Gina A. Zurlo (eds), *World Christian Database* (Leiden/Boston: Brill), accessed January 2020.

prevalence of Christian faith owes its origins to evangelism carried out in the nineteenth century, which also explains the variation in ecclesiastical geography between the three atolls. Atafu was evangelised by the London Missionary Society, particularly through Sāmoan teachers and evangelists who were active there from the 1840s. The commitment of the people to the Congregationalist tradition of the LMS was cemented by the visit of the Revd Samuel James Whitmee in 1870. As a result, a large majority of the population of Atafu belong to the (Congregationalist) Church in Tokelau.

Nukunonu, by contrast, was evangelised by Roman Catholic missionaries, who came from Wallis Island, and remains a majority-Catholic island. Fakaofa was exposed to both traditions and includes strong representation of both Congregationalists and Catholics in its population. The Catholic Church in Tokelau falls under the Metropolitan Archdiocese of Sāmoa-Apia. The Catholic parish on Nukunonu is administered by a priest, while the parish on Fakaofa is administered by a catechist with the faculties of a deacon.

Overall almost two-thirds of the Tokelau population are Congregationalists while just over one-third are Catholics. There are also small numbers of Presbyterians, Seventh-day Adventists and Jehovah's Witnesses. The only non-Christian religion with representation is the Bahá'í faith. The influence of Sāmoan Christianity has been strong, to the extent that church worship and all important religious and civic functions are conducted in the Sāmoan language, with Tokelauan featuring only in more mundane settings. However, in 2003 the four gospels were translated into Tokelauan for the first time, and work is proceeding on the translation of the Old Testament. Christianity remains an important part of Tokelauan identity, both in the homeland and in the diaspora.

Bibliography

Ekalesia o Elise [Ellice Islands Church], *Te 100 Tausanga o te Tala Lei i Elise. 1861–1961. The Centenary of the Coming of the Gospel to the Ellice Islands* (Funafuti, 1961).
Ernst, Manfred (ed.), *Globalization and the Re-shaping of Christianity in the Pacific Islands* (Suva: Pacific Theological College, 2006).
Kofe, Laumua, 'Palagai and Pastors', in Hugh Laracy (ed.), *Tuvalu: A History* (Suva and Funafuti: Institute of Pacific Studies and Tuvalu Ministry of Social Services, 1983), 102–20.
Munro, Doug and Michael Goldsmith, *The Accidental Missionary* (Christchurch: Design and Print Services, 2002).
Thomas, A. I. Tuia and Judith Huntsman (eds), *Songs and Stories of Tokelau: An Introduction to the Cultural Heritage* (Wellington: Victoria University Press, 1990).

Kiribati and Nauru

Soama Tafia

The Republic of Kiribati, formerly known as the Gilbert Islands, lies astride the equator in the central Pacific. Kiribati comprises 33 coral atolls, together with Ocean Island, which is of raised limestone. The country is divided into three main groups: the Kiribati Group, the Phoenix Group and the Line Group. Christmas Island is the largest, with a total land area of 363.4 square kilometres. Kiribati as a whole has a total land area of 719.6 square kilometres and claims a 320-kilometre economic zone around the islands, so that the total surface area comes to more than 3 million square kilometres.

Kiribati has limited resources. The phosphate deposits were exhausted by the time the country gained independence from Britain in 1979. Today, fish and copra represent the bulk of production and exports. Due to the limited natural resources, the government has put in place initiatives to strengthen the economy. According to the national census, the population increased from 72,335 in 1990 to 113,100 in 2018. In view of the growing population, the government has developed the Kiribati Vision for the next 20 years (known as KV20), which is an attempt to find a way forward toward sustainable development that will create hope for a better standard of living, health, peace and security. The government together with Christian churches and civil society seek to work together in mutual understanding and cooperation toward achieving the goals and aspiration of KV20.

The Coming of Christianity

The coming of Christianity to the shores of Kiribati can be traced to the 1830s, when whaling ships, beachcombers and traders (including slave traders) from the Western world began to visit regularly. These early contacts were not propitious, as the newcomers exploited the life and culture of the people. Through barter local people acquired weapons that were used in civil wars and family disputes. The new conditions led to the spread of prostitution and alcoholism. Permanent traders who benefited from high profits cheated the locals, paying out very little to them.

The first Christian missionary work in Kiribati began in 1857, when the American Board of Commissioners for Foreign Missions (ABCFM) started work in the northern Kiribati islands. Hiram and Clarissa Bingham were the first resident missionaries. Their appointment resulted from visits carried out by the ABCFM in 1852 and 1855. These visits were organised by the Micronesian mission in consultation with the Hawaiian mission and the headquarters in Boston to search for a suitable place and centre for the ABCFM to operate in northern Kiribati. The Binghams' work was assisted by Hawaiian pastors who worked and served in different islands in north and central Kiribati.

The London Missionary Society (LMS) arrived in 1870 and began work in the southern Kiribati islands. There was no resident European missionary, but a band of Sāmoan pastors were placed in each of the five southern islands of Arorae, Tamana, Nikunau, Onotoa and Beru. The first resident missionary from the LMS, William Goward, arrived in 1900 and established schools for boys and girls. Later he founded a training institution for preparing local pastors to assist with the work of evangelisation in Kiribati.

The early spread of Christianity in Kiribati was attributable mainly to the work of the two Protestant mission boards who introduced the faith to the islands and supported the first converts. The spread of Christianity throughout the islands enabled the inhabitants of Kiribati to embrace the new faith in large numbers. A report by G. E. Eastman during the jubilee celebration in 1920 marking the completion of 50 years of the LMS's work in the southern islands revealed that significant progress had been made.

The two Protestant mission boards worked separately until 1917, when the LMS took over the work of the ABCFM. This was viewed as an achievement and as a step forward toward an Indigenous Christian church. The transition into an Indigenous church was a sign of trust and confidence on the part of the LMS and a step toward giving locals leadership and authority to plan and manage the mission and ministry of Christianity in Kiribati. The Kiribati Protestant Church became fully independent in 1968.

Christianity in Kiribati, 1970 and 2020

Tradition	1970		2020		Average annual growth rate (%), 1970–2020
	Population	%	Population	%	
Christians	50,000	97.7%	119,000	96.9%	1.7%
Independents	50	0.1%	20,300	16.6%	12.8%
Protestants	24,600	48.1%	47,400	38.7%	1.3%
Catholics	23,900	46.7%	56,800	46.4%	1.7%
Evangelicals	2,100	4.2%	5,200	4.2%	1.8%
Pentecostals/Charismatics	540	1.1%	10,000	8.2%	6.0%
Total population	**51,200**	**100.0%**	**122,000**	**100.0%**	**1.8%**

Source: Todd M. Johnson and Gina A. Zurlo (eds), *World Christian Database* (Leiden/Boston: Brill), accessed January 2020.

The Roman Catholic Church was first introduced to Kiribati by two locals who worked at the plantations on Tahiti. When they returned in 1881, they brought with them the Roman Catholic faith. However, the Roman Catholic mission officially started only when priests from France arrived in 1888, a generation later than the first Protestant missionaries. The Roman Catholic mission started from the island of Nonouti in central Kiribati and spread to northern Kiribati. Today it remains the case that the Roman Catholic Church is particularly strong in northern and central Kiribati, while Protestant strength is concentrated in southern Kiribati. For more than 100 years, priests from France ministered in the Catholic parishes, latterly supported by priests from the Australian Missionaries of the Sacred Heart. Today, however, most of the priests are nationals, known as I-Kiribati. Their parish network extends throughout the Kiribati islands, except the two southern islands of Arorae and Tamana, which have no Roman Catholic priest.

Catholicism in Kiribati is marked by very strong devotion to the Virgin Mary. The training of I-Kiribati priests in Rome and at the Pacific Regional Seminary in Suva, Fiji, has greatly strengthened the Roman Catholic mission in Kiribati. These I-Kiribati priests have replaced most of the priests from France and Australia. The Roman Catholic Church in Kiribati and Nauru was headed by a bishop from France until 1978, when an I-Kiribati was selected to take over the leadership of the Church. In 1979, Paul Mwea became the first I-Kiribati to be consecrated Bishop of Kiribati and Nauru.

Ministry and Evangelism

The work of ministry and evangelism in the early years of Christianity in Kiribati depended very much on the ordained pastors. Though the model of European ministerial work was used as a template, the people had to conform, as this was a new venture as regards their way of life and culture. Both the ABCFM and the LMS introduced the same pattern of Christian ministry, whereby the pastors were seen as dominating figures in the life of the church, even after the LMS was given responsibility for the work in Kiribati when the ABCFM withdrew in 1917.

The attempts to train local personnel by the ABCFM in the northern islands and the LMS in the southern islands aimed to strengthen the work of evangelism and replace Hawaiian and Sāmoan pastors with local ones. Steady progress with the establishment of Christian ministry and extension of evangelistic work resulted in the growth of churches throughout the Kiribati islands. A holistic approach to Christian mission was taken for granted, with the establishment of church schools being widely recognised as a contribution of Christianity to the people as well as the government of Kiribati.

After the independence of the Kiribati Protestant Church in 1968, the pattern of Christian ministry was revised according to the rapid changes taking place in the country. The structure of the church has helped to bring together the pastors, deacons, women and youth to work jointly to maintain the integrity of Christianity in Kiribati.

Currently, the pattern of Christian ministry has been revised to combat the problem of sectarianism. A significant and successful initiative in the twenty-first century has been the development of team ministry. This aims toward the nourishment of faith, broadening of members' understanding of Christian doctrines and provision of assistance in addressing family problems. The age of pioneer evangelism has passed, and the new concept and definition of evangelisation as nourishment and sustainability of faith has emerged to broaden Christian influence in Kiribati.

From the missionary period there was a long history of hatred between Protestants and Roman Catholics in Kiribati. However, the way Protestants and Roman Catholics have reacted to each other has changed since the Second Vatican Council in the 1960s. The establishment of the Kiribati National Council of Churches in 1988 provided a forum for healthy ecumenical relations between Protestants and Catholics. Today they are able to come together to celebrate Gospel Day, marking the coming of Christianity to Kiribati. The Protestants have their major celebration on 18 November each year to mark the coming of Christianity to the shores of Kiribati, through the arrival of Hiram and Clarissa Bingham from the ABCFM.

Denominational Profile

The results of the 2018 census indicate that the vast majority of the population identify as either Protestant or Catholic. In 2016 a split occurred in the Protestant Church when the general assembly passed a motion to change the name of the Kiribati Protestant Church to the Kiribati Uniting Church. The change of the name was based on a vision of sustainable development of church ministry and expansion of God's mission work to all spheres of life in Kiribati. The motion was passed by majority vote, and most congregations and Island Church Councils complied with the general assembly resolution to change the name. However, a minority did not accept the change of name and broke away to continue as a separate denomination, retaining the name Kiribati Protestant Church. They maintain that the name 'Kiribati Protestant Church' must be retained because the term 'Protestant' was introduced by the early missionaries and has its roots in the Reformation. The 2018 census indicates that 23,387 belong to the Kiribati Uniting Church, while 10,560 belong to the Kiribati Protestant Church.

More than half of the population, 65,772, belong to the Roman Catholic Church. Other churches have relatively few members. The Church of Jesus Christ of Latter-day Saints (Mormons) has 6,552 members, while the Seventh-day Adventists have 2,191 members. Though relatively small in number, both the Latter-day Saints and Seventh-day Adventists are gradually increasing their membership each year. Pentecostal groups are also small but growing.

Worship and Spirituality

Churches and places of worship are fully occupied during Sunday morning worship. Fewer people attend afternoon and mid-week services. The cool temperatures of the morning hours provide more favourable conditions for worship. Daily worship also takes place in many families. Most Christian homes hold their devotions in the evening, while some prefer the morning. Christian festivals such as Easter and Christmas are high points of the year in Kiribati. The Protestants on each island often come together to celebrate Christian festivals, as planned by the Island Church Council. Roman Catholics similarly gather together to celebrate the great festivals of the Christian year.

People hold different views and perceptions as regards personal spirituality. Some see the Christian life as a matter of being faithful to church rules, and attending worship on Sundays and mid-week services. Others stress financial contributions and other forms of service to the church. Others again emphasise the need for repentance and profession of faith as a communicant member. There is a need to cultivate a spirituality that fosters worship, hope and love while reckoning with such twenty-first-century challenges as the impact of climate change, high cost of living and sexually transmitted diseases.

Theological Education and Ecumenism

Theological education in Kiribati is provided by Tangintebu Theological College for Protestants and by the Kiribati Pastoral Institution for Roman Catholics. These institutions not only prepare candidates for ministerial work but also provide training for deacons to assist pastors in their work.

Though the Kiribati National Council of Churches is a national ecumenical body, the meaning of ecumenism is far from being realised by the people. The two major denominations come together for worship only on the Kiribati national day. No programmes have been designed to strengthen ecumenical relationships between Roman Catholics, Protestants and other religious bodies. The National Council of Churches needs to take further steps to work toward a full realisation of ecumenism in Kiribati and to express what it means to be a Christian nation.

Nauru

Christianity was introduced to the tiny island of Nauru in 1887. The first pioneer missionary, appointed by the ABCFM, was a Kiribati man named Tabwia. His ministry was not very successful, yet he began the process that led the people to be converted to Christian faith. Little is known about how Christianity progressed in Nauru, but it appears that the training of local people played a very significant role. Itubwa Amram, the first local ordained minister, was trained in Australia and returned to Nauru to take up the work of leading the emerging church, known today as the Nauru Congregational Church.

Today the two major churches are the Congregational Church and the Roman Catholic Church, which has a substantial number of parishioners, though there is only one priest serving on the island. Some smaller churches have a presence but have very few members. A challenging issue for the Nauru Christian church has been phosphate mining, which has caused environmental catastrophe on the island while yielding very little benefit to the islanders.

A lack of trained pastors has inhibited the growth and development of the church in Nauru. The Council for World Mission (CWM), during a visit to the Nauru Congregational Church in 2014, found only two ordained ministers and two probationary pastors, none of whom was located in a village congregation. The turnout for Sunday worship was poor, and most of those attending were women or children. The CWM team encouraged the Congregational Church to give priority to building up the ministry. The church is facing problems of lack of church attendance, drinking among young people and other related issues. The 2014 CWM visit resulted in the development of a strategic mission plan, with an emphasis on establishing and sustaining an effective and efficient ministry.

Christianity in Nauru, 1970 and 2020

Tradition	1970 Population	%	2020 Population	%	Average annual growth rate (%), 1970–2020
Christians	5,300	82.3%	8,300	74.2%	0.9%
Anglicans	150	2.3%	450	4.0%	2.2%
Independents	0	0.0%	830	7.4%	9.2%
Protestants	2,700	41.6%	5,400	47.7%	1.4%
Catholics	1,200	18.5%	3,300	29.4%	2.0%
Evangelicals	120	1.8%	790	7.0%	3.9%
Pentecostals/Charismatics	0	0.0%	1,600	14.4%	10.7%
Total population	**6,500**	**100.0%**	**11,200**	**100.0%**	**1.1%**

Source: Todd M. Johnson and Gina A. Zurlo (eds), *World Christian Database* (Leiden/Boston: Brill), accessed January 2020.

Bibliography

Garrett, John, *Footsteps in the Sea* (Geneva and Suva: WCC, 1992).

Garrett, John, *To Live Among the Stars* (Geneva and Suva: WCC, 1982).

Lange, Raeburn, *Island Ministers: Indigenous Leadership in Nineteenth Century Pacific Islands Christianity* (Canberra: Pandanus Books, 2007).

Tafia, Soama, 'The Kiribati Protestant Church', unpublished thesis, Pacific Theological College, Suva, 1982.

Thorogood, Bernard (ed.), *Gales of Change: Responding to a Shifting Missionary Context* (Geneva: WCC, 1994).

Guam, Federated States of Micronesia, Marshall Islands, Northern Mariana Islands and Palau

Francis X. Hezel SJ

In June 1668, six Spanish Jesuits, along with a group of some 30 lay helpers, landed on Guam to begin evangelising the people of the Mariana Islands. Guam is the largest of the numerous islands scattered throughout the western Pacific north of the equator, an extensive area known as Micronesia. The area includes what today are known as the island nations of Palau, the Federated States of Micronesia (FSM) and the Republic of the Marshall Islands, along with the US-affiliated Territory of Guam and the Commonwealth of the Northern Mariana Islands. The term 'Micronesia' is sometimes extended to the nations of Kiribati and Nauru as well, but these latter islands are treated separately in the preceding essay.

The arrival of the Jesuit missionary band not only marked the beginning of evangelization in Micronesia but also represented the earliest sustained attempt to bring Christianity to any part of the Pacific. Only at the close of the eighteenth century, more than 100 years later, was any serious missionary effort made elsewhere in the Pacific.

The launch of this initial mission to the Marianas was marked by a serious population decline – resulting from the diseases that the Europeans introduced – as well as a long series of hostile encounters popularly known as the Chamorro-Spanish Wars. By the end of the seventeenth century, virtually the entire population was converted and concentrated in towns on the two southernmost islands of Guam and Rota. Both the flag and the faith were planted, and Spain retained the Marianas as a colony for the next 200 years. Later, Augustinian Recollects took responsibility for the mission and until the end of the nineteenth century regularly dispatched priests from the Philippines to continue the work.

Meanwhile, the rest of Micronesia remained unevangelised. It was only in the mid-nineteenth century that Christianity was introduced to the other island groups of Micronesia. Islands such as Pohnpei and Kosrae (located in the eastern part of what is now known as the FSM), which served as popular recreation ports for American whaling ships, were already gaining the attention of mission groups. The American Board of Commissioners for Foreign Missions, which had successfully brought Christianity to Hawaii a generation earlier, founded a mission in these islands in 1852.

Over the course of the next few decades, the missionaries established flourishing Congregational churches on Pohnpei and Kosrae and extended their work to the Marshall Islands through Hawaiian pastors. In the latter group of islands it was Kaibuki, a paramount chief who had been renowned for his unprovoked attacks on Western ships, who became the patron of the new mission. By the early 1870s, the American Board missionaries had opened a pastoral school and trained a group of Pohnpeian mission teachers, a few of whom were deployed to Chuuk in the west (also part of the FSM) to bring the church there. By the end of the century, the Congregational Church was solidly established throughout the eastern part of Micronesia – the Eastern Carolines (Pohnpei, Kosrae and Chuuk) and the Marshall Islands.

When Spain pressed its claims for formal title to the Caroline Islands in 1885 against the counter-claims of Germany, the islands were awarded

Christianity in Guam, 1970 and 2020

Tradition	1970		2020		Average annual growth rate (%), 1970–2020
	Population	%	Population	%	
Christians	80,700	96.2%	158,000	93.6%	1.4%
Anglicans	500	0.6%	1,200	0.7%	1.8%
Independents	1,700	2.0%	8,800	5.2%	3.4%
Protestants	11,000	13.2%	13,900	8.2%	0.5%
Catholics	68,000	81.1%	138,000	81.6%	1.4%
Evangelicals	5,700	6.8%	10,000	5.9%	1.1%
Pentecostals/Charismatics	2,700	3.2%	12,000	7.1%	3.0%
Total population	**83,900**	**100.0%**	**169,000**	**100.0%**	**1.4%**

Source: Todd M. Johnson and Gina A. Zurlo (eds), *World Christian Database* (Leiden/Boston: Brill), accessed January 2020.

Christianity in Micronesia, 1970 and 2020

Tradition	1970		2020		Average annual growth rate (%), 1970–2020
	Population	%	Population	%	
Christians	57,600	93.8%	102,000	94.5%	1.1%
Independents	320	0.5%	9,000	8.4%	6.9%
Protestants	27,300	44.4%	49,000	45.5%	1.2%
Catholics	20,000	32.6%	65,000	60.3%	2.4%
Evangelicals	4,800	7.9%	19,500	18.1%	2.8%
Pentecostals/Charismatics	260	0.4%	10,800	10.0%	7.7%
Total population	**61,400**	**100.0%**	**108,000**	**100.0%**	**1.1%**

Source: Todd M. Johnson and Gina A. Zurlo (eds), *World Christian Database* (Leiden/Boston: Brill), accessed January 2020.

to Spain by papal arbitration. Within a year or two, Spanish Capuchin missionaries were stationed on most major island groups in an effort to establish the Catholic Church there. In the Western Carolines (Yap and Palau) this was to be the initial contact of islanders with Christianity. In the east, Catholic missionaries would contest the fields in which American Protestant missionaries had already laboured for two or three decades.

Building Churches under Changing Flags

At the end of the Spanish–American War in 1898, the political map of Micronesia was redrawn, as it would be a few more times during the twentieth century. When Germany acquired the islands that the Spanish had once ruled, German Capuchin priests and brothers replaced their Spanish confreres in their effort to extend Catholicism throughout the region. Their field included the Northern Marianas, which had been brought under German rule at the same time. In 1911, German priests were sent to Chuuk, where they rapidly gained adherents. Meanwhile, Missionaries of the Sacred Heart took up work in the Marshalls, focusing mainly on the islands of Jaluit and Likiep. The Congregational churches were by this time operating largely on their own, under local pastors. The

Christianity in the Marshall Islands, 1970 and 2020

Tradition	1970 Population	%	2020 Population	%	Average annual growth rate (%), 1970–2020
Christians	19,200	94.1%	50,300	94.4%	1.9%
Independents	140	0.7%	10,200	19.1%	9.0%
Protestants	14,500	71.1%	50,000	93.9%	2.5%
Catholics	2,000	9.8%	5,500	10.3%	2.0%
Evangelicals	5,100	25.2%	35,600	66.9%	3.9%
Pentecostals/Charismatics	4,000	19.6%	37,500	70.4%	4.6%
Total population	**20,400**	**100.0%**	**53,300**	**100.0%**	**1.9%**

Source: Todd M. Johnson and Gina A. Zurlo (eds), *World Christian Database* (Leiden/Boston: Brill), accessed January 2020.

Christianity in Northern Mariana Islands, 1970 and 2020

Tradition	1970 Population	%	2020 Population	%	Average annual growth rate (%), 1970–2020
Christians	12,900	98.0%	43,100	77.9%	2.4%
Independents	0	0.0%	11,000	19.9%	15.0%
Protestants	1,100	8.5%	7,300	13.2%	3.8%
Catholics	11,400	86.8%	41,300	74.6%	2.6%
Evangelicals	170	1.3%	5,000	9.0%	6.9%
Pentecostals/Charismatics	0	0.0%	8,000	14.5%	14.3%
Total population	**13,100**	**100.0%**	**55,300**	**100.0%**	**2.9%**

Source: Todd M. Johnson and Gina A. Zurlo (eds), *World Christian Database* (Leiden/Boston: Brill), accessed January 2020.

number of American and Hawaiian missionaries had dropped sharply over the years and fell off even more in the early twentieth century.

Meanwhile, German evangelical Liebenzell missionaries entered the region in 1907. They first established themselves in the Eastern Carolines, and then, in 1929, expanded their work to include the Western Carolines. Their mission soon spread throughout the area from Palau to the outer islands of Chuuk, serving in effect as a counterbalance to the Catholic efforts there.

Guam was annexed as a territory of the USA after the Spanish–American War and administered by the US Navy. In 1910, the first Protestant church (Methodist) was established on Guam. Yet Catholics continued to make up the vast majority of the native population of this island, originally evangelised two and a half centuries earlier. The Catholic Church remained the centre of village life, as was the case in many other former Spanish colonies. This close integration of cultural and religious features continues to the present day and is expressed in many distinctive ways: the observance of religious feast days by means of the traditional fiesta and procession following the statue of the patron saint; the importance of veneration of saints; and the recital of the rosary in common. Especially important is the remembrance of the dead through the novenas celebrated by family and friends. All Souls Day on 2 November is marked by prayers at grave sites and masses held in the cemeteries of the island.

Japanese acquisition of all the islands in Micronesia except Guam at the outbreak of the First World War in 1914 had little negative impact on church work initially. Local pastors in the Congregational Church were encouraged to continue their work. Although German Catholic missionary priests and sisters were soon repatriated, Japan appealed to the Vatican for replacements. Spanish Jesuits arrived in force in 1921 to assume control of the field, and two years later one of their number, Mgr Santiago de Rego, was named the first bishop of the mission area (which had been expanded

Christianity in Palau, 1970 and 2020

Tradition	1970		2020		Average annual growth rate (%), 1970–2020
	Population	%	Population	%	
Christians	11,300	98.0%	20,600	91.6%	1.2%
Independents	4,400	38.7%	2,400	10.7%	−1.2%
Protestants	2,600	22.8%	9,300	41.4%	2.6%
Catholics	4,000	34.8%	8,200	36.5%	1.4%
Evangelicals	2,500	21.5%	5,700	25.4%	1.7%
Pentecostals/Charismatics	88	0.8%	2,200	9.8%	6.6%
Total population	**11,500**	**100.0%**	**22,400**	**100.0%**	**1.3%**

Source: Todd M. Johnson and Gina A. Zurlo (eds), *World Christian Database* (Leiden/Boston: Brill), accessed January 2020.

to include, in addition to the Carolines, the Marshalls and Northern Marianas). Mission schools remained closed, to permit children to attend the mandatory public school system, but otherwise churches were granted freedom to operate as they had under Spain and Germany. Indeed, a handful of Japanese Methodist pastors were sent to work in the Eastern Carolines. It was only in the late 1930s, as the Second World War loomed, that the Japanese government imposed restrictions on the movement of missionaries. After war broke out, foreign missionaries were confined, and later, as Allied forces were poised to launch their decisive attack on the islands, six Spanish Jesuits were executed in Palau.

With the transfer of the islands from Japan to the USA at the end of the war, churches were again obliged to make administrative and personnel changes. For Catholics, the Northern Marianas were placed under the jurisdiction of Guam, while American Jesuits took over responsibility for the mission of the Carolines and Marshall Islands. Congregations of sisters soon entered the field: Maryknoll Sisters in Palau and Yap, and the Mercedarian Missionaries of Berriz (MMB), who had begun a mission in the islands even before the war. Catholic mission schools were reopened and island girls were soon entering the MMB convent.

Meanwhile, German missionaries from Liebenzell resumed work in the Western Carolines. The best known was probably the Revd Edward Kalau, who founded Pacific Missionary Aviation during his long service on Yap before continuing his work for years on Pohnpei. In the eastern part of Micronesia, the Congregational churches continued under local pastors, even as American representatives from the United Church Board worked with them to develop schools and stronger links between local churches.

The post-war years also saw the arrival of a number of smaller churches in the region. Seventh-day Adventists began a mission on Guam in 1950. Within a few years the church had spread to all the major islands throughout the area, opening schools at the same time. Baptists and the Assemblies of God also became established during this time, with the Assemblies of God becoming especially strong in the Marshalls. Latter-day Saints initiated work on Saipan in 1975, and soon after extended their ministry to nearly all major islands in Micronesia.

Local Leadership

From the outset of its missionary activity in the nineteenth century, the American Board set as its goal the establishment of churches in the islands that would be 'self-financing, self-governing and self-propagating'. Accordingly, the Congregational training school continued to turn out pastors, deacons and teachers to provide leadership for the church over the years, despite the frequent changes of colonial government. Liebenzell, soon after its return to the Western Carolines and Chuuk, also offered training programmes for local pastors so that these pastors could soon staff all the churches.

Things were much different in the Catholic Church, which remained reliant chiefly on missionaries through much of the twentieth century. Indeed, just one priest was ordained in the region before that time: Fr Jose Palomo, trained in the Philippines and ordained in 1859, who served his people on Guam for 60 years before his death in 1919. Two other Guamanian priests were ordained before the Second World War: Fr Oscar Calvo and Fr Jesus Duenas. Fr Duenas was executed by the Japanese just months before the end of the war.

After the Second World War, as American Capuchins assumed responsibility for the church in Guam and the Northern Marianas, the first Catholic seminary was opened. Over the next few decades, local vocations to the priesthood multiplied sufficiently to staff many of the island parishes, with Capuchin missionaries providing pastoral assistance as needed. The Catholic Church on Guam reached another landmark in 1970 when Mgr Felixberto Flores was consecrated as the first local bishop. Not long afterward, the Northern Marianas was constituted a diocese in its own right, with an island priest, Mgr Tomas Camacho, named as the first bishop.

In the Carolines the transition to local leadership took longer. For a time, the mission had only two local priests, both Jesuits: Fr Paulino Cantero, a Pohnpeian ordained shortly before the war, and Fr Felix Yaoch, a Palauan who began his priestly service there in 1967. Then, beginning in the late 1970s, a number of young island men were ordained to the priesthood. The late surge in vocations was aided by the minor seminary, established on Guam in 1968, that Jesuits operated for more than 30 years. Finally, in 1995, with the appointment of Amando Samo as Bishop of the Caroline Islands, the diocese had its first local bishop. By this time most of the parishes finally had Micronesian pastors. In that same year the Marshall Islands, where Catholics remained a small minority, was entrusted to the Missionaries of the Sacred Heart, the order that had opened the first Catholic mission in the island group a century before. To date, no local priests have been ordained in the Marshalls.

Contribution to Society: Education

Formal education represents perhaps the greatest contribution by the churches to society. The first school anywhere in the Pacific was opened on Guam the year after the arrival of the first missionaries. The Congregational missionaries in the Carolines operated small schools throughout the region in the mid-nineteenth century, long before a public school system existed.

During the latter half of the twentieth century, Catholics and Protestants redoubled their efforts in education. Several of the Catholic schools
founded on Guam during this period remain among the best on the island.
They include Father Duenas Memorial School, a boys' high school, and
two superior girls' schools: Our Lady of Mercy Academy and Notre Dame
Academy. St John's Academy, arguably the best school in the region, was
founded by the Episcopal Church during the same period. Other notable
schools opened since are Grace Baptist and Harvest on Guam, as well as
St Paul's Academy and Mt Carmel School on Saipan.

After the Second World War, when American Jesuits assumed authority
over the mission, they set up elementary schools and later high schools
throughout the Carolines and Marshall Islands. The best-known and most
highly regarded were Xavier High School in Chuuk, which was founded
in 1952, and Pohnpei Agriculture and Trade School, opened in 1965.
Both accepted students from every island group throughout the region.
On every major island group today can be found a Catholic high school
and an elementary school. Seventh-day Adventists also operate schools in
each of the island groups. Today, private church-run schools in the FSM,
Palau and the Marshall Islands enrol about 10% of all schoolchildren in
the region, perhaps half of the proportion that they educated during the
early 1960s, the heyday of mission schooling.

Inculturation

The Catholic Church in the Carolines and the Marshall Islands from the
early 1970s espoused the goal of indigenisation – that is, blending the
faith with cultural practices from the islands. The church consciously
began to make liturgical adaptations aimed at making use of cultural
symbols. Flower leis were placed on the heads of the newly baptised to
signify the title they were receiving with the sacrament, and leis also were
presented with the usual gifts of bread and wine to the one presiding at
the Eucharistic liturgy. Dances and chants were incorporated into various
parts of the services on special occasions. On Pohnpei, *sakau* (kava) is used
in reconciliation services, as it would have been when forgiveness was
being asked of a chief. In Yap, famous for its dignified dances, distinctive
island wailing and stately women's dances were introduced into the Holy
Week services.

Congregational churches have also adopted cultural practices, although
not to the same extent. During the week before Easter, churches will
normally exchange pastors. The visiting pastors are feted during the week
and sent off with gifts from the community that hosted them. Christmas
celebrations are distinctive in each island group. In Kosrae, the congregation practices months ahead of time for a glittering marching display

that is offered in the main church by various subgroups, all performed in beautifully tailored uniforms and dresses.

Church music, in the meantime, has undergone changes of its own. At first it was a cappella congregational singing of numbers translated from the standard European or American hymnals. Soon, however, islanders themselves began composing hymns with a distinctive island sound. Instrumental music, absent at first, was eventually supplied by organs, guitars and often enough today by keyboards. The richness and variety of religious music today represents church inculturation at its best.

In Guam and the Northern Marianas, which remain predominately Catholic, inculturation tends to look backward to reflect those practices identified with Spanish Catholicism: that is, the novenas, processions, village feast days and even the music from an earlier age.

Church and Society

To suggest that the church has become a significant part of the social landscape in the islands is to understate the fact. Indeed, in many places it is the dominant institution in the daily life of the people. The church calendar regulates much of the life of villagers; its choirs perform at community events; its pastors call down blessings at the onset of projects and the dedication of buildings; its policies are invoked as norms for community behaviour.

Church involvement in social issues, however, must be understood in the light of cultural practices rather than modern political rights. The Congregational Church in the Eastern Carolines struggled to limit the obeisance to chiefs, opposed the use of kava in traditional ceremonies and curtailed the trafficking of young women to foreign ships. The Catholic Church in the Western Carolines opposed traditional clubhouses with their prostitution and attempted to stamp out spirit mediums. Perhaps its most generally lauded contribution was to bring peace to islands embroiled in local warfare. In accomplishing this, the Christian churches altered the cultural landscape in an effort to make it more compatible with the tenets of Christianity.

In recent decades, many of the churches have engaged in public education to assist the local population to make enlightened choices on contemporary issues. The Catholic Church, for instance, instituted mobile teams to make yearly visits to villages to lead reflection on social issues. In some island groups Baptists and Catholics produced weekly radio programmes on contemporary life issues, although this has fallen off in the twenty-first century. Social justice workshops brought together Christian leaders from different parts of the region to reflect on what the church might do to assist its members in responding to today's concerns.

One recent focus of church efforts has been casino gambling, proposed by some governments as a means of expanding tourism. Another is environmental protection, particularly in the light of global warming and the danger that rising sea levels present to the low islands of the area. The churches are not so much spearheading the campaign against climate change, however, as supporting the efforts of the governments to deal with the issue. In Guam and the Northern Marianas, most Christian churches openly oppose abortion and same-sex marriage, both of which have been legalised under US law.

One of the dominant issues has been change resulting from social and religious pluralism. Guam and the Northern Marianas, along with Palau, have seen their populations become more ethnically heterogeneous. Meanwhile, smaller church groups, most of them Evangelical, have sprung up nearly everywhere in the region. This was happening just as a new spirit of collaboration was reached among older denominations, with Catholics and Congregationalists working together to translate the Bible into the major local languages. Attempts by some small islands to preserve their social and religious unity by forbidding other denominations were overruled by the new constitutions. Although the adherents of these newer church groups remain relatively few – representing a combined 4–10% of the total population – the older denominations are clearly challenged to extend the ecumenism that they have achieved with one another to these newer groups.

Current Status of Christianity

All the island groups in the region today remain overwhelmingly Christian. Although Bahá'í centres can be found in a few of the islands and Buddhist shrines have been built on Guam and Saipan, the percentage of non-Christians in the islands is tiny. Hence, the relationship between Christians and other world faiths remains basically a non-issue in the region.

Guam and the Northern Marianas both remain heavily Catholic (c. 80%), with a scattering of smaller churches: Baptist, Congregational, Episcopal and Iglesia Ni Kristo, the latter with a membership almost exclusively Filipino. Latter-day Saints, Seventh-day Adventists and Jehovah's Witnesses are also represented, along with a number of small Evangelical churches. Since the 1970s, growing secularisation has cut into church membership, although the majority of non-practising members continue to identify as Christians.

The Marshall Islands remains predominately Congregational (c. 90%), although the Congregational Church split into two factions some years ago. The remainder of the population includes a small Catholic minority (*c.* 7%) and a few smaller Evangelical churches. The Assemblies of God has shown the fastest growth of any of the smaller church groups over the past few decades.

The status of Christianity in the Caroline Islands, which include Palau and the FSM, varies across the island groups, each with its own history and culture. Kosrae, at the eastern end of the FSM, is heavily Congregational (87%), although five smaller churches are also found there, the largest of which is the Church of Jesus Christ of Latter-day Saints, with almost 4% of the population. In both Pohnpei and Chuuk, the largest states of the FSM, Catholics make up 55% of the population, while the Congregational Church follows, with 41% in Chuuk and 36% in Pohnpei. Palau, like Yap, is predominately Catholic, more so Yap (82%) than the former. But versions of the traditional religious belief remain strong through a local religious system (*Modekngei*) in Palau and in spirit-veneration practices still observed in parts of Yap.

Overall, the impact of Christianity on the island groups in Micronesia has been enormous and is recognised as such by islanders themselves. The effects today, however, are not so much represented by institutional battles over issues like gender rights or environmental protection, as might be the case in Western societies. Church-led protest marches and social challenges are generally muted in Micronesia in accordance with cultural practice in small island societies. Even so, the real force of Christianity is unmistakable, not only in the way that it has already altered the social landscape but in the impact it continues to make on daily life in these island societies today.

Bibliography

Forman, Charles, *The Island Churches of the South Pacific: Emergence in the Twentieth Century* (Maryknoll: Orbis Books, 1982).

Garrett, John, *To Live Among the Stars: Christian Origins in Oceania* (Suva: Institute of Pacific Studies, 1982).

Hezel, Francis X., *The Catholic Church in Micronesia* (Chicago: Loyola University Press, 1991).

Sullivan, Julius, *The Phoenix Rises: A Mission History of Guam* (New York: Seraphic Mass Association, 1957).

Zimmermann, Anna R., *Sixty Years Liebenzell Mission* (Schooley's Mountain: Liebenzell Mission, 1960).

New Caledonia, and Wallis and Futuna Islands

Nathalie Cawidrone

New Caledonia is an archipelago in the south-west Pacific, south of Vanuatu and 1,210 kilometres east of Australia. It comprises the main island of Grande Terre, the Loyalty Islands, the Chesterfield Islands, the Belep Archipelago, the Isle of Pines and some remote islets. Its population comprises the Indigenous Kanak inhabitants, people of European (mainly French) descent, Polynesians and Southeast Asians. France took possession of New Caledonia in 1853. An independence movement with strong Kanak support has so far been unsuccessful.

The presence of Christianity in New Caledonia can be traced back to missionary work that began in the 1840s. In the Loyalty Islands, Protestant missions came first, when Tataio and Taniela, two Oceanian catechists serving with the London Missionary Society (LMS), arrived at Maré in 1841. The France-based Société des Missions Evangéliques de Paris (SMEP) later took up the work of its British counterpart with the arrival of the missionary Edmond Langereau in 1892. Catholic mission in the Loyalty Islands did not begin until the late 1850s, since access to the Islands was forbidden by the governor of that time to avoid conflicts with the British Protestants who were already installed.

In Grande Terre, the opposite occurred: Catholic missionaries arrived in 1843, 10 years before the French colonial state, while Protestant work did not begin until the 1890s. Unlike the Loyalty Islands, which were spared colonisation, this part of the country was greatly affected. In September 1853 Admiral Auguste Febvrier-Despointes took possession of Grande Terre, and for almost a century the natives were subjected to restrictive regimes imposed by the French colonial administration: land spoliation, an Indigenous code, confinement to reserves and other forms of exploitation.

With French colonial rule came Catholic missionary activity. Protestantism was not officially introduced until 1898, by Governor Paul Feillet. The first Protestant evangelists came from the Loyalty Islands and were known as *nata* – native pastors. They were initially advised by Pastor Philadelphe Delord, an SMEP missionary stationed at the Ro mission in Maré. Later they were directed by Pastor Maurice Leenhardt of the same missionary society, from his arrival in Houaïlou in 1902 until the 1920s.

It was not until 1946 that New Caledonia became a French overseas territory and the Kanaks acquired citizen status with the right to vote. Indeed, this period also marked a turning point in the history of the country on the political level, especially for the Kanaks as they entered political life. The role of both Catholic and Protestant missions was significant in supporting the Kanak people as they organised themselves to assert their identity and defend their rights. Today in New Caledonia, Christianity is represented by a range of churches.

The Roman Catholic Church

In December 1843 the first Catholic missionaries landed at Balade (Pouébo) in the far north of the Caledonian archipelago, led by Mgr Guillaume Douarre. Pope Gregory XVI had entrusted the evangelisation of the central and western Pacific to the Marist fathers of the Nascent Society of Mary. In terms of church administration, New Caledonia was separated from Central Oceania in 1847 to become a distinct apostolic vicariate. On the Isle of Pines, the first Mass was said in 1847, but it was not until the late 1850s that the first Catholic presence was established in the Loyalty Islands. The first three decades were extremely difficult times for Catholic missionary action. It was not until 1872 that the situation began to recover gradually, which continued even during the period of persecution inflicted by Governor Paul Feillet during the early 1900s.

Today, official statistics of the Roman Catholic Church indicate that there are some 144,000 Catholics in New Caledonia, approximately half the population. The Metropolitan Archdiocese of Nouméa is led by Archbishop Michel-Marie-Bernard Calvet. It has 32 parishes, 27 priests, 24 deacons and 79 lay religious (22 brothers, 57 sisters). Catholicism is characterised by its social commitment, with Catholic Relief and the Society of Saint Vincent de Paul undertaking significant charitable work. The Catholic Church also plays an active role in education, health, student and

Christianity in New Caledonia, 1970 and 2020

Tradition	1970 Population	%	2020 Population	%	Average annual growth rate (%), 1970–2020
Christians	96,300	91.5%	243,000	84.8%	1.9%
Anglicans	50	0.0%	280	0.1%	3.5%
Independents	4,000	3.8%	25,000	8.7%	3.7%
Protestants	17,900	17.0%	43,100	15.0%	1.8%
Catholics	73,600	69.9%	144,000	50.1%	1.3%
Evangelicals	3,900	3.7%	19,500	6.8%	3.3%
Pentecostals/Charismatics	1,300	1.2%	19,000	6.6%	5.5%
Total population	**105,000**	**100.0%**	**287,000**	**100.0%**	**2.0%**

Source: Todd M. Johnson and Gina A. Zurlo (eds), *World Christian Database* (Leiden/Boston: Brill), accessed January 2020.

university chaplaincy, as well as working with Caledonian youth through scouting. Like the Protestant churches, the Catholic Church has always been involved with the Kanaks in their political struggle and in matters of reconciliation and civil peace. It has, however, been badly hit by a vocations crisis. The percentage of Catholic faithful has also been declining.

The Church of Ecône

The Church of Ecône resulted from a schism within the Roman Catholic Church following the Second Vatican Council (1962–5). The Society of Saint Pius X was created in Switzerland in 1970 by Mgr Marcel Lefebvre, who opposed several fundamental texts of the Council. He opened a seminary in Ecône, in the Swiss Valais, to train his priests in what he considered to be the authentic tradition of the church.

This fraternity has existed for more than 35 years in New Caledonia. In 1983 the first priest, Fr François Laisney, disembarked following a request to Mgr Lefebvre by a tribal chief. Its chapel is located 20 kilometres from Nouméa, in Katiramona (Païta). This community has around 150 faithful, who are served by an 'integrist' priest from New Zealand who has no official relationship with the Catholic Church. Even if Catholicism has experienced dissent, it has always set a premium on unity, unlike Protestantism, which is marked by its plurality. Hence the Church of Ecône has not lacked its critics.

Reformed Churches

During the 1950s, two main factors caused the birth of two Protestant churches: first, the drive of the native churches to become autonomous; and second, the missionary crisis experienced by the Protestant Church due to interpersonal conflicts among SMEP missionaries concerning financial issues. This crisis provoked a split. In 1958, the Evangelical Free Church, also known as Charlemagne after the name of its founder, was formed. Two years later, in 1960, the SMEP granted the Protestant Church its autonomy and it became the Evangelical Church in New Caledonia and the Loyalty Islands (EENCIL). Since then, two Calvinist churches have existed in New Caledonia. The EENCIL was renamed the Protestant Church of Kanaky New Caledonia (EPKNC) on 17 August 2013 at the Thuahaik Synod in Lifou.

The Protestant Church of Kanaky New Caledonia (EPKNC)

A diverse missionary heritage has shaped New Caledonian Protestantism. The imprints of Anglo-Saxon puritanism, German pietism and Wesleyan Methodism still remain decisive in the Loyalty Islands, while Caledonian Protestantism was strongly marked by the spiritual and social Christianity inherited from the missionaries of the SMEP, notably Maurice Leenhardt. Even though the EPKNC has a presbyterian-synodal system of government, this does not prevent occasional tensions between two ecclesial regimes, namely the Congregationalism inherited from the LMS and the presbyterian-synodal tradition of the SMEP. It is a form of Protestantism attached to the traditions of the church and also those of Kanak culture. The church finds it difficult to break away from tradition and adapt to the modern era.

Of all the Protestant churches in the country, the EPKNC is the one that stands out for its support for the Kanak people in their struggle against colonial oppression and in their effort to assert their identity. It took a strong stance in favour of independence at the Synod of Guarou (Houaïlou) in 1979. It supported the Kanak people not only by its interventions on the ground during acute conflicts but also through biblical and theological reflection on political conditions in the country. The 70,000 members of the EPKNC are almost 95% Kanak and represent about a quarter of the national population. It has around 60 pastors, including four women, distributed in 87 parishes or posts of specialised ministry.

The Free Evangelical Church (EEL)
This Protestant Church was born as a result of conflicts among missionaries of the SMEP.

After the split, the Free Evangelical Church was born and organised. The Federation of Protestant Free Education (FELP), which is intended for the education of Kanak youth, was founded shortly after the founding of the Free Church. At the beginning, this was aimed at pastoral training and theological education of Kanak pastors. Later it became a decentralised training centre also open to the laity.

The Free Evangelical Church has been greatly affected by three acute conflicts. The first took place in 1976, between Pastor Raymond Charlemagne and a group of native pastors who accused him of monopolising the leadership of the church. This first conflict led to the dismissal of the protesters. The second was caused by a dispute between the Steering Committee and a Kanak pastor who was refused permission to launch a Bible programme that he wanted to lead. This led to a split and gave birth to the Church of Sion, recently renamed Antioch Evangelical Church. The third major conflict, about issues of church management, took place in 2004 between two Kanak pastors, both members of the church's steering committee. This last conflict led to the closure, for some time, of the Church of the Mount of Olives in Nouméa.

Even if these conflicts were followed by successful reconciliations between the opposing camps, it proved difficult for the church to recover fully. The history of the Free Evangelical Church has also been marked by changes in its theological orientation. In 1980 the church, through its synod, questioned baptism by sprinkling and opted for baptism by immersion for adults only, hence rejecting paedobaptism. From its initial Calvinist orientation, the church moved to a Baptist position, adopting a more literal interpretation of the Bible. Some parishes that disagreed with this decision returned to the EENCIL. These experiences have had a negative impact on its progress today and the church is struggling to maintain itself. It currently has 72 parishes, 20 pastors and some 18,000 members.

The Māòhi Protestant Church in New Caledonia (EPM-NC)

The Evangelical Church of French Polynesia originated in the work of Protestant mission societies, the LMS from 1797 and the SMEP from 1863 in Tahiti. It became autonomous in 1963, with Samuel Raapoto as first president. In 2004, it was renamed the Māòhi Protestant Church. The decision to found a Tahitian Protestant parish was born following the large-scale immigration of Mao'his seeking study opportunities or employment in Nouméa in the 1950s.

In 1957, Pastor Autai Tumata was sent to Nouméa to take care of the Tahitian Protestant community. Pastor Hunter Joseph took over in 1962 and it was under his mandate that the church and presbytery were built, both inaugurated in 1965. The Tahitian Protestant parish located in the Tir Valley in Nouméa constitutes the eighth district of the Māòhi Protestant Church. It has two outstations, Thio and Poro.

Pentecostals

Pentecostalism arrived in New Caledonia with a Portuguese Pentecostal by the name of Rodrigues after the Second World War. Alone and having found no Pentecostal place of worship, he first attended Protestant churches. He then settled in Nouméa and began to hold Pentecostal meetings. Siméon Rousseau, a teacher at the Protestant mission in Maré, and his wife Lydie heard about this beginning of Pentecostal work and wrote to their son, Paul Augustin, then pastor of the Assemblies of God church of Lens and Liévin in northern France. In March 1955, Paul Rousseau returned to New Caledonia and began to develop a Pentecostal presence. After his death in 1961, the work was taken over by Pastor Jean Ledru and his wife Simone. On 7 October 1965, the 'Assembly of God' was officially declared a religious association with the object of spreading the teachings of Christ.

Soon afterward, Western Pentecostal missionaries came to serve in New Caledonia. Ronald and Joy Killingbeck from the USA arrived in 1967, Howard and Charlotte Fox, also from the USA, in 1969, and Maurice and Denise Poncet from France in 1976. The Pentecostal movement spread quickly over the whole country as evangelistic tours multiplied. Unlike Reformed Protestants, who are established in specific places, Evangelicals and Pentecostals are scattered all over the country, including in parishes historically identified as Catholic or Reformed. From the south to the north of the archipelago, passing through the Loyalty Islands, churches and fellowships have been established. While the Reformed churches comprise almost entirely Kanaks, the Pentecostal communities are made up of all ethnic groups.

Pentecostalism experienced considerable growth in the 1980s. Despite conflicts and persecutions, it continues today to be very active and to grow year by year throughout New Caledonia. It places evangelism, the proclamation of the Word, at the centre of missionary activity, with the aim of converting the masses. Christianity is presented in a modern idiom that has proved attractive but keeps a distance from the political and cultural realities of the country. It also sends missionaries overseas, both to other parts of Oceania and to France.

Seventh-day Adventist Church (SDA)

In 1953 the Adventists were officially allowed to begin work in New Caledonia, permitting the arrival of pastors to lead the community. Official recognition as a church followed in 1962. With financial support from Adventists in Australia, a church was built in the Valley of the Settlers in Nouméa and inaugurated in July 1967. The SDA is multi-ethnic, made up of Kanaks, Tahitians, Wallisians, West Indians, Europeans and Vanuatuans. Its seven pastors care for more than 2,000 members.

Contemporary Challenges

Two contemporary challenges call for attention. The first is the vocations crisis that has affected the churches for more than 20 years. Among Catholics there is a shortage of priests and nuns. Among Reformed Protestants, the vocation of pastor is maintained but with few new recruits, no more than 10 per year. EEL no longer educates pastoral students but instead provides decentralised training for lay preachers. Secondly, Catholic numerical decline and Protestant increase are marked features of Christianity in New Caledonia. The proportion of the population professing to be Catholics decreased from 67% in 1980 to 51% in 2015. Protestants and Independents, on the other hand, accounted for 24.5% in 1980 and by 2020 had reached 35%. In quantitative terms, the past 40 years have seen Protestants and Independents gaining ground while Catholicism has receded.

A variety of factors lie behind these developments, such as secularisation, individualisation and social change, as well as the advent of new forms of faith. The changes that Caledonian society is undergoing are not without effect on the spirituality and vigour of the churches. It is also possible that the departure of church members to new spiritual movements is due to deficiencies within the older churches. Perhaps it is time for the churches to reflect on what might be the appropriate means to proclaim the gospel in the modern era. Perhaps it is time for the Protestant churches to work together, to coordinate efforts to meet the current challenges facing Caledonian society.

Wallis and Futuna Islands

Wallis and Futuna is a French-speaking and Catholic archipelago (centred around the islands of Uvea and Futuna) in an English-speaking and Protestant South Pacific. It has a land area of 142 square kilometres and a population of 11,558 (2018 census). It is made up of three volcanic islands split into two island groups separated by 260 kilometres (Wallis Islands in the north-east, Futuna and Alofi Islands in the south-west). The culture is Polynesian, similar to that in neighbouring Sāmoa and Tonga. Eighty per cent of the population is engaged in subsistence agriculture; deforestation is a major challenge. All human rights and civil liberties are fully respected on the islands. Although traditional pre-Christian religion has a few remnant adherents, and there are a few other non-Christian religionists, virtually the entire population has become Catholic.

Fr Pierre Bataillon, a Marist priest, established the first mission on Wallis (Uvea) in 1837, and there are now stations at Mata-Utu, Malaetoli and Lano. Futuna was reached later and is served by mission centres at Sigave and Alo. Upon their arrival, the missionaries studied the Wallisian and Futunan languages while building mission stations from scratch with the invaluable help of their coadjutor brothers. As soon as the missionary-linguists mastered the basics of these two languages, they wrote dictionaries and grammars while preaching. In Wallis, Fr Bataillon

Christianity in Wallis and Futuna Islands, 1970 and 2020

	1970		2020		Average annual growth rate (%), 1970–2020
Tradition	Population	%	Population	%	
Christians	8,700	98.9%	11,200	97.0%	0.5%
Independents	0	0.0%	60	0.5%	3.6%
Protestants	0	0.0%	200	1.7%	6.2%
Catholics	8,400	95.0%	11,000	95.0%	0.5%
Evangelicals	0	0.0%	40	0.3%	7.7%
Pentecostals/Charismatics	0	0.0%	340	2.9%	7.3%
Total population	**8,800**	**100.0%**	**11,600**	**100.0%**	**0.5%**

Source: Todd M. Johnson and Gina A. Zurlo (eds), *World Christian Database* (Leiden/Boston: Brill), accessed January 2020.

obtained the support of Tu'ugahala, principal chief of Mua and grand cousin of King Vaimua. Conversions multiplied in 1838, with the baptism of the lavelua (king) on 30 October 1842, and almost all Uveans converted in the months that followed. At Futuna, things happened differently. Despite his desire for inculturation, Fr Pierre Chanel gradually denounced certain customary or religious practices, which resulted in his martyrdom in 1841. Nonetheless, by 1845 most Futunans had become Catholic.

Over time, traditional wars, polygamy of the chiefs and voluntary mutilation of the phalanges of the women and daughters of the chiefs have disappeared. The chiefs gradually lost their ancient spiritual power as receptacles of the gods of the major deities of the Polynesian pantheon. The Marist mission favoured both the emergence of a Western-style state organisation in Wallis and the integration of Wallis and Futuna within the framework of a protectorate which, on 29 July 1961, became a French overseas territory.

In the 1980s, a small Protestant community settled in Vele, south of Futuna. It was created by migrants returning from New Caledonia. Since 1975, Jehovah's Witnesses, Evangelicals and Pentecostals have planted small congregations. Seventh-day Adventists started work on Wallis in 2008; there is a small congregation with one permanent pastor ministering on the island. Adventists still do not have government permission to work on Futuna.

Christianity in the islands manifests itself through collective prayers and the values of mutual aid, exchange, sharing and generosity, which resonate with Polynesian culture. Religion is also present in primary education, and parents instil respect for elders and religion at home. On both Uvea and Futuna, villages and families are vying for the construction of new churches and chapels. In a world where religious vocations are increasingly rare, becoming a priest or a nun is an honour to which many young people aspire.

At the start of the third millennium, it appears that the French citizens of Wallis and Futuna have successfully adapted to their Western modernity while retaining their inherited identities and their complex relationship to traditional culture. And, if there is a certain inevitable duality between a secular state and a Christian or Catholic territory, there has been peaceful co-existence of the five interwoven powers that are religion, custom, trade, administration and, since 1961, politics.

Bibliography

Angleviel, Frédéric, 'Wallis-et-Futuna: l'alliance de la grande chefferie et de la croix dans la République', in Florence Faberon and Jean-Yves Faberon (eds), *Religion et société en Nouvelle-Calédonie et en Océanie* (Clermont-Ferrand: Centre Michel de l'Hospital, 2013), 139–51.

Bertram, Robert, 'Le pluralisme religieux en Nouvelle-Calédonie et ses structures', in Florence Faberon and Jean-Yves Faberon (eds), *Religion et société en Nouvelle-Calédonie et en Océanie* (Clermont-Ferrand: Centre Michel de l'Hospital, 2013), 403–6.

Delbos, Georges, *L'Eglise Catholique à Wallis et Futuna: généalogie d'une chrétienté (1837–2003)* (Suva: CEPAC, 2004).

Kohler, Jean-Marie, *Le Christianisme en Nouvelle-Calédonie et aux Iles Loyauté: présentation sociologique*, Profils du christianisme dans le Pacifique (Nouméa: Orstom, 1980).

Vidal, Gilles, 'L'autonomie de l'Eglise Evangélique en Nouvelle-Calédonie et aux Iles Loyauté en 1960: imbrications politico-religieuses', in Salvador Ezeyo'o and Jean-François Zorn (eds), *L'autonomie et l'autochtonie des Eglises nées de la mission, XIXe–XXIe siècles* (Paris: Karthala, 2015).

Grateful acknowledgement is made of the work of the Revd Billy Wetewea in translating this chapter from French to English. The chapter has also been helpfully informed by the Revd Wetewea's translation from French of the above-cited essay on Wallis and Futuna by Frédéric Angleviel.

Fiji

Rusiate Tuidrakulu

Fiji is an archipelagic state in the Pacific Islands of the global South comprising citizens from diverse ethnic, cultural and religious backgrounds. It comprises more than 300 islands, with a population of approximately 900,000, most of whom live on the two main islands of Viti Levu and Vanua Levu. Early European contact came through blackbirding (forced labour) and the presence of Christian missionaries, who began arriving in the 1830s. Fiji became a British colony in 1874 and was under colonial rule until attaining independence in 1970. A feature of British rule was the importation of large numbers of Hindus and Muslims from South Asia, most of them indentured, in the late 1800s and early 1900s. By this time many of the Indigenous people had become Christians, often Methodists, so that in the twentieth century Fiji developed as a multiracial and multireligious nation. Underlying ethnic tension has characterised Fijian politics and resulted in three military coups, two in 1987 and one in 2000.

Fijian Identity

Identity is an issue that is always present in Fiji. Indigenous Fijians have a strong sense of belonging to the land, and it is from this that they draw a definitive sense of what it means to be a human being. It is not so much a matter of finding meaning as belonging to the *vanua* (land or place), the basis of life on earth. A person does not own the land; rather, the *vanua* owns him or her. Therefore, Fijian Taukei (Indigenous people) identify themselves on the basis of the inseparable union between the three strands of *vanua* (land), *lotu* (church) and *matanitu* (state). The union of these three is so complete that if one is affected, the whole is affected. Indigenous Fijians do not think of themselves as belonging within certain frontiers but as originating from the place – the *vanua*. The close relation between *vanua* and *lotu* during the last century and a half in Fiji has been greatly appreciated and valued, for it has brought about much-needed unity among the Fijian people from the early days of Christian presence. This remains true today. Their link and relative harmony helped promote civilisation and wellbeing in villages and islands and continues to do so.

For Indigenous Fijians, Christianity has become a permanent part of the local culture. Therefore, drastic social changes are bound to affect not only the Christian faith but also the local culture, of which the faith is now an integral part. Fijians have also had to come to terms with the multi-racial and multi-religious make-up of their country. A major emphasis in national life has been recognition that all people of Fiji are people of the land, irrespective of race, religion or ethnicity. The naming of all Fiji citizens as 'Fijian' has been an important process in uniting the different racial and religious strands to achieve a sense of shared community. The secular approach of the current government presents a challenge, calling for a re-description of Christian identity in the islands. What does it mean to live as Christians and as a Christian community at this point in time in Fiji? This question is asked as Fijian political life passes through turbulent waters. The ongoing 'coup culture' in Fiji's politics has seen three elected governments overthrown and raises profound questions about the structure of democracy in the country. Since the first coup, national life has been directed not in the interests of justice for all but rather to serve the agenda of the few. Furthermore, as in most 'Third World' countries, Fiji's elected government leaders are only puppets of unfriendly market forces, who claim to be guardians of social justice. During the twenty-first century, the churches have often clashed with the state on issues of justice, but to little effect.

Concerns include lack of freedom of expression through tight control of the media and disarray in the arrangements for parliamentary elections. The major political event in Fiji in recent years has been the return, in 2014, to a form of political democracy after eight years of military rule. The big turn-out in the 2016 election showed an enthusiasm for participation and the sense of freedom that arose from a return to civilian rule. However, the future role of the military with respect to parliament will not be clear for some time as, at present, the bonds between government and military are very strong. Tension between church and state continues to be evident. The government under Prime Minister Frank Bainimarama has been

Christianity in Fiji, 1970 and 2020

Tradition	1970		2020		Average annual growth rate (%), 1970–2020
	Population	%	Population	%	
Christians	263,000	50.5%	598,000	64.6%	1.7%
Anglicans	6,500	1.2%	7,300	1.0%	0.7%
Independents	4,700	0.9%	114,000	12.3%	6.6%
Protestants	187,000	36.0%	408,000	43.9%	1.6%
Catholics	43,500	8.4%	115,000	12.4%	2.0%
Evangelicals	47,500	9.1%	181,000	19.6%	2.7%
Pentecostals/Charismatics	20,800	4.0%	200,000	21.6%	4.6%
Total population	**521,000**	**100.0%**	**925,000**	**100.0%**	**1.2%**

Source: Todd M. Johnson and Gina A. Zurlo (eds), *World Christian Database* (Leiden/Boston: Brill), accessed January 2020.

critical of religious groups for their support of opposition parties. In 2017, the Republic of Fiji Military Forces issued a press release stating that the Methodist leaders were advocating for the country to become 'a Christian nation' and that this could cause societal unrest. A significant stand-off between the Methodist leaders and the government administration raised the question of whether the army will be loyal and subservient to the government when a different party comes to power in the future.

Globalisation and Church Life

It is not possible to understand changes in Fiji without considering how it is influenced by global trends. The world has become increasingly interconnected, especially in recent decades, so that what happens in one country or region often has significant impact on other countries. Fr Frank Hoare of the Roman Catholic Archdiocese of Suva, a former faculty member of the Pacific Regional Seminary, has observed that this web of interconnections has three dimensions: political, economic and technological. At the political level, the fast-changing situation in Fiji has to be understood in relation to the Pacific 'sea of islands' as it relates to a globalising context. Economically, the dominance of the capitalist system, expressed through the power of the great multinational companies, puts pressure on Fiji to deregulate its labour market. The result is that the increasing worldwide divide between rich and poor is increasingly evident at the national level. Technologically, Fiji is not exempt from the compression of time and space that have been effected by television, the internet and the mobile phone. One result of global connectedness and global awareness is mass migration of peoples. Fiji is increasingly affected by the outmigration of doctors, nurses and carers, rugby players, soldiers and security officers, who are attracted overseas by higher salaries to reward the skills they possess.

Technological advances have benefited people through better health care, better education and more opportunities for personal development and achievement. But they come with negative effects also. Modern life and globalisation have increased individual autonomy. This increased individualism runs counter to the traditional communal culture of Pacific people and on current trends is likely to weaken it further. Traditional values of obedience, respect, duty and hospitality are vulnerable to the much more individualistic philosophy of life shown on popular media.

Celebrity culture is increasingly influential as the media celebrate film stars from Hollywood and Bollywood and contemporary sporting heroes. Fashion shows and beauty contests have grown in popularity, as have awards nights and glitzy social events held in expensive hotels. The attention of young people is gripped by images of success and attainment, rewarded by big money, prestige and self-aggrandisement. Materialism is seducing people and personhood is being defined by the material goods you own, and what you produce, control and consume. An alienating individualism is being promoted by the mass media that feeds our minds daily. We feel ambiguous about the changes happening around us. Out of this ambiguity we have to do theology, read the scriptures and preach our homilies.

Becoming aligned with a globalised economy is also having disastrous consequences for the health of local communities. They are moving away from locally produced root crops, vegetables and fruits toward the consumption of processed fatty and salty imported foods. This has resulted in a very high incidence of non-communicable diseases like type 2 diabetes, heart ailments and runaway obesity rates. The large number of early deaths and amputations is a source of growing concern. At the same time, international networks have made the islands more vulnerable to global pandemic diseases.

Climate Change

Like all the Pacific Islands, Fiji is being negatively affected by climate change. The destructive changing weather patterns, with severe hurricanes, flooding and the incursion of the sea in low-lying areas, threaten life in all its aspects. The category-5 Cyclone Winston that rampaged through half of the country in 2016 highlighted the need to relocate the coastal villages to higher ground. The churches have taken on an advocacy role as regards the dangers of climate change, working through regional and national meetings to press for urgent action at the global level.

The people of Fiji have an important role to play in spreading this awareness because they possess values of community and solidarity to show to the world. Therefore, Fijians try to live lightly on the land and sea and make their voices heard in all international forums, calling for the reduction of carbon pollution in the atmosphere as a matter of extreme urgency. The Pacific Council of Churches has been addressing this issue since the early 1970s, when there was no such term as 'climate change' and few were concerned about the threat posed by the modern industrial economy to the integrity of creation. Today, the need for effective advocacy on behalf of the Pacific is greater than ever.

New Christian Movements

Today in Fiji there is a great variety of Christian denominations. Besides the traditional mainline churches there are vigorous new movements such as the New Methodists and the Pentecostals. There is a shift from worship in traditional church buildings to outdoor church gatherings at bus stands and in stadiums and housing estate parks. The new movements often emphasise the gifts of the Holy Spirit, healing, lively singing and praying. They also promote a moral life and oppose the consumption of the traditional drink, *yaqona* (kava), and alcohol. They challenge the traditional churches in the areas of apologetics, liturgy, relevant preaching and better family life. Their strict morality and strong bonding have an appeal in the new context of globalisation. Personal morality is emphasised, with a view to benefiting from the gospel of prosperity. If people fall short, this is a sign that they are not part of the elect to which others are called. To critics, it appears that religion has become another market commodity. Good presentation and enticement are vital to success in a competitive market.

The new movements are geared to the urban environment, to which growing numbers of young people are migrating. For many in Fiji, the village is experienced as dull and over-regulated, with irritating communal responsibilities to be undertaken. The cities, with their bustle and colour, shops and cinemas, pool halls and parks, seem like paradise. However, village youths who come to the city or towns often cannot find jobs and live with relatives in overcrowded housing. No one bothers whether they go to church, whereas in the village there was pressure to attend worship. They are uprooted and unchurched and find it easy to drift into crime, prostitution and drugs. This provides a mission field for the new Christian movements. Many of their members are trained in how to approach strangers, how to detect openness and how to introduce their church appropriately. Conversion takes place when a fresh and relevant presentation of the gospel is related to the present context of the lost souls. Many who join these churches report that personal invitations triggered their conversion.

While the teaching of the new movements is persuasive to the younger generation, the traditional churches are uncertain how to recover and develop their own mission. Traditional church members are slow to share their faith and usually lack the confidence to give testimony to others of their faith experience. There is a need for reawakening and for the emergence of a new generation of apologetics to reach people affected by economic and social exclusion, political exclusion, exclusion on the basis of race and gender, and exclusion in terms of religious affiliation.

Despite their apparent success, the new Christian movements have been criticised by their traditional counterparts for being overprotective and oppressive and for lacking a fully biblical theology. Christians formed within more traditional church life also sense that the new movements are little engaged with the many different social, economic and political problems of the present or future Pacific. They appear to accept the economic and political status quo and preach an individual but not a social ethics. Commonly, they are strong in condemnation of the current society but see no reason to try to improve it because they expect Christ to come again soon and abolish the world.

Notwithstanding such criticisms of their theology and spirituality, the new Christian movements are proving attractive to many Fijians, particularly in the younger generation. This presents a significant challenge to the mainline churches and their concerns for the future of the Pacific Island nations and their people.

Faith and Society

The I Taukei (Indigenous people) now have a clear majority in multi-ethnic and multicultural Fiji. Race relations can be expected to improve as the I Taukei's fear of losing the land and of being dominated by Indo-Fijians recedes. In the 2014 and 2016 general elections, the strategy of Indigenous-founded parties like the Social Democratic Liberal Party to appeal to the traditional loyalties and aspirations of the I Taukei alone seemed to fail in the face of the development vision of the newly formed FijiFirst party. The establishment of a common roll (ethnicity-based electoral registration), which was previously a highly divisive topic, has been well accepted by all and has proved beneficial to race relations. The country seems to have matured socially, making it harder in the future for leaders to win votes by playing the race card or posing as the saviour or leader of one ethnic group only.

Fiji is a country where three of the main world religions, Christianity, Hinduism and Islam, live side by side. There has been an increase in Indo-Fijians becoming Christians (almost exclusively from Hinduism) in recent decades. The Anglican and Methodist churches are gaining moderately from this, but they are overshadowed by the Evangelical and fundamentalist Pentecostal churches, with their emphasis on healing and exorcisms. Conversions from one religion to another take place in both directions while collaboration on issues of common humanity is valued on all sides.

Some inter-religious dialogue has continued in Fiji through Interfaith Search, but this has not really touched ordinary church members or members of the other world religions. Yet opportunities exist to bring members of different religions together to work for the poor, for justice and human rights and for a greater ecological awareness. The mainline churches can do more to promote this kind of cooperation to build understanding, unity and peace in Fiji's multicultural and multireligious society.

Significant numbers of people are affected by spirit possession, witchcraft or sorcery, *mate ni vanua* (non-hospital sicknesses) and divination. Connected with these crises are discernment or treatment rituals involving ecstasy, trance and speaking in tongues. These cultural crises have been occurring from time immemorial and are still being experienced today. They are common in both rural and urban Fiji but affected members of mainline churches tend to go to traditional healers or to Pentecostal churches for healing. Psycho-cultural healing and physical healing are other reasons why people join the Pentecostal churches. This is especially true of Indo-Fijians. Greater attention to these cultural dis-eases is needed in the training of pastors and priests in all the churches.

Another acute social concern is the violence suffered by women and children. Many cases of domestic violence are reported in the media and courts, but many more cases go unreported. Domestic violence has exposed the lack of sound family values. Children from such families are vulnerable to many social and educational problems. Rape figures are frightening and, despite the marches, protests and publicity, they are not decreasing. Sexual, emotional and physical abuse of children is also far too common and has traumatic effect on the lives of the victims.

Both major races, the Indigenous I Taukei and the Indo-Fijians, have patriarchal and hierarchical cultures, which is an underlying cause of violence against women. Even negligent, lazy men can demand subservience from their wives and attempt to enforce this by physical violence. Reluctant neighbours and traditional reconciliation rituals were used in the past instead of court trials to resolve these issues. Today, the churches are taking significant steps to address this matter. A curriculum resource 'Violence against Women' designed by the South Pacific Association of Theological Schools in 2006 is taught in theological institutions. Strategically it is important for the church to build alliances in this work with agencies of the state and non-governmental organisations (NGOs).

Young People

Fiji's current ruling party has understood the importance of young people in electoral politics. In the last two elections the FijiFirst party has targeted youths in training and even in involving them in key areas of the decision-making of society. Offering free education, free school transport and free books has made education available to all as an answer to the quest of today's young generation. However, the issue of urbanisation is still taking its toll on children staying in crowded conditions with relatives in towns in order to attend secondary school. Inevitably, the lack of a satisfactory home environment contributes to an increase in rebellious behaviour.

Modern conditions have brought negative lifestyle changes among young people. Mobile phones connecting them to the internet and social media mean that they are more influenced by friends than by their parents. Pornography is readily available on mobile phones. Abuse of *yaqona* and alcohol by youths often leads to sexual relations, with the resulting spread of HIV-AIDS and other sexually transmitted diseases. The situation is exacerbated by high levels of unemployment among young people – a problem that both church and state are struggling to address effectively. There is need for government, NGOs and churches to work together to motivate and facilitate youth to find productive and fruitful goals and community belonging.

Church ministry to youth offers little to counteract these problems. For example, in a church conference of a mainline church, youths themselves named the abuse of *yaqona* drinking as one of the main weaknesses in their youth clubs. Parents are understandably slow to let their children attend and the youth groups feel unsupported. Where some churches have well organised programmes of Bible study, prayer, music and singing, charity and service work, and skills programmes, most Catholic groups are still focused on social activities and fund-raising for social events.

Churches still face a huge challenge to align their youth programmes to be relevant to the context of the youth of today. In 2016, the Roman Catholic Church redesigned its programme on discipleship and personal and spiritual development. The Methodist Church organises annual rallies as preparation for the Pacific Methodist youth rally, which brings together young people from Tonga, Sāmoa, Fiji and other, smaller islands. However, there is more to be done to meet the needs of the young generation and lessons to be learned from the work of the new Christian movements in this area.

Conclusion

On the face of it, Fiji is presently living through a relatively peaceful social situation. However, the church is facing huge challenges from the changes that come with globalisation. Lack of effective response from the mainline churches has favoured the leadership elites and allowed them to undermine the traditional values of communal life in Fiji. The change of the religious landscape to accommodate individualism, materialism and consumerism reflects changing social relationships as we are seduced into accepting an unequal society of 'haves' and 'have-nots'. Social analysis and cultural analysis would seem to be important skills for our communities and leaders.

New Christian movements are aggressively challenging traditional spiritual and social leadership. The church needs to analyse the reasons for their success and learn some lessons from them. New vision and structures are greatly needed to help our members deepen their faith and grapple with the rapid social change that they are experiencing. Young people generally, and especially urban unemployed youths, need understanding, facilitation and pastoring.

Bibliography

Ernst, Manfred (ed.), *Globalization and the Re-shaping of Christianity in the Pacific Islands* (Suva: Pacific Theological College, 2006).

Ernst, Manfred, *Winds of Change: Rapidly Growing Religious Groups in the Pacific Islands* (Suva: Pacific Theological College, 1994).

Hoare, Frank, 'Social Context in the Church Mission in Fiji', *Pacific Journal of Theology*, Series 2, No. 57, (2019), 1–16.

Tuidrakulu, Rusiate, 'God Mana in Fijian Democracy', unpublished article, 2007.

Tuwere, Ilaitia Sevati, *Vanua: Towards a Fijian Theology of Place* (Suva: Institute of Pacific Studies, University of the South Pacific, 2000).

Vanuatu

Randall Prior

Vanuatu is located in the South Pacific and comprises 83 islands, 66 of which are inhabited. It has a population of around 300,000, with an average annual population growth of 2.6%. Lying 2,000 kilometres east of northern Australia, its islands form a Y shape running some 900 kilometres from the Torres Islands in the north to Hunter Island in the south. Its nearest neighbours are New Caledonia, 400 kilometres to the south-west, and Fiji, 800 kilometres to the east.

Although in recent decades people have been migrating into the two main urban centres, Port Vila on the island of Efate and Luganville on the island of Santo, still more than 70% are spread across the islands in small communities. The cultures of the people are predominantly Melanesian, comprising autonomous tribal groups, each with its own language, culture and structure. Vanuatu has more than 100 different and distinct languages and cultures, and some 600 dialects. Migration history has determined that there is also some presence of Polynesian cultural groups. Called the New Hebrides under the joint colonial rule of Britain and France, the name Vanuatu (meaning 'our land forever') was adopted on independence in July 1980.

Colonial and Mission Background

In terms of its colonial and mission history, Vanuatu was first visited in May 1606, by Ferdinand de Quiros, who, with six Franciscan priests and four monks on board his ship, landed in Big Bay on the northern island of Santo and claimed the land 'for God and for Spain'. They constructed a small chapel and began to say Mass, but their authoritarian and insensitive manner among the local people generated hostilities. After less than two months, they departed.

Missionaries began to appear in earnest in the first half of the nineteenth century, originally through the London Missionary Society (LMS). In 1839 John Williams landed on the island of Erromango, where he and his companion, James Harris, were famously clubbed to death. Through the early 1840s further attempts were made by the LMS to spread the gospel on the islands, but it was not until the arrival of John Geddie from the Presbyterian Church of Nova Scotia that the first Christian church was founded. Geddie landed on the southern island of Aneityum in July 1848. A great enthusiast for mission, he remained until 1872. By that time the whole island community had been embraced by the Christian mission, which now included churches, schools and medical clinics.

The LMS continued a missionary involvement in the New Hebrides, sending up to 100 Polynesian converts as catechists and evangelists, until 1880. However, after the effective establishment of the mission on Aneityum, the Presbyterian Church took the lead in spreading the Christian faith. Over the coming decades, mission work was established by Presbyterians (from Canada, Scotland and, later, Australia and New Zealand) across the southern islands and extending into the central islands of the group. These early initiatives guaranteed that the Presbyterian Church would subsequently become the church with the greatest adherence among local inhabitants.

The Anglican Church, under the enlightened leadership of George Selwyn in New Zealand, established a mission to the Melanesian nations in the late 1840s. Committed to cooperation with other mission initiatives, Selwyn, and later his successor John Patteson, worked in supportive partnership with the early Presbyterians, choosing to establish the Anglican mission cause in other Melanesian lands. A modification of this agreement was reached in 1881 whereby the Anglicans were given mission access to the islands in the north of the New Hebrides. Subsequently, the Anglican mission successfully established a firm and lasting presence, with church communities most prominent in the north.

Roman Catholics of the Order of St Mary (Marists) made a short-lived attempt to establish a settlement on the southern island of Aneityum from 1848, but it was fraught with difficulty, leading to their departure in 1852. They did not reappear in the New Hebrides until 1885, with the arrival of a Marist mission on the central island of Efate. Coupled with the serious expansion of French colonial interests in the New Hebrides,

Christianity in Vanuatu, 1970 and 2020

Tradition	1970		2020		Average annual growth rate (%), 1970–2020
	Population	%	Population	%	
Christians	78,000	91.3%	275,000	93.5%	2.6%
Anglicans	10,000	11.7%	36,500	12.4%	2.6%
Independents	9,100	10.7%	30,200	10.3%	2.4%
Protestants	37,000	43.3%	189,000	64.4%	3.3%
Catholics	13,200	15.4%	33,000	11.2%	1.9%
Evangelicals	15,400	18.0%	111,000	37.8%	4.0%
Pentecostals/Charismatics	4,600	5.4%	110,000	37.4%	6.5%
Total population	**85,400**	**100.0%**	**294,000**	**100.0%**	**2.5%**

Source: Todd M. Johnson and Gina A. Zurlo (eds), *World Christian Database* (Leiden/Boston: Brill), accessed January 2020.

the French-speaking Marist missionaries were now able to secure their mission work. The development of the mission was consolidated further by the official establishment, in 1906, of the Condominium of the New Hebrides, which formally prescribed a parallel structure of French and British government across the whole island group. This guaranteed a strong French presence and an expanding Roman Catholic Church across the islands. The fact that Roman Catholics were aligned with French interests and Protestants with British interests exacerbated existing religious tensions between Protestants and Catholics. These political and religious tensions persevered through to the time of independence in 1980, and beyond.

Although there was resistance at times and missions sometimes failed, the missionary work ultimately created a strong foundation for an enduring Christian allegiance among the great majority of the population. At the time of independence, more than 90% of the population claimed to be Christian, the three mainstream mission churches together claiming around 70% allegiance. Currently these same three traditions account for 56% of the population: 27.9% Presbyterian, 15.1% Anglican and 13% Roman Catholic.

Alongside the three mainstream churches, other Christian traditions have also established a foothold. The earliest of these, just after the turn of the twentieth century, was the Churches of Christ, which has sustained a stable membership of around 4.5% of the population. In 1912 the first Seventh-day Adventist (SDA) missionaries, Calvin and Myrtle Parker from the USA, arrived in the New Hebrides. Today, the SDAs have more than 90 churches, and their number is estimated at around 12.5% of the population and growing.

After the Second World War, missionaries from the Apostolic Church in Australia were invited to affiliate with a small emerging independent church on the island of Ambae. This Pentecostal church now claims the allegiance of around 2.2% of the country's population. Assemblies of God (AOG) missionaries from the USA first arrived in the New Hebrides via Fiji in 1968. With an energetic commitment to 'born-again Christianity', the AOG gained converts, primarily from the established churches. Currently the membership of the AOG numbers around 4.7% of the population.

More recently, a number of marginal or sectarian Christian groups have taken root in Vanuatu. Neil Thomas Ministries (NTM), formerly known as the Holiness Fellowship, has developed into a network of 130 churches from the Banks and Torres down to Aneityum. Neil Thomas died in 2014 and was succeeded his son. Despite some recent controversy around their founder's inappropriate behaviour and questionable financial practices, NTM has retained a membership base of around 3.1% of the population.

Since its beginnings in 1973 the Church of Jesus Christ of Latter-day Saints has steadily expanded, with its impressive facility in Port Vila running programmes for youth, welfare activities and a family history centre. Their impact is greater than their numbers might suggest (around 1% of the population). The Jehovah's Witnesses consolidated their presence during the 1950s. Their numbers have remained small but relatively stable; currently there are 17 congregations and around 800 members.

The category of 'Custom' in Vanuatu refers to two separate groups: those who have never been exposed to or responded to invitations to change their traditional beliefs, and those who have reclaimed aspects of traditional belief around a particular movement. In the former category, there remain tribal communities, mainly in remote areas on the islands of Santo and Malekula, who have been untouched by any of the mission activities of the churches. In the latter category, the most prominent of these belong to the John Frum Movement on the island of Tanna. This movement arose in the late 1930s after a strange appearance on a mountain slope of someone claiming the name of John Frum and promising the arrival of a day of great prosperity for its followers. Over the years, this movement has had a colourful and controversial history – a period of persecution, rises and falls of membership, internal divisions, and both conflict with and cooperation with the local church communities. At its height around the turn of the century, it numbered 8,000 adherents.

Church, Politics and Religious Freedom

The strong interconnection between church life and political life is grounded in the Melanesian cultural heritage, whereby the leaders of the tribal communities oversaw the whole of the life of the community, without drawing any distinctions between religious and political affairs. The divisions between church and state, familiar to the Western world, had no place in Vanuatu. After independence, the people elected into government leadership were those who had been church leaders. Thus the Vanuatu constitution recognises both Melanesian values and Christian practice as foundational to national life. This integration has remained over the years since independence, even if the religious and political allegiances of those in leadership have diversified. Political leaders remain sympathetic to church interests, and those in church leadership feel that they have an effective voice in political affairs.

On matters of religious freedom, this relationship has sometimes been uneasy. The Vanuatu constitution provides for freedom of religious expression. However, from time to time, the Vanuatu Christian Council expresses its concern about the arrival of new religious groups that might disturb the existing church communities or undermine the Christian foundations of the nation. Despite these concerns, there has been little hindrance to the free expression of religious observance in Vanuatu, including the growing presence of other faiths, such as Islam, Buddhism and Hinduism.

Globalisation and Political Influence

Over the last generation, the lifestyle of the people of Vanuatu has been exposed to global influence. Increased opportunity for locals to travel to other destinations and greater hospitality to visitors from other nations have gone hand in hand. One of the obvious impacts has been the rapid growth of technology across the islands, especially among the younger generation, bringing greater exposure to diverse lifestyles and cultures. This has been most concentrated in urban areas, where the strength of traditional cultures has been more difficult to sustain and where there is greater scope to embrace changing global trends. The mainstream churches feel the challenge of these influences as the younger generation turn toward other expressions of the Christian faith or, in line with trends in the Western world, distance themselves from any Christian affiliation.

While the lifestyle and preferences of people are impacted by globalisation, shifts of political influence are also taking place. After the domination of Britain and France during the colonial period, Vanuatu determined, following independence, to make its own political decisions and establish its own political alliances. However, like other island nations that are dependent on economic support, Vanuatu has remained vulnerable to external political influence and a target for competing interests between global powers. In particular, the rapidly growing influence of China on the world stage is having its impact also in Vanuatu, raising concerns for Western allied nations like Australia.

Gospel and Culture

The relationship between the Christian gospel and the traditional beliefs and customs of the people remains a matter of unresolved tension across the churches. Did the Christian faith really become embedded within the cultural context of the local people, or was it a superficial imposition of a foreign missionary version of the faith? Does the Christian faith prohibit traditional cultural practices, does it embrace them, or does it sit uneasily alongside them? These questions have been debated since the early days of mission but became acute at the time of national independence in 1980 when, both politically and culturally, the newly independent peoples expressed a determination to take hold of their own destiny and to give their own shape to the Christian gospel, at the same time rejecting colonial domination. A Gospel and Culture Movement was initiated by the Presbyterian Church soon after independence and has produced some fruitful work on this theme, most recently on the controversial topic of Women in Leadership.

Shifting Religious Allegiance

Accurate figures for membership of the various Christian traditions and other religions in Vanuatu are notoriously difficult to obtain. The situation is exacerbated by the relative fluidity of allegiances and the ease with which people move from one group to another. Evidence suggests that up to one-quarter of the population has changed religious affiliation in the last 30 years. Some have moved from the traditional mainstream mission churches into more recently established groups. It is notable, for example, that the proportion of Presbyterian members has dropped from close to 40% at the time of independence to around 28% today, while Roman Catholic allegiance has dropped from 16% to 12.7%.

There are a number of reasons for this shifting religious affiliation. Allegiance is not grounded so much in the fundamental beliefs or doctrines of the institution as it is in both relational forces and perceived benefits. A person of persuasive influence can be a catalyst for people changing their allegiance. The person might be someone of power or influence within the family or community or a figure from a foreign country who is publicly impressive and draws people as followers. The cultural disposition of local people makes them more vulnerable to such influence. It can mean that persons with influence can start up new groups and attract their own followers. Equally, people might be persuaded by the apparent benefits of leaving their existing community and joining another group. This could be because they have become disaffected within their own community or because they will gain something of importance from the new group. In some cases, this gain is about a deeper sense of meaning and purpose in their lives. In others it has been because of an experience of conversion that enables them to move beyond an unwelcome past. In others again it has come in the form of material gain or opportunity. The possibility of financial benefit, the opportunity for education or travel, the offer of a position of power or influence, the healing of disease or ailment are all reasons for changing allegiance. The cultural disposition of ni-Vanuatu has elements of a 'cargo cult' mentality: people are open to the possibility of greater prosperity in the form of promised gifts from afar.

These influences have also led to the rapid increase and diversification in religious groups. Any new Evangelical group that comes into Vanuatu is able to generate a following. Equally, in certain circumstances, existing groups can easily splinter into new offshoots. Over recent decades, each of the mainstream Christian groups has spawned one or more new churches, so that the number of churches operating in Vanuatu is constantly increasing. For a nation of only 300,000 people, there is a dazzling array of distinct and different church traditions. In the last decade of the twentieth century, 48 churches and religious groups were registered. At least another 30 different Christian groups have appeared since then. Strongly Evangelical Korean churches have been especially prominent. One Korean group founded its own missionary training college on Santo and aims to engage with unchurched communities in remote bush areas.

The Vanuatu Christian Council, founded in 1967, fosters mutual cooperation among the church traditions, a common voice in liaising with the government on religious matters, and pooling resources to address issues of social or political concern. Around the time of independence, its influence was significant. More recently, however, due to rapid growth of church groups with no interest in cooperation, the evolution of other religious faiths and the decline in the influence of mainstream churches, the influence of the Council has diminished.

Gender

One of the areas of emerging change in Vanuatu is the place of women in family, cultural and political life. Increasingly, women are taking up roles of leadership, even if Vanuatu remains one of very few nations currently with no women members of parliament. While the contribution of women in changing roles has been welcomed by many, the cultural heritage of clear role distinctions between men and women has provided a background for the potential abuse and exploitation of women. Within village communities, where the peace and stability of the community are paramount, the changing role of women tends to be controlled and authorised communally. However, within the urban environment, where there is less traditional community oversight, the scope for conflict between men and women over these changes is greater. While it is by no means confined to urban life, instances of domestic abuse of women have increased alarmingly, to the point where various church and other groups have launched programmes of education and welfare to deal with this. This is the underside of a slow but certain change in the historical place of women in Vanuatu life, a change that will continue to evolve as generations of younger and more educated women embrace non-traditional postures.

Conclusion

The people of Vanuatu find themselves increasingly in a global context where there is constant interaction between traditional cultural lifestyles and contemporary world influences. In terms of religious affiliation, the traditional mainstream churches, dominant until independence, have been forced, mostly unwillingly, to face the challenges brought by growing numbers of diverse and sometimes competing Christian groups. At the same time, Christians face a threat from a small groundswell of other world faiths. Especially in the urban environment, the forces of Western globalism will pose their own challenge to the ongoing strength of Christian affiliation.

Going by recent trends, over the next generation, church affiliation in Vanuatu will continue to be fluid and potentially decline. However, despite the changes that have taken place, the Christian churches between them still claim the allegiance of around 90% of the population. Their involvement in sustaining and supporting most aspects of local and national life is critical to the welfare of the people, and their influence in matters of political governance remains significant. Churches will continue to have a strong involvement in national education, partnering in the government's determination to provide improved standards of, and access to, education for every child. This provides some assurance that the next generation of ni-Vanuatu people will be shaped by the Christian faith, even if that comes through a kaleidoscope of church traditions.

Bibliography

Ernst, Manfred (ed.), *Globalization and the Re-shaping of Christianity in the Pacific Islands* (Suva: Pacific Theological College, 2006).

Miller, J. Graham, *Live: A History of Church Planting in the New Hebrides. Books 1–7* (Sydney: General Assembly of the Presbyterian Church of Australia, 1978–90).

Prior, Randall (ed.), *Gospel and Culture in Vanuatu, Vols 1–5* (Melbourne: Gospel Vanuatu Books, 1998–2006).

Regenvanu, Sethy John, *Laef Blong Mi: From Village to Nation. An Autobiography* (Suva: Institute of Pacific Studies, University of the South Pacific, 2004).

Whyte, Jennie (ed.), *Vanuatu: Ten Years of Independence* (Rozelle: Other People Pty Ltd, 1990).

Solomon Islands

Brian Macdonald-Milne

The Solomon Islands are an archipelago east and south-east of the island of New Guinea. Like the Sāmoan islands, they were divided politically into two parts. After agreement between the German and British empires, when they were extending their influence in the Pacific Islands in the latter part of the nineteenth century, the westernmost islands of the long chain – the largest of which is Bougainville – became the German Solomon Islands. The rest became the British Solomon Islands Protectorate, being gradually annexed between 1893 and 1899. After the First World War, the German Solomon Islands became part of the Mandated Territory of New Guinea, administered (with the former British colony of Papua) by Australia. They became part of the independent country of Papua New Guinea in 1975 but are still seeking their own independence.

The British Solomon Islands became independent in 1978, retaining the name 'Solomon Islands'. After the depredations of diseases introduced by Europeans and the earlier recruiting of islanders to work on plantations in Fiji and Queensland, the population numbers gradually recovered; the population since the beginning of the twenty-first century has grown to about 650,000, with one of the highest birth rates in the Pacific area. This makes the Solomon Islands the third largest in population of any of the Pacific's island states, after Papua New Guinea and Fiji. However, its land area, at 27,540 square kilometres, is larger than that of Fiji and it has a geographical extent of over 1,667 kilometres. Part of the country is separated from the rest by 400 kilometres of ocean – a cluster of islands sometimes known as the Santa Cruz Group, but nowadays more often as Temotu, form the Outer Eastern Solomons. In total there are 992 islands, of which 347 are inhabited.

Papua New Guinea and the Solomon Islands are distinctive in having been populated over many millennia by different waves of immigrants, leading to academics increasingly describing them as 'near Oceania', while the remainder of the Pacific Islands have been classified as 'remote Oceania'. People began to arrive in the Solomon archipelago about 30,000 years ago from New Guinea, gradually spreading eastward through the chain of islands. A later migration of people who were seafarers from an area around Taiwan began about 4,000 years ago and led to the population of the outer islands, especially the atolls, by people now known as Polynesians, the rest of the population generally being called Melanesians. This admixture of peoples has led to a vast variation in skin colour, from black to near white; to the development of nearly 80 Indigenous languages, belonging to two language families, Papuan and Austronesian; and to a great deal of inter-ethnic and inter-island rivalry and conflict. There was no overall political or social structure; local chiefs exercised authority over comparatively small areas, their power depending largely on their skill in warfare. Headhunting and cannibalism were practised in some areas.

This geographic and social diversity affected the country's religious and colonial history, and indeed the Solomon Islands and the Santa Cruz Group were the first of the Pacific Islands to be explored and named by Europeans, when the Spanish arrived in the latter part of the sixteenth century seeking gold. Alvaro de Mendaña's first expedition arrived in the Solomon Islands in 1568, and many of the islands still bear Spanish names, including the main island of Guadalcanal. His second expedition, in 1595, came across the island they named Santa Cruz, where they attempted to establish a Spanish colony in the area they named Graciosa (Thanksgiving) Bay. Due to sickness and the hostility of the inhabitants, it was soon abandoned, and both groups of islands remained unknown to the outside world for nearly 200 years.

Besides hoping for more gold (which was indeed later discovered on Guadalcanal), the Spanish authorities also hoped that they would be able to start the evangelisation of the islands, and they ensured that both expeditions were accompanied by Franciscan friars, who would have conducted worship on board ship and also probably ashore at Santa Cruz. This was the first Christian worship offered in any of the Pacific Islands.

The Roman Catholic Church was very aware of the need to follow up this early initiative, especially as it had been successful in establishing itself from the sixteenth century onward north of New Guinea in the

Christianity in the Solomon Islands, 1970 and 2020

Tradition	1970 Population	%	2020 Population	%	Average annual growth rate (%), 1970–2020
Christians	150,000	93.8%	615,000	95.0%	2.9%
Anglicans	49,000	30.6%	200,000	30.9%	2.9%
Independents	7,300	4.6%	45,000	7.0%	3.7%
Protestants	47,300	29.5%	235,000	36.3%	3.3%
Catholics	30,800	19.2%	132,000	20.4%	3.0%
Evangelicals	36,000	22.5%	165,000	25.5%	3.1%
Pentecostals/Charismatics	4,800	3.0%	105,000	16.2%	6.4%
Total population	**160,000**	**100.0%**	**647,000**	**100.0%**	**2.8%**

Source: Todd M. Johnson and Gina A. Zurlo (eds), *World Christian Database* (Leiden/Boston: Brill), accessed January 2020.

Philippines – which, although situated in the Pacific, were considered to be part of East Asia. Pope Gregory XVI invited the recently founded French religious order (or congregation) the Society of Mary to undertake evangelistic work in the central and western Pacific Islands, with its island base in what soon became the French territory of Wallis and Futuna, north-east of Fiji. This was the last island group in Polynesia not yet reached by Protestant missionaries, the first of whom had arrived in the Tahiti area in 1797, sent by the London Missionary Society (LMS).

The Marists served this new mission territory, the Vicariate of Western Oceania, founded in 1836. In 1844, with the assent of Rome, they established new vicariates of Melanesia and Micronesia. Jean Baptiste Épalle, from Lyon in France, was appointed Vicar Apostolic of Melanesia and consecrated as bishop, and then seven priests and six lay brothers set out for the Solomons, hoping that the mission there would later be able to extend its work onward to New Guinea. Épalle was killed on the island of Santa Ysabel (now called Isabel) in 1845, and the mission party returned to the island of San Cristobal. However, sickness and conflict with some of the islanders, which had led to the withdrawal of the Spanish, also led to their mission being withdrawn from the Solomons and its departure for Woodlark Island near New Guinea in 1847. This was only for a short period, before they were removed again. The Marists did not return to the Solomons until 1898.

George Augustus Selwyn had become the first Anglican bishop of New Zealand in 1841 and arrived from England in 1842. His vast diocese included the islands of Melanesia to the north, and to encourage their evangelisation he established the Melanesian mission in 1849, on the understanding that the main work of evangelisation would be carried out by Melanesians. He obtained, through regular visits by ship to the islands, young men whose parents had been persuaded, with gifts and certain reassurances, to allow them to go. The first to be trained were from the Loyalty Islands, near New Caledonia, and from the New Hebrides (now known as Vanuatu). The mission ship's visits extended into the Solomon Islands, and in 1850 a Solomon Islander from San Cristobal (also known as Makira) showed interest in being trained. Those who came assumed that it would be one way of acquiring trade goods and also of understanding how white men acquired their power, influence and skill in technology. However, the benefits of embracing the Christian faith and receiving some basic education increasingly came to be appreciated, and more students and prospective Indigenous missionaries agreed to come for training, especially when the mission school – known as St Andrew's College and later as St Barnabas's – moved from Kohimarama, near Auckland in New Zealand, to Norfolk Island, south of the New Hebrides, in 1866/7.

Thereafter, some young women came for training as well, along with an increasing number of Solomon Islanders, especially from San Cristobal, Florida (Gela) and Santa Ysabel.

The leadership of the Melanesian mission had increasingly been entrusted by Bishop Selwyn to a young English priest, John Coleridge Patteson, who had joined him in 1855 and had been consecrated as the first Anglican bishop of Melanesia, in 1861. He believed deeply in Indigenous ministry and ordained George Sarawia from the Banks Islands north of the New Hebrides as a deacon in 1868, the first Melanesian ordained a minister of any Christian denomination. The bishop was, tragically, killed – and almost immediately hailed as a martyr by his Anglican colleagues – on the island of Nukapu in the Reef Islands in the Santa Cruz Group on 20 September 1871, by those 'for whom he would willingly have given his life'. Two others died with him: Joseph Atkin, a New Zealand priest, and Stephen Taroaniara from San Cristobal, whom Patteson hoped would become the first ordained minister from the Solomon Islands. He is venerated as the first Anglican Melanesian martyr from the Solomon Islands; others were killed later, but only he is referred to as 'Saint'. One notable feature of Anglican spirituality in Melanesia has been its recognition and commemoration of its saints and martyrs, whether Indigenous or expatriate. The Anglicans reached out to nearly all parts of the present Solomon Islands (except some western parts of the country) until the arrival of other missions. They came with the agreement of the new Protectorate Government, established at the end of the nineteenth century, starting in 1898.

The Roman Catholics established themselves at this time on the island of Guadalcanal, and the priests and brothers of the Society of Mary were assisted by the Missionary Sisters of the Society of Mary. Their first Indigenous priest, Fr Michael Aike, was ordained in the 1960s. The original Vicariate of the South Solomons, established in 1912, eventually became the Diocese of Honiara in 1966, and new dioceses were later established for Malaita and for the western Solomons. The latter is called the Diocese of Gizo and is managed by the Dominicans. After the Second Vatican Council (1962–5), a bishops' conference was established for Papua New Guinea and the Solomon Islands, and not long afterward the See of Honiara was raised to the status of an archbishopric in 1978. A 'native sisterhood', the Daughters of Mary Immaculate, serves the church in the Solomons.

In 1902 the Revd George Brown, general secretary of the Australian Wesleyan mission board, entered the western Solomons with the Revd John F. Goldie, a man of great force of character and with strong ideas about how mission should be conducted. Goldie stayed for many years. Brown had made a comity agreement with Cecil Wilson, the Bishop of

Melanesia, so that mission work was left to the Methodists in that part of the Solomons. The Roman Catholics and the Seventh-day Adventists did not enter into such agreements and, unusually for them, the Adventists initiated primary evangelism in parts of that area and extended their work later to other islands, especially Malaita, and became one of the five main denominations. A smaller, localised denomination developed after the Second World War after Goldie had departed. One of his students, Silas Eto, disillusioned with developments in the Methodist mission, started a breakaway movement that led to the foundation in the 1960s of the Christian Fellowship Church, with himself as its leader, known as the Holy Mama (Holy Father). In 1962 the Papua Ekalesia (founded by the LMS), the Methodist Church in Papua New Guinea and the Solomon Islands, and the United Church in Port Moresby became the United Church of Papua New Guinea and the Solomon Islands, with a bishop for the Solomon Islands region.

On the island of Malaita, there had been other developments after the return of labourers from Queensland, where some had been converted to Christianity through the Queensland Kanaka Mission founded by Florence Young, who had been inspired by the China Inland Mission. The returned labourers on Malaita (and also on Guadalcanal and San Cristobal) did not want to join the Anglican Church on those islands, and so the South Seas Evangelical Mission was established, later becoming the autonomous South Seas Evangelical Church (SSEC). After the arrival of European traders, a pidgin language developed to enable better communication and this is known to nearly all Solomon Islanders nowadays, and widely used in conversation. It is not recognised as an official language, although the pidgin languages of Papua New Guinea and Vanuatu (formerly the New Hebrides) are. It is known as Solomon Pijin, or Pijin blong Solomon Aelan, and the Solomon Pijin translation of the whole of the Bible was published by the Bible Society of the South Pacific in 2008, complementing Scriptures and liturgical material in the Indigenous island languages. Pijin was probably widely used by the returned labourers.

After the Anglican Diocese of Melanesia's synod on Ugi Island in the Eastern Solomons in 1965 had backed the establishment of the New Hebrides Christian Council, it was agreed to approach other denominations in the Solomon Islands to form a similar body. At the same time, the Second Vatican Council was meeting in Rome, and approval was given for Roman Catholic participation in such bodies, so the Solomon Islands Christian Association was established in 1966 with three members – the Anglican, Roman Catholic and Methodist churches – and two associate members – the South Seas Evangelicals and the Seventh-day Adventists. SICA, as it become known, led to close cooperation between the churches, and the SSEC later became a full member. The government increasingly expected it to deal with all ecumenical matters, especially concerning Christian bodies wanting to operate in the country, such as the Bible Society, Summer Institute of Linguistics, Child Evangelism Fellowship and Mission Aviation Fellowship (which flew there for a short while, then withdrew).

The churches, especially those in the western and central Solomons, had been deeply affected by the Second World War in Papua New Guinea and the Solomons. The capital was moved from Tulagi, off the coast of Big Gela (Nggela Sule), to Honiara on Guadalcanal, and the Roman Catholics and Anglicans established their headquarters and main cathedrals there. In 1975 the Anglican Province of Melanesia was formed with four dioceses, three in the Solomon Islands and one in the New Hebrides. The dioceses later grew in number to nine in the Solomons and two in Vanuatu, one of which included New Caledonia. All the bishops are now Indigenous. In the 1970s, the number of Anglican religious orders increased. The Melanesian Brotherhood, established in 1925 by Ini Kopuria of Guadalcanal, was complemented by the arrival in 1970 of the Anglican Franciscan Brothers of the Society of St Francis and the Community of the Sisters of the Church and, later, by the locally founded Community of the Sisters of Melanesia. The Revd Dr Charles Elliot Fox, who joined the Diocese of Melanesia in 1902, became for a time the only white member of the Melanesian Brotherhood, but two others joined later. The Brotherhood is now the largest religious order for men under traditional vows in the Anglican communion.

At the same time, the influence of the Charismatic movement grew, and bodies like the Assemblies of God and the Church of the Nazarene were recognised and formed part of a group of churches that did not belong to SICA. There is a small Chinese community, a few of whom are Christians, and some Jehovah's Witnesses.

Almost all the population of the Solomon Islands who are Melanesian or Polynesian belong to one of the churches or Christian movements, the last people practising the Indigenous animistic religion having been on Malaita. Much work among the animists in the mountainous areas of Guadalcanal and Malaita was carried out by the Indigenous Melanesian Brotherhood.

However, the widespread acceptance of Christianity did not prevent a tragic civil war from 1998 to 2003. Known as the 'ethnic tension', it was partly caused by the migration of people from the other islands to the developing capital, Honiara, and other parts of Guadalcanal after political independence in 1978, which had been achieved peacefully. In the aftermath of the conflict, in which the Anglican and Roman Catholic religious orders had provided sanctuary and acted as peacemakers, seven members of the Melanesian Brotherhood were killed in 2003 on the south coast of Guadalcanal by a rebel leader who had not accepted the peace agreement made in 2000 and also some of his followers. This shocked the whole country, which took years to recover. Its recovery was aided by the Regional Assistance Mission to the Solomon Islands, led by Australia, with participants from New Zealand and other Pacific countries. The Solomon Islands Christian Association coordinated the peace efforts of the churches, and the national and denominational women's organisations pleaded for peace to be restored. A truth and reconciliation commission was established with the help of the churches, chaired by the dean of the Anglican Provincial Cathedral. It was opened by Archbishop Emeritus Desmond Tutu, former Anglican Archbishop of Cape Town, South Africa.

A significant drawing together of the churches has been occurring since the 1960s, and they have influenced one another. As a result of ministers of different denominations sometimes being sent to train at the ecumenical Pacific Theological College in Fiji, the churches have accepted that some training can be shared in local situations. The United Church in the Solomons sees its future as being more closely related to the Anglicans and contributes to the teaching and training at the Bishop Patteson Theological College on Guadalcanal. The Anglicans have established the John Coleridge Patteson University, which is open to those of all denominations. It is gradually developing, as is the Solomon Islands National University. The South Seas Evangelical Church has now adopted the title of 'bishop' for its chief ordained minister, as the United Church had earlier done.

Greater contact has led to a wider appreciation of Solomon Islands art, music and culture – including dance, which had always been an accepted part of Anglican practice (including in its liturgy nowadays) but was not often accepted by the Methodists, and usually not approved by the SSEC or the SDA. Prohibitions were usually, though not always, introduced by foreign missionaries and church leaders. As Indigenous leaders have taken their places, they have begun to question and re-examine some of these policies.

The churches still run a number of key schools throughout the country, as well as some of the medical services. The Anglican women's orders and the Mothers' Union set up a refuge for abused women and their children called the Christian Care Centre with the active encouragement of the government. The Anglicans form about a third of the population, with the Roman Catholics and SSEC coming next in size, and the United Church and the Seventh-day Adventists being fewer in number overall. All play important roles in their areas. The churches have a key role in the Solomons in providing basic unity for a very diverse population. As Christians form such a large part of the population, it is usually not difficult for them to cooperate with the national and provincial governments, which appreciate all that the churches are able to provide socially, culturally, educationally and medically, as well as spiritually and liturgically. There is, for example, cooperation in broadcasting. The churches and SICA also contribute to Christian cooperation more widely in the Pacific, especially through the Pacific Conference of Churches and the Pacific Theological College. If peace can be maintained, the country will have much to contribute to the region and to the world church in the future.

Bibliography

Joseph, Keith R. and Charles Brown Beu, *Church and State in Solomon Islands* (Canberra: Australian National University Press, 2008).

Laracy, Hugh, *Marists and Melanesia: A History of Catholic Missions in the Solomon Islands* (Canberra: Australian National University Press, 1976).

Macdonald-Milne, Brian James, *The True Way of Service: The Pacific Story of the Melanesian Brotherhood 1925–2000* (Leicester: Christians Aware and The Melanesian Brotherhood, 2003).

Tippett, Alan, *Solomon Islands Christianity: A Study in Growth and Obstruction* (London: Lutterworth, 1967).

Whiteman, Darrell, *Melanesians and Missionaries: An Ethnohistorical Study of Social and Religious Change in the Southwest Pacific* (Pasadena: William Carey Library, 1983).

Papua New Guinea

Jack Urame

Papua New Guinea is made of up many different tribal groups speaking more than 800 languages. There was no unifying religion before Western contact began in the 1800s. The spread of Christianity on the islands is connected with the colonial history. Three colonial powers penetrated what was then known as New Guinea. The Dutch took over the western end of the island, now West Papua (Indonesia), the British took over the southern end of the island, and the Germans took over the northern end. German rule lasted for only a short period; Australian troops captured the German territory in 1914, following the outbreak of the First World War. After the war the British and German territories merged and came under the Australian government from 1923 until the country gained political independence in 1975.

In the 1800s, at the height of the European colonial invasion of the Pacific Islands, a variety of missionaries from the West arrived in Papua New Guinea and began to evangelise the Indigenous people. The earliest group were Catholic missionaries. Members of the Marist congregation arrived in Woodlark and Rooke (Umboi) islands in 1847. London Missionary Society work among the Motu people was begun by William Laws in 1871. Methodist Mission Society work in Duke of York Island was started by George Brown in 1875. The current United Church in Papua New Guinea is the result of a 1968 merger between the London Missionary Society and the Australian Methodist Mission. On the main island, the Lutheran presence in Finschhafen was initiated by Johannes Flierl in 1886, and the Anglican Church traces its origins to the arrival of Copeland King and Albert Macklaren in Dogura in 1891. The Seventh-day Adventist Church spread to Australasia in 1906 and reached Papua New Guinea in 1910 under the leadership of S. W. Carr and his wife.

The Evangelical Church of Papua New Guinea began in Balimo in 1934. In 1948, the Assemblies of God became the first Pentecostal church to be represented in Papua New Guinea when Don Westbrook and Hugh Davidson started their work in the Sepik area. The Baptist presence began in Baiyer River in 1949. The Evangelical Brotherhood Church began in Minj in 1954, and the Apostolic Church began in Enga that same year. Other groups have also established their churches in various parts of the country.

Growth, Contraction and Engagement of Churches

The country is predominantly Christian, but Christianity is not a state religion. However, the government recognises Christianity as the religion of the majority, and the Department for Community Development and Religion works together with the churches. There is space for dialogue and cooperation between the government and the churches. The constitution of the country explicitly upholds freedom of religion. Although it is not acknowledged by law, the majority of the people accept Christianity as an official religion. Other religious groups are present, but they are small minorities and found mainly in towns and cities.

Around 95% of the total population of nearly 9 million profess to be Christians. More than 100 Christian churches and groups operate in the country. The Roman Catholic Church is the biggest, while the Evangelical Lutheran Church is the largest among the Protestant churches. Some of the churches still have missionaries from overseas serving in the country, but the number of overseas workers has declined sharply, while local leaders have taken over many of the responsibilities that were earlier exercised by foreign missionaries. Some churches, especially the mainline groups, have trained and sent missionaries overseas to serve in other countries. Through this exchange, ecumenical relationships and partnerships with overseas churches remain strong.

Because freedom of religious expression faces no legal restrictions, movement of people within and between churches enjoys great flexibility. There are two notable forms of religious movement. One is a movement that fosters cooperation among church groups. The other is the movement of new religious groups both within and outside of existing groups. As a result of these movements, church membership fluctuates, as some lose while others gain in numbers.

Christianity in Papua New Guinea, 1970 and 2020

Tradition	1970 Population	%	2020 Population	%	Average annual growth rate (%), 1970–2020
Christians	2,390,000	94.6%	8,338,000	95.2%	2.5%
Anglicans	60,000	2.4%	230,000	2.6%	2.7%
Independents	21,300	0.8%	440,000	5.0%	6.2%
Orthodox	200	0.0%	400	0.0%	1.4%
Protestants	918,000	36.3%	4,050,000	46.3%	3.0%
Catholics	694,000	27.4%	2,300,000	26.3%	2.4%
Evangelicals	370,000	14.6%	2,300,000	26.3%	3.7%
Pentecostals/Charismatics	109,000	4.3%	1,950,000	22.3%	5.9%
Total population	**2,528,000**	**100.0%**	**8,756,000**	**100.0%**	**2.5%**

Source: Todd M. Johnson and Gina A. Zurlo (eds), *World Christian Database* (Leiden/Boston: Brill), accessed January 2020.

The Christian churches and groups present in the country fall into a number of categories, including historic mainline churches, breakaway groups, established groups and emerging new groups. New religious groups include Pentecostals, renewal groups and local churches. Local churches are formed as a result of breaking away from the established churches. Since the 1980s, Pentecostal groups have been spreading very rapidly across the country. Many of the leaders of these groups originally belonged to the mainline churches, particularly the Lutheran and Catholic churches. The pattern is that they became dissatisfied with their leaders or felt that they did not have the space to participate in the church as they wished. By breaking away they created their own space to express their faith and promote their religious identity.

Many of the large churches in the country are known for their engagement in social work as a strategy of holistic mission. They establish learning institutions such as schools, colleges and universities to spread the Word of God and promote their Christian values and teachings. They also establish health centres and hospitals. Almost half of the schools and health facilities in the country are owned and operated by the churches. Some churches engage in social, economic and development programmes to empower the communities as part of their mission. Their mission is not confined to the religious domain but extends to the wider social and economic fields. Because of this, the government recognises them as partners in social, spiritual and economic development of the people. The government has also developed a partnership policy with the churches to strengthen the cooperation and dialogue between the two bodies. This relationship is active, and the churches appreciate the openness of the government to work in partnership for the common good of the people.

The Papua New Guinea Council of Churches, established by the mainline churches, includes the Roman Catholic Church, Evangelical Lutheran Church, Baptist Union, Anglican Church, Good News Lutheran Church, United Church and Salvation Army. This body was established to strengthen ecumenical cooperation. It also serves as a platform for the churches to raise their collective voice on national issues affecting people in the country. Through the Council they speak out on such matters as social injustices, climate change, corruption and extractive industries that cause social, environmental and ecological harm.

Religious Movements

Religious proliferation is a notable phenomenon in the country. The rapid expansion and spread of new groups continues to put pressure on the established mainline churches, who see the trend as competition and as counterproductive to their mission. Several movements have spread across the country. Some have proved to be enduring, while others lasted only for a short time before they declined or split up, often leading to the emergence of new groups with new names. Religious movements can cause division and fragmentation within families and social groups. Families who belong to the mainline churches break away from their social foundation to join new religious groups. One of the major reasons for this is the greater flexibility offered by the growing number of new groups and movements. They offer new forms of spirituality and worship styles that have wide appeal. They sing and dance with loud music and prayer. Many people are attracted to this kind of free worship style compared with the guided liturgical forms of the established churches. Over the years, several waves of movements have developed at different stages. The following are the major types of movements since Christianity began in the country.

Evangelisation/conversion movements began with the arrival of missionaries from the West with the aim to spread Christianity and convert the Indigenous people who were still rooted in their traditional religion and untouched by the Christian message. This was the earliest Christian movement and led to the establishment of the present mainline churches in the country.

Messianic movements developed out of a feeling of captivity and desperation among Christians. This led to a deeper search for salvation, which the followers believed was imminent. These movements focused on the expected advent of a Saviour who would soon deliver them from their miseries. These movements began in various parts of the country during the colonial era and continued into the post-independence period. Today such movements are still active in some parts of the country.

Cargo cult movements developed out of a feeling of economic desperation mixed with Christian belief and the quest to acquire material blessings. These movements have emerged dynamically since contact with Europeans, Western civilisation and Christianity. The movement has both Christian and traditional religious elements. The followers believed that there was material deficiency or that they lacked the 'cargo' (material). Therefore, they engaged in the movements in anticipation of the coming of abundant blessings, to be brought by the ancestors or God. Cargo cult movements are found mainly among isolated communities in rural areas. Today the movements are still prevalent in many places, especially where people remain isolated from modern change and where people lack understanding of the modern economic system.

Independent local church movements grew out of a feeling that the larger established churches, especially the mainline churches, were not meeting people's physical and spiritual needs and expectations.

Some members broke away from the mainline churches and established their own local churches. The leaders of the movements have no formal pastoral and theological training but they can read and interpret the Bible. The preachers are called pastors, even when they lack formal training and qualification.

Pentecostal movements grew from a desire for spiritual renewal and a deeper search for truth. They began with the arrival of American missionaries and have spread rapidly across the country since the 1970s. This is the fastest-growing group of movements, attracting many followers. One of the common characteristics of these movements is speaking in tongues as one of the physical signs of receiving the Holy Spirit. Some operate only within the country, while others have international connections, particularly to similar groups in Australia and the USA.

Charismatic/revival movements grew out of the other churches. These movements are similar in character to the Pentecostal stream. Their emphasis is on renewal and spiritual empowerment. The Charismatic movements spread rapidly, and their membership has increased swiftly during recent decades. The various movements that fall under this category are identified as Revival Churches. Some have been formed locally and call themselves Revival Centres of Papua New Guinea, while others have links to similar ministries overseas and are known as Revival Centres International.

Renewal movements have been started within the established churches when their members have been influenced by Pentecostal churches. They adapt elements of spirituality and worship styles from others and try them out in their own churches. This often creates confusion and tension between those favouring innovation and those resisting, often leading to division and instability within the churches. Some churches accept these movements out of fear of losing their members, but others reject them. Within the Lutheran Church the movement led to the creation of a new offshoot called the Lutheran Renewal group.

Pro-Israel movements grew out of a desire for spiritual renewal that sought identity with God's chosen people, the Jews. This is a recent emerging movement under various names and is spreading rapidly across the country. Followers seek to relocate their history with the Jewish people and the Holy Land. They accept the Pentateuch and attempt to follow the Old Testament tradition with the belief that God's blessing comes to his people and can be extended to others by linking to God's chosen people. The followers believe that God and the Christian churches are secularised, the essence of Christianity has declined and people have lost sight of God's covenant with Abraham, Isaac and Jacob and have turned away. Therefore, people have been afflicted by the evils of the world and human suffering has increased. Further, they believe that the country is not blessed and development is lacking or not progressing. Consequently, followers of these movements attempt to find answers by returning to the Old Testament tradition in order to seek blessings and progress in life. Christianity thus is used as a convenient channel to construct new pathways to respond to complex development issues.

Across the country, religious movements create much instability and confusion among the churches. There is a rise in new theological ideas, forms of worship and ways of interpreting the Bible. In a country where many people are affected by unfavourable social, economic and political conditions, people seek ways to find answers by recourse to their Christian belief. Religious movements obviously relate to the diverse social and economic challenges such as poverty, injustice, inequality, violence, sickness and many other negative forces that confront people today. Shaped by their worldview, spirituality and encounter with the Bible, Papua New Guineans use Christianity as a convenient lens through which to seek answers.

With the arrival of new Pentecostal, Renewal and Fundamentalist groups, the mainline churches are facing a new challenge of losing members. Through the influence of the new groups, the movement of people between churches continues. The mainline churches see this trend as a threat because their members leave and join the new groups. The new groups are influential because of their character of worship and preaching style. They emphasise holiness and obedience as means to obtain spiritual and physical blessing.

The new movements expand in numbers because they go out to the public in the streets, towns and cities and preach openly, while the mainline churches confine their preaching to their own members in their church buildings. The public open-air preaching, praying, healing, speaking in tongues and emphasis on holiness attract many people. Some people have moved between several churches already in their lifetime. They feel that in their former churches they did not experience blessing and the power of the Holy Spirit and that the worship life was dead or not active. Therefore, they search for a church that can meet their spiritual needs and expectations.

Ecumenical Cooperation

One of the characteristics of the Christian churches in Papua New Guinea is their strong ecumenical spirit of cooperation. There are two types of cooperation. One is the inter-church bodies formed among some of the existing churches to work together. Notable among these interfaith bodies are the Papua New Guinea Council of Churches, Bible Translation

Association, Christian Leaders Training College, Christian Radio Mission Fellowship, Melanesian Institute, Melanesian Association of Theological Schools, Christian Education Council, Christian Medical Council, Evangelical Alliance, Evangelical Missionary Association, Christian Media Production, National Council of Pentecostal Churches, PNG Evangelical Association, Operation Mobilisation PNG, Ecumenical Religious Education, City Mission, Word Publishing, Religious Television Association and Body of Christ.

The other type is the international non-denominational bodies. Created by various Christian groups to work together to extend the gospel without church affiliation, notable examples include Missionary Aviation Fellowship, Bible Society, Scripture Union, Summer Institute of Linguistics, Tertiary Students Christian Fellowship, World Vision, Young Men's Christian Association, Young Women's Christian Association, Youth With A Mission and Campus Crusade for Christ.

Recently the mainline churches have developed a concept to work together called the Church Partnership Programme. The members of this programme are the Anglican Church, Baptist Union, Roman Catholic Church, Evangelical Lutheran Church, United Church, Salvation Army and Seventh-day Adventist Church. Leaders of these churches meet several times a year to discuss common concerns and have closer cooperation than with the Pentecostal groups. The Pentecostal churches have also developed closer cooperation. Recently they have created the Body of Christ PNG to strengthen their cooperation. However, the mainline churches consider this as competition with the Papua New Guinea Council of Churches. This creates misunderstanding and confusion between the mainline and the Pentecostal churches.

Culture, Society and Politics

The encounter between Christianity and culture has played a significant role in people's response to Christianity. Traditional religion and cultures have provided the basis for the spread of Christianity in Papua New Guinea. Elements of traditional belief in spirits, gods, myths of creation and other elements of spirituality and culture enabled people to connect them with the biblical narratives of God, creation and humanity. Christianity has transformed society, yet over time the influence of Christianity has contributed to the decline of the traditional beliefs, cultures and values. Today Papua New Guineans appreciate the positive contribution of Christianity to society but also express concern at the loss of many positive cultural values and practices.

Different churches have different ideas about culture; therefore, their attitudes to local cultures differ. Mainline churches are sensitive to local cultures and integrate some cultural elements in their mission. Generally, they accept the positive elements as God's gifts but reject the negative elements that are harmful to people and contradictory to the teaching of the Bible. Pentecostal and other smaller churches consider culture as bad or evil. They reject elements such as traditional dances, songs, rituals, ceremonies, symbols of spirits and totems of clan spirits, and traditional carvings with cultural and religious motifs. They have even encouraged government leaders to remove traditional carvings and paintings from the National Parliament House.

Christianity also plays a major role in the political life of the people. There is a clear demarcation between church and state, but people do not draw a clear line between religion and politics. When Christians become political leaders they integrate politics in their religious life or blend politics and Christianity together. Christian prayers are offered in political meetings and gatherings. In church conferences and gatherings, political leaders are invited to participate and address the delegates. This reflects the Melanesian worldview of interconnectedness of life and the cosmos. Papua New Guineans see the social, religious and cultural aspects of life in a web of relationship.

Papua New Guinea is a country of diverse language groups and cultures, but Christianity plays an important role as a unifying force. It breaks down social and cultural barriers and unites people of many societies into a new community. Yet religious proliferation creates perplexities within the Christian communities. Church buildings of one denomination or another are visible in towns and villages. Along the main roads church buildings are located every few kilometres, with many different name-tags, symbolising the denominational diversity in the country.

Today Christianity still has a big influence in Papua New Guinea. People value Christianity and appreciate its contribution to the country and see it as an important agent of societal transformation. Christians joyfully worship together, engage in prayer groups and participate in church activities. In the congregations they appreciate the communal life of sharing, caring and living together. While Papua New Guineans appreciate the positive benefit Christianity offers, they are also anxious about the increased trends of globalisation and secularisation that bring new challenges to church and society. Christians are concerned about how the changing dynamics of society today will shape the future of Christianity in the country.

Bibliography

Gibbs, Philip, *Bountiful Harvest: The Churches in Papua New Guinea*, Occasional Paper of the Melanesian Institute No.13 (Goroka: The Melanesian Institute, 2007).

Macdonald-Milne, Brian, *Christianity in Papua New Guinea*, Pacific Churches Research Centre Paper No. 2 (Port Vila, Vanuatu: Pacific Churches Research Centre, 1980).

Tromp, Garry, *Melanesian Religion* (Cambridge: Cambridge University Press, 1998).

Tromp, Garry, *Melanesian Religion and Christianity*, Melanesian Mission Studies No. 4 (Goroka: The Melanesian Institute, 2008).

Zocca, Franco, *Melanesia and its Churches: Past and Present* (Goroka: The Melanesian Institute, 2007).

New Zealand

Geoffrey Troughton

Geographically, New Zealand lies at the southernmost reaches of the globe. Situated 'down under', 1,500 kilometres to the south-east of Australia, it is a last staging post for visitors to Antarctica, as far removed physically from Europe as it is possible to be. It was from Europe, and primarily the UK, however, that Christianity reached New Zealand in the nineteenth century through processes of missionisation, settlement and colonisation. Those origins and influences configured New Zealand Christianity in far-reaching ways. For much of the nation's history, the vast majority of New Zealanders identified as Christians. This situation changed from the second half of the twentieth century, and New Zealand is now often cast as a highly secular country with high rates of non-religion. In this context, the various impacts of secularisation, developing Pentecostal and Charismatic movements, growing ethnic diversity and trajectories connected with Māori expressions of faith are among the most important influences reshaping contemporary Christianity. This chapter provides an overview of the development of Christianity in New Zealand and an exploration of these contemporary dynamics.

Nineteenth-century Beginnings

New Zealand Christianity is often understood to have developed in two main streams. The earliest of these grew out of mission among the Indigenous Māori people prior to colonial rule. At the instigation of Samuel Marsden, the leading Church of England clergyman in the New South Wales penal colony in Australia, a first Church Missionary Society (CMS) settlement was established in 1814 in the Bay of Islands under the protection of Ngāpuhi chief Ruatara. This mission experienced early difficulties but became more settled and effective from the 1820s under the leadership of Henry Williams.

In 1822, Wesleyans joined the CMS in the upper North Island; French Roman Catholics of the Society of Mary also arrived in 1838 under the leadership of Bishop Jean-Baptiste Pompallier. There was fierce competition between the Protestant and Catholic missions, and some rivalry between the CMS and the Wesleyan Methodist Missionary Society, despite their commonalities. Tensions stimulated activity but also led the missions to seek distinct spheres of influence, which shaped subsequent geographies of affiliation.

From the 1830s, a significant turning occurred as younger Māori in particular embraced Christianity, engaging seriously with new ideas, practices and lifeways. One observer in 1845 estimated the total Māori population to be 110,000, of whom about 65,000 attended services in one of the mission churches. Indigenous evangelists were critical agents of change, often extending the reach of Christian teaching beyond the regions of European missionary contact. In the early decades, these evangelists included 'redeemed slaves' who received instruction through the missions before returning to their own *whānau* (extended family) and *hapū* (kinship group). Some, such as Piripi Taumata-a-Kura, showed no particular interest in Christianity so far as CMS missionaries could discern. Yet on his return, Taumata-a-Kura became the first and most influential evangelist to Ngāti Porou on the east coast of the North Island, which became an important and enduring heartland of Māori Anglicanism. Elsewhere, other evangelists reached effectively beyond tribal boundaries, establishing distinctly Māori expressions of Christianity.

A second stream of Christianity was established through European settlement from 1840. Protestant missionaries also facilitated this development by helping convince the British government to intervene in New Zealand and through pivotal contributions to the Treaty of Waitangi, which secured Māori agreement to British annexation on the promise of British citizenship, protection and continuing exercise of traditional authority. Massive growth in British immigration followed in the second half of the century. By 1901, Māori numbered just 43,112 in a population of 815,865. The remainder were almost all of European descent, 95% of whom affiliated with a Christian denomination.

Christianity in New Zealand, 1970 and 2020

Tradition	1970 Population	%	2020 Population	%	Average annual growth rate (%), 1970–2020
Christians	2,688,000	95.4%	2,619,000	54.2%	−0.1%
Anglicans	876,000	31.1%	590,000	12.2%	−0.8%
Independents	85,900	3.0%	334,000	6.9%	2.8%
Orthodox	5,500	0.2%	14,800	0.3%	2.0%
Protestants	837,000	29.7%	710,000	14.7%	−0.3%
Catholics	426,000	15.1%	543,000	11.2%	0.5%
Evangelicals	756,000	26.8%	590,000	12.2%	−0.5%
Pentecostals/Charismatics	28,200	1.0%	420,000	8.7%	5.5%
Total population	**2,818,000**	**100.0%**	**4,834,000**	**100.0%**	**1.1%**

Source: Todd M. Johnson and Gina A. Zurlo (eds), *World Christian Database* (Leiden/Boston: Brill), accessed January 2020.

New Zealand attracted a diverse array of 'transplanted' denominations and traditions. The four largest were Anglican (Church of England), Presbyterian, Roman Catholic and Methodist; much changed and, representing smaller proportions of the population, these denominations remain the main face of 'traditional' Christianity. Up until the Second World War, 40% of the population claimed an Anglican affiliation. Anglicanism was never the state religion in New Zealand – a reality Anglicans recognised in their 1857 constitution, adopted under Bishop George Selwyn's leadership. Nevertheless, a de facto status as the national church persisted in some minds. Anglicanism's links to the Crown and numerical predominance led to prominence in state and civic ceremonies. That role continues to some degree, though the Anglican Church's cultural status and influence are greatly diminished, even in Canterbury, which was originally designed as an Anglican settlement (1850). Church cultural authority was symbolised there by the central-city location of Christchurch's cathedral, which became a key icon of civic identity. After the cathedral was destroyed in a devastating earthquake in 2011, its future became a focus of intense dispute; community and political leaders opposed the diocese's plans to build a new cathedral, forcing it to rebuild the original instead. At the time of writing the cathedral remains in ruins.

Presbyterians made up nearly a quarter of the population in the century from 1840. The Otago settlement (1848) was founded by the Otago Association, which was an outgrowth of the Evangelically oriented Free Church of Scotland. The southern Synod of Otago and Southland joined with the Northern Church to form a national Presbyterian Church of New Zealand in 1901, but Otago-Southland remains a heartland of New Zealand Presbyterianism – culturally, numerically, financially and otherwise.

Roman Catholics constituted less than 15% of the population over the same period. French priests led the early Catholic expansion in New Zealand, and it was a French-born religious, Suzanne Aubert, who founded New Zealand's home-grown congregation, the Daughters of Our Lady of Compassion, in 1892. If her cause, currently in process with the Congregation for the Causes of Saints, is recognised, Aubert will become New Zealand's first canonised saint. From the 1860s, Irish migration increased substantially, and with clergy also increasingly drawn from this source, an Irish flavour characterised New Zealand Catholicism before a more multicultural church emerged late in the twentieth century.

The fourth-largest tradition was Methodism, the various streams of which united into one body in 1913. Nimble Methodist organisation, with its emphasis on lay leadership and heartfelt spirituality, was well suited to the conditions associated with mass immigration and expanding settlement. Methodism thrived in the nineteenth century, growing to about

10% of the population by 1900, but slowly declined proportionally thereafter. By 2018, it represented just 1.6% of the population and was deeply
fractured along cultural and theological lines.

Other groups proliferated, with Baptist, Congregational, Lutheran,
Brethren and Quaker communities among the largest of the smaller
groups. Some exercised greater influence on New Zealand culture and
religiosity than numbers alone indicate. The Brethren, for example,
evangelised effectively in pioneer rural settlements and were significant
contributors to overseas mission as well as Evangelical networks and
institutions; Brethren networks, commitments and finances continue
to be influential in these areas. The Salvation Army, whose first mission
commenced in 1883, established a high profile in New Zealand through
welfare provision, occasional activism and colourful evangelism.
It remains one of the most distinctive and widely respected public
expressions of Christianity, despite its very small size – just 8,000 in 2018 –
and declining affiliation. A number of Baptist churches have also thrived,
exercising nationally significant ministries, while Carey Baptist College
is now the largest and arguably most influential of the denominational
theological education providers.

North American influences have also shaped New Zealand Christianity – for example, through new churches that arrived from the nineteenth
century. These include the Church of Jesus Christ of Latter-day Saints and
the Seventh-day Adventists, which are now sustained by very high levels
of support from Māori and Pacific peoples. Anglo-American revivalist
preachers and social campaigners established institutions and movements
that influenced the ethos and social commitments of New Zealand
Christians for decades. It was after the Second World War, however, that
North American influences became particularly widespread, especially
through Evangelical and Pentecostal networks and in movements like
Youth for Christ.

Māori Christianity

Māori Christianity developed in distinct ways after the early missionary
era, shaped by internal logics as well as the effects of colonisation. Growing
tensions over disputes connected to European settlement, land and sovereignty led to the creation of a Māori King Movement (Kīngitanga) that
was promoted by Māori Christians such as Wiremu Tāmihana Tarapīpipi
Te Waharoa. Tensions erupted spectacularly, however, when the Crown
prosecuted war in Taranaki in 1860, supporting settler aspirations in
a disputed land claim. Some Anglicans, including Octavius Hadfield,
protested vigorously, but the churches overwhelmingly supported the
Crown and rejected the Kīngitanga movement. At the end of the war

Methodists found that 90% of Māori members had departed, and the Anglican mission was effectively destroyed.

After the wars, some Māori turned from the churches altogether. Others embraced rival denominations, including the Church of Jesus Christ of Latter-day Saints, or other expressions of Indigenous Māori Christianity. The latter included prophet movements that proliferated from the 1860s, whose Christian influences and dimensions are clearer now than they were to contemporary European commentators. Among the best-known and most enduringly influential of the prophets were: Te Ua Haumēne, founder of the Pai Mārire faith; Te Kooti Rikirangi, founder of the Ringatū Church; Te Whiti-o-Rongomai and Tohu Kākahi, who established the once large and thriving pacifist community of Parihaka, which was sacked by government troops in 1881; and Rua Kēnana, who was baptised in 1906, styled himself Te Mihaia Hou (the New Messiah) and sought to build Te Hiruhārama Hou (the New Jerusalem) at Maungapōhatu, the sacred mountain of Tūhoe.

The emergence of the Rātana Church in the 1920s was especially significant. From 1918, Tahupōtiki Wiremu Rātana embarked upon a healing and prophetic ministry following a dramatic spiritual experience. By 1925, his ministry had developed into an independent church and a political movement. It called for renewed commitment to the Treaty of Waitangi, which had been marginalised since the mid-nineteenth century. From 1943 to 1996, Rātana held all the Māori seats in parliament. It continues as a political force, with annual celebrations at the Rātana settlement near Whanganui drawing political leaders from across the spectrum, alongside religious supporters and other church leaders. With more than 40,000 census affiliates in the 2018 census, Rātana is also the largest Māori church.

Rātana's popularity influenced other churches, notably by hastening recognition and promotion of Māori leadership. Anglicans had been slow to ordain Māori in the nineteenth century, but in 1928 F. A. Bennett was appointed first Bishop of Aotearoa as an assistant to the Bishop of Waiapu. Whakahuihui Vercoe was ordained the first full bishop in 1981. An outspoken advocate for Māori and promoter of the Treaty, Vercoe was a key influence in the formation of a new Anglican constitution in 1992, which restructured the church into three *tikanga* (ways, styles, cultural modes) – for Māori, Pākehā (Europeans) and Pasefika (Pacific Peoples, in the Diocese of Polynesia). This was envisaged as a means of enabling 'partnership' in decision-making and facilitating mission and ministry within these cultural groups. This change proved controversial and challenging, but the new structure also represented one of the earliest and most substantial attempts at institutional decolonisation in New Zealand and has been widely praised as such.

Anglican constitutional change occurred in the context of a broader 'Māori renaissance', political activism and renewed recognition of the Treaty of Waitangi from the 1970s. It built upon the introduction of a new Prayer Book in 1989, which aimed to combine traditional liturgy with modern prayers and a distinctively New Zealand sensibility that included Māori visual design elements and bilingual text. More broadly, Treaty principles of partnership, protection and participation had become part of government discourse. Churches generally were forced to wrestle with the challenges of postcolonial critique of Christianity and the implications of a Treaty that some Māori referred to as a sacred covenant.

Recognition of Christian complicity in colonialism, and the ongoing legacies of injustice and marginalisation that this produced, haunts contemporary Christianity. Pākehā Christians have been slow to recognise these issues, but there is evidence in recent years of a profound shift in outlook. Within the broader culture, Māori language (te reo Māori), culture, values and *tikanga* (protocols, procedures) are increasingly regarded as integral to New Zealand's future. For many Christians these have also come to be imagined as central to the emergence of a vibrant, authentic and distinctively New Zealand Christianity. The shift is evident in greater use of te reo Māori in *waiata* (song) and *karakia* (prayers), as well as wider acknowledgement that issues relating to resource distribution, reconciliation and recognition of Māori leadership remain outstanding. While these matters are often articulated as questions of justice and integrity, greater openness to Tikanga Māori has also been fostered by demographic changes, the collapse of Christian cultural influence (accompanied by critique of the failures of 'the Church') and growing disillusionment with elements of the political and socio-economic status quo.

Secularisation and Disaffiliation

Secularisation and rapid disaffiliation from the churches were defining challenges of the late twentieth century and continue to reverberate. In 1896, 0.25% of the New Zealand census population claimed 'no religion', and there was little sign of change to this for more than half a century. After the Second World War, church-building and fund-raising campaigns proliferated and many new parishes were created in the burgeoning suburban developments. Dynamic new youth movements emerged, while a tour by US evangelist Billy Graham in 1959 garnered support from across the denominations – with sponsorship from the National Council of Churches, which had formed in 1941 – and met with great success.

From the 1960s, however, the churches were confronted by challenges to their authority and relevance and were forced to grapple with their changing place in society. The upshot involved considerable grief, contestation and fragmentation, as well as creative new forms of expression. A symbolic watershed occurred in 1967 when Lloyd Geering, principal of the Presbyterian Theological Hall, was tried by the church for 'doctrinal error' for championing liberal views of the resurrection and publicly stating that 'man has no immortal soul'. The trial was a national media sensation. Differences between liberal and conservative Christians sharpened and questioning of the cultural salience of Christianity intensified. Description of New Zealand as a 'secular' nation also became more common and increasingly referred to cultural and religious realities as well as political arrangements. Geering became New Zealand's prophet of modernity and secularisation. In 2006 he was awarded the nation's highest honour as a member of the Order of New Zealand.

Growing disaffiliation from Christianity was an obvious marker of change as disavowal of religious identity became a cultural norm. In the 40 years from 1966 to 2006, the proportion of New Zealanders identifying as census Christians declined from 89.1% to 54.2%. By 2018, this had fallen to 38.6%. Between 1966 and 2018, those claiming 'no religion' rose from 1.2% to 48.6% of the population, though the proportion of 'no religionists' aged under 30 is substantially higher. The total number of professing Christians dropped less dramatically, but nominal Christian identification is no longer culturally valued. This change is reflected in the collapse of affiliation with the historic denominations: Anglicans dropped from 33.7% in 1966 to 6.8% in 2018 and Presbyterians from 21.8% to 5.2% (including Congregational and Reformed Christians). Catholic affiliation also fell, but at a much slower rate, so that by 2013 Catholics were the single largest religious group – 10.1% in 2018. Census data are limited but do capture a dramatic shift that has affected the experience and practice of Christianity.

For a range of reasons, denominational loyalty has ceased to be a central marker of identity, as evidenced in the census category 'Christian nfd' (Christian not further defined), which has grown against the general trend to 6.7% of the population in 2018. Those who identify as Christian but specify no denomination tend to be younger and highly identified with their faith, and also of European ethnicity. They often connect to churches of a conservative theological hue, including newer Independent and Pentecostal ones. Since the 1990s, these kinds of church have increasingly repudiated traditional church 'brands' in favour of contemporary styling in order to retain members and attract new ones. Some historic churches are self-consciously emphasising denominational values as part of a missional orientation. In the Anglican Diocese of Wellington, this approach nevertheless involves substantial reconfiguration of traditional Anglicanism, drawing from radical resources that re-imagine the church as a kind of social movement.

The relative strength of Catholicism partly reflects that church's investment in education. Concerned about Protestant hegemony influencing national 'secular' state schooling, Catholics established an independent education system in the nineteenth century. This aimed to inculcate Catholic faith in connection with the parishes. From 1975, Catholic schools became state integrated, allowing them access to state funding while retaining their special character. Such education remained popular, and 8.7% of children were educated in Catholic schools in 2011. Yet this popularity belies major challenges. Catholic youth report very low levels of identification with their faith, and their participation beyond the school system is limited. Their loyalty to the church has been further tested, with others, by the clergy abuse crisis that has rocked New Zealand as elsewhere. Shortages of priests, declining Mass attendance and parish consolidations all point to a more uncertain future for Catholicism.

A range of other Christian educational institutions exist. Denominational schools, mainly Anglican and Presbyterian, grew as secondary education flourished in the twentieth century, though most of these are private and supported largely by the elite. From the 1960s, concerns about secular 'humanism' in state education led to the development of other Christian schools. About 90 of these now connect with the NZ Association for Christian Schools. Home schooling has also flourished, drawing extensively from Christian support. Secularity in state primary schools severely restricts teaching about religion, and there are long-running tensions and disputes about the current system of voluntary church-run teaching that still operates legally in a large number of schools. Concerns about the likely eventual demise of this system will be partly mitigated only if it is replaced by a pluralist religious studies curriculum, since many conservatives seek to preserve a particular status for teaching of the Christian faith. At the tertiary level, Evangelical Christian institutions like Laidlaw College and Bethlehem Tertiary Institute have developed well respected teacher training programmes, as well as counselling and social work training. Laidlaw is also the largest theological education provider in the country, although Otago's Theology Programme has a wide reach and strong academic reputation as the only dedicated theology programme based in a university.

Changes associated with secularisation have contributed to sectional fragmentation, including polarisation between conservative and liberal Christians – theologically and on social issues. Christians were in the vanguard supporting a range of socially liberal causes, including justice-related reforms related to race and sex equality, as well as New Zealand's landmark anti-nuclear legislation, in the 1970s and '80s. They also initiated conservative movements, often focused on questions of sexual morality.

Numerous, invariably short-lived, political parties have appeared since the late 1980s with a conservative orientation, though none has achieved electoral representation. Their ongoing proliferation reflects anxiety about a loss of Christian identity, and influence, within the nation. Yet since the 1990s such parties have tended to downplay their Christian basis, which also reflects the limited electoral appeal of overt religious politics in New Zealand.

Debates about sexuality continue to polarise. In the mid-1980s, churches were divided over homosexual law reform, with strong and public conservative Christian opposition to this legislation pitted against liberal support. Disputation within the denominations followed. The Presbyterian AFFIRM movement began in 1993, stimulated in part by resistance to initiatives to ordain homosexual ministers. Methodist contestation over the same issue led Evangelicals to form the Wesleyan Methodist Movement in 1998. Protracted Anglican debates culminated in May 2019 with a split, when a small GAFCON-aligned group established the Church of Confessing Anglicans in New Zealand, based in Christchurch.

Pentecostal and Charismatic Christianities

Pentecostal and Charismatic Christianity grew and became influential in the late twentieth century, and a large portion of active churchgoers are now in churches connected with this stream. The earliest explicitly Pentecostal influences drew from late-nineteenth-century Holiness spirituality and trans-Atlantic revivalist movements, introduced to New Zealand through evangelistic tours, prophecy-oriented movements and healing ministries such as those associated with John Alexander Dowie. A distinctive Pentecostal movement is usually dated to Smith Wigglesworth's visits in 1922 and 1923–4. A. C. Valdez's tour in 1924–5 was particularly crucial since it led to the establishment of the Pentecostal Church of New Zealand (PCNZ), a body from which the most influential subsequent Pentecostal churches derived – notably the Assemblies of God and the Apostolic Church. Other early Pentecostal churches included the Elim and Apostolic Churches, and the Christian Revival Crusade initiated by the Australian Leo Harris. A series of 'Indigenous' churches also developed after the Second World War, ultimately developing into the New Life Churches, which later grew in numerical significance.

From the 1960s, the Charismatic movement within the historic churches had a profound impact in New Zealand, and this also benefited the Pentecostal churches through crossover growth from the denominations. Pentecostal religiosity became more acceptable and respectable, and often less determinedly sectarian as it sought to reach out to middle New Zealand. In the 1980s and '90s, Charismatic churches were the fastest-growing congregations in most denominations. The movement also led to many conflicts and splits, and new alignments formed within and between churches. While exercise of Charismatic gifts has become less prominent, characteristically informal, contemporary styles of church service and music have become widely entrenched.

Churches of the Pentecostal-Charismatic type were mission-oriented, and often effective at attracting youth, their style cohering with wider cultural changes that favoured emotional expression, spontaneity and informality. From the 1970s, 'Scripture and Song' music had a wide global influence, and the production of new music has continued to be a feature and focus for many of these churches. Numerous independent fellowships appeared from the 1990s with aspirations to mega-church style and influence. These include C3, City Impact and the Life Churches in Auckland, and Arise Church in Wellington.

Pentecostalism had mixed success among Māori communities, though the Apostolic Church was particularly effective in nurturing Māori support. From the 1990s, Destiny Church, led by Brian Tamaki, had particular success. Tamaki had previously been an apostle in the Apostolic Church; his departure contributed to a weakening of the Māori presence in that church, in part because a number of churches left the Apostolic fold to join Destiny. Tamaki was sometimes likened to the nineteenth-century prophets, on account of his charismatic style and political aspirations. His personality and desire for media attention, and the church's combination of prosperity teaching and conservative politics, also led to substantial public criticism, ridicule and parody.

In 2018, 1.75% of the New Zealand population identified as Pentecostal, but the boundaries of the tradition are fluid and this figure does not capture the size or influence of the broader stream. A substantial proportion of such believers simply identify as 'Christian', either because they eschew other labels or because no other suggested category makes sense of their affiliation. Churches in this tradition are often highly activist and have initiated broad-ranging community outreach and humanitarian activities. They have also proven attractive to new migrants in a more multicultural New Zealand. A network of Sāmoan Assemblies of God developed from 1965 and numbered 90 churches by 2005, while nearly 10% of census Pentecostals claim an Asian ethnicity. A wide range of ethnic Pentecostal churches have appeared among migrants from Africa, Asia and elsewhere.

Ethnic Diversification

Another relatively rapid shift may be described as the ethnicisation of New Zealand Christianity. This change occurred in the wake of broader transformations to New Zealand's ethnic and cultural make-up as a consequence of changing immigration policies in the second half of the twentieth century. It reshaped the geography of Christianity, its institutional expression in individual churches as well the traditional denominations, and relationships with other faiths.

At the beginning of the twentieth century, 93% of New Zealand's population was born in New Zealand, England, Ireland or Scotland, and for much of the twentieth century immigration policies favoured British immigration. Some non-British European migration occurred in the wake of the Second World War, though it was very limited in scale compared, for example, with Australia. In 1944, 845 Catholic Polish refugees, 734 of them orphan children, were kept at a camp in Pahīatua in the lower North Island prior to acceptance for permanent settlement. Some Greek post-war migration led to a rise in the small Orthodox community, which was part of the Greek Orthodox Archdiocese of Australia and New Zealand from 1924 to 1970. An influx of migrants from the Netherlands connected initially with the Presbyterian Church but left in 1952–3 to establish the Reformed Churches of New Zealand.

Pacific immigration was a more distinctive feature and had a more substantial overall influence. Some early migration from Niue and the Cook Islands followed inclusion from 1901 in what was then the Colony of New Zealand. After the Second World War, labour shortages and decolonisation increased such migration dramatically. A Treaty of Friendship in 1962 enabled immigrants from Western Sāmoa to enter New Zealand under a quota scheme. Restrictions relaxed during the economic prosperity of the 1960s. Despite a backlash in the mid-1970s Pacific migration continued, and in fact grew and diversified in the decades that followed. By 2018, Pacific peoples made up 8.1% of the population, with some projections anticipating a rise to 10% by 2026. This growth was concentrated mainly in the North Island – particularly Auckland, where nearly two-thirds of New Zealanders who identify with at least one Pacific ethnicity live. By contrast, only 7% live in the South Island. Almost two-thirds of Pacific peoples in New Zealand are now New Zealand-born, and they are also considerably younger than the national average. The highest rates of Christian affiliation are among New Zealand's Pacific peoples.

Institutionally, Pacific migration reshaped the denominations, particularly the Methodist, Presbyterian and Congregationalist churches. The first ethnic Pacific Island church, Newton Pacific Islanders Congregational Church (PICC), was founded in Auckland in 1947. A few multicultural parishes emerged, but 'ethnic' churches became more common and were often more successful in retaining members, particularly among first-generation migrants. Migrants associated with the former churches of the London Missionary Society in Sāmoa, Niue and the Cook Islands initially connected with the Congregational Church in New Zealand. In 1969, Pacific members accounted for 6,000 of the nearly 7,000 Congregationalists who left to join the Presbyterian Church. A small Congregational Union still exists, with a strong Pacific flavour. Numerically, New Zealand Methodism in now very largely Pacific in make-up. European membership has aged and declined precipitously, but Tongan, Fijian and Rotuman congregations in particular have flourished within the different strands of contemporary Methodism – strands that proliferated along cultural, institutional and theological lines.

From the late 1980s, further changes to immigration policies led to a rapid influx of immigrants from other parts of the world, notably from Asia. In 2002–3, 40% of immigrants to New Zealand were from Asia. Different waves brought successive concentrations of Malaysian, South Korean, Chinese, Filipino and South Asian populations, among others. By 2018, the combined Asian ethnic group represented 15.1% of the New Zealand population, only slightly less than Māori (16.5%) and up from 9.2% in 2006. Much of this migration also focused on Auckland: in 2013, people of Asian ethnicity constituted 23% of the city's population, but only 11.8% of the national population. Nearly two-thirds of those who identify ethnically as Asian lived in Auckland in 2018. A significant proportion of them were believers: in 2013, 28.5% of those identifying as Asian also identified as Christian.

All the denominations experienced growth in membership among people of Asian ethnicity, though this growth was not evenly distributed. It was particularly apparent among Catholics, Baptists and Presbyterians but was negligible in the Anglican Church. Chinese and Japanese congregations also proliferated, in contrast to the distinct minority status of Christianity in those nations of origin. Theologically, the Asian churches, like migrant churches generally, were more conservative in orientation. Asian migration also increased the presence of other religions, notably Hinduism (2.7%), Islam (1.3%), Buddhism (1.1%) and Sikhism (0.9%), which has influenced public attitudes and policy-making. The extent and implications of Christian identification among Asian New Zealanders, however, are often less well understood.

Conclusion

Public, media profiles typically frame New Zealand Christianity through its most novel, eccentric and controversial forms, or in relation to narratives concerning the demise of religion that oversimplify the complex processes of secularisation. The present situation is much more dynamic and interesting than such accounts suggest, as old forms and new patterns of religious critique, identification and globalisation converge, conspiring to change the face of Christianity in New Zealand. Many New Zealand Christians mourn the loss of what they perceive as the Christian social and moral order of an earlier era. There is grief and a degree of confusion about a new minority status, and some data suggest an increasing sense of embattlement and victimisation among Christians. Despite secularisation, Christian presumptions and imaginations continue to shape cultural outlooks, and the churches' activities, including extensive welfare, humanitarian and community work, still impact deeply upon New Zealanders' lives. Yet critique of New Zealand's colonial past has become central to contemporary reconfigurations of New Zealand identity, and this postcolonial nation-making is stimulating new questions, including more widespread and deliberate consideration of what Māori values, theologies and cultural practices might contribute to a distinctively New Zealand Christianity. If such a Christianity does emerge in the coming decades, it will take place in dynamic conversation with the more ethnically diverse global Christianity that is already present.

Bibliography

Davidson, Allan, *Christianity in Aotearoa: A History of Church and Society in New Zealand*, 3rd edition (Wellington: Education for Ministry, 2004).

Lineham, Peter, *Sunday Best: How the Church Shaped New Zealand and New Zealand Shaped the Church* (Auckland: Massey University Press, 2017).

Morrison, Hugh, Lachy Paterson, Brett Knowles and Murray Rae (eds), *Mana Māori and Christianity* (Wellington: Huia Publishing, 2012).

Troughton, Geoffrey and Stuart Lange (eds), *Sacred Histories in Secular New Zealand* (Wellington: Victoria University Press, 2016).

Troughton, Geoffrey and Hugh Morrison (eds), *The Spirit of the Past: Essays on Christianity in New Zealand History* (Wellington: Victoria University Press, 2011).

Australia

Andrew Dutney

Australia is a secular society. It has no established church, and no religion is privileged over the others. However, Christianity has had a 200-year head start over other religions in influencing the development of Australia's culture and institutions. Australia is a multicultural society that has been built on migration and celebrates its cultural and linguistic diversity. At the same time, the British and Irish have aggressively colonised the continent since the late eighteenth century, shaping Australian culture and institutions to serve that imperial project. Today just over half of all Australians identify as Christian; almost as many identify with another religion or none. Australian Christians report affiliation to one of more than 90 denominations, while a growing number report no denominational identity, describing themselves simply as 'Christian'. A quarter of Australian Christians were born overseas – about half in greater Europe, a quarter in Asia and substantial numbers in the Pacific, Africa, the Middle East and Central and South America. Of those Australians who identify as Christian, only a small minority attend worship regularly, and of that minority of attenders more than a third were born overseas, mostly in non-English-speaking countries. However, until the 1960s the overwhelming majority of Australians identified as Christian, almost all of whom were Anglican, Catholic, Methodist or Presbyterian, and attended their church.

Christianity in Australia is in a liminal phase. It is not what it once was. It is not yet what it is becoming. This liminality has different aspects. It involves both the decline of the established and assumed and the emergence of new and renewed forms of Christianity. Australians, including Australian Christians, have been so mesmerised by the decline of churches as they have known them that they generally do not notice the emergence and vitality of new and renewed forms of Christianity.

Measuring Christianity in Australia

Over the last generation, the proportion of Australians indicating an affiliation with Christianity has decreased from about three-quarters to about half. This ongoing decline first became evident in the late 1970s. Until then the proportion of Australians identifying as Christians had remained relatively stable, at between 86% and 89%. But in the 1976 census it dropped suddenly to 79%. This was the first opportunity to measure the impact in Australia of the 1960s crisis in Western society and religion. The sudden statistical change was not really a surprise at the time. Neighbourhood by neighbourhood, town by town, Australian congregations had been experiencing in their own life and witness the shift from near-universal denominational affiliation toward religious voluntarism and indifference in the emerging cultural economy of consumption, entertainment and self-improvement. Church affiliation has only continued to fall since then.

Another indicator of this decline is the rise in the number of Australians reporting 'no religion' in the census. At 30%, 'no religion' is now the largest category of Australian 'religion', well ahead of the next largest: Catholic (23 per cent), Anglican (13%) and Uniting Church (4%). 'No religion' includes a tiny minority of those who explicitly identify as, for example, atheist, agnostic, rationalist or spiritual. But more than 98% offer no explanation of their identification as 'no religion'. It is nobody's business, and they make themselves unavailable for enlistment into anyone's ideological or religious campaign. The census question about religion was optional, yet the vast majority of respondents chose to answer it. This suggests that Australians continue to be engaged with matters of religious identity (including non-identity).

This picture includes an important generational dimension. Young adults are least likely to report affiliation to Christianity and most likely to report affiliation to another religion or no religion. At the same time, older Australians are most likely to report affiliation to Christianity and least likely to report affiliation to another religion or no religion. It seems likely, then, that the numerical decline of Christianity will continue in Australia as 'the generations rise and pass away'.

The growth of other religions has implications for the place of Christianity in Australian society. This growth is due almost entirely to patterns of migration. The proportion of people reporting affiliation with

Christianity in Australia, 1970 and 2020

Tradition	1970 Population	%	2020 Population	%	Average annual growth rate (%), 1970–2020
Christians	11,945,000	93.0%	13,744,000	54.1%	0.3%
Anglicans	3,777,000	29.4%	3,488,000	13.8%	−0.2%
Independents	343,000	2.7%	800,000	3.1%	1.7%
Orthodox	328,000	2.6%	1,100,000	4.3%	2.5%
Protestants	1,899,000	14.8%	2,372,000	9.3%	0.4%
Catholics	3,038,000	23.7%	5,900,000	23.2%	1.3%
Evangelicals	2,516,000	19.6%	2,553,000	10.1%	0.0%
Pentecostals/Charismatics	102,000	0.8%	1,550,000	6.1%	5.6%
Total population	**12,843,000**	**100.0%**	**25,398,000**	**100.0%**	**1.4%**

Source: Todd M. Johnson and Gina A. Zurlo (eds), *World Christian Database* (Leiden/Boston: Brill), accessed January 2020.

non-Christian religions, while still relatively small, has increased significantly, from 2% in 1986 to 8% in 2016. The largest of these are Islam, Buddhism, Hinduism and Sikhism. While these continue to be relatively small communities within the Australian population as a whole, they are now present in numbers comparable to the smaller Christian denominations. For example, both Muslims and Buddhists are more numerous than Presbyterians or the Eastern Orthodox. There are more Hindus than Baptists or Lutherans, and more Sikhs and more Jews than Jehovah's Witnesses or Seventh-day Adventists.

However, this is only part of the story of Australian Christianity. The census also has been tracking growth in the Australian church. Over the decade between the 2006 and 2016 censuses, the number of Australians identifying as Christian decreased by 7% while, against that trend, the very small Assyrian Apostolic and Oriental Orthodox denominations grew dramatically, reflecting the increase in Christian migration from the Middle East. Neighbourhoods in capital cities in which these migrants have settled have become used to the presence of their thriving congregations, their priests and festivals and schools, while the congregations themselves are meeting the challenges of a period of exponential growth. So too the census continues to record the growth of Pentecostalism in Australia. At the end of the 1960s, the number of Pentecostals was too small to record. At the 2016 census they became the fourth-largest religious group, equal to the Uniting Church, which was formed in 1977 through the union of Congregational, Methodist and Presbyterian churches, and smaller than only 'no religion', Catholic and Anglican. 'Other Protestant', which includes independent congregations and new or very small denominations, also showed significant growth. And, against the trends among other established Protestant churches of British origin, Baptists increased by 9%.

Interestingly, the undefined 'Christian' grouping almost doubled. It is within this category that most of the Pentecostal movement is concealed. Just as those recording 'no religion' generally do not nominate any preferred philosophical or spiritual alternative, the vibrant, growing part of the Australian church is increasingly indicating, by silence, detachment from denominationalism.

The demographic dimension to this data suggests further growth in these communities. While a little over a third of all Christians are under 35, the proportion of people under 35 in most of these growing communities is much higher, around half. By contrast, in two of the largest denominations, the Anglican Church and Uniting Church, the proportion of people under 35 is only around one-third. These are indicators of the emergence in Australia of a different Christian profile, as the dominance of Anglican and British Protestant churches comes to an end.

The flourishing diversity that is Australian Christianity is reflected in worship. The renewed Catholic rites are celebrated in parishes across the continent, making use of images and music that reflect the Australian context. The liturgical expectations of a parish's larger cultural group are usually reflected as well, be it Filipino, Italian, Irish or Tiwi. Anglican worship is usually based on *A Prayer Book for Australia*, although many congregations of the Sydney Archdiocese, or with a similar theological orientation, worship in the style of contemporary Evangelical communities. The ancient liturgy of the Eastern and Oriental Orthodox churches has been delivered into Australian cities and suburbs, where it is celebrated much as it is in Greece, Egypt or Persia. Hillsong is Australia's largest Pentecostal community and is now a denomination in its own right, with multiple campuses in Australia and overseas. The influence of its music in Australian worship could hardly be overestimated, as Christian gatherings in cities, suburbs, towns and isolated settlements try to replicate the heartfelt, prayerful singing they listen to on CDs or experienced firsthand at the Hillsong Conference.

In previous generations there was a sameness about congregational worship. Wherever you attended on a particular Sunday, congregations tended to follow denominational forms. Those days are long gone, as migration and social change deliver constant surprises. A 'prayer meeting' does not necessarily refer to a handful of people seated in a circle in a closed room with heads bowed and eyes closed. When Sudanese congregations hear 'prayer meeting' they picture hundreds of people up all night singing, dancing, drumming and pouring out their hearts before God. The relaxed egalitarianism for which Australians are famous is set aside in Fijian, Tongan, Cook Island or Sāmoan congregations that maintain a traditional formality in relationships between minister and people, men and women, elders and young adults. At the same time, they gladly include people of other cultural traditions in their passionate singing, praying, fasting, preaching, dancing and feasting. An inner-city congregation might use prayer stations. A town's botanical gardens might host an eco-congregation. A suburban congregation might worship in Korean as well as English. Worship with Aboriginal people is typically a heady mix of old-time Gospel, Pentecostalism, country music and radical politics – largely unstructured, highly participatory, multi-generational, lots of stories, laughter and tears. Their worship is not led by the head or the clock but by the heart and the Spirit. It lasts as long as it lasts and includes whatever it needs to include as the community brings its suffering, loss and grief to God, whom they experience as reaching out to them in love.

A key indicator of the changed profile of Australian Christianity is the modest increase in the number of Australians identifying as Catholic in each census. In the 1986 census Catholics became the largest religious group in Australia – reaching 26% of Australians, ahead of Anglicans at 24%. Although the Catholic proportion of the Australian population declined to 23% in the 2016 census, over the same period the Anglican proportion, still the second-largest Christian denomination, declined to 13%. The Catholic proportion has stayed as high as it is only because of steady numerical growth over the whole period. Catholics now comprise 43% of Australian Christians, while Anglicans now comprise 25%. Migration is the primary source of this growth. In that 1986 census, almost 1 million of the 4 million Catholics had been born overseas. These people came from 22 countries – the greatest variety of birthplaces of all the religious groups. Almost a quarter of them were born in Italy, with significant numbers in Yugoslavia, Malta, Poland, the Philippines, Lebanon and India. This reflected the impact of changes in Australian migration patterns, especially after 1947 as government policy responded to needs and opportunities presented in post-war European migration, and the winding up of the White Australia policy in 1966. Catholics are now by far the largest, most multicultural religious community in Australia.

Both of these facts – that the Catholic community is now far larger than the Anglican and British Protestant community and that it is strikingly multicultural – indicate clearly that Christianity in Australia is no longer what it once was and is well advanced in becoming something new.

Irish Catholics and British Protestants

A significant Irish Catholic minority has been part of the Australian community since the establishment of New South Wales as a penal colony in 1788. Irish convicts were among those in the First Fleet, including some who had been transported for political crimes. They were compelled to attend Church of England services conducted by the chaplain to the settlement, the Revd Richard Johnson, since no provision had been made for Catholic ministry. It was never likely to have been.

The Catholic Church and its priests, religious and people were discriminated against under British law and, in the context of the Irish conflict, were regarded as seditious. The first Catholic priests to arrive in Australia came as convicts, sentenced because of their connection to the 1788 Irish Rebellion. One of them, Fr James Dixon, eventually was permitted to celebrate the first Catholic Mass, in 1803. However, that permission was revoked after the Irish-led Castle Hill Rebellion of 1804. Another priest, Fr Jeremiah O'Flynn, entered the colony in 1817 without the necessary authorisation. Having promised not to act as a priest until the matter was clarified by the British Colonial Office, he was found to be secretly administering the sacraments, arrested and deported to London. O'Flynn's conflict with the Colonial Office drew attention in Britain to the spiritual neglect of Catholics in the colony, putting pressure on the British government to allow Catholic chaplains to be sent to New South Wales for the first time in 1820. This long delay in making provision for the large Irish Catholic minority in the colony reflected both the disenfranchisement of Catholics under British law and the repressive English colonisation of Ireland. Anti-Catholic attitudes persisted in the political, economic and social establishment until the 1960s.

Catholic emancipation in Britain (1829) restored civil rights to Catholics in the colonies also, and the New South Wales Church Act (1836) placed the Catholic Church, Church of England and Presbyterian churches on equal footing with respect to receiving funding to employ clergy and build churches. The Methodist Church was later included in this arrangement. However, while making space for the development of a thriving Irish Catholic subculture in Australia, these developments coincided with a tacit agreement between the government and the Anglican and Protestant churches in both Britain and Australia. During the nineteenth century, urbanisation and the emergence of a new middle class provided the opportunity for loyal Anglican and Protestant congregations to become the site at which the social capital necessary to participate and advance was generated and accumulated. It was where one met people who mattered, learned about new opportunities as they appeared, and established one's credentials for industry, reliability and leadership. It was where women could step forward to contribute and lead, now that they had largely been excluded from employment and leadership in the new middle class. The state encouraged and supported the expansion of these loyal churches and the churches nurtured the culture and norms of the new social class. By the time of Federation, in 1901, Catholics made up 24% of Australian Christians but Anglicans constituted 41%. Presbyterians, Methodists and other British Protestant churches made up almost all the remainder, except for a small, vigorous German Lutheran community and a handful of Greek Orthodox families. This was in a context in which 96% of non-Indigenous Australians identified as Christian. This 'Protestant Ascendancy' was transplanted from Britain – both the term and the attitudes and practices signified – and persisted in Australia until the 1960s, nurturing the bitter sectarianism that had stained Australian society and Christianity until then.

The 1986 census confirmed the end of that Protestant Ascendancy. It confirmed the end of the dominance of Anglican and British Protestant denominations in Australian Christianity. Subsequent censuses confirm the continuing decline of that established form and assumed understanding of Christianity in Australia, and also the emergence of new and renewed forms of Christianity.

What Australians know as Christianity is now shaped by the reality of a very large proportion of Catholic Christians and their institutions. While rates of attendances at Mass are lower than the church would like, and continue to decline, parish churches still flourish in most Australian neighbourhoods. And although there is an unsustainably low number of vocations from within Australia, priests and religious from other countries – especially from the Majority World – are being recruited to serve in what is now a strikingly multicultural Catholic community. Catholic schools comprise the second-largest national education system after government schools, and Catholic Health Australia is the nation's largest non-government grouping of health, community and aged-care service providers. Institutions included in these networks are one of the primary ways in which the general community interacts with the Catholic Church. It remains to be seen what will be the lasting impact of the appalling revelations of child sexual abuse by Catholic clergy and the shameful details of corruption and mismanagement in the church's response to the complaints of survivors. The Royal Commission into Institutional Responses to Child Sexual Abuse (2013–17) has provided the opportunity for the Catholic Church – and the other churches, community groups and government agencies – to demonstrate genuine contrition and to enact meaningful reforms.

The decline of the Anglican and British Protestant churches has been accompanied by the growth of Pentecostal, Independent, Orthodox and other Protestant churches. Alongside these has been a proliferation of 'missional communities', 'house churches' and 'fresh expressions' that are sometimes associated with an existing congregation or denomination but are just as likely to be entirely independent. Even those denominations that have been declining have been energetically adapting to the new reality, seeking sustainable ways to witness and serve without the social advantages they once enjoyed. Within the constraints and leveraging the advantages of their particular denominational heritage, they focus on intentional mission, evangelism and discipleship formation, highly participatory worship that engages the heart as well as the mind, and reliance on lay participation and leadership. They also embrace the multicultural character of twenty-first-century Australia while relativising the denomination's British heritage. Most of the larger denominations make provision for migrant congregations within their organisation – especially for communities of Christians from the Majority World. For example, the Uniting Church recognises 12 'National Conferences' that provide fellowship for congregations and their leaders: Tongan, Sāmoan, Fijian, Indonesian, Korean, Tamil, Chinese, South Sudanese, Filipino, Niuean, Vietnamese and Middle Eastern. At the same it is important to recognise that many, if not most, mono-cultural migrant congregations are not connected to an Australian denomination, being either independent or responsible to a denomination in their country of origin.

Christianity and the First Peoples

The national census has identified one further development over the last generation that is a crucial element in the emerging profile of Christianity in Australia in the twenty-first century. According to the census, the percentage of Aboriginal and Torres Strait Islander people identifying as Christian is slightly greater than the percentage of the total Australian population identifying as Christian and has been consistently so over recent decades. This is a surprising finding given the history of contact between Australia's First Peoples and Christianity.

The continent of Australia was colonised by Britain from the end of the eighteenth century (1788). A business case had been presented for the establishment of a new settlement in what the English explorer James Cook had called 'New South Wales'. The settlement was to be a penal colony comprising convicts, marines, officers and some others. It was not primarily a response to the pressure of overcrowded British prisons and the recent loss of the American colonies as a destination for transported convicts, as is often suggested. Many of the convicts to be sent to New South Wales had been convicted of minor offences, but because they were farmers or had other useful trades or skills they were sentenced to transportation in the expectation that they would contribute to establishing a new colony to further enrich the British imperial economy.

At that time, hundreds of Indigenous nations and clans were living in a highly sophisticated network of cultural, economic and political relationships across the whole continent of Australia and its associated islands. No part of Australia was legally unaccounted for or ambiguous. Australia was in no sense *terra nullius*, as the High Court finally confirmed in the landmark 'Mabo decision' (1992). Estimates of the total population range from 300,000 to more than 1 million. These First Peoples had cultural and legal characteristics that distinguished them from each other and included hundreds of different language groups. However, there was sufficient coherence in their relationship to their lands, their kinship structures and Songlines to facilitate travel, trade and diplomacy between the nations. The First Peoples were more like multinational Europe than today's multicultural Australia. These nations had lived in their lands and practised their law for up to 60,000 years. They were, and are, the world's oldest continuous human cultures.

The initial contact between First Peoples and a Christian culture was probably early in the seventeenth century, when Dutch explorers began investigating opportunities in *Terra Australis* – which they began to call 'New Holland'. However, the primary engagement between First Peoples and Christianity was with the British colonists – convicts, marines, officers, chaplains and, eventually, free settlers – as they violently dispossessed and gradually displaced the First Peoples and established their own settlements, farms and systems of economy and law across the entire continent as agents of the British Empire.

Although the fleet of 1788 did include an Evangelical chaplain from the Church of England, no particular thought had been given to any mission to the Indigenous people the colonisers would encounter. This was in contrast to the long-established British colonial policy of encouraging missionaries to accompany settlers, with the task of converting Indigenous people to Christianity. In the absence of any such strategy, the contact between Australia's First Peoples and the Christian colonisers in this first phase was haphazard and frequently violent, confirming the Aboriginal impression that the white invaders were lawless, degraded and hostile. White religion was just another dimension of that experienced reality.

After a full generation, in 1821, the first missionary appointed to work with the Indigenous people arrived in New South Wales. William Walker represented the Wesleyan Missionary Society and would be followed by missionaries of Anglican, Catholic, Congregational and Lutheran backgrounds. In this second phase of contact between First Peoples and Christianity the missions were directed toward Aboriginal communities already displaced or in fresh conflict with the spreading settlements. Indeed, they were promoted as a possible solution to Aboriginal 'hostility'. The objectives were to gather Indigenous people into centres separate from white settlements, teach them to read and write, convert them to the Christian faith and train them to be productive members of white society. By 1848 all of these missions had been abandoned in failure.

In spite of this failure, some Christians continued to feel concern for the welfare of the declining Aboriginal populations in the settled areas. In the last quarter of the nineteenth century such concern was directed toward people still living on their own lands, remote from existing settlements. It was hoped that missions to such Aboriginal people, converting them to the Christian faith and providing training in the ways of white society and work, would prepare them for the inevitable contact and mitigate the most damaging effects of colonisation. In this phase the initiative did not come from British missionary societies but from the churches, which had now established their own structures within Australia. This phase of Aboriginal missions coincided with, and was supported by, almost a century of government policies of deliberate cultural genocide. To some extent the missionaries accepted the underlying premises of these policies.

However, in the interests of evangelism and of the practical management of the missions, the centres they established also became places where significant linguistic work was done and from which Aboriginal people were able to absent themselves periodically to conduct ceremonies and law. So, while the missions were at the service of the government's genocidal policies, paradoxically they were also often centres of Aboriginal society and culture. It is striking that most of the missions established in this phase continue to function as Aboriginal communities today.

In this third phase of contact between First Peoples and Christianity, the 'whiteness' of that religion was still a liability, expressed as it was in the implementation of government policies intended to suppress Aboriginal culture and languages and, implausibly, assimilate Indigenous people into the deeply racist dominant culture. However, the missions also provided a relatively safe context in which culture, language and law could be surreptitiously practised and maintained. In the 1933 census, 'mixed race' Aboriginal people were subsumed under the total population, reflecting the official policy of extinguishing their Aboriginal identity and relationships. That census found that 18% of 'full-blood Aboriginals' identified as Christian, in comparison with 87% of the total population. All things being equal, that was a remarkably large proportion of Aboriginal people to identify themselves with the white missionaries' religion. However, they could do so without rejecting their own culture, language and law.

It was only in the late 1970s, in a fourth phase of contact between First Peoples and Christianity, that widespread conversions to Christianity occurred in Aboriginal communities. This wave of conversions was related to two changes in the circumstances of Aboriginal people living on missions. One of these was the government's epochal change from the ill-conceived policy of 'assimilation' to the untried, but manifestly just, 'self-determination' policy. It brought the mission era to an end, transferring those communities and their administration to local councils and suddenly introducing a cash economy. Without the (paternalistic) protections of the missionaries and mission managers, catastrophic increases in alcohol consumption and petrol sniffing and the associated violence, disease and social disruption followed. Where it was embraced, conversion to Christianity specifically involved 'going off the grog' and committing oneself to being a good, positive member of one's family and community. It did not necessarily involve rejecting one's Aboriginal identity and heritage. On the contrary, it was a way of recovering the relationships to family and country that are at the heart of Aboriginal identity.

The other significant change was the formation of Indigenous Christian leaders during the 1950s and 1960s. These Aboriginal leaders were networking together within their denominations and inter-denominationally, developing a shared vision for Aboriginal Christianity that embraced the gospel and the Christian way of life, but in an authentically Aboriginal way and without being under the wing or in the shadow of white Christians. One important moment in this process was the creation of the Aboriginal Evangelical Fellowship (AEF) in January 1971. The AEF was not a church or a denomination but a national vehicle enabling Aboriginal Christian leaders to support one another in ministering without the supervision of white Christians. Many of these people became pastors of a diverse range of Aboriginal churches across Australia. The combination of experiencing a desperate need to be freed from the personal and social disruptions of the post-mission era, and hearing the gospel preached by Aboriginal people, in Aboriginal languages and vernacular, and addressing the circumstances and needs of Aboriginal people resulted, in the timing and under the influence of the Holy Spirit, in an unprecedented spiritual revival. It began in Galiwin'ku, in East Arnhem Land, in 1979 and spread swiftly to Western Australia, central Australia and Queensland. The critical difference in this fourth phase was that the Christianity with which the First Peoples were coming into contact was black Christianity – specifically, Aboriginal Christianity.

Today, most Aboriginal Christians identify as Anglican or Catholic (33% and 32% respectively). In addition, a large number identify as Uniting Church (6%), as is unsurprising given the history of missionary involvement with Aboriginal communities and trends in the wider population. It is significant that 10% of Aboriginal Christians identify as Pentecostal, a much higher proportion than in the general Christian population. Also significant is that 70% of Aboriginal Christians are less than 35 years old. While this reflects the age distribution in the wider Aboriginal community, it also suggests potential for the continuing growth of Aboriginal Christianity in Australia.

Aboriginal Christianity remains diverse in its presence and expression. The relationship between the gospel and Aboriginal culture is still being explored and contested within Aboriginal churches. Over several decades Aboriginal Christian leaders and elders have documented their insights and commitments, primarily in short occasional writings. These leaders include Pastor Don Brady, Pastor Bill Hollingsworth, the Revd Charles Harris, Dr Patrick Dodson, the Revd Djiniyini Gondarra, Dr Anne Pattel-Gray and the Revd Denise Champion, as well as many others. Music and communal singing are at the heart of Aboriginal Christian life. The power of this music has been brought to public attention through the film *Song Keepers* (2018), which documents the way the Central Australian Aboriginal Women's Choir took hymns introduced and translated by German missionaries in the 1870s back to Germany, sharing them in their own

Pitjantjatjara and Western Arrarnta languages. So too the incomparable Dr Geoffrey Yunupingu (1971–2017) made best-selling, award-winning recordings of worship songs in his own Yolŋu languages. Along with music, Aboriginal painting is recognised as a powerful medium for the communication of Aboriginal Christian faith, akin to the writing and reading of icons. Examples of this kind of work are published in *Our Mob, God's Story* (2017).

And of signal importance are the face-to-face gatherings of Aboriginal Christians to worship, share their faith and testimonies, encourage emerging leaders, and negotiate future initiatives in ministry. These happen locally and regionally, but there are key national meetings too, such as the non-denominational Grasstree Gathering series. Even the organisers of non-Indigenous events are recognising how important the presence and meaningful participation of Aboriginal Christians is to their activity. For example, the influential non-denominational young adult gathering Surrender insists that building genuine relationships with Indigenous Australians is 'at its core'. Indeed, Surrender has become a major gathering for young Aboriginal Christians. Among local congregations, in the meantime, there is a growing movement to mark Australia Day by holding church services with Aboriginal people. Initiated by Aunty Jean Phillips, the purpose of the prayer services is to hear Aboriginal stories of dispossession, lament with them and seek reconciliation.

Christianity in Australia is in a liminal phase. It is not what it once was. It will become what it is becoming as Aboriginal Christianity learns and teaches the churches what it is to be Christian in this place. As Pope John Paul II said to a gathering of Aboriginal and Torres Strait Islander Christian leaders in Alice Springs in 1986, 'The Church herself in Australia will not be fully the Church that Jesus wants her to be until you have made your contribution to her life and until that contribution has been joyfully received by others.'

Bibliography

Bouma, Gary, *Australian Soul: Religion and Spirituality in the Twenty-First Century* (Melbourne: Cambridge University Press, 2006).

Budden, Chris, *Why Indigenous Sovereignty Should Matter to Christians* (Unley: MediaCom Education, 2018).

Champion, Denise with Rosemary Dewerse, *Yarta Wandatha* (Salisbury: Denise Champion, 2014).

Lake, Meredith, *The Bible in Australia: A Cultural History* (Sydney: NewSouth, 2018).

Sherman, Louise and Christobel Mattingly (eds), *Our Mob, God's Story: Aboriginal and Torres Strait Islander Artists Share Their Faith* (Sydney: Bible Society Australia, 2017).

Major Christian Traditions

Anglicans

Brenda Reed

The Christian tradition called Anglicanism developed from the practices, liturgy and identity of the Church of England following the English Reformation. Followers of Anglicanism are known as Anglicans or Episcopalians. Traditions of church life and how these manifest themselves in this region will be discussed with regard to the Anglican Church of Australia, which from 1962 to 1981 was known as the Church of England in Australia, an independent Australian church within the Anglican Communion. Also discussed is the Anglican Province of New Zealand, which is now called the Anglican Church of Aotearoa, New Zealand and Polynesia. The name change followed a change in the church constitution in 1992. The church now includes the Diocese of Polynesia as a full partner. The Anglican Diocese of Polynesia comprises the Anglican Church in the nations of Fiji, Tonga, Sāmoa and American Sāmoa. Both the Anglican Church of Australia and the Anglican Church of Aotearoa, New Zealand and Polynesia are branches of the Anglican Communion. They are individual members of the World Council of Churches and are members of the national organisations of churches in their own nations. The following traditions and customs associated with Anglicans in this region will be highlighted: British connections and Anglican evangelism; bicultural relationships; Anglican missions; church schools; women's ordination; and same-sex relationships.

British Connections and Anglican Evangelism

Henry VIII became head of the church in 1534 as King of England and Ireland. The break from the Roman Catholic Church began the Reformation in the church in England, which culminated during the reign of Elizabeth I in the sixteenth century by taking the form of Anglicanism which still exists today. The Anglican Church is often referred to as the middle way between Roman Catholic and Protestant churches and said to look Catholic but sound Protestant. Today, all Anglican churches belong to the Anglican Communion, which comprises national, independent and autonomous churches throughout the world that observe the teachings of Anglicanism.

Certain traditions instituted from the Elizabethan era are still practised wherever Anglicanism is found. For example, Anglicans adhere to a threefold order of ministry – comprising bishops, priests or presbyters, and deacons – and believe in Apostolic succession. The voice of the laity is also valued in decision-making in the church, and this is accomplished in different ways in each diocese. The New Zealand Anglican Church was one of the first to specifically state this, in its constitution of 1857, and it is included in the fundamental provisions of the 1992 revised constitution of the Anglican Church in Aotearoa, New Zealand and Polynesia:

> There shall be a Representative Governing Body for the management of the affairs of the Church to be called the General Synod of the Branch of the United Church of England and Ireland, in the Colony of New Zealand, which shall consist of three distinct Orders, viz the BISHOPS, the CLERGY, and the LAITY, the consent of all of which Orders shall be necessary to all acts binding upon the Synod, and upon all persons recognising its authority. [1857]

Anglicans refer to their official church meetings attended by bishops, clergy and laity as synods. An important feature of Anglican identity is the Book of Common Prayer, of which the prayer book of 1662 represents the official version of the Church of England. The 1662 prayer book has been revised and adapted to suit the different audiences and cultures of the Anglican Communion but still retains the basic structure and format of the original prayer book. The Anglican churches in Australia and New Zealand have developed their own prayer books. Different services from the New Zealand prayer book are now available in Māori, Fijian, Hindi, Tongan and Sāmoan languages. In addition to the prayer book, the Holy Eucharist remains the central act of Anglican Christian worship.

British colonisation in the late eighteenth and nineteenth centuries facilitated the spread of the Anglican confession throughout the Pacific and Oceania. However, it was not through direct evangelism, but rather the English church taking care of the spiritual needs of English settlers who rushed to the new-found lands in search of a better life. This was especially true of the situations in Australia and New Zealand. The Anglican Church of Australia developed from the churches established

Anglicans in Oceania, 1970

Region	Total population	Christian population	Anglican population	% of region Anglican	% of Christians Anglican
Oceania	19,718,000	18,250,000	4,781,000	24.2%	26.2%
Australia/New Zealand	15,661,000	14,633,000	4,653,000	29.7%	31.8%
Melanesia	3,399,000	2,978,000	126,000	3.7%	4.2%
Micronesia	248,000	237,000	650	0.3%	0.3%
Polynesia	410,000	402,000	1,400	0.3%	0.3%
Global total	3,700,578,000	1,229,309,000	47,394,000	1.3%	3.9%

Source: Todd M. Johnson and Gina A. Zurlo (eds), *World Christian Database* (Leiden/Boston: Brill), accessed January 2020.

by the English settlers in Australia in the eighteenth century. The first settlers were convicts sent from England to settle the country in 1788. They were accompanied by a chaplain. As new prospects were discovered in Australia, more settlers and priests followed. The first diocese in Australia was founded in 1836 and the first bishop consecrated. Today, the Anglican Church of Australia consists of 23 dioceses, with bishops and archbishops appointed to be responsible for each one. Their primate, the President of the General Synod of the Anglican Church of Australia, is currently the Archbishop of Adelaide. The 2016 census found that Christianity continues to be the major religion in Australia, with 52% of Australians classifying themselves as Christian. Twenty-five per cent of this number distinguished themselves as Anglican, while the largest share identified as Catholic (43%).

The Anglican Church in Aotearoa, New Zealand developed from two pathways. The Church Missionary Society (CMS), founded by Anglican Evangelicals in 1799, was set up in London to sponsor Anglican missions and enabled the spread of the gospel to the Pacific. Samuel Marsden, an Anglican priest and member of the CMS, was pivotal in the spread of Anglicanism to the Māori people of New Zealand. He was not only the chaplain but also the magistrate for Sydney's penal colony in the early 1800s. Through Marsden's friendship with a young Māori chief, missionaries came to New Zealand, landing at Oihi in the Bay of Islands on Christmas Day in 1814. This marked the beginning of the mission to the Māori, the Indigenous people of Aotearoa, in their native language. Twenty-eight years later, in 1842, George Augustus Selwyn, Bishop of the United Church of England and Ireland, arrived to administer and cater for the spiritual needs of the numerous English settlers who had migrated to New Zealand seeking better prospects. The bicentennial of the church was celebrated in 2014, and Bishop John Bluck's *Wai Karekare – Turbulent Waters: The Anglican Bicultural Journey 1814–2014* marked the occasion.

The Anglican Church in Aotearoa, New Zealand and Polynesia embraces the area described in its title and is a constitutionally independent member

Anglicans in Oceania, 2020

Region	Total population	Christian population	Anglican population	% of region Anglican	% of Christians Anglican
Oceania	42,384,000	27,606,000	4,556,000	10.8%	16.5%
Australia/New Zealand	30,233,000	16,363,000	4,078,000	13.5%	24.9%
Melanesia	10,909,000	10,069,000	474,000	4.4%	4.7%
Micronesia	541,000	501,000	1,700	0.3%	0.3%
Polynesia	701,000	673,000	2,300	0.3%	0.3%
Global total	7,795,482,000	2,518,834,000	99,662,000	1.3%	4.0%

Source: Todd M. Johnson and Gina A. Zurlo (eds), *World Christian Database* (Leiden/Boston: Brill), accessed January 2020.

of the worldwide Anglican Communion. The present 1992 constitution of the church stipulates for the three partners the opportunity to order their affairs within their own cultural context. Tikanga Pakeha covers seven dioceses and Tikanga Māori covers five Amorangi, whose boundaries are different from those of a diocese. Tikanga Pasefika, also known as the Diocese of Polynesia, covers Fiji, Tonga, Sāmoa and the Cook Islands. The Anglican Church was long the dominant Christian denomination in New Zealand; the 2013 and 2016 censuses, however, showed that the largest Christian denomination is now the Roman Catholic Church.

The Polynesian Islands, in contrast, are home to relatively few Anglicans. The interdenominational London Missionary Society (LMS) sent the first missionaries to the region in the late eighteenth century. By the nineteenth century, the LMS had set up missions in Tahiti, Sāmoa and the Cook Islands and the Methodists (Wesleyan) in Fiji and Tonga. As an active supporter of the Anglican (CMS), LMS and Methodist missions in Australia, Samuel Marsden initiated a comity agreement among the various denominations that in essence meant the denominations would not compete with each other's missions. Thus, there were no active Anglican missions in the Polynesian Islands in the nineteenth century. Anglicans who were already in the islands, mainly white settlers and colonial officials, were ministered to by priests, who were referred to as chaplains.

The first Anglican priest in Polynesia, William Floyd, came from Melbourne to Levuka in Fiji in 1870 in answer to an appeal by planters and traders there for an Anglican priest to minister to them. Floyd found an untouched mission field in Fiji. He pioneered the two main missionary ventures within the Diocese of Polynesia to the descendants and remaining members of 'blackbirded' Solomon Islanders and the Fiji Indians. These Solomon Islanders had been brought to work on cotton plantations during the 1860s. They were discarded when sugar became the main cash crop and indentured labourers from India were brought in to work on the sugarcane plantations instead. Floyd was able to befriend Fijian villagers

Changes in Anglican in Oceania, 1970–2020, growth rate, % per year

Region	Total population	Christian population	Anglican population
Oceania	1.54%	0.83%	−0.09%
Australia/New Zealand	1.32%	0.22%	−0.26%
Melanesia	2.36%	2.47%	2.70%
Micronesia	1.57%	1.51%	1.88%
Polynesia	1.08%	1.04%	1.05%
Global total	1.50%	1.45%	1.50%

Source: Todd M. Johnson and Gina A. Zurlo (eds), *World Christian Database* (Leiden/Boston: Brill), accessed January 2020.

who gave some land for the Solomon Islanders who had been left landless, starving and destitute around Levuka. From this was born the first of the Anglican Melanesian settlements in Fiji. The majority of Anglicans in Fiji in the twenty-first century are of Solomon Islander or Fiji Indian descent.

The Anglican Church in Tonga was established by Bishop Alfred Willis by invitation from a group of Anglicans in Tonga in 1902. At the time, Willis was the Bishop of Honolulu and had been chaplain to the royal family in Hawaii. In 1898, the royal family was deposed when Hawaii became annexed as a territory to the USA. Willis had given his oath to the Queen of England, so the invitation to Tonga was a welcome alternative to the USA. The Anglican community was small and began with a primary ministry to expatriates. Willis was able to translate the Book of Common Prayer of the Episcopal (American) Church, and with the Tongan Bible and the help of Tongan lay readers they were able to grow their community. In 2017, the first bishop of the newly constituted Episcopal Unit of Tonga was consecrated. Tonga has six Anglican parishes.

The Anglican Church in Sāmoa initially functioned as a chaplaincy for Anglicans or those who wanted to be Anglicans. Individuals and families with Anglican connections had been living in Sāmoa since the mid-nineteenth century. The Sāmoan Anglicans were from families of German ancestry who had been Lutherans and had become Anglicans, as well as families with British connections and visiting expatriates. There was no permanent church and Anglicans were dependent on visiting naval chaplains and visiting clergy for baptisms and confirmations. In 1932 a permanent chaplaincy was established with the appointment of a young priest from Britain, and the quest to build a permanent church began in earnest. The Anglican community in Sāmoa continued to grow in size and dedication under the guidance of an Australian priest, Fr Charles William Whonsbon-Aston, who came as chaplain in 1943. By 1958, the All Saints Anglican Church building now standing at Leifiifi, Apia, was consecrated. The church also sent its first candidate for ordination, Jabez Bryce, for training in New Zealand. He became the first Indigenous Bishop of Polynesia in 1975.

The founding of the Diocese of Polynesia was fortuitous. In the early days of mission, any Anglican parish that was not part of an existing diocese of the Church of England was accountable to the Bishop of London and the Archbishop of Canterbury. William Floyd had come to Fiji under the approval of the bishops of Melbourne, Sydney and Melanesia. However, they had no official jurisdiction in Fiji. The Anglican Church in Polynesia grew despite the 'comity of missions' principle. This presented a dilemma for the Archbishop of Canterbury in addition to having Bishop Willis in Tonga and Fiji becoming a British colony in 1874. In 1902, he consulted the primates of New Zealand, Australia and the USA, who recommended making the whole area, including Fiji, a diocese. Consequently, the Archbishop set up a new diocese, although the boundaries were unclear and settled only 52 years later. The diocese had no endowments and little financial backing and did not have a bishop. In 1908, the Archbishop of Canterbury appointed the Revd T. C. Twitchell of Kent as the first Bishop of the Diocese of Polynesia. Bishop Stanley Kempthorne followed from 1923 to 1961. He was originally from New Zealand, and his personal connections enabled an uncomplicated acceptance of the Diocese of Polynesia as an associated missionary diocese of the Province of New Zealand. The Diocese of Polynesia remained in this ad hoc status until the revised constitution of 1992.

Today, the Diocese of Polynesia (Tikanga Pasefika) consists of five nations – Fiji, Tonga, American Sāmoa, Sāmoa and the Cook Islands – connected by the *moana* (the Pacific Ocean). Most of the Anglicans in the Pacific are in Fiji (two bishoprics and one archdeaconry), Tonga (one bishopric), American Sāmoa (two parishes) and Sāmoa (one parish). There is no permanent Anglican church in the Cook Islands. There is also an archdeaconry in New Zealand with two Tongan, two Sāmoan, one Indo-Fijian and one Fijian parish in Auckland and one Tongan parish in Christchurch. The wide area covered by the diocese and the national borders create communication difficulties as regards travel, and getting visas is often problematic.

Bicultural Relationships

Bicultural relationships within New Zealand are part and parcel of the Anglican Church of Aotearoa and New Zealand, and are a complex issue. Although New Zealand is home to many different peoples with different cultures, the officially recognised ones are the dominant Pakeha (European) culture and the Indigenous Māori culture. The history of Anglicans in Aotearoa has been a bicultural journey, a connection of two cultures. The English version of Christianity that the missionaries brought was rapidly accepted and propagated and became the Māori church called Te HaHi Mihinare, the church of the missionaries. At the time, the foremost people in the land were Māori. After the Treaty of Waitangi was signed in 1840 the white settlers, who arrived in their thousands, became dominant and the Anglican Church became predominantly a white settler or Pakeha church. British colonisation, disregard for the Treaty and Māori civil rights, and increased settler influence resulted in land wars and other disturbing events that affected relationships within the church. The 1992 Anglican constitution with its *tikanga* (customary Māori laws and values) model is regarded as a way forward for the two cultures. However, the threads of past injustices and voices of biculturism have been woven into the mix and are always present. It has been almost 30 years since the 1992 constitution, and issues regarding the relationships within the three *tikangas* are still prevalent.

Anglican Missions

The Five Marks of Mission that were developed by the Anglican Consultative Council (ACC) in 1984 have been widely adopted by Anglicans as an understanding of contemporary mission in daily life. The Five Marks are: (1) to proclaim the Good News of the Kingdom; (2) to teach, baptise and nurture new believers; (3) to respond to human need by loving service; (4) to seek to transform unjust structures of society, to challenge violence of every kind and to pursue peace and reconciliation; and (5) to strive to safeguard the integrity of creation and sustain and renew the life of the earth. The wording of the Fourth Mark, including the need for Christians to challenge violence and pursue peace, was added by the ACC in 2012. Dioceses and other denominations use the Five Marks as the basis of action plans and innovative mission ideas. Most of the work and activities carried out in the community by the Anglican churches are related to these Marks of Mission.

Supporting ecumenical relationships is one of the dedicated aims of Anglicanism, and both the Anglican Church of Australia and the Anglican Church of Aotearoa, New Zealand and Polynesia are individual members of the World Council of Churches. Anglicans are active promoters of Christian unity, as is evident in local communities where Anglican churches are situated. This aspect of Anglicanism reflects the first three Marks of Mission. Anglicans are involved at the national level in encouraging and forming national conferences of churches or organisations. For example, even in Sāmoa, where there is only one parish, the Anglican Church is a founding member of the National Council of Churches (NCC) and the women's wing of the NCC. Anglicans have something in common with most expressions of the Christian faith and readily connect with Roman Catholic, Orthodox and Protestant leaders in theological discussion and joint liturgy. Anglican clergy and lay personnel in Australia and New Zealand are also much involved with interfaith relationships and community activities, where they 'respond to human need by loving service' as stated in the Third Mark of Mission.

The Fourth Mark of Mission – to seek to transform unjust structures of society, to challenge violence of every kind and to pursue peace and reconciliation – also finds active expression in this region. For example, the former Archbishop of Polynesia declared the diocese 'violence free' in 2016, and from then onward many programmes have been initiated in the diocese, such as the House of Sarah initiative to stop violence faced by women and children. The international White Ribbon Day campaign on 25 November for the Elimination of Violence Against Women is widely supported by the Anglicans in the region, as is the 16 Days of Activism campaign. White Ribbon Day began as a day for men to stand up and be willing to show they do not condone abusive and violent behaviour toward women and children. In March 2020, the House of Sarah and the leaders of the Roman Catholic, Anglican and Free Wesleyan churches of Tonga spoke out publicly against gender-based violence. This was a historic occasion, since it was the first time that faith leaders spoke out on this issue on national television in Tonga. The campaign was the result of partnership between the House of Sarah and the Pacific Conference of Churches and was supported by the UN Women Fiji Multi-Country Office and the Pacific Partnership to End Violence Against Women and Girls.

The Fifth Mark of Mission has been a paramount area of mission for the Pacific Islands this century, especially in view of climate change and its effect on rising sea levels and the loss of low-lying atolls. In March 2017, the primate of Australia invited the primates of the Oceania region to *talanoa* (discuss) common issues and to consider opportunities for support and collaboration. The first Oceania Anglican Fono (gathering, meeting or council) was attended by the Archbishop of the Anglican Church of Australia, the Archbishop of the Anglican Church of Papua New Guinea, two archbishops of the Anglican Church in Aotearoa, New Zealand and Polynesia and the Archbishop of the Anglican Church of Melanesia. The 2017 statement arising from this first meeting made a commitment to the continuation of the Oceania Anglican Fono. They also 'agreed that as whole nations of ocean people lose their island homes, Climate Justice advocacy and action must become the most urgent priority for Oceanic Anglicans'.

The next Oceania Anglican Fono was hosted by the Anglican Church in Aotearoa, New Zealand and Polynesia and held in Suva, Fiji, from 25 March 2018. In addition to the original five primates, Justin Welby, Archbishop of Canterbury, was also invited, along with other key executives of the Anglican Communion, including the bishop for Hawai'i and Episcopal Diocese of Micronesia. This signalled the magnitude of the climate change issue for the church as a whole. The statement arising from this 2018 meeting addressed regional priorities in the areas of climate change, family violence, disaster preparation and relief, and opportunities for leadership development and capacity building.

The young people of the Diocese of Polynesia have been very proactive and diligent as advocates for climate change issues. For example, during the last World Council of Churches meeting in Busan, Republic of Korea, in 2013, youth from the Diocese of Polynesia as well as from Tuvalu and Kiribati, gave cultural performances and spoke out avidly about the effects of climate change on their islands.

In August 2019, young members of the Diocese of Polynesia were invited to attend the 'Moana – Water of Life: Navigating Climate Change for Planetary Health' conference held by the Diocese and University of Lincoln. They reported on a project they had carried out in Tonga with the University of the South Pacific in 2017 on how to assess the vulnerability of a community and set plans for when a natural disaster or crisis strikes. Their assessment was crucial in ensuring the community was ready and resilient when Cyclone Gita struck Tonga in February 2018.

The Anglican Church has a long history of assisting the disadvantaged and vulnerable in the community. Many established Anglican missions serve the communities in Australia, New Zealand and the Pacific. They are independent organisations that are active in the church nationally, assisting and undertaking various forms of mission and ministry. These may operate beyond the church's national structures and so are directly accountable neither to the General Synod nor its standing committee. Some operate in both Australia and New Zealand and some are specific to one nation, like the Association of Anglican Women in New Zealand and Polynesia, and the Australian National Aboriginal and Torres Strait Islander Anglican Council. The latter is affiliated internationally with the Anglican Indigenous Network, which has a seat at the United Nations. Other organisations include Anglicare, Church Army, Anglican Missions Board, Anglican Cursillo movement of Australia, Church Missionary Society, Anglican Mothers Union, Society of St Francis, the Society for Promoting Christian Knowledge – Australia, Mission to Seafarers Council – Australia, Anglican Men's Society, and the Defence Force Board – Australia.

Church Schools

The establishment of schools in addition to churches is evident as a practice of Anglican mission. Anglicans believe that education matters and Anglican schools are active contributors in the mission of the church, fostering and encouraging young people to respect and contemplate their response to the Christian faith and to develop an appreciation of other religious traditions.

In Australia, almost 155 Anglican schools are located in 20 dioceses across the nation. The Anglican schools educate more than 155,000 pupils and are one of the largest schooling sectors in Australia, after government and Catholic schools. The Anglican Schools Australia (ASA) is a network to which all Anglican schools can belong. It is an interconnected body involving a wide range of schools: urban, regional and rural; low-fee through to high-fee; single-sex and co-educational; independent and systemic; day-tuition and boarding. Assisting the socially disadvantaged through bursaries and scholarships, Indigenous education initiatives, community service and seeking ways to expand school activities into local communities and parishes is a dedicated service of the ASA.

Forty-six schools are supported by the Anglican Schools' Office of the Anglican Church of Aotearoa, New Zealand and Polynesia. Ten are under Tikanga Polynesia, with eight in Fiji, one in Tonga and the newest, number 46, in Apia, Sāmoa. The rest are in New Zealand, two under Tikanga Māori and the rest under Tikanga Pakeha. The three-*tikanga* model poses the question of whether there is anything that Anglican schools can offer that is different from state schools. The official page for the Anglican Schools' Office states:

> One of the hallmarks of the Anglican Church is a spirit of kindness, compassion and respect for all people. This expresses itself in healthy relationships in our school and towards the wider community. Concern for the common good is shown through community service, care of the environment, celebration of our tikanga partnership, and healthy relationships with those of other faiths. Our school is a welcoming and safe place. Our school quickly identifies and responds appropriately to any member of our school community who is in need of support, healing and wholeness.

Fiji is a good example of how the provision of schools through the church assisted the plight of disadvantaged people – namely the children of Melanesian (Solomon Islands), Indian and Chinese residents – from the twentieth century to present times. St Andrew's secondary school in Tonga, founded in 1905, is now highly productive academically and represents significant service of the Anglicans in the community.

Women's Ordination

The ordination of women is still a controversial subject in many Anglican churches, as is the consecration of women to be bishops. The Anglican Church in New Zealand in December 1977 became the fourth province of the Anglican Church to decide to ordain women priests. In 1990, Penny Jamieson became the first female diocesan bishop in the Anglican Communion when she became Bishop of Dunedin. The Council for Anglican Women's Studies of the Church in Aotearoa, New Zealand and Polynesia produced a book of essays to mark the twenty-fifth anniversary of this event in 2015. The Council is also producing a book to commemorate the fortieth anniversary of the ordination of women in the province, celebrated in 2017.

The Anglican Church of Australia consecrated Kay Goldsworthy as their first woman archbishop, for the Archdiocese of Perth, in 2017. She was also the first female Anglican bishop in Australia, having been appointed an assistant bishop of Perth in 2008. Her other firsts include ordination as the first female deacon (1986) and first female priest (1992). The General Synod of the Anglican Church of Australia approved legislation permitting dioceses to choose whether to ordain women to the priesthood in 1992. That same year, 90 women were ordained in Australia and two others who had been ordained overseas were acknowledged. This revealed tremendous support for women's ordination. However, there are still dioceses in Australia, like the Diocese of Sydney, that do not ordain women.

The first ordained woman in the Tikanga Polynesia was a nurse from England who was recruited by the Diocese of Polynesia as a nurse evangelist in 1961 and ordained in 1985. The first Indigenous woman ordained was from Fiji, in 1995. To date, 37 women have been ordained in the Diocese of Polynesia. The first cohort of seven women held specific positions and roles in the diocese in the area of administration and management.

After a long gap, more women were ordained in 2011. Thirty-two have been ordained since, making the ministry of ordained women in the Diocese of Polynesia a very young one. In 2017, 80% of women priests were in their first six years of ministry. Most of the women clergy are 'worker priests' or non-stipendiary. Very few women are responsible for parishes. They mostly assist the full-time male priests in the parish with Sunday services and pastoral care.

Same-sex Relationships

Ordination to the priesthood and consecration as bishop of persons who are in same-sex relationships continue to be issues of contention in the Anglican Church. Also contentious are same-sex marriages. The nations of Australia and New Zealand have passed laws to legalise same-sex unions and marriage. In New Zealand, same-sex marriage has been legal since 19 August 2013. In Australia, same-sex marriage became legal in December 2017. Legislation to allow same-sex marriage, the Marriage Amendment (Definition and Religious Freedoms) Act 2017, was passed by the Australian parliament on 7 December 2017 and received royal assent the next day. Although these are the laws of the land, they are not automatically applicable to the church, which has its own constitution, canons and acts. Opposition to same-sex marriage is strong in some Australian dioceses, such as the Diocese of Sydney.

The General Synod of the Anglican Church of Aotearoa, New Zealand and Polynesia issued a resolution in 2018 that allows churches in New Zealand to bless same-sex relationships. This came after much discussion and debate, during and in between the synods of 2014 and 2016. The resolution, which was called Motion 29, states clearly that 'the Church's teaching on the nature of marriage [which] is to affirm marriage as between a man and a woman, should not change.' It indicated that individual bishops should be free to use provisions already within the province's canons for 'a non-formulary service' to allow for the blessing of same-sex relationships. The resolution also calls for changes to the canons so that no member of the clergy can face disciplinary action either for agreeing to bless such relationships or for refusing to do so.

The change does not apply to the Diocese of Polynesia – the province's Tikanga Pasifika. A separate motion, passed without opposition, acknowledged that the Pacific Island countries within the diocese – Sāmoa, Tonga and Fiji – did not recognise unions between people of the same gender. It was also noted that a recent Polynesia diocesan synod had signalled the disapproval of its members to the blessing of same-sex relationships.

Following the decision by the Anglican Church in Aotearoa, New Zealand and Polynesia to allow the blessing of same-sex marriages and civil unions, some members left the church. A new Church of Confessing Anglicans Aotearoa, New Zealand grew out of the New Zealand branch of the Fellowship of Confessing Anglicans and was established on 17 May 2019.

Conclusion
The Anglican Churches in the Pacific-Oceania region uphold connections to the Anglican Communion, although they are autonomous. Their ties are due to descent and church structure. Anglicans are very active in missions in the community, especially in helping the vulnerable and disadvantaged. The Anglican schools provide crucial education for the socially and financially deprived. Although Anglicans are fewer in number than other church denominations in Polynesia, the impact of their services in the community through schools and social interaction is renowned. The global issues that beset the Anglican churches throughout the world also impact this region. Matters concerning relationships – be they related to culture, gender, sexual orientation, or health and welfare – are integral to a ministry where people are central to its purposes.

Bibliography
Anglican Church of Aotearoa, New Zealand and Polynesia, Diocese of Polynesia, *Celebrating 100 Years: Diocese of Polynesia, 1908–2008. Celebrating our Journey of Faith Yesterday–Today–Tomorrow* (Suva: Diocese of Polynesia, 2008).
Blombery, Tricia, *The Anglicans in Australia* (Canberra: Australian Government Publishing Service, 1996).

Bluck, John, *Wai Karekare – Turbulent Waters: The Anglican Bicultural Journey 1814–2014* (Auckland: Anglican Church in Aotearoa, New Zealand and Polynesia, 2012).

Church of the Province of New Zealand/Te Haahi o te Porowini o Niu Tireni, *A New Zealand Prayer Book/He Karakia Mihinare o Aotearoa* (Auckland: Collins, 1989).

Davidson, Allan K., *Christianity In Aotearoa* (Wellington: New Zealand Education for Ministry Board, 1991).

Independents

Kenneth R. Ross

Oceania has provided fertile ground for a wide variety of Independent church movements that maintain an identity distinct from the Western-originated churches that derive from European settlement or missionary work. Some began with an anti-colonial inspiration, seeking to embrace and express Christian faith while cherishing Indigenous tradition and resisting colonial domination. Others emerged in response to a charismatic local leader and a spiritual movement that could not be contained within existing ecclesiastical structures. Others again arose in response to international movements on the fringes of Christianity that proved to have appeal in the context of Oceania. These different threads could sometimes be interwoven in the same movement. Usually they represented an intense and passionate spirituality, often one that challenged orthodox doctrine and church order – sometimes to breaking point. Their independent spirit and willingness to rethink the faith in their own terms could lead to questions about whether or not they remained authentically Christian. However, in most cases the biblical faith has been a central reference point and has continued as an anchor even when some adventurous variations from classical orthodoxy have arisen.

A good example is the Rātana Church in New Zealand. Its inspirational founder, Tahupōtiki Wiremu Rātana, came from a Methodist background and emerged as a prophet and healer in New Zealand in the years following the First World War. He taught that the Māori people are one of the lost tribes of Israel, who eventually settled in New Zealand after a long migration. He sought to form a church that would represent a distinctly Māori appropriation of Christianity. Rātana's leadership played an important part in fostering Māori consciousness, and he later led a political movement in order to champion the interests of the Māori. The church, founded in 1925, developed a distinctive blend of Christian and Māori beliefs, established its own hierarchy of religious officials and venerated Rātana as the mouthpiece of God. Initially condemned as syncretistic by mainstream Christian leaders, in the 1960s it sought to recover its original biblical beliefs and achieved some rapprochement with the mainstream churches. It began to attract White as well as Māori members. Today it has a membership of some 40,000 in New Zealand, where it continues to be significant in national politics. It also has several thousand followers in Australia.

Another church that traces its origins to the ministry of a charismatic leader is the Christian Fellowship Church. It emerged in the 1950s on New Georgia in the western Solomon Islands as a spiritual movement that was critical of colonialism. Initially a movement within the Methodist mission, it was registered as a separate church in 1964. It was founded by former Methodist pastor Silas Eto (c.1905–84), also known as Holy Mama, who stressed the ministry of the Holy Spirit, exercised healing powers and gave expression to Melanesian identity and culture. He also championed communal ownership of land and promoted programmes of environmental stewardship, such as reforestation. When Unilever extended its logging operations into the western Solomons in the 1970s, the Christian Fellowship Church played a prominent part in the resistance until Unilever was forced to withdraw in 1986. Today, the church is led by Eto's son, Ikan Rove (b. 1984), who holds the title 'Spiritual Authority'. With more than 15,000 members, it combines Evangelical spirituality with Melanesian cultural values, remains strongly independent and wields significant political influence in the western Solomon Islands.

By contrast with such Indigenously inspired church movements, some Independent-type churches that originate elsewhere also have found wide appeal in Oceania. Foremost among them is the Church of Jesus Christ of Latter-day Saints, informally known as the Mormons, which was initiated by Joseph Smith in upstate New York in the USA in the 1820s. It departs from orthodox Christianity on some central tenets of belief such as the trinitarian nature of God, but its members self-identify as Christians and regard their church as a restoration of the original church of Jesus Christ. Its strongly evangelistic orientation has found a positive response throughout Oceania, perhaps particularly because of its capacity to frame Pacific Island populations as lost chosen people now discovering their true destiny. Today its adherents number almost 150,000 in Australia, around

Independents in Oceania, 1970

Region	Total population	Christian population	Independent population	% of region Independent	% of Christians Independent
Oceania	19,718,000	18,250,000	542,000	2.8%	3.0%
Australia/New Zealand	15,661,000	14,633,000	429,000	2.7%	2.9%
Melanesia	3,399,000	2,978,000	46,400	1.4%	1.6%
Micronesia	248,000	237,000	6,600	2.7%	2.8%
Polynesia	410,000	402,000	60,400	14.7%	15.0%
Global total	3,700,578,000	1,229,309,000	89,480,000	2.4%	7.3%

Source: Todd M. Johnson and Gina A. Zurlo (eds), *World Christian Database* (Leiden/Boston: Brill), accessed January 2020.

112,000 in New Zealand, almost 80,000 in Sāmoa, some 64,000 in Tonga, around 27,000 in French Polynesia, a similar number in Papua New Guinea and more than 20,000 in Fiji. It is represented in most of the Pacific Islands. In some, such as Kiribati, where there are almost 20,000 Latter-day Saints, they form a significant proportion of the population.

The Jehovah's Witnesses, another movement that originated in the USA in the nineteenth century, are non-trinitarian in doctrine, self-identify as Christian and are strongly evangelistic in orientation. They, too, are widely represented in Oceania today, their appeal perhaps strengthened by their strongly millenarian beliefs that strike a chord with traditional spirituality in the Pacific. Generally, their membership is lower than that of the Latter-day Saints, but with more than 100,000 members in Australia, almost 25,000 in New Zealand, some 16,000 in Papua New Guinea and around 6,000 in the Solomon Islands, their presence is not insignificant. Both the Latter-day Saints and the Jehovah's Witnesses are growing churches, even in contexts like Australia and New Zealand, where secularising trends have brought about decline in the historic mainstream churches.

Another category of Independent-type churches that originate elsewhere are those that are identified with a particular nation or ethnic group. Korean Presbyterian churches, found in Guam and the Northern Mariana Islands, are strongly Independent in character. Chinese churches, unaffiliated with any historic denomination, are also present in the Northern Mariana Islands. Likewise, Filipino Baptist churches, unconnected with any parent denomination, have flourished among Filipino immigrants in the Northern Mariana Islands.

Also Independent in character are churches that have broken away from historic denominations as a result of differences on matters of doctrine or church order. These include, for example, the Anglican Catholic Church in Australia, which broke away from the Anglican Church when the latter introduced the ordination of women to the priesthood; and the Church of the Torres Strait, which also broke away from the Anglican Church

Independents in Oceania, 2020

Region	Total population	Christian population	Independent population	% of region Independent	% of Christians Independent
Oceania	42,384,000	27,606,000	2,096,000	4.9%	7.6%
Australia/New Zealand	30,233,000	16,363,000	1,134,000	3.8%	6.9%
Melanesia	10,909,000	10,069,000	654,000	6.0%	6.5%
Micronesia	541,000	501,000	62,500	11.5%	12.5%
Polynesia	701,000	673,000	246,000	35.1%	36.6%
Global total	7,795,482,000	2,518,834,000	391,125,000	5.0%	15.5%

Source: Todd M. Johnson and Gina A. Zurlo (eds), *World Christian Database* (Leiden/Boston: Brill), accessed January 2020.

in Australia in order to maintain traditional Anglican church order. The Seventh-day Adventist (SDA) Church has also spawned splinter groups, such as the Seventh-day Adventist Reform Movement in Australia and the Sāmoan SDA Church. A similar pattern is evident with regard to the Apostolic Church. Determination to maintain a conservative theological position often, though not always, prompts the formation of a new church that dissents from the direction being taken by the parent denomination. Exceptions include Methodist breakaway churches in Tonga that have sought a more Indigenous expression of the faith and the Nauru Independent Church, which broke away from the Nauru Congregational Church in order to accommodate a commitment to Charismatic spirituality.

A growing sector of Christianity in Oceania is the Pentecostal movement, which has spawned Independent churches across the region. Many of these are still in their first generation and have grown from small beginnings to become a significant presence. In 1990 in Fiji, a Charismatic church called Christian Mission Fellowship was founded and has grown rapidly, doubling in number from 30,000 to 60,000 between 2000 and 2015. The Alofa Tunoa Pentecostal Church in American Sāmoa was founded in 1980 and has grown at a rate of more than 8% per annum, so that today it has around 1,600 members in its three congregations. In Papua New Guinea, the Christian Revival Crusade, a church with Baptist and Pentecostal features, has seen its membership grow from 1,000 in 1970 to more than 100,000 today. Vineyard Churches Australia, a Charismatic church with emphasis on signs and wonders, started in 1990 and has grown at almost 10% per annum and counts around 4,000 members today. Across the region, Independent churches that express Pentecostal/Charismatic spirituality are rapidly becoming a significant feature on the religious landscape. These include many very small churches, often, though not always, affiliated to networks of like-minded churches.

A striking example of rapid growth is offered by C3 Church Global, which began in 1980 as a single congregation founded by Phil and Chris Pringle on the northern beaches of Sydney, Australia. It positioned itself

Changes in Independents in Oceania, 1970–2020, growth rate, % per year

Region	Total population	Christian population	Independent population
Oceania	1.54%	0.83%	2.74%
Australia/New Zealand	1.32%	0.22%	1.96%
Melanesia	2.36%	2.47%	5.43%
Micronesia	1.57%	1.51%	4.59%
Polynesia	1.08%	1.04%	2.85%
Global total	1.50%	1.45%	2.99%

Source: Todd M. Johnson and Gina A. Zurlo (eds), *World Christian Database* (Leiden/Boston: Brill), accessed January 2020.

as contemporary, relevant and 'anointed', with an emphasis on the leadership of its founders, dynamic communal life and a modern style of music. It declares its guiding vision to be one of saving the lost, making disciples and building the church. By 2018 it had grown at a rate of more than 18% per annum to become a community of 520 churches in 64 countries, including almost 30,000 members in Australia. The network provides strong oversight relationships for its participant churches, which in turn exercise discipline over their members. From its base in Australia it exercises worldwide reach and is ambitious about future expansion.

Independent churches in Oceania are by no means homogeneous. Their independence from 'mainline' forms of Christianity takes a variety of forms. What they have in common is a search for a more authentic spirituality, which can lead them to uphold traditional expressions of the faith during times of change, to attempt a deeper inculturation of the faith, or to connect with an international movement on the fringe of Christianity. Paradoxically, they are sometimes able to embrace what appear to be opposites. Pentecostal forms of spirituality, for example, represent a determined rejection of traditional cultural values yet at the same time offer a form of religious expression that resonates with magical and millennial elements in Indigenous religious consciousness in Oceania. In one way or another, Independent churches are effectively addressing the spiritual quest of a small but not insignificant proportion of the population in Oceania.

Bibliography

Ernst, Manfred, *Winds of Change: Rapidly Growing Religious Groups in the Pacific Islands* (Suva: Pacific Conference of Churches, 1994).

Henderson, James Mcleod, *Ratana: The Man, The Church, The Movement* (Auckland: A. H. & A. W. Reed, 1963).

Trompf, Garry W., 'Independent Churches in Melanesia', *Oceania*, 54:1 (1983), 51–72.

Trompf, Garry W., 'New Religious Movements in Oceania', *Nova Religio, The Journal of Alternative and Emergent Religions*, 18:4 (2015), 5–15.

Tuza, Esau, 'Silas Eto of New Georgia', in Garry Trompf (ed.), *Prophets of Melanesia: Six Essays* (Port Moresby: Institute of Papua New Guinea Studies, 1977), 65–87.

Orthodox

Doru Costache

To talk about Orthodoxy in Oceania is as difficult as on the worldwide scale. Various churches claim this name, but they do not seem to acknowledge each other as such. Overall, there are three major Orthodox families, walking their separate ways since the fifth century. To outside observers, what keeps them apart is a matter of theological semantics. That is, they represent Jesus Christ in different, not contradictory, ways.

Specifically, the Eastern (or Byzantine) Orthodox churches, adherent to the Council of Chalcedon (451), speak of Christ as 'one in two natures', divine and human, without the natures being either mingled or separated. These churches share with the Oriental Orthodox churches – which reject Chalcedon – the conviction that Jesus's mother, Mary, is *theotokos*, 'She who gave birth to God'. The Oriental Orthodox churches, in turn, speak of Christ as 'one nature', by which they refer to the divine Logos become a human being, but, again, without divinity and humanity being either mingled or separated. Furthermore, the Assyrian Church of the East, which has journeyed by itself since the Council of Ephesus (431), speaks of the two natures of Christ who is one person; this church does not refer to Mary as *theotokos*, preferring to call her 'the Mother of Christ, who is both God and man'. Observers are bewildered by the reasons that prevent these churches from attaining fellowship, even from interacting in a constructive way, but nevertheless theirs is the longest-lasting division in Christian history.

However, in Oceania as elsewhere, there is more to their story. Within each ecclesial family can be found further differences, which have their origins in other factors, not of a theological nature. Across these churches, furthermore, one discovers both shared values and an enriching diversity.

The Oriental Orthodox

Sometimes, what causes a parting of the ways are merely national borders or ethnic distinctiveness. Case in point, the Ethiopian Orthodox Tewahedo Church and the Eritrean Orthodox Tewahedo Church are one church become two after Eritrea won independence in 1991. Both are increasingly present in Australia and New Zealand, making their mark in the region. As members of the Oriental Orthodox family, both are historically and theologically related to the Coptic Orthodox Church, with which they have ecclesial fellowship. And while they operate as independent entities, some cooperation seems to occur at the parish level, especially with regard to youth education and activities. The same goes for the Armenian Apostolic Church, the Syrian Orthodox Church of Antioch and the Indian Orthodox Church, present in small numbers in the region, primarily in Australia and New Zealand. While they all share in the Oriental Orthodox heritage, cultural distinctiveness causes them to walk differently. The same happens in the churches of Byzantine tradition, discussed below.

The Oriental Orthodox churches develop an intense activity, catechetical and educational, aimed at preserving their ethnic and cultural identity. Most of their members are recent migrants. However, the Armenian and the Coptic communities have been present in the region for several generations and are therefore better integrated. All develop programmes of youth ministry. Given the ethnic and cultural focus of the Oriental churches in Oceania, their main form of cooperation is through the ecumenical movement. The Assyrian Church of the East is no different in this regard. It caters to its membership, refugees from Iran, Iraq, Lebanon and Syria whose activities unfold around several parishes in Australia and New Zealand. It, too, is very ecumenically involved.

Some of these churches, such as the Assyrian and Coptic ones, have established networks of primary and secondary schools. These are open both to their own members and to the broader community. Also, both churches have founded theological colleges, which offer tertiary degrees. In Australia, the Coptic Church trains future clergy, teachers and youth ministers at St Athanasius College (University of Divinity, Melbourne) and at St Cyril's College (Sydney College of Divinity). The Assyrian Church recently established Nisibis College (currently on its way to receiving tertiary accreditation through the Sydney College of Divinity). All three theological colleges welcome staff and students from their own constituencies and from the wider community.

Before turning to the churches of Byzantine tradition, it is noteworthy that offshoots of several Oriental and Eastern churches – or indeed whole churches – encountered in Australia and New Zealand are in full

Orthodox in Oceania, 1970

Region	Total population	Christian population	Orthodox population	% of region Orthodox	% of Christians Orthodox
Oceania	19,718,000	18,250,000	333,000	1.7%	1.8%
Australia/New Zealand	15,661,000	14,633,000	333,000	2.1%	2.3%
Melanesia	3,399,000	2,978,000	200	0.0%	0.0%
Global total	3,700,578,000	1,229,309,000	141,930,000	3.8%	11.5%

Source: Todd M. Johnson and Gina A. Zurlo (eds), *World Christian Database* (Leiden/Boston: Brill), accessed January 2020.

communion with the Roman Catholic Church. Such is the case of the Maronite and the Melkite churches (largely of Lebanese background), the Syrian and the Syro-Malabar churches (of Syrian and Indian background), the Chaldean Church (of Assyrian ethnicity) and pockets of Armenian, Coptic, Romanian and Ukrainian believers. As the Assyrian Church of the East is also in the process of union with Rome, sacramental fellowship and pastoral cooperation with the Chaldean Catholic Church is now possible. All the churches of this group maintain their traditional faith and liturgical particularities but cooperate within the framework of the Catholic family. In turn, the relation between them and other Orthodox churches is overall cold, sometimes tense.

The Eastern Orthodox

By and large, the Eastern Orthodox churches of Byzantine tradition that are present in Oceania mirror the situation of the Oriental family. They are organised independently, according to ethnic and cultural particularities. As none of them owns autocephalous status – namely, they are not self-ruled – these churches obey foreign headquarters, with their jurisdictional interests and national agendas. For example, most clergy and certain lay employees of the Romanian Orthodox Church receive wages from the Romanian government for contributing to the cultural consciousness of ethnic Romanians living in the region. To reciprocate, together with maintaining a website in its mother tongue only, the Romanian Orthodox Diocese of Australia and New Zealand organises annual collections for the benefit of the Romanian Patriarchate's 'national' building undertakings in Bucharest. In like manner, the two regional outposts of the Ecumenical Patriarchate of Constantinople – the Greek Orthodox Archdiocese of Australia and the Greek Orthodox Archdiocese of New Zealand – support with funding the Patriarchate's headquarters in Istanbul, as well as various ecclesiastical organisations in Greece. As with the Romanian example, the Greek Orthodox churches in the region also develop cultural and ethnic activities of no ecclesial significance. In the same vein, other Eastern Orthodox churches with dioceses in Oceania – such as the Antiochian,

Orthodox in Oceania, 2020

Region	Total population	Christian population	Orthodox population	% of region Orthodox	% of Christians Orthodox
Oceania	42,384,000	27,606,000	1,115,000	2.6%	4.0%
Australia/New Zealand	30,233,000	16,363,000	1,115,000	3.7%	6.8%
Melanesia	10,909,000	10,069,000	400	0.0%	0.0%
Global total	7,795,482,000	2,518,834,000	292,132,000	3.7%	11.6%

Source: Todd M. Johnson and Gina A. Zurlo (eds), *World Christian Database* (Leiden/Boston: Brill), accessed January 2020.

Macedonian and Serbian – follow overseas directives, working hard at maintaining their ethnic distinctiveness. The same goes for the small pockets of other ethnic Orthodox, that is, Bulgarian, Russian (Moscow Patriarchate) and Ukrainian. In turn, small dioceses and parishes of mixed ethnic background tend to migrate between the larger jurisdictions, seemingly not aligning to foreign nationalist policies.

A special case is the Russian Orthodox Church Outside Russia (ROCOR), which, while dependent on the Moscow Patriarchate, has a very dynamic diocese in Australia and New Zealand. Its parishes and monasteries, of Russian liturgical tradition, appear to be less ethnocentric than other Eastern churches. Most of these parishes develop a robust mission in the region, welcoming Orthodox and potential converts regardless of their ethnic, cultural or linguistic background. The main language of many of these parishes is English, which facilitates communication within their congregations as well as with society at large. It is beyond any doubt that the use of English explains ROCOR's missional success and progress towards Antipodean contextualisation, including its organising the first Orthodox parish for Australia's First Nations.

Other Eastern Orthodox parishes that use English include Antiochian, Greek, Romanian and Serbian. However, only a very few are English-only. Of these, the majority are Antiochian, especially parishes whose clergymen are converts to Orthodoxy; this also is the case of one Serbian parish in Ballarat, Australia. In only two other parishes – one Romanian and one Serbian, both in Sydney's suburbs – do ethnic clergy minister in English for missional and pastoral purposes, welcoming faithful regardless of their cultural background. In turn, most parishes that combine English and other idioms are not free of the ethnocentric agendas of their foreign headquarters. Ethnocentrism prevents most of these churches both from developing missions in the region and from cooperation. It should not come as a surprise, therefore, that only two of them – the Antiochian Archdiocese of Australia, New Zealand, and the Philippines, and the Greek Archdiocese of New Zealand – operate in the broader Oceania. Further problems, of pastoral nature, are caused by the feuds between the

Changes in Orthodox in Oceania, 1970–2020, growth rate, % per year

Region	Total population	Christian population	Orthodox population
Oceania	1.54%	0.83%	2.44%
Australia/New Zealand	1.32%	0.22%	2.45%
Melanesia	2.36%	2.47%	1.40%
Global total	1.50%	1.45%	1.45%

Source: Todd M. Johnson and Gina A. Zurlo (eds), *World Christian Database* (Leiden/Boston: Brill), accessed January 2020.

overseas headquarters of some of these churches, whose faithful are no longer welcomed across the jurisdictional borders.

The overseas centres are largely responsible for another development. Specifically, several Eastern Orthodox churches have recently withdrawn from the ecumenical movement in Australia, either nationally or at the state level. Currently, three churches – the Antiochian, Greek and Romanian – have membership with the National Council of Churches in Australia. Two – the Antiochian and Greek – are members of the New South Wales Ecumenical Council, four – the Antiochian, Bulgarian, Greek and Romanian – are members of the Victorian Council of Churches, and two – the Greek and Romanian – are members of the Council of Churches of Western Australia as well as of Queensland Churches Together. This isolationist trend corresponds to the current rise of Orthodox fundamentalism, in Australia and abroad. And while the Eastern Orthodox churches are out of sync with each other because of nationalism and the calendric schism (half of them adopted the new calendar in the 1920s, while the other half follows the calendric rhythms of late antiquity), fundamentalism keeps them apart from other Christians and from regional societies. True, the official churches mentioned above are not openly fundamentalist. However, many of their offshoots whose canonical status is uncertain – usually self-styled 'true orthodox' – outrightly oppose everything that falls outside their narrow scope. Either way, the combined impact of ethnocentrism and fundamentalism is detrimental to the wellbeing of these churches and to their regional destiny.

But the outlook is not entirely bleak. Recently, the Greek, Romanian and Serbian churches managed to reconcile with some of their 'true orthodox' and other political offshoots in the region. Most churches of the Eastern Orthodox family are active, within Australia, in the areas of education and healthcare. From this viewpoint, some of them, such as the Antiochian and Greek churches, make a positive impact beyond their constituencies. Under the leadership of a genuine holy man, Fr Nektarios Zorbalas, the Greek parish and community of Newtown, Australia, feeds hundreds of homeless and other disadvantaged people daily. The youth of several Antiochian parishes in the greater Sydney area do the same on a weekly basis, ministering to the homeless in the Central Business District.

In turn, the monasteries promote Orthodox spirituality beyond their immediate ecclesial perimeter. Pantanassa Monastery (Mangrove Mountain, New South Wales, Australia) has an iconographical workshop in which the monks, guided by Fr Arsenios Pantanassiotis, experiment with Indigenous painting techniques. The Greek Church's St Andrew's Theological College (Sydney College of Divinity) and ROCOR's Sts Cyril and Methodius Institute (Adelaide College of Divinity) tentatively have begun to educate their students in ways relevant to the Oceanic context. It is hoped that both will seek cooperation with one another and with their Coptic and Assyrian counterparts. Alongside these tertiary institutions, the Australian Institute for Orthodox Christian Studies (Sydney), an independent organisation, provides publications and free-access tools for the exploration of the Orthodox tradition within the Antipodean context. Much more must be done, however, by all involved, in order to achieve a genuine rapprochement and indigenisation of the various forms of Orthodoxy in Oceania.

Bibliography

Angold, Michael (ed.), *The Cambridge History of Christianity, Vol. 5: Eastern Christianity* (Cambridge: Cambridge University Press, 2006).

Casiday, Augustine (ed.), *The Orthodox Christian World*, The Routledge Worlds (London: Routledge, 2012).

Lamport, Mark A. (ed.), *Encyclopedia of Christianity in the Global South*, vol. 2 (Lanham: Rowman & Littlefield, 2018).

McGuckin, John Anthony (ed.), *The Encyclopedia of Eastern Orthodox Christianity* (Oxford: Wiley-Blackwell, 2011).

Parry, Ken (ed.), *The Blackwell Companion to Eastern Christianity* (Oxford: Blackwell, 2007).

Protestants

Graham Joseph Hill

The Pacific Islands

Protestantism has entrenched itself across the Pacific since Protestant missionaries established themselves and their ministries in the Pacific Islands in the late eighteenth century. The earliest Protestant missionaries were associated with the London Missionary Society, the Wesleyan Methodist Missionary Society and the American Board of Commissioners for Foreign Missions. Local peoples met their presence with a mixture of welcome and hostility. Like the Catholics before them, the Protestant missionaries brought European customs, moral and sexual sensibilities, dress codes and social expectations that seemed strange to local peoples. Protestant Christianity and the European colonial enterprise were enmeshed.

Protestant Christianity did not thrive and grow throughout the Pacific, however, until Pacific Islanders made it their own. European individualism, anthropocentrism, formality and monotheism contrasted with Pacific cultures. Such cultures were mostly communal, creation-centred and polytheistic. Indigenous, local and grassroots Pacific Islander missionaries played the most significant role in spreading and establishing Protestant Christianity across the Pacific. Takamoa College in the Cook Islands, established in 1839, was crucial in training and sending out Indigenous missionaries in the Pacific. Soon, other local theological colleges were set up in other parts of the Pacific. Local missionaries and Indigenous-led churches contextualised the faith in creative and appealing ways, leading to the rapid spread of Protestant Christianity throughout the Pacific.

The story of Protestant Christianity in the Pacific is a mixed one. It is a story shaped by colonial expansion, military conquest and notions of cultural and religious superiority. But it is also a history of stunning conversion to Christianity; by the end of the nineteenth century, most of the Pacific had become Christian. It is a story of widespread Evangelical and Charismatic renewal, of Indigenous Pacific Islander leaders taking the gospel across the Pacific and the globe, and of extensive Bible translation into numerous languages. Some 1,500 languages are spoken in the Pacific (almost 25% of the world's languages), so the work of Bible translation is enormous. Papua New Guinea alone has 851 languages, and more than

300 language groups do not have the Bible in their mother tongue. But the work of Bible translation in the Pacific has been one of the most impressive in the world, and it is ongoing.

During the twentieth and twenty-first centuries, Pacific Islander churches moved increasingly from colonial and foreign missionary control to independence and self-identity. This shift reflected the broader decolonisation happening in the region. Resisting and discarding colonialism and imperialism did not lead to the rejection of Christianity. Instead, Christianity has remained deeply embedded in many of the cultures and societies of the Pacific, taking on more Indigenous forms, theologies and leadership, especially since the 1960s. In over three-quarters of the countries of the Pacific, more than 90% of the population self-identify as Christian. The extent to which this Christianity is genuine discipleship to Christ is open for discussion. Still, one could say the same for Christianity in Australia, the UK and the USA. A remaining challenge is to help Christianity make sense not only to literate cultures but also to the oral cultures of the Pacific.

Over recent decades, Pacific theologians have written theological works characterised by Indigenous, postcolonial, liberationist, relational, familial and eco-theological themes. Such theology is profound and timely, especially given the ecological and social challenges facing our world. Pacific Islander theology tends to emphasise oral traditions, the earth, family and (w)holistic approaches to faith. Such theology is not wedded to rationalistic and Enlightenment categories and is done in conversation with local churches and with attention to creation.

Protestant theologians like Ama'amalele Tofaeono of Sāmoa challenge the church worldwide, and especially the churches of Oceania and the Asia-Pacific, to address issues related to climate change, rising sea levels and environmental destruction. For too long, Western Christian theology has been too supportive of economic growth, human dominion over creation and the neglect of the planet. Tofaeono says that traditional Pacific cultures value the whole of creation, guiding humans toward

Protestants in Oceania, 1970

Region	Total population	Christian population	Protestant population	% of region Protestant	% of Christians Protestant
Oceania	19,718,000	18,250,000	4,242,000	21.5%	23.2%
Australia/New Zealand	15,661,000	14,633,000	2,736,000	17.5%	18.7%
Melanesia	3,399,000	2,978,000	1,207,000	35.5%	40.5%
Micronesia	248,000	237,000	83,900	33.8%	35.4%
Polynesia	410,000	402,000	215,000	52.4%	53.4%
Global total	3,700,578,000	1,229,309,000	204,506,000	5.5%	16.6%

Source: Todd M. Johnson and Gina A. Zurlo (eds), *World Christian Database* (Leiden/Boston: Brill), accessed January 2020.

interdependence of all living things and the entire earth. Pacific theologies often emphasise the sacredness of the land, seas and animals and the biblical vision of communion between God, humans and all living things. Tofaeono notes that Sāmoans have a concept called *aiga*, which means 'family'. *Aiga* includes the whole family of creation. *Aiga* includes God, spiritual beings, humans, the whole earth and all living creatures. *Aiga* is the 'household of life' and the whole household of creation. God invites his people to enter into a loving, sustaining, prayerful stewardship and communion with *aiga*, the household of life.

Pacific Protestant theologians like Ama'amalele Tofaeono are engaged in one of the essential theological projects of our time. They invite Christians to theologise about climate change, environmental degradation, rises in sea level and the neo-colonial, capitalistic, consumeristic forces that threaten the earth. When it comes to climate change, the Pacific Islands are a particularly threatened region. Pacific theologians such as Tofaeono remind the church that Christian witness is directly connected with our care for the most vulnerable in societies, and with our respect for the whole family of creation, the entire household of life. Anthropocentric and colonising faith can be destructive for people and the planet. God has given us Indigenous faith, practices and wisdom for the sake of all humans and the whole earth. Christian leaders and theologians can tap into these insights and practices to raise ecological awareness and to seek justice and liberation for the poor and the planet. Pacific theologians offer guidance on how liturgy and worship can lead to environmental awareness, stimulate a passion for creation care and honour the voices of Indigenous communities and local peoples. These Pacific Protestant theologians paint a vision of an eco-ethical Christian spirituality that can address some of the most significant issues facing humanity and the planet.

Protestant churches have played a significant role in shaping the social, public and political life of the nations of the Pacific. Sometimes these churches are too closely connected with political parties and ethno-nationalistic movements. At other times, Protestant church leaders have

Protestants in Oceania, 2020

Region	Total population	Christian population	Protestant population	% of region Protestant	% of Christians Protestant
Oceania	42,384,000	27,606,000	8,526,000	20.1%	30.9%
Australia/New Zealand	30,233,000	16,363,000	3,082,000	10.2%	18.8%
Melanesia	10,909,000	10,069,000	4,925,000	45.1%	48.9%
Micronesia	541,000	501,000	182,000	33.7%	36.4%
Polynesia	701,000	673,000	337,000	48.0%	50.1%
Global total	7,795,482,000	2,518,834,000	485,935,000	6.2%	19.3%

Source: Todd M. Johnson and Gina A. Zurlo (eds), *World Christian Database* (Leiden/Boston: Brill), accessed January 2020.

taken the lead in challenging military coups, human rights abuses, domestic and family violence, depletion of natural resources, and policies that disadvantage the poor and minorities. The secular–religious divide is blurry in the Pacific, and Pacific Island cultures have usually seen the spiritual, natural and social worlds as interwoven and interdependent. This view of the integration of all things has affected the way Protestant Christianity relates to nation and politics.

Aside from Indigenous Pacific cultures, it has been mostly European, Australasian and North American cultures, politics and religions that have influenced Pacific societies over the last 200 years. The evidence of this is apparent in many of the ministries, liturgies, missions and theologies of the Protestant churches. But China has become increasingly interested and influential in the Pacific. China has strategic cultural and economic interests in the South Pacific, and possibly military interests too. China became much more muscular and assertive in the region over the 2010s, becoming an important partner to many governments in the Pacific. The Pacific nations are fragile, their economies are small, and climate change and natural disasters take a toll. Many rely on foreign aid and development. While Australia has been the biggest donor to the region, Pacific nations often feel ignored, and the USA does not have the influence or footprint in the area it once did.

This geopolitical environment is uncertain and rapidly changing. Protestant Christian leaders in the Pacific, Australia and New Zealand are in conversation about the role the church must play in these uncertain times of climate change, pandemic and shifting cultural and political forces. These trends impact Pacific cultures, societies and Christianity, and Protestants from the region are trying to figure out how to respond, together. Every year, for instance, Pacific and Australian Christian leaders join together in Micah Australia's Voices for Justice to spend a week in Canberra lobbying Australian politicians to respond to issues of injustice, poverty, economic fairness and climate change. This joint action is one example of the dynamic and crucial partnerships forming between Protestant Christians and their leaders across Oceania.

Changes in Protestants in Oceania, 1970–2020, growth rate, % per year

Region	Total population	Christian population	Protestant population
Oceania	1.54%	0.83%	1.40%
Australia/New Zealand	1.32%	0.22%	0.23%
Melanesia	2.36%	2.47%	2.85%
Micronesia	1.57%	1.51%	1.56%
Polynesia	1.08%	1.04%	0.91%
Global total	1.50%	1.45%	1.75%

Source: Todd M. Johnson and Gina A. Zurlo (eds), *World Christian Database* (Leiden/Boston: Brill), accessed January 2020.

Australia

Understanding Australian culture and history is crucial in order to appreciate the condition of Australian Protestantism. Much of Australian culture is profoundly suspicious of institutions, including institutionalised religions, but it is not a secular culture. It was once popular to say that Australia is one of the most secular societies on the planet. In the 2016 Australian census, 30% of people said they had no religion, up from 22% in 2011 and 16% in 2001. Yet, recent research has shown that Australians have a deep interest in spirituality.

The cultural divide between the churches and Australian culture has historical roots. The British Empire established Australia as a convict settlement and military outpost. The Church of England received significant cultural, financial, property and political privileges in the early Australian colony. It was often in competition with the Catholic Church for cultural and political power. The British and European churches were planted in a sectarian way. Australians often saw them as representatives of an oppressive empire and aristocracy. Churches were perceived to be serving as 'God's moral police', patrolling culture, morality, political allegiances and social debates. Many people in the early Australian colonies grew suspicious and antagonistic toward the churches and their leaders. They considered political, religious and social institutions suspect. This posture has never left Australian society and remains widespread.

Protestant churches never developed deep roots in Australian culture and society. Australians tended to see them mainly as places for 'hatches, matches and dispatches' (baby christenings, wedding ceremonies and funerals). Religious and ethnic diversity existed in the early Australian colony. This diversity included Christian convicts, pioneers and soldiers, Jewish convicts, Mormon missionaries, Buddhist migrants, Unitarians, Theosophists and many others. When people tell the story of the early Australian settlement, they often overlook this fact. Rationalist views also flourished, pushing Christianity aside. 'Religions' or spiritualities of culture and informality grew. Australians often saw these informal approaches to spiritual and social life as more important than established churches and religions, and they still do.

These informal Australian spiritualities include the following: (1) jingoism – a spirituality of patriotism, especially as it relates to real or perceived foreign threats; (2) mateship – a spirituality of loyalty, equality and friendship, framed around egalitarianism and sometimes masculinity; (3) ANZAC – a spirituality of remembering and revering Australians and New Zealanders who have served together in wars, conflicts and peace-keeping operations; (4) recreational culture – a spirituality shaped around the beach, surf, bushland, sun, BBQs, travel, relationships and alcohol;

(5) sport – a spirituality built upon a shared commitment to sport, which is significant in Australian life; and (6) individuality – a spirituality expressed through a common, robust, fierce individualism, as seen in Australia's eccentric cultural heroes and personalities, and also seen in 'do-it-yourself' approaches to religions and spiritual movements. Homegrown Australian Protestant mission and church life have sought to respond and adapt to these informal spiritualities in a variety of ways, with mixed success.

What we are painting is a complex cultural picture. But from the earliest days, Australians have been suspicious of institutions and organised religions. Australians often see Protestant churches as complicit in the abuse of Aboriginal peoples and their rights, in the removal of Aboriginal children from their families (for many decades of the last century) and in an unwillingness to address institutionalised forms of child abuse. Meanwhile, Australians also often perceive the churches to be judgemental on issues of sexuality, alcohol and gambling.

Many Australians self-identify as Christians during a census but would never enter a church, except possibly for special occasions. The proportion identifying as Christian in the national census declined from 96.1% in the 1901 census to 52.1% in the 2016 census. But most researchers estimate that only 5% of Australians attend a church weekly. McCrindle Research indicates that as few as 8% of Australians attend church once per month, with 92% of Australians not attending church regularly. Across all denominations, those who identified as Christian fell from 13.1 million (61%) to 12.2 million (52.1%) between 2011 and 2016. That includes 600,000 fewer Anglicans and 147,500 fewer Catholics in five years. In 2020, the figure appears to be 54.1% Australians self-identifying as Christian, with only 8% attending church regularly. But analysts will need to confirm this after the next Australian census. In the 2016 census, 29.6% of Australians (almost 7 million people) selected 'no religion'.

In 1970, 93% of Australians claimed to be Christian. This percentage fell to 54.1% by 2020. The number of Australians who claimed to be Christian grew from 11,945,000 in 1970 to only 13,744,000 in 2020, which was far outstripped by population growth. Of the Australians who self-identified as Christian in 2020, 25.4% were Anglican, 17.3% were Protestant, 5.8% were Independent, 7.6% were unaffiliated Christians, 18.6% were Evangelical, 11.3% were Renewalist, 42.9% were Catholic and 8% were Orthodox. Some, of course, were double-affiliated.

Australians are primarily concerned about the quality of life and close friendships. They believe in the separation of church and state, and many are indifferent or ignorant about the church. But it would be a mistake to suggest that Australia is highly secular. Australian society is rapidly changing, with the increase of many identifying as 'spiritual but not religious', the growth of religions other than Christianity, the religious changes created by immigration and the rise of Pentecostalism. Australian Protestantism itself is in rapid evolution, with the rising influence of Evangelical, Pentecostal, Independent and Renewalist movements, the decline of mainline Protestant churches and the spread of post-denominational sentiment. Belief in God – or at least in a 'higher power' – is widespread in Australia, even if church attendance is low. Given this environment, there is a startling shortage of contextualised forms of Australian Protestant theology, mission and ways of being church. This lack of contextualisation is beginning to change, as evidenced in the pioneering work associated with the Forge Mission Training Network Australia, Arrow Leadership Australia and the creative forms of church planting among the Baptists.

McCrindle Research (led by Mark McCrindle) and Hugh Mackay are two social researchers respected in Australia. Protestant churches, denominations and organisations, as well as Australian media organisations, often turn to McCrindle Research for analysis of social trends and demographic forecasts. The leadership team at McCrindle find their roots in Australian Protestantism, but the organisation serves the wider Australian society.

Aboriginal and Torres Strait Islander Australians are the oldest continuous human culture on earth. At the time of European arrival, more than 250 Aboriginal languages were spoken among 500 Aboriginal and Torres Strait Islander nations, with numerous distinct cultures, languages, traditions and beliefs. Protestant missionary activity in early Australia (or the lands we now call Australia) was complicit in Aboriginal and Torres Strait Islander suffering. Many Protestant missionaries were well meaning but, overall, the early Protestant missionaries were complicit in the brutality shown to Aboriginal peoples by European settlers. Missionaries often treated Aboriginal peoples, cultures, spiritualities, sacred sites and traditions as inferior, barbaric and a danger to Christianity. Missionaries colluded with Australian federal and state governments to forcibly remove Aboriginal and Torres Strait Islander children from their families (sometimes called the Stolen Generation or the Stolen Children). To be fair to the Protestant missionaries, many individuals acted with compassion and respect for the humanity of Aboriginal peoples. But, overall, the picture is one of collusion, abuse and failure. The legacy of this period lives on. Given this history, it is remarkable that in the 2016 Australian census, 54% of Aboriginal and Torres Strait Islander peoples reported a commitment to Christianity.

Brooke Prentis is an Aboriginal Christian leader who is a descendant of the Waka Waka peoples. Prentis is also the chief executive officer of Common Grace, a movement of 50,000 Australian Christians seeking to call the Australian church and nation to acts of mercy, justice and compassion. She describes how Aboriginal Christianity can show the Australian and worldwide church that mission, church and theology must be done collectively and in community. Aboriginal Christians remind God's church that God invites it into a loving, dynamic community with all humanity and the whole creation. Many Aboriginal and Torres Strait Islander Christians challenge the Australian church and its leaders to get behind a formal treaty between the Australian government and Indigenous peoples. They remind the churches that they reside on stolen lands. Reconciliation and justice begin when Australians tell the truth about the extraordinary depth and treasures of Aboriginal and Indigenous cultures, spiritualities, courage, wisdom, graciousness and pioneering spirit, and when Christians invite Aboriginal and Indigenous leaders to teach the church how to follow Jesus Christ.

One such effort is the Grasstree Gathering, an event that brings together emerging and established leaders from among Aboriginal and Torres Strait Islander Christians. It is national in scope, encompassing participants from all over Australia, as well as inter-denominational and non-denominational, with attendees from across denominations and churches. Grasstree Gathering's vision is to 'celebrate, encourage, equip and inspire an emerging generation of Aboriginal and Torres Strait Islander Christian Leaders'.

Change the Heart services are held in January each year. These lead up to the official national day of Australia, celebrated on 26 January. Aunty Jean Phillips is one of the most senior Aboriginal Christian leaders in the country. She invites Australian Christians to attend #ChangeTheHeart services of acknowledgement, lament and prayer in advance of Australia Day, which Aboriginal and Torres Strait Islander peoples experience as a day of mourning. Common Grace holds Aboriginal-led prayer services in every Australian capital city and several regional centres. Aboriginal Christian leaders are calling church and society to repentance, justice and changed hearts.

The Royal Commission into Institutional Responses to Child Sexual Abuse has shown the extent of child sexual abuse in institutions managed by or affiliated with Protestant churches and denominations. The abuse was on a horrific scale. There is little doubt that these sickening actions and revelations have done significant damage to the churches and to their credibility and reputation. The Royal Commission has made extensive recommendations to Protestant and Catholic religious institutions to prevent and deal with such abuse. The recommendations amount to sweeping reforms.

Several groups with Protestant roots are active in politics. Political parties include Australian Christians, the Christian Democratic Party

(Australia) and the Family First Party (which dissolved in 2017). The Australian Christian Lobby is a conservative Christian lobby group operating out of Canberra.

Several other groups with Protestant origins and mostly Protestant constituencies are also active in politics and public life. We have already mentioned Common Grace, which is a movement of 50,000 Australian Christians focused on justice issues surrounding people seeking asylum, Aboriginal and Torres Strait Islanders, domestic and family violence, and climate change. Surrender Conference is a collective of Christian organisations and people seeking to address issues of poverty, marginalisation, justice, and Aboriginal and Torres Strait Islander leadership. Micah Australia runs Voices for Justice in Canberra each year, enabling Christians to lobby politicians on issues of global and regional poverty. Micah Australia is a movement of Australian Christians advocating for the world's most impoverished, vulnerable, sick, forgotten and oppressed. World Vision Australia and TEAR Australia are also charities fighting poverty and injustice.

Other groups involved in public life include the Centre for Public Christianity and the Australian Centre for Christianity and Culture. The first is a Protestant group connected with the Bible Society Australia, while the second is a university centre led by Protestants and Catholics together.

Associated with the University of Divinity in Melbourne, the Global Church Project profiles Majority World, Indigenous and diaspora Christian voices and ministries. The Global Church Project is also developing catalogues of female theologians from around the globe. These lists include African, Asian, Latin American, US Latina, Arab, African-American, Oceanian, Australian and New Zealand female theologians. Pertinent to the present essay, the Global Church Project has a blog post called '160+ Australian and New Zealander Women in Theology You Should Know About'. These women were then asked to nominate 20 of their peers whom Christians should read. This led to a follow-up post representing the 20 female theologians nominated by their peers, called '20 Australian and New Zealander Female Theologians You Should Get to Know in 2020'.

The largest theological consortia in Australia are the Australian College of Theology (ACT) and the University of Divinity (UD). The ACT has 17 Protestant seminaries in Australia and one in New Zealand, with more than 3,000 students combined. The UD has seven Protestant, three Catholic and one Orthodox seminary, with more than 2,000 students combined.

When we examine church attendance in Australia (as opposed to those who claim affiliation with a denomination but rarely attend church), we see significant shifts. Twenty-five years ago, Anglicans were the second-largest denomination, after Catholics. But going by church attendance, the largest denominations in Australia in 2016 were Catholics (39%), Australian Christian Churches, which are Pentecostals (12%), Anglicans (10%), Baptists (7%) and the Uniting Church (6%). The Uniting Church was formed through the union of many Methodist, Presbyterian and Congregational churches. This shift puts Pentecostal church attendance larger than Anglican attendance, and Pentecostal churches continue to grow. Over the last 25 years, Catholic, Anglican, Uniting, Lutheran and Presbyterian churches have declined. Baptists, the Salvation Army, Adventists and Churches of Christ have experienced a plateau or moderate growth. Pentecostals, on the other hand, have doubled in size during the same period.

The most reliable source of data on trends in Australian church life is the National Church Life Survey (NCLS Research), which has taken place every five years for the past 25 years (1991, 1996, 2001, 2006, 2011 and 2016). NCLS surveys church attendance, leadership, worship and more, across more than 20 Christian denominations and traditions. In 2016 this involved 3,000 local churches, 260,000 adult attenders, 10,000 child attenders and 7,000 lay and clergy church leaders. The survey is conducted in 10 languages: English, Chinese, Vietnamese, Korean, Tongan, Italian, Arabic, Dinka (Sudanese), Burmese Chin and Burmese Karen. NCLS reports that ethnic and cultural diversity is on the rise in Australian churches. In 2016, 36% of Australian church attenders were born outside of Australia, up from 28% in 2006. Of Australian church attenders, 27% were born in a non-English-speaking country. NCLS reports that 31% of Australian churches are involved in ministry toward migrants and that 23% of Australian churches are multi-ethnic or multicultural (compared with 14% in the USA). Linguistic, cultural and ethnic diversity are transforming Australian Protestant churches. Some of the fastest-growing and most missionary and vibrant Australian Protestant churches are multicultural or led and populated by people who were not born in Australia.

New Zealand

European Protestant mission in New Zealand dates back to the early nineteenth century. Samuel Marsden established the Church Mission Society (Anglican) in New Zealand in 1814. Other Protestant denominations followed, the most notable of which was the Scottish Presbyterian church. In the late nineteenth and early twentieth centuries, Scottish Presbyterians joined with Baptists, Methodists, Brethren, the Church of Christ, the Salvation Army and Congregationalists to form an Evangelical alliance. This coalition became influential in New Zealand society, and its cultural struggle was more often with Anglicans and Catholics than secularists.

In 1970, 95.4% of New Zealanders claimed to be Christian. This percentage had fallen to 54.2% by 2020. Fewer total people claimed to be Christian in New Zealand in 2020 than in 1970. Like the case in Australia, most researchers estimate that only 5% of New Zealanders attend a church weekly and perhaps 10% once a month. Of the 2,619,000 New Zealanders who self-identified as Christian in 2020, 22.5% were Anglican, 27.1% Protestant, 12.8% Independent, 17.2% unaffiliated Christians, 22.5% Evangelical, 16% Renewalist, 20.7% Catholic and 0.6% Orthodox. Some, of course, are double-affiliated.

In the 2018 census, 2 million New Zealanders said they had 'no religion' (48.2% of the population). The percentage of New Zealanders ticking 'no religion' in the census has been steadily growing, from 29.6% in 2001 to 34.6% in 2006, 41.9% in 2013 and 48.2% in 2018.

Protestant Christian groups are trying a range of pioneering initiatives to recapture the hearts and minds of New Zealanders. Innovative experiments include 'alt worship' experiences (involving art, dance and liturgy), community development projects and café and pub churches. 'New monastic movements' are growing, where young adults live in contemplative and missionary communities. New Zealand Protestant young adults are exploring fresh ways to live out relevant, prophetic public faith. Such witness includes non-violent peace activism, human rights and reconciliation campaigns, speaking out about issues of ecological and social justice concern and offering a spirituality of engagement with society.

This kind of innovative New Zealand Protestantism has impacted Christianity across Oceania and the globe. One example is Parachute Music. From 1992 to 2014, Parachute Music ran the annual summer Parachute Festival, with more than 25,000 people attending the four-day event. Parachute Music and Records continues to have a significant influence on Christian music and witness worldwide.

Indigenous Māori Christian movements grew in the late nineteenth and early twentieth centuries, with the most prominent being the Rātana and Ringatū movements. The Rātana church is a Māori Christian religious and political movement founded by Tahupōtiki Wiremu Rātana in 1925. This church claims over 50,000 followers. As many as 120,000 Māori might be involved in the Rātana movement. The Ringatū church is a Māori Christian church founded by Te Kooti Arikirangi te Turuki in 1868, with roughly 13,000 members.

New Zealand Protestant denominations have increasingly recognised the damaging role they played in colonisation and the injustices suffered by Māori peoples. Protestants were complicit in the introduction of diseases, the theft of Māori lands and the suppression of culture.

Protestant involvement in the Treaty of Waitangi (Te Tiriti o Waitangi) was mixed and often driven more by European rivalries rather than concern for Māori.

Protestants with Enlightenment-shaped, European-origin Christianities have often struggled to honour Māori culture and spirituality appropriately. Yet there is a growing movement among New Zealand Protestants to listen and learn from Māori. There is an increasing desire to learn from Māori perspectives on Jesus and the Spirit, ecology and creation care, land and place, harmony and unity, community and family, and spirituality and prayer. Māori culture enriches and guides Christian faith and witness, with a Māori focus on customs and protocol (*tikanga*), hospitality and kindness (*manaakitanga*), and respect and guardianship of the earth and all living things (*kaitiakitanga*). Māori teach us about the interdependencies and shared genealogies and spiritualities of every natural element and all living things. These are crucial insights, enhancing our understanding of Christian faith and helping humanity address pressing issues such as climate change, social isolation and rising conflicts. Those who spend time among New Zealand Protestants are often struck by the respect they show for Māori language (Te Reo Māori), customs, culture, theology and faith.

New Zealand is a culturally and ethnically diverse society. While the majority of New Zealanders are of European descent (70.2% of the population in 2018), Māori, Asian, Pacific Islander, African, Latin American and Middle Eastern communities are growing. Aside from those with European descent, the largest groups in 2018 were Māori (16.5%), Asian (15.1%) and Pacific Islander ethnic groups (8.1%). Auckland is the largest city in New Zealand and one of the most ethnically diverse cities in the world. In Auckland, roughly 50% of people are of European descent, 30% Asian, 15% Pacific Islander and 12% Māori (some people identify with more than one ethnicity). Of the population of New Zealand, 24% were born outside the country, and this rises to 40% of the inhabitants of Auckland. More than 200 ethnic groups call New Zealand home.

This ethnic, linguistic and cultural diversity is transforming the Protestant church in New Zealand. New arrivals lead and populate some of the fastest-growing Protestant churches in New Zealand. Most Protestant denominations now recognise that the future of their churches will be multi-ethnic and multicultural, and possibly multi-linguistic. Dr George Wieland, who directs Carey Baptist Theological College's Centre for Mission Research and Training, is a leading voice on the theology and practice of multi-ethnic churches. The Aotearoa New Zealand Association of Mission Studies also studies Christian mission within and beyond New Zealand, including the missional responses to an ethnically and spiritually changing society. The Anabaptist Association of Australia and New Zealand (AAANZ) is a community of Christians across those two countries exploring the theology and practices of the Anabaptist tradition and its relevance for rapidly changing and diversifying cultures. New Zealand Protestants are recognising that growing multicultural and ethnically diverse churches is not a pragmatic strategy: it is a matter of faithfulness to the gospel.

Protestantism is Changing

Protestantism in Oceania is changing rapidly. Many factors are shaping this transformation. Such influences include ethnic and religious diversification, environmental issues and climate change, refugees and asylum seekers, immigration, Indigenous issues and revelations about institutionalised forms of abuse. Other reasons include global and local politics, concerns about gender and sexual equality, the rise of post-denominationalism, secularisation and the growth in numbers of those who claim to have 'no religion'.

Many Millennial Protestants in Oceania care about addressing climate change and welcoming asylum seekers and refugees. They challenge the church and society to eradicate poverty and honour Indigenous peoples and cultures. They are less nationalistic and more hospitable than earlier generations. These Millennial Protestants tend to welcome diversity and multicultural church and society. They care about economic equality, immigration reform and police brutality. They advocate for universal healthcare and neighbourhood transformation. These younger Protestants call for fairer access to education and welfare as well as justice for minorities and those who are poor. Protestantism in Oceania faces many challenges, but it is also going through a period of exciting and welcome transformation.

Bibliography

Ernst, Manfred, 'Changing Christianity in Oceania: A Regional Overview', *Archives de Sciences Sociales des Religions*, 57:157 (2012), 29–45.

Harris, John, *One Blood: Two Hundred Years of Aboriginal Encounter with Christianity* (Fullarton: Australians Together, 2018).

Rainbow Spirit Elders, *Rainbow Spirit Theology: Toward an Australian Aboriginal Theology* (Adelaide: ATF Press, 2012).

Tate, Henare, *He Puna Iti I Te Ao Marama: A Little Spring in the World of Light* (Auckland: Libro International, 2012).

Tofaeono, Ama'amalele, *Eco-Theology: Aiga – The Household of Life: A Perspective from Living Myths and Traditions of Sāmoa* (Erlangen: Erlanger Verlag für Mission und Ökumene, 2000).

Catholics

Rocío Figueroa and Philip Gibbs

The Pacific Islands

Christian evangelisation in the Pacific began during the period of Iberian expansion, when in 1668 Jesuit priests and brothers came from the Philippines to Guam, in the Mariana Islands – then known as the Ladrones (Thieves) Islands. The missionaries accompanied a military garrison intended to protect Spanish trade. Growth of the Catholic Church in the region in the nineteenth century closely followed colonial expansion there. In Micronesia, missionary influence depended very much on the colonial interests of several nations. On the Micronesian island of Yap, Spanish Jesuit missionaries came in 1710 and again in 1731, at a time when Spain controlled shipping in the region. Their mission was interrupted when the missionaries were killed. A century and a half later, in 1899, the Spanish–American war ended with Spain selling the Caroline Islands and Mariana Islands to Germany. With the exit of the Spanish, German missionaries began again the evangelisation of Yap. In 1921, after the First World War, Spanish Jesuits replaced the German Capuchin missionaries, only to be replaced themselves after the Second World War by American Jesuits. Each change of political control brought about a change in church personnel, with their different approaches and varied access to resources.

Britain became influential throughout Polynesia following the three exploratory voyages of Captain James Cook between 1768 and 1779. A British colony was established in Fiji in 1872. The Gilbert and Ellice Islands were administered as a British protectorate from 1892 and Niue from 1900. However, Catholic missionaries to the South Pacific in the nineteenth century were predominantly French. France raised its flag on New Caledonia in 1844 and again in 1854, turning it into a penal colony from the 1860s to the end of the transportations in 1897. With the declaration of a protectorate over Tahuata in 1842, France regarded the entire Marquesas Islands as French. These political moves opened the way for evangelisation by Catholic missionaries, particularly those belonging to the Society of Mary, commonly known as Marists. Jean-Baptiste Pompallier played a key role in founding the Catholic Church in the South Pacific. He was appointed Vicar Apostolic of the new Vicariate of Western Oceania in 1836 by Pope Gregory XVI. Pompallier initially intended to visit the Tahiti and

Tonga islands and then go to New Guinea. Later he changed his plans, starting his mission in New Zealand instead.

After the Second World War, the position of the Catholic Church in many parts of the Pacific was strongly influenced by the movement from colonialism to independence and the establishment of the local church. France was engaged in nuclear testing in the Pacific and was insisting that its colonies remain as overseas French territories. Whereas a century before, links with Western powers, particularly France, had proved to be advantageous in forcing recognition of freedom of religion, now, in the postcolonial era, the church found that links to Western powers provoked suspicion on the part of Indigenous people.

Currently, the Catholic Church serves throughout Oceania. The table on the following page shows how the Catholic population varies, with the church being a major presence in a few countries, such as Guam and parts of French Polynesia – for example, Wallis and Futuna; a major player in the Federated States of Micronesia, the Northern Mariana Islands and parts of French Polynesia and Papua New Guinea (PNG); and very much in the minority in countries such as Tuvalu and in some provinces of PNG.

Typically, religiosity is an orthodox and often-taken-for-granted component of Pacific identity and, by extension, public life. Papua New Guinean Catholic philosopher and former cabinet minister Bernard Narokobi, author of the book *The Melanesian Way* (published by the Institute of Papua New Guinea Studies in 1983), argues that differentiation between religious and non-religious experiences is foreign to many people of the Pacific, who view the world as an integrated whole. Thus, many Pacific countries have not gone through the experience of modernity – distinguishing sacred and secular – that has shaped modern European-oriented cultures and Christian faith. While in theory there might be a separation of church and state, in practice that is far from the case. In Papua New Guinea, as in many Pacific nations, the secular has a negative connotation and religious language is notable in public discourse. The public role of the church in Melanesia, in a country such as Papua New Guinea, is most probably aided by the Catholic Church's important role as a primary provider of more than a third of the educational and health facilities in the country, and the exclusive provider in many isolated rural areas.

Theologians worldwide have developed different approaches to interpreting their context. Where Classical Western theology often employs rational discourse based on revealed truth, Indigenous theologies in Oceania tend to look to human experiences as the locus for theology, and 'life' as their own distinctive key to meaning. The concept can have a range of meanings, from the cosmic concept of life as found in primal religions to the struggle for life in the urban and semi-urban settlements of the

Archdioceses and dioceses in Oceania

	(Arch)diocese	State/country	Catholic population (2017)	% of total population
Micronesia	Agaña	Guam	140,593	85.0
	Caroline Islands	Federated States of Micronesia	66,339	52.2
	Chalan Kanoa	Northern Mariana Islands	71,850	59.8
	Marshall Islands (Prefecture Apostolic)	Marshall Islands	5,100	9.7
Polynesia	Suva	Fiji	63,762	7.3
	Rarotonga	Cook Islands	2,255	19.0
	Tarawa & Nauru	Kiribati and Nauru	68,406	54.0
	Funafuti (Mission Sui Iuris)	Tuvalu	110	1.0
	Tonga & Niue	Tonga and Niue	14,691	14.2
	Sāmoa-Apia	Sāmoa	31,221	16.6
	Sāmoa-Pago Pago	American Sāmoa	12,600	20.7
	Tokelau (Mission Sui Iuris)	Tokelau	535	38.5
	Papeete	French Polynesia	105,780	38.2
	Taiohae ou Tefenuaenata	French Polynesia	8,997	90.1
	Nouméa	New Caledonia	132,015	48.7
	Port Vila	Vanuatu	34,320	12.0
	Wallis and Futuna	Wallis and Futuna	10,450	95.4
Melanesia	Honiara	Solomon Islands	61,400	22.2
	Auki	Solomon Islands	45,600	28.4
	Gizo	Solomon Islands	15,214	11.2
	Port Moresby	Papua New Guinea (PNG)	207,623	31.7
	Alotau-Sideia	PNG	54,795	17.3
	Bereina	PNG	94,000	68.2
	Daru-Kiunga	PNG	48,352	23.1
	Kerema	PNG	26,700	16.4
	Madang	PNG	180,224	34.6
	Lae	PNG	35,600	5.2
	Aitape	PNG	153,460	75.4
	Vanimo	PNG	38,476	33.7
	Wewak	PNG	215,700	48.4
	Mount Hagen	PNG	195,617	29.7
	Mendi	PNG	77,096	8.6
	Wabag	PNG	75,947	16.7
	Kundiawa	PNG	123,300	31.9
	Goroka	PNG	16,250	2.7
	Rabaul	PNG	354,004	43.9
	Kimbe	PNG	286,720	80.0
	Kavieng	PNG	102,900	52.2
	Bougainville	Autonomous region of PNG	157,000	62.5

regions. The search for the maintenance and celebration of life is present behind almost all efforts in Indigenous theology in Oceania. Aside from Australia and New Zealand, the majority of the population in Oceania are Indigenous people who are guardians of land, forests and one-third of the earth's water. Hence theological issues related to climate change and environmental issues reveal a passion derived from their personal experience and close identity with the natural world.

In November 1998, the Catholic bishops from Australia, New Zealand, the Pacific Islands, Papua New Guinea and Solomon Islands travelled to Rome to attend the Special Assembly of the Synod of Bishops for Oceania. The focus of the synod was the person of Jesus Christ and how to walk his way, tell his truth and live his life. Synods had previously been held for the bishops of Africa, Asia and the America, and a synod for Europe was in the final stages of preparation. However, the synod for Oceania was special in a number of respects. It was the only synod to which all the bishops of the region had been invited, and in fact all except three participated. Most of the bishops already knew one another, many having met at the Federation of Catholic Bishops Conferences of Oceania assembly in Auckland in 1994. The impressive opening Mass in St Peter's Basilica included dancing and music from the Pacific, notably Sāmoa. That some Roman officials were rather critical of tattooed Sāmoan men in traditional dress dancing in the Basilica is perhaps symbolic of a cultural gulf, with sights that are quite 'normal' in the Pacific appearing scandalous to some members of the Roman Curia. In his speech at the presentation of *Ecclesia in Oceania*, the papal exhortation following the synod, Cardinal Williams – from New Zealand but with many years of experience in Sāmoa – noted that communion, inculturation and a renewed proclamation of the gospel in ways appropriate for the peoples of Oceania were the key themes and insights that emerged from the 1998 Synod of Bishops for Oceania.

Most governments in the Pacific have adopted neo-liberal economic concepts and terminology, such as 'deregulation' and 'user pays'. Leaders are conscious of being part of global interests, particularly involving the

Catholics in Oceania, 1970

Region	Total population	Christian population	Catholic population	% of region Catholic	% of Christians Catholic
Oceania	19,718,000	18,250,000	4,546,000	23.1%	24.9%
Australia/New Zealand	15,661,000	14,633,000	3,464,000	22.1%	23.7%
Melanesia	3,399,000	2,978,000	855,000	25.1%	28.7%
Micronesia	248,000	237,000	131,000	52.6%	55.1%
Polynesia	410,000	402,000	96,500	23.6%	24.0%
Global total	3,700,578,000	1,229,309,000	658,556,000	17.8%	53.6%

Source: Todd M. Johnson and Gina A. Zurlo (eds), *World Christian Database* (Leiden/Boston: Brill), accessed January 2020.

USA and China, with some influence from Australia and New Zealand. Migration is an important aspect of life, with more Sāmoans living today in Auckland than in the Sāmoan capital, Apia. The majority of Cook Islanders live permanently in New Zealand. Church leaders are also aware of being part of a global movement of 'born-again' Christians, with increasing cross-national contacts between them and the centres of Evangelicalism in the USA, Australia and New Zealand. Churches in the Pacific region are confronted by the attraction of the 'gospel of prosperity' proclaimed by some Pentecostal churches and are challenged to put the Catholic Church's social teaching into practice. In the Pacific, a theology of integral human development was the equivalent of liberation theology.

The Micronesian island states survive on a still widespread subsistence economy centred on fish, coconuts and foreign aid. Melanesia is an international source for timber and minerals. The Polynesian islands are helped by remittances from relatives living abroad and tourism. The growth of tourism and hospitality has meant investment in global alliances with air companies, hotels and tour operators. It has helped expose people to different cultures and to cross-cultural communication. Local specialties are valued in order to establish identities that differentiate them from other tourist destinations. However, this can be at a cost for local people, with the commercialisation of culture leading to undignified ways of seeking a livelihood, such as opening up sacred sites to the public and paid performances of Indigenous rituals.

Where, previously, missionary priests and sisters had come from Europe and other Western countries to the Pacific, now the reverse has been happening, and Pacific Islanders are migrating to so-called developed countries, bringing new life to the church there. In reality there is a noticeable difference now between the life of the church in what at times is a post-Christian reality in Australia and New Zealand, on the one hand, and the raw realities in Papua New Guinea, the Solomon Islands and the Pacific Islands, on the other. The contrast is apparent in recent effects of and responses to the coronavirus.

Catholics in Oceania, 2020

Region	Total population	Christian population	Catholic population	% of region Catholic	% of Christians Catholic
Oceania	42,384,000	27,606,000	9,690,000	22.9%	35.1%
Australia/New Zealand	30,233,000	16,363,000	6,443,000	21.3%	39.4%
Melanesia	10,909,000	10,069,000	2,724,000	25.0%	27.1%
Micronesia	541,000	501,000	318,000	58.7%	63.5%
Polynesia	701,000	673,000	205,000	29.2%	30.5%
Global total	7,795,482,000	2,518,834,000	1,239,909,000	15.9%	49.2%

Source: Todd M. Johnson and Gina A. Zurlo (eds), *World Christian Database* (Leiden/Boston: Brill), accessed January 2020.

Australia

The first Catholics arrived and settled in Australia with the First Fleet in 1788. Most of them were Irish convicts; the majority were ordinary criminals and a small number were political rebels. The formal establishment of the Catholic Church in Australia began with the arrival of two chaplains, Fr John Joseph Therry and Fr Philip Connolly, appointed from London in 1820. Although the first Australian bishop – John Bede Polding, appointed in 1842 – was an English Benedictine monk, most of the priests were Irish and tried to create a Catholic model in Australia that was very similar to the Irish one. However, by the 1930s the number of Australian-born priests outnumbered the Irish clergy.

Early Catholic settlers in Australia had little regard for the Aborigines. The first missions, established by Bishop Polding, completely failed. During the nineteenth century, the missionaries wanted to 'civilise' the Aboriginals. Unfortunately, we can now see in hindsight that the Catholic Church's methods were intimately linked to European colonialism in Australia. European colonialism eventually caused the Aboriginal people to lose their cultures, languages, rights and land. Polding spoke about the injustices inflicted on the Aborigines by the white man, but many missionaries were clearly aligned with the colonialist power. For example, the church played a shadowy role in the infamous 'Stolen Generations' era of Australia's past by providing homes to Indigenous children taken from families. The 'Stolen Generations' were the children of Australian Aboriginal and Torres Strait Islander descent who were removed from their own families by the Australian government and church missions between 1910 and 1970. On 13 February 2008, Prime Minister Kevin Rudd, on behalf of the Australian people, expressed a national apology in parliament to the Aboriginal peoples for all historical wrongs done to them. It was an act for national reconciliation and had a huge impact on the national consciousness. The Catholic Church has also been working on this national reconciliation and acknowledging its own wrongs in this 'Stolen Generations' affair.

Changes in Catholics in Oceania, 1970–2020, growth rate, % per year

Region	Total population	Christian population	Catholic population
Oceania	1.54%	0.83%	1.53%
Australia/New Zealand	1.32%	0.22%	1.25%
Melanesia	2.36%	2.47%	2.35%
Micronesia	1.57%	1.51%	1.80%
Polynesia	1.08%	1.04%	1.52%
Global total	1.50%	1.45%	1.27%

Source: Todd M. Johnson and Gina A. Zurlo (eds), *World Christian Database* (Leiden/Boston: Brill), accessed January 2020.

In the nineteenth and twentieth centuries the Australian constitution had discriminatory references against the Aboriginal people. An overwhelming 'yes' vote in a 1967 national referendum demanded change in the constitution to recognise and allow the Commonwealth to make laws about Aboriginal Australians and include them in the census. These societal changes and the Second Vatican Council (1962–5) influenced the Catholic Church in Australia. The Second Vatican Council's new missionary approach introduced the concept of inculturation, which affirmed the need to incarnate the gospel in different cultures while appreciating and integrating the values within that culture. With this new approach, Catholic missionaries attempted to adapt to Aboriginal congregations. For example, an experimental Aboriginal Mass was developed that included Indigenous music, dance art and a specially composed Aboriginal Eucharistic Prayer.

Boniface Perdiert was ordained Australia's first Indigenous deacon in 1974 and Pat Dodson was the first ordained Indigenous priest in 1975. However, much remains to be done in this regard. According to the Aboriginal author Graeme Mundine, the history of the Catholic Church in Australia is one of indifference, toward subjects of mission in the past and toward subjects of social justice issues more recently. For Mundine, the fact that Australia has non-Indigenous leadership and no authentic participation of Aboriginal people in their own inculturation process causes deep barriers. That is why the future of Indigenous Catholics is an important challenge for Catholicism in Australia. Indigenous people number 460,000 in Australia and make up 2.4% of the Australian population. In the census of 2016, there were 133,540 Indigenous Catholics.

Pope John Paul II's visit to Australia in 1986 was pivotal in the journey of Indigenous Catholics. His address to Aboriginal and Torres Strait Islander people sparked a recognition of Aboriginal and Islander ministries:

> Your Christian faith calls you to become the best kind of Aboriginal people you can be…. Only then will you make your best contribution to all your brothers and sisters in this great nation. You are part of Australia and Australia is part of you. And the Church herself in Australia will not be fully the Church that Jesus wants her to be until you have made your contribution to her life and until that contribution has been joyfully received by others.

After John Paul II's visit, an Aboriginal Catholic ministry in Melbourne was born, and many Aboriginal Catholic ministries grew in other states and territories. The National Aboriginal and Torres Strait Islander Catholic Council, an advisory body to the Australian Catholic Bishops on issues relating to Aboriginal and Torres Strait Islander Catholics, was founded in 1992. At present there are Aboriginal and Islander ministries in every state and territory of Australia. In each of these ministries the traditional owners are striving to incorporate the gifts of their culture, rituals and symbols into the liturgy and the life of the church. For example, Aboriginal art and items are being used as altar cloths and vessels. In some communities, rituals such as water blessings and smoke ceremonies are culturally appropriate to incorporate into the Mass.

Vicky Walker Clark, a descendant of the Mutthi Mutthi tribe of southwest New South Wales, has dedicated decades of her life to increasing understanding of aboriginal spirituality and defending the rights of the Aboriginal. A coordinator at the Aboriginal Catholic ministry in the Archdiocese of Melbourne until 2015, she has lamented the fact that the Aboriginal contribution has not been fully accepted by the Australian Catholic Church. From her perspective, Aboriginal culture and symbols of the land continue to be viewed with suspicion, and there is a reluctance to adopt them into mainstream everyday Catholic life.

The Catholic Church in Australia has five provinces: Adelaide, Brisbane, Melbourne, Perth and Sydney. It has 35 dioceses comprising geographic areas, as well as the military diocese and dioceses for the Chaldean, Maronite, Melkite and Ukrainian rites. The national assembly of bishops is the Australian Catholic Bishops Conference, presently headed by Brisbane's Archbishop Mark Coleridge. In total, 175 Catholic religious orders operate in Australia, affiliated under Catholic Religious Australia, presently headed by Sr Monica Cavanagh.

The latest national census, in 2016, revealed that Christianity remains the most common religion (57.7% of the population). Catholicism is the largest Christian group in Australia, accounting for almost a quarter (22.6%) of the population. One of the dominant features of the Australian Catholic community today is the plurality of cultures from different parts of the world. The 2016 census showed that the ancestries with which Australian Catholics identified were extremely varied, the largest being English (1.49 million), Australian (1.12 million), Irish (577,000), Italian (567,000) and Filipino (181,000). Other important immigrant Catholic groups come from Croatia, India, Vietnam and Malta. According to the National Church Life Survey of 2016, which sampled Mass attendees in Catholic parishes all over Australia, immigrant people felt a stronger sense of belonging to the Catholic Church than their Australian counterparts, and their participation in the church has helped them to settle into the nation. Despite these positive results, however, many of the third generation of current migrants are not following the religious practice of their parents and grandparents and are highly secularised. The Catholic Church continues to be challenged by the diversity of its community. In a pluralistic society it is not easy to incorporate the values of each culture. The 2016 census statistics showed also that nearly one in five Catholics (19.1%) were born outside of Australia in non-English-speaking countries, while 5.6% were born overseas in English-speaking countries. This situation gives the Catholic Church an opportunity to be a space of intercultural dialogue, receiving the faith and values that refugees and migrants bring from all over the world. Around Australia Mass is celebrated in more than 35 different languages every Sunday. This trait certainly helps immigrants – but is it aiding them in truly assimilating into a foreign culture, and, further, is it possibly isolating Australians from the benefits of diversity? Another challenge to consider is that many communities have been importing so-called 'international priests'. There are now more 'international priests' than locally born priests in Australia.

The Catholic Church in Australia is the largest non-governmental provider of welfare services. Catholic Social Services Australia aids some 450,000 people annually and is the Catholic Church's most important national social-services body. It advocates for the most disadvantaged and campaigns for a fair and just society. The St Vincent de Paul Society, with 40,000 volunteers, is the largest volunteer welfare network in the country.

Catholic presence in Australian political life is also important. Historically, Catholics have been a considerable presence in leadership positions. In the late nineteenth century, the Catholic community had an allegiance with the Labour Party. In the 1950s and 1960s, the Catholic politicians concentrated their fight against communism, breaking away from the Labour Party to form the Democratic Labour Party from 1957 to 1978. From 1980 onward, Australian Catholics have had no allegiances and individual politicians have followed their own values and choices. The fact that politicians do not receive any ecclesial support or preference today has aided a healthy autonomy between religious and political identity. Australia has had several Catholic prime ministers (most recently Malcolm Turnbull, 2015–18). Because Australian political life is based on a democratic liberal foundation, Catholic politicians have room to act according to their faith.

Education has been a pillar of the Catholic Church in Australia. An important proportion of faith-based schools and children's homes were run by Catholic entities after the Second World War. In 2016 the church had some 760,000 students in more than 1,700 schools. The education of young people has been one of the most important means for the Catholic Church to transmit the gospel. However, the enormous and fruitful presence of the church in educating generations of Australians has also become its Achilles' heel. It enabled one of the darkest chapters in Australian church history: the sexual abuse of minors by clergy. In the twenty-first century the Australian Catholic Church is facing a deep crisis due not only to these crimes of sexual abuse but also to the extensive cover-up of those crimes at the institutional level. The Australian government's Royal Commission into Institutional Responses to Child Sexual Abuse (2013–17) handed down its final report in December 2017. Sixty-two per cent of the survivors who were abused in religious settings were abused in Catholic institutions.

Theologian Robert Gascoigne has analysed the causes of the sexual abuse crisis in the Australian Catholic Church. Gascoigne considers the problem to be that the church received the tools of liberal society but at its core remained hierarchical and authoritarian. According to him, before the nineteenth century, Catholics in the British Empire suffered from restrictions and sanctions, but due to the development of liberalism they finally obtained civil freedom. For example, Governor Richard Bourke's Church Act in New South Wales (1836) allowed Catholics to become a social group with their own identity and civil rights. However, the church's internal structure did not change along with the new political structures of liberalism. Unfortunately, the combination of clericalism, the massive engagement with young people and the freedom that the church in Australia had won enabled these crimes to occur without any accountability. Failing to prosecute offending religious clergy, the church operated in a realm separate from the public sphere, where secular law did not apply. The findings of the Australian Royal Commission not only illuminated the crimes of sexual abuse but also exposed major failures in ecclesial government and leadership, and it also recommended a review of church governance at a national level.

It is highly likely the crisis of sexual abuse has had a strong impact on the faith and trust of Australian Catholics. Although the Catholic Church is the largest Christian denomination in Australia, with 5,439,268 people, the 2016 census found a fall in both overall numbers and the percentage of Catholics: around 22.6% of the population in 2016, down from 25.3% in the 2011 census.

Following the Royal Commission's advice, the Catholic Church undertook an independent review of governance. This report, published confidentially to the Australian Catholic Bishops Conference in May 2020, is titled *The Light from the Southern Cross: Promoting Co-responsible Governance in the Catholic Church in Australia*. The report proposes a co-responsible synodal model of church with much more participation of lay people, particularly women, at all levels. Could this report and the coming Australian synod, originally scheduled for October 2020 but delayed by the coronavirus pandemic, lead the Australian church on a path of justice for victims and institutional transformation? The bishops will discuss this report and take their ideas to the plenary council. The plenary council will be the first to be held since the Second Vatican Council. The first phase, 'Listening and Dialogue 2018', features the voices of the faithful who participated, contributing 17,457 submissions. During the second phase, 'Listening and Discernment 2019', Catholics all over Australia participated in writing and discernment sessions. Due to the COVID-19 pandemic, the plenary council 2020 has been postponed until 2021–2.

Although the crisis has been very difficult for believers, this situation could be an opportunity for renewal and change. If the Australian Catholic Church takes on a new co-responsible model we perhaps could expect a future in which the church can serve as an example for other Catholic communities around the world. Time will tell.

New Zealand

New Zealand is about 2,000 kilometres east of Australia across the Tasman Sea and 1,000 kilometres south of the Pacific Island areas of New Caledonia, Fiji and Tonga. Due to its remoteness, it was one of the last lands to be settled by humans. New Zealand's isolation has led to its distinct biodiversity of animal and plant life. The country's varied topography and its sharp mountain peaks, such as the Southern Alps, are the result of rapid tectonic uplift of land and volcanic eruptions.

The date of the first settlement is a matter of debate. Some affirm that the earliest settlement of Aotearoa took place up to 1,000 years before James Cook's arrival in 1769, but current understanding is that the first arrivals came in the late thirteenth century. The ancestors of modern-day Māori made their way from the Southeast Asian and Micronesian regions into what came to be known as Polynesia in the Pacific. They travelled northward to Hawaii and to Rapanui (Easter Island) in the east and likely made their way to New Zealand from more than one Polynesian island. Europeans did not become aware of the country's existence until later, in 1642. Abel Janszoon Tasman, a Dutch captain, sighted 'a large land, uplifted high', probably referring to the Southern Alps. Four of Tasman's party were killed by Māori from the Ngāti Tūmatakōkiri tribe and the Dutch captain responded by shooting and hitting one Māori. The Dutch ship was forced to leave.

The first Catholics known to have set foot in New Zealand arrived in 1769 aboard James Cook's barque *Endeavour*. From the 1790s, New Zealand was visited by British and French whaling and trading ships. Their crews traded European goods, including guns and metal tools, for Māori food, water, wood and flax.

Māori in New Zealand have had a strong religious life and spirituality. For them, human beings and everything in creation have a *wairua*, a divine sparkle that comes from the gods; respect for nature and creation is a natural consequence of this belief. Māori believe in supernatural and immortal beings. For them, Atua is the supreme God that is beyond any knowledge. Atua can also mean Rangi and Papa – the Sky Father and the Earth Mother – and the different forces of nature. A strong connection exists between the material world and the spiritual world; they are not separated worlds. *Whakapapa* (genealogy) links animate and inanimate things, terrestrial and spiritual worlds, and is what binds all things, interconnecting them. In Māori culture the land has a deep meaning. It belongs to their ancestors and has ethical implications; land has *mauri* or *wairua* force. The spiritual values of *atua, wairua, whanau* (family) and *mana* meant that it was not hard for many Māori to accept the Christian faith brought by Europeans; they felt that Christian values were similar to their own.

In the 1820s and 1830s New Zealand attracted Australian Catholic migrants to Hokianga, the Kaipara, the Bay of Islands and the Bay of Plenty. The best-known and most respected of these early New Zealand-Irish Catholics were Thomas and Mary Poynton. The Poynton family became a point of reference to their Māori neighbours and the migrant Catholics in Hokianga. They gathered many Catholics in their house on Sundays to pray together and be instructed by Thomas Poynton. By 1838 Poynton estimated 40 or 50 Catholics lived in Hokianga alone.

The Catholic Church was slow to send clergy to New Zealand, however. Between the suppression of the Jesuits, the French Revolution and the Napoleonic Wars, its attention was focused elsewhere. The first real plan for sending missionaries began in 1830. Rome approved the new mission territory of the South Sea Islands (south of the Equator from Easter Island to New Zealand) and appointed Fr Gabriel Henri Jérôme de Solages as responsible for missions in the region. Although Solages never actually went to the region, Rome declared that New Zealand was part of the mission of the French church.

In January 1836 Rome established the Vicariate of Western Oceania, which included New Zealand, and then began finalising arrangements for missionaries to staff it. At that time the Society of Mary (Marists) was seeking official recognition as a religious congregation. Rome offered its approval while also requesting the Marists to accept the new mission field of Western Oceania. Eastern Oceania was given to the Congregation of the Sacred Hearts of Jesus and Mary (Picpus Fathers). Jean-Baptiste Pompallier, a young French bishop, was entrusted with the mission in New Zealand, arriving with a few priests and brothers of the new congregation. Pompallier, a handsome and charismatic 36-year-old, arrived in 1838 with Fr Catherin Servant and Br Michel Colombon and began his mission in Northland. From Hokianga they soon moved east to the Bay of Islands and later south to the new capital, Auckland.

Pompallier, Servant and other Marists very quickly learned Māori. Some Māori converted to Catholicism, in many cases because rival tribes had become Anglicans or Methodists. Pompallier urged his priests to build Catholic belief around Māori customs. The missionaries set up a printing press and printed books in the Māori language. Their focus was to evangelise the Māori. During the period 1838–43 almost 40 members of the Society of Mary arrived in New Zealand. Bishop Pompallier had many qualities that attracted the Māori people, but he was less accomplished with respect to administration and finance. In 1842 the Catholic Church was in a financial crisis, and some of the Marists priests complained about Pompallier: they felt abandoned, overworked and under-resourced. The tensions grew between Pompallier and Jean-Claude Colin, the Superior General of the Marists, and in 1848 Rome decided to divide New Zealand into two dioceses, Auckland and Port Nicholson (Wellington). Pompallier oversaw Auckland while the Marist Philippe Viard took over Port Nicholson. As more European settlers arrived in New Zealand, many of them Irish Catholics, the Catholic Church became more of a settler church than a Māori mission.

According to the 2013 census the Catholic Church represents 12.6% of the total population, with 492,384 members. In New Zealand there is one archdiocese, in Wellington, and five suffragan dioceses: Auckland, Christchurch, Dunedin, Hamilton and Palmerston North. The church is overseen by the New Zealand Catholic Bishops' Conference.

In 2013, Māori who were Catholic numbered 71,700 – or 10.7% of the Māori population. New Zealand has had one Māori bishop: Pā Max Takuira Māriu's ordination in 1988 fulfilled a long-held desire of Māori. When Bishop Māriu died in 2005, both Māori and the church in Aotearoa New Zealand strongly felt his loss. Not many vocations to the priesthood or religious life have come from the Māori community. It seems that the Catholic Church has not been able to reach Māori people nor to integrate the faith with Māori values and culture. Catholic Māori Deacon Karatea-Goddard affirmed, 'We always have had a Māori translation of the Mass but it has never been inculturated. Māori elements and expressions were never included formally in the Mass' (*New Zealand Catholic*, 2018).

For generations, as in many Western countries, Indigenous people have suffered from discrimination, and that is no different in New Zealand. In response to this discrimination, Māori New Zealanders are experiencing a renaissance in their own identity and spirituality. The Catholic community must find a way to present faith and worship in a way that makes sense to Māori culture. Te Rūnanga o te Hāhi Katorika ō Aotearoa, the national Māori advisory group appointed by the bishops, advises the bishops on the pastoral care of Māori. Māori pastoral care is organised in different ways in the six dioceses. Some dioceses have a vicar for Māori, while others have a Māori chaplaincy, and all have Catholic *marae* (meeting grounds).

The main trait of the Catholic Church in New Zealand has been its focus on education. Catholic missionaries set up many church schools from 1877. The early Catholic Church in New Zealand belonged largely to the lower end of the socio-economic scale. Recognising this, the missionaries used education as a tool to raise the economic and social status of Catholics, producing doctors, lawyers, priests and other professionals. Bishop Patrick Moran of Dunedin (1823–95) was one of those who in the nineteenth century promoted and built many schools. He affirmed, 'Build your schools and churches must follow, neglect your schools and your churches must close'. By 1895 the Diocese of Dunedin had 27 Catholic schools for 2,000 children. In 1877 the government decided to withdraw all subsidies from church schools, making schooling free, secular and compulsory. It was only in 1975 that religious schools were integrated into the state system and again received state funding. Today, 8.5% of primary and secondary students in New Zealand attend the nation's 237 Catholic schools, which equates to about 70,000 students.

Besides education, the Catholic Church has been committed to social services. Catholic Social Services began in Auckland in 1923 and has offices in different dioceses. It has a commitment to the community and provides professional services in counselling, parenting assistance, prison chaplaincy, mitigating poverty and working for justice.

The minority status of the Catholic Church within the New Zealand population has brought both benefits and disadvantages to the Catholic community. Without a national established church, all religious denominations have been on an equal footing. On the other hand, because the Catholic Church operates independently of political power, its influence and societal impact are weaker than in other countries.

Recent migration from the Pacific, Asia, the Middle East and Latin America has boosted numbers in the Catholic Church. New Zealand society is very tolerant of cultural diversity, but the challenge for the Catholic Church is to have communities that integrate the values and traditions of different nationalities. Another challenge is the very low number of New Zealand seminarians, which has forced the church to import priests or seminarians from overseas. Will overseas-born priests be able to understand and reach New Zealand's secular society? Perhaps a possibility for the future is that lay people, especially women, assume responsibilities and even ministries within the church.

Conclusion

Oceania is a unique area covering almost one-third of the earth's surface. It has vast areas of water and is marked by outstanding natural beauty. It has high proportions of both migrants and Indigenous peoples. Two important commitments of the Catholic Church are most relevant for this region: ecological, protecting the land for future generations, and social, promoting the equality and dignity of all the people of God from different cultures, nations and traditions.

Bibliography

Ernst, Manfred (ed.), *Globalization and the Re-shaping of Christianity in the Pacific Islands* (Suva: Pacific Theological College, 2006).

Gascoigne, Robert, 'The Mystical and the Political: Challenges for the Australian Catholic Church', *Australasian Catholic Record*, 95:1 (January 2018), 20–34.

Gibbs, Philip, 'Emerging Indigenous Theologies in Oceania', *Concilium*, 5 (2010), 34–44.

King, Michael, *God's Farthest Outpost: A History of Catholics in New Zealand* (Auckland: Penguin Books, 1997).

Ormerod, Neil, Ormond Rush, David Pascoe, Clare Johnson and Joel Hodge (eds), *Vatican II: The Reception and Implementation in the Australian Church* (Mulgrave: Garratt Publishing, 2012).

Evangelicals

Stuart Lange

Oceania involves some 20 different countries (most of them surrounded by vast expanses of sea), a myriad of Christian denominations, many different cultures (Indigenous as well as Western) and various fusions of culture. Evangelicalism in Oceania has a great variety of different strands and shades but shares characteristics common to Evangelicalism around the globe: an emphasis on the Bible and its authority, and its use in preaching and personal devotion; a focus on the gospel, the cross, salvation by grace, faith in Christ and new birth; emphases on holy living, prayerfulness and evangelism; doctrinal and moral conservatism; a tendency toward simplicity and fervour in worship; and a commitment to global mission.

Evangelical Christianity should not simply be equated with Fundamentalism. Evangelicalism exists on a spectrum, with varying degrees of narrowness and breadth of spirit. Evangelical beliefs and practices largely overlap with those of Charismatic and Pentecostal Christianity, but (in Oceania at least) most Pentecostals primarily think of themselves as 'Pentecostal' rather than as 'Evangelical'. Evangelicalism in Oceania includes some who explicitly identify as 'Evangelical'. Many more rarely identify themselves as such, because their primary identity is cultural or denominational (or they are not quite sure what the word 'Evangelical' means), but are nonetheless Evangelical because their Christian faith and practice exhibit the usual hallmarks of Evangelical faith. Still others reflect some characteristics of Evangelicalism, along with those of other cultural, theological and ecclesiastical traditions. At the same time, some denominations include the word 'Evangelical' in their names but might not be theologically Evangelical in the usual sense.

People across Oceania become Evangelical for many different reasons, such as an Evangelical upbringing, a conversion experience, a search for certain answers in an uncertain world, an appreciation of biblical teaching, the attraction of clear beliefs and conservative morality, disillusionment with liberal or traditional churches, the style of worship and music, and many personal and social factors.

This essay discusses Evangelical Christianity across Oceania, with closer reference to a subset of countries. Ethnically and culturally, Oceania can be conceptualised in two blocs, in which the cultural and ecclesiastical contexts for Evangelical churches are very different: (1) Australasia, where both countries (Australia and New Zealand) are developed, affluent and mainly populated by non-Indigenous people, and (2) Melanesia, Micronesia and Polynesia, where the populations are largely Indigenous and the countries are both developing and less prosperous.

Australia and New Zealand

As a continent with 25 million people, primarily of European ethnicity and culture, Australia is atypical of countries in Oceania. Only 3% of the population is Indigenous. In settler Australia, which was overwhelmingly Anglo-Celtic until the late twentieth century, Evangelical Christianity has always been an important part of the religious and cultural mix. Australian streams of Evangelicalism were strongly shaped by British antecedents, especially those in the Anglican, Methodist and Baptist denominations and among Scottish and Irish Presbyterians. It has also been influenced by the more emotionally intense styles of American Evangelicalism. Evangelical piety was bolstered by fervent preaching, much use of the Bible, prayer meetings, Bible conferences and countless evangelists and revivalists. A later peak of Evangelical influence occurred around the time of the 1959 Billy Graham crusades.

The largest Protestant affiliation in Australia is Anglican. The Sydney diocese is predominantly conservative Evangelical in character, in the Puritan tradition. Sydney Evangelicalism reaches as far back as the Port Jackson penal colony begun in 1788, with its Evangelical chaplains including Samuel Marsden (whose reputation in Australia has been mixed, but who later took Christianity to New Zealand). The Sydney Evangelical tradition has been strengthened by successive archbishops and the diocese's Moore College. The diocese has emphasised biblical authority, expository preaching and evangelism. It does not ordain women. It has had an influence on other denominations and on the wider Anglican Church. Elsewhere in Australia, though, Evangelical Anglicanism co-exists with other Anglican traditions.

Evangelicals in Oceania, 1970

Region	Total population	Christian population	Evangelical population	% of region Evangelical	% of Christians Evangelical
Oceania	19,718,000	18,250,000	3,788,000	19.2%	20.8%
Australia/New Zealand	15,661,000	14,633,000	3,272,000	20.9%	22.4%
Melanesia	3,399,000	2,978,000	473,000	13.9%	15.9%
Micronesia	248,000	237,000	20,600	8.3%	8.7%
Polynesia	410,000	402,000	21,800	5.3%	5.4%
Global total	3,700,578,000	1,229,309,000	111,809,000	3.0%	9.1%

Source: Todd M. Johnson and Gina A. Zurlo (eds), *World Christian Database* (Leiden/Boston: Brill), accessed January 2020.

The second largest mainline Protestant affiliation is the Uniting Church (UCA), formed in 1977 through a merger of Methodists, Presbyterians and Congregationalists. The UCA is predominantly liberal. In 2006, Evangelicals in the UCA, upset by UCA decisions in relation to same-sex issues, formed the dissident Assembly of Confessing Congregations. Many in the UCA's Uniting Aboriginal and Islander Christian Congress are Evangelical, as are many Tongan and Asian congregations.

The two next largest Christian streams in Australia, the Baptists and Pentecostals, are generally Evangelical in doctrine and practice. The Hillsong mega-church in Sydney has considerable influence across Oceania. The Presbyterian Church of Australia, that part of the Presbyterian Church which did not enter the UCA in 1977, is conservative Evangelical, often with a Reformed flavour. Numerous smaller Australian denominations, mostly in the Holiness tradition, are Evangelical. These include the Wesleyan Methodist Church, Nazarene Church, Christian and Missionary Alliance, Salvation Army and Open Brethren.

Many movements and institutions help foster Australian Evangelicalism. These include the Australian Fellowship of Evangelical Students, the Church Missionary Society, numerous theological and Bible colleges, and gatherings such as the Katoomba Christian Convention. Organisations such as World Vision and the Bible Society are Evangelical at heart. Many newer Christian arrivals in Australia, from Asia and the Pacific, are theologically and morally conservative and often join Evangelical types of church. Through books and internet, conferences and visiting speakers, Australia Evangelicalism is continually influenced by British and US Evangelicalism (the American influence has increased since the 1960s). A number of new churches have been established by some (including Pacific Islanders) migrating from New Zealand.

In recent decades, both society and churches in Australia and New Zealand have felt the strong social and ideological winds that have been blowing across many other Western societies: religious scepticism, a relativistic view of religious truth, biblical illiteracy, a broadened

Evangelicals in Oceania, 2020

Region	Total population	Christian population	Evangelical population	% of region Evangelical	% of Christians Evangelical
Oceania	42,384,000	27,606,000	6,063,000	14.3%	22.0%
Australia/New Zealand	30,233,000	16,363,000	3,143,000	10.4%	19.2%
Melanesia	10,909,000	10,069,000	2,777,000	25.5%	27.6%
Micronesia	541,000	501,000	81,800	15.1%	16.3%
Polynesia	701,000	673,000	61,400	8.7%	9.1%
Global total	7,795,482,000	2,518,834,000	387,026,000	5.0%	15.4%

Source: Todd M. Johnson and Gina A. Zurlo (eds), *World Christian Database* (Leiden/Boston: Brill), accessed January 2020.

spirituality, suspicion of the institutional church, rejection of traditional sexual morality, a pervasive emphasis on individual freedom and experience, secular public discourse, and the burgeoning popularity of declaring 'no religion' (30% of Australians in the 2016 census and 48.2% of New Zealanders in 2018). In the face of such shifts, most churches have lost members, but Evangelical churches have often been more resilient, especially when they have retained an Evangelical theology while adopting a more contemporary style.

In New Zealand (population 4.78 million in 2019), Evangelicalism is broadly similar to that in Australia, shares many of the same roots, and faces similar post-modern and secular challenges. But the denominational configurations are different, and Indigenous Māori people and the large number of Pacific Islanders (especially in Auckland) also bring distinctive flavours. From the 1830s, many Māori adopted Christianity and incorporated it into Māori culture. Many Māori today have an Evangelical faith, but on the whole Māori Christianity is currently not especially Evangelical. Some younger Māori Christians are grappling with how the gospel sits within Māori culture and spirituality. Older Pacific Islanders in New Zealand are usually quite traditional in their faith and practice, at least within mainline denominations, but many of them – especially younger (and New Zealand-born) Pacific Islanders – are very active in Evangelical, Charismatic and Pentecostal churches.

The Anglican Church in New Zealand lacks any major Evangelical concentration equivalent to Sydney Anglicanism. The diocese of Nelson is largely Evangelical, with an Evangelical bishop, but it has only one city and is mainly rural. In addition, the diocese of Christchurch has been home to numerous Evangelical parishes. Following the general synod decision in 2018 to allow blessings of same-sex relationships, some Evangelical parishes and clergy have joined the new Church of Confessing Anglicans Aotearoa New Zealand (2019). The second major Protestant denomination, the Presbyterian Church of Aotearoa New Zealand, has

Changes in Evangelicals in Oceania, 1970–2020, growth rate, % per year

Region	Total population	Christian population	Catholic population
Oceania	1.54%	0.83%	0.95%
Australia/New Zealand	1.32%	0.22%	−0.08%
Melanesia	2.36%	2.47%	3.60%
Micronesia	1.57%	1.51%	2.80%
Polynesia	1.08%	1.04%	2.09%
Global total	1.50%	1.45%	2.51%

Source: Todd M. Johnson and Gina A. Zurlo (eds), *World Christian Database* (Leiden/Boston: Brill), accessed January 2020.

liberal elements, but its prevailing theological character is broadly Evangelical. In recent decades the denomination has been divided about the same issues affecting most mainline denominations but has opted for a more conservative approach.

The next largest Protestant denomination in New Zealand, the Baptist Union, is overwhelmingly Evangelical in theology and often also Charismatic. Churches from the Open Brethren movement (with many linked as the Christian Community Churches of New Zealand) are Evangelical, as are most of the Salvation Army, the Christian Churches, the Congregational Union and the Lutheran Church. Other smaller Evangelical denominations in New Zealand include the Nazarene Church and the Grace Presbyterian Church. The Methodist Church is the smallest and most liberal of New Zealand's mainline denominations; in 2000, many Evangelical ministers and members left the Methodist Church and formed the Wesleyan Methodist Church, which is strongly Evangelical. New Zealand also has a large number of Pentecostal and Charismatic churches. Some are organised into denominations but many are independent.

Institutions and organisations that foster Evangelicalism in New Zealand include the Tertiary Students Christian Fellowship, Tandem Ministries, Scripture Union, Laidlaw College, Carey Baptist College, Bethlehem Training Institute, the New Zealand Christian Network, Rhema Media and many para-church and mission organisations. Some observers feel that Evangelical faith in New Zealand is now more often assumed than clearly articulated, and that in response to changing moods in society and church there has been some drift away from explicit Evangelical identity and doctrine, from a strong emphasis on biblical authority and exposition, and from Evangelical disciplines of Bible reading, prayer, regular church attendance, evangelism and conservative morality. New priorities include personal fulfilment, community, connection with non-Christians and social justice.

Papua New Guinea and the Pacific Islands

Across Papua New Guinea (PNG) and the Pacific Islands, the basic religious context is different from that prevailing in Australasia: instead of the largely non-Indigenous and significantly secularised contexts of Australia and New Zealand, people in PNG and the Pacific Islands still live in largely Indigenous and predominantly Christian societies. The dynamics for Evangelicalism are thus different. Secularism has yet to make deep inroads. In many Pacific Islands, the historic mainstream denominations are deeply intertwined with Indigenous cultural traditions and have become less able to adapt to modernising island societies. But denominational plurality has become established, and new religious movements are rapidly growing, at the expense of the older denominations. New churches include many that are Evangelical, Charismatic or Pentecostal (along with the rapid growth of such movements as Latter-day Saints). The ecclesiastical landscape in most Pacific nations is thus undergoing significant change. Manfred Ernst has related this to the processes of 'globalisation', an ongoing modernising in which every place becomes more connected with the wider world, in which traditional patterns and authority are weakened, in which various dislocations accentuate yearnings for religious certainties, in which older churches are unable to compete, and in which new churches (Evangelical, and especially Pentecostal) are generally thriving. Except in the smallest and most remote of the Pacific Islands, the domination of the historic denominations is steadily eroding.

Papua New Guinea, with 8.78 million people in 2019 and by far the largest Melanesian nation, illustrates a number of aspects of what is happening more widely with Evangelical Christianity in the Pacific region. As in most other Pacific nations, more than 95% of the PNG population identify with a Christian denomination. In the nineteenth century, the first wave of missionaries to PNG – from the London Missionary Society (LMS), Lutherans and Wesleyans – were Evangelical, but in the twentieth century the churches they founded became more liberal. The second wave of missionaries, after the Second World War and mainly in the Highlands, were almost entirely from Evangelical denominations (such as Baptists, Christian Brethren and the Swiss Evangelical Brotherhood) or from interdenominational Evangelical missions (like the South Seas Evangelical Mission, New Tribes Mission and Wycliffe Bible Translators). The churches they established have remained Evangelical. From the 1980s onward, a third wave of missions arrived in PNG, of mainly Pentecostal groups, especially in urban areas. The Evangelical Alliance is a union of 22 Evangelical PNG denominations, including the Baptists. Indigenous denominations such as the Christian Union Church and Tiliba Christian Fellowship are also Evangelical. The Seventh-day Adventist Church is also well established (as it is in many other Pacific nations) and can in its own way be seen as Evangelical. Evangelical agencies working in PNG include the Christian Leaders' Training College (CLTC, an Evangelical theological college), the Mission Aviation Fellowship, Tertiary Students' Christian Fellowship, Campus Crusade, Christian Books Melanesia, Christian Radio Missionary Fellowship and World Vision. As with many other Pacific nations, overseas input into newer PNG churches has been very international, but many influences and personnel have come from Australia, New Zealand and the USA.

As elsewhere in Oceania, mainline churches in PNG are losing members, and Evangelical and Pentecostal churches (especially the latter) are growing. Unlike the older churches, the Evangelical and Pentecostal churches are active in evangelism and recruitment. Their emphasis on spiritual power and experience resonates well with underlying Melanesian spirituality. In an era of urbanisation and social dislocation, the Evangelical emphases on clear belief, the authority of the Bible and on changed lives all have appeal, as does the more lively style of worship. The older denominations are often seen – by those leaving them – as nominal, too bound to cultural tradition and rather dull. For those who have moved from their villages to the large towns, the new churches also provide a new community to belong to – and a community that is chosen, rather than culturally mandated. Such churches also often provide freedom from Melanesian cultural obligations such as bride-price and compensation payments.

Similar religious dynamics to those in PNG are found across other parts of Melanesia: the animistic background, the high percentage of Christian affiliation, nominalism, syncretism, increasing denominational choice, the decline of the historic mainline churches and the growth of Evangelical and (especially) Pentecostal churches. But the particularities of each nation are unique. In the Solomon Islands, for instance, where the Anglican Church is the largest Protestant denomination, 17% of the population (and 50% on the principal island of Malaita) identify with the long-established South Seas Evangelical Church (SSEC), which had its beginnings in the nineteenth century with an interdenominational Evangelical mission to blackbirded Melanesians (forced labourers) in Queensland. The SSEC emphasises Bible teaching and is morally strict. It forbids alcohol, smoking and chewing betel nuts. In the 1970s, it experienced revival. It runs several Bible schools and also sends students to CLTC. Several smaller evangelical and Pentecostal denominations have established a presence in the Solomon Islands, including the Nazarenes, Baptists, Christian Outreach Centre and Assemblies of God.

In Vanuatu, the largest Christian denomination (32%) is the Presbyterian Church of Vanuatu (PCV), pioneered by devout Evangelical missionaries such as John Geddie and John Paton. The twentieth century saw the arrival of some liberal influences but also the impact of conservative Evangelicals from the Presbyterian churches in New Zealand and Australia, such as the Revd J. G. Miller. Talua Theological Training Centre has an Evangelical flavour. The characteristic Melanesian respect for the Bible prevails in the PCV, along with religious and moral conservatism. Evangelical Reformed doctrines of grace and conversion are held, but in the context of a Christian-ised and communal culture, conversion is often seen as moral reformation and a resumption of church involvement. Evangelical elements in Vanuatu can also be found in some other denominations and through the influence of such para-church groups as the Gud Nius Yunivesiti Felosip, Cru Vanuatu and Youth With A Mission (YWAM).

In the French (and mainly Catholic) territory of New Caledonia, Melanesians are now less than 40% of the population. Many French settlers are secular. The principal Protestant church – the Église Protestante de Kanaky Nouvelle-Calédonie (EPKNC) – had its beginnings with the LMS and later French missionaries. Its name reflects the continental sense of 'Protestant' and 'Reformed', but it is not Evangelical in any biblicist or conversionist sense. Largely Melanesian, the EPKNC is culturally traditional and understandably drawn toward both indigenisation and liberation theology. As elsewhere, newer independent, Charismatic and Pentecostal churches – many linked with the Conseil Chrétien – are usually more focused on Bible teaching, evangelism and contemporary worship songs.

Fiji is different again, with its sizeable Indian (and mainly Hindu) minority. The dominant church in Fiji is the Methodist Church, composed primarily of Indigenous Fijians, which reflects some fusion of Christian faith and traditional culture. It is also biblically conservative and contains numerous Evangelicals. The Methodist Church has an Indian division, which includes many who are Evangelical. A wide range of smaller Protestant denominations, many of them Evangelical or Pentecostal, is also present. These include the Fiji Gospel Churches (Brethren), Fiji Bible Church, Baptists, Nazarene Church, Salvation Army, South Pacific Evangelical Fellowship and Covenant Evangelical Church, along with Pentecostal churches such as the Christian Mission Fellowship, All Nations Christian Fellowship, Kingdom Ambassadors, Assemblies of God (AOG), Apostolic churches and New Life. The College of Theology and Evangelism Fiji serves Evangelical churches regionally. The AOG's South Pacific Bible College likewise caters to students from Fiji and beyond.

In the Polynesian context, Sāmoa and Tonga exemplify similar patterns. Ninety-eight per cent of Sāmoans profess themselves Christian. The dominant Christian Congregational Church of Sāmoa (CCCS/EFKS) is a key presence in Sāmoan villages, and its life and practice is closely interwoven with *fa'a Sāmoa*, traditional Sāmoan culture. Overall, the EFKS is theologically and morally conservative. Worship is solemn and reverent. As in other Pacific societies where almost everyone identifies as Christian, EFKS churches are very active (with programmes for all age groups) but are not obviously evangelistic. Preaching emphasises Christian living and service rather than conversion. The EFKS is losing members to newer churches. Fairly or otherwise, such leavers often see the EFKS as too subject to culture and tradition, a bit old-fashioned and insufficiently focused on the gospel. The competitive system of giving can be a financial burden for some, and the income of ministers is sometimes critiqued. New Evangelical, Charismatic and Pentecostal churches are flourishing in Sāmoa and include Sāmoa Evangelism, Bible Study Fellowship, Open Brethren, Christian Community Church, the Peace Chapel, Worship Centre, Assemblies of God, Elim and New Life. In varying degrees, such churches are biblicist, evangelistic, innovative, less connected with Sāmoan cultural obligations and exuberant in their worship. Most embrace globalised contemporary Christian music. Supporting organisations and institutions include Youth for Christ, Every Home for Christ, South Pacific Nazarene Theological College, Graceland Broadcasting Network, Rhema Bible College and YWAM. In Sāmoa, as in other Polynesian nations, the historic denominations regard the newer churches with much suspicion and argue that they are destroying the unity of Sāmoan communities and families.

In Tonga almost everyone attends church, and basic Christian beliefs and values are deeply embedded in Tongan culture. Thirty-five per cent of Tongans are affiliated with the largest Methodist denomination, the Free Wesleyan Church (FWC). Its official doctrines reflect historic Evangelical Wesleyanism. FWC leadership is theologically mixed, and the FWC maintains close links with its (more liberal) sister denominations in Australasia. At the congregational level, however, lay people remain pervasively conservative in relation to the Bible. Evangelical influences in Tonga include the Tokaikolo Fellowship, Scripture Union and Navigators.

Conclusion

Across Oceania, mainline churches founded through Evangelical mission often retain elements of their Evangelical DNA but have also become significantly shaped by cultural and ecclesiastical traditionalism, and in some places by an element of theological liberalism. In a more globalised world, most parts of Oceania have also seen the emergence of many new and culturally adaptive churches and organisations exhibiting key features of Evangelical Christianity, such as strong emphases on the authority and use of the Bible, evangelistic zeal, and conversion and spiritual experience; some of these movements would describe themselves as 'Evangelical', while others would primarily see themselves as Charismatic or Pentecostal. Such movements are significantly changing the face of Pacific Christianity. In Oceania's two more-Westernised and secularised societies, Australia and New Zealand, Evangelical Christianity remains a significant presence within some mainline denominations as well as in many smaller denominations, independent churches and Pentecostal denominations. In those two countries, the main challenge to Evangelicalism is not cultural traditionalism but the new winds of thought that are affecting all Western societies.

Bibliography

Ernst, Manfred (ed.), *Globalization and the Re-shaping of Christianity in the Pacific Islands* (Suva: Pacific Theological College, 2006).

Ernst, Manfred, *Winds of Change: Rapidly Growing Religious Groups in the Pacific Islands* (Suva: Pacific Conference of Churches, 1994).

Garrett, John, *Where Nets Were Cast: Christianity in Oceania since World War II* (Suva: Institute of Pacific Studies, 1997).

Lange, Stuart M., *A Rising Tide: Evangelical Christianity in New Zealand, 1930–1965* (Dunedin: Otago University Press, 2013).

Piggin, Stuart and Robert D. Linder, *Attending to the National Soul: Evangelical Christians in Australian History, 1914–2014* (Melbourne: Monash University Publishing, 2019).

Pentecostals/Charismatics

Kevin Hovey

This essay on Pentecostals and Charismatics within Christianity in Oceania immediately subdivides into two very different situations: the highly secularised Western nations of Australia and New Zealand, compared with the 21 Pacific Island nations comprising the balance of Oceania, sub-grouped as Melanesia, Micronesia and Polynesia. For the majority Caucasian populations of Australia and New Zealand, the initial outpouring of the Holy Spirit was often in response to the spiritual hunger of existing Christians seeking a deeper experience of God. By contrast, the churches and movements in the Pacific Island nations typically were the result of expatriate missionaries, and the local workers they trained, preaching a Pentecostal message of salvation and a Holy Spirit-empowered life to people who had an awareness of the spirit world.

In the 110 years of their history in Oceania, the Pentecostal and Charismatic churches, leaders and members have been willing to pay a price to see the growth of what they have considered to be 'the kingdom of God' rather than just their denominations. To them it was simply the cost of discipleship, as the Lordship of Christ, lived in the power of the Holy Spirit, has been challenged in many places in Oceania. Two quotations from pastors in Papua New Guinea will illustrate the level of commitment that underlies the growth of these movements across Oceania.

First, as told to me by Johannes: 'After the gang beat me unconscious for the third time, because I would not stop preaching, I slowly regained consciousness. Then it dawned on me: "Oh, they didn't kill me. That's good; I can keep preaching."'

And then, in dialogue with Pedro: 'The gang told me not to come to my wife's village on Sunday to conduct the service in the church I'd planted. They said that if I come, they will kill me.' 'What do you plan to do?' I asked with concern. The answer was given without hesitation: 'I've decided not to take my wife and children to church when I go on Sunday.'

Through such costly commitment, the Pentecostal and Charismatic churches in Oceania have grown.

Beginnings

The early Pentecostal movement in the majority-Caucasian populations of Australia and New Zealand began in the early 1900s, in response to a widespread spiritual hunger being experienced among earnest Christians. This was frequently enhanced by their own study of the scriptures regarding the Holy Spirit or news of the outpouring of the Holy Spirit in other countries. Sarah Lancaster, seen as the primary person of influence in the initial proliferation of the Pentecostal message in Australia, is one such person, but representative of many others.

For the islands of the Pacific, however, the missionary activity of Pentecostal members and movements from Western nations was a highly significant factor. Albert (Australian) and Lou (American) Page were the first Pentecostal missionaries in the islands of Oceania, starting ministry in Fiji in 1913. This phenomenon was extended in a more organised way in 1926, when Assemblies of God USA (AGUSA) missionaries were sent to American Sāmoa.

Some of these Pentecostal missionaries worked in remote locations where the gospel was previously unknown, such as the Assemblies of God Australia (AGA) missionaries who began ministry in Papua New Guinea (PNG) in 1948, or the other Pentecostal movements (International Church of the Foursquare Gospel and Apostolic Church Australia, in particular) who subsequently began ministry in PNG in the decade after the Second World War. These can be described as 'first wave' Pentecostal missions. Living close to village communities in rural areas and ministering in languages other than English, they were sensitised to community needs. This led to their involvement in a number of programmes of a development nature: literacy for Bible study, which led to the development of educational programmes; medical ministry, which led to health benefits; and trading, which both served the remote communities and limited the impact of unscrupulous traders who took advantage of the local people. However, other Pentecostal missionaries found themselves in areas where other denominations had existing churches. This brought another set of dynamics, such as inter-denominational competition – and tribal allegiances that sometimes exploited it.

Pentecostals and Charismatics in Oceania, 1970

Region	Total population	Christian population	Pentecostal/ Charismatic population	% of region Pentecostal/ Charismatic	% of Christians Pentecostal/ Charismatic
Oceania	19,718,000	18,250,000	289,000	1.5%	1.6%
Australia/New Zealand	15,661,000	14,633,000	130,000	0.8%	0.9%
Melanesia	3,399,000	2,978,000	140,000	4.1%	4.7%
Micronesia	248,000	237,000	7,600	3.1%	3.2%
Polynesia	410,000	402,000	10,900	2.7%	2.7%
Global total	3,700,578,000	1,229,309,000	57,637,000	1.6%	4.7%

Source: Todd M. Johnson and Gina A. Zurlo (eds), *World Christian Database* (Leiden/Boston: Brill), accessed January 2020.

One factor common to both situations described here is the way the missionaries focused on planting churches and training leaders for those churches, whether formally or informally. This has resulted in large, strong Indigenous Pentecostal movements, with the Assemblies of God Papua New Guinea being the largest Pentecostal movement in all of Oceania. Approximately 500,000 congregants gather in its more than 2,000 congregations each weekend.

Whether first contact or secondary contact, the dynamics of the spread of Pentecostalism in the Pacific Island nations were quite different from those in the Christian-background nations of Australia and New Zealand. Churches and movements in the Pacific Island nations were predominantly the result of the missionaries and the local workers they trained preaching a Pentecostal message of salvation and a Holy Spirit-empowered life to people who had an awareness of the spirit world. This knowledge typically included a deep-seated dread of the spirit world as they knew it and the willingness to consider a message that provided answers to that dread.

Impact amidst Diversity

The Pentecostal expression of Christianity in PNG challenges description and is also representative of Pentecostal and Charismatic ministry in other parts of Oceania. By 1980, more than 20 different Pentecostal denominations could be found in PNG. The first to arrive were the Assemblies of God in 1948, followed by the Apostolic Church and the International Church of the Foursquare Gospel in the 1950s. Subsequently, other movements such as Faith Mission, CRC International, Revival Centres of PNG and United Pentecostal Assemblies of PNG have established themselves.

Pentecostal churches generally represent a flexible approach to ministry that can result in denominational splits and amalgamations, allowing for the movement of workers or even congregations between one denomination and another. To an outsider, this 'fluidity' often looks like instability.

Pentecostals and Charismatics in Oceania, 2020

Region	Total population	Christian population	Pentecostal/ Charismatic population	% of region Pentecostal/ Charismatic	% of Christians Pentecostal/ Charismatic
Oceania	42,384,000	27,606,000	4,536,000	10.7%	16.4%
Australia/New Zealand	30,233,000	16,363,000	1,970,000	6.5%	12.0%
Melanesia	10,909,000	10,069,000	2,384,000	21.9%	23.7%
Micronesia	541,000	501,000	82,100	15.2%	16.4%
Polynesia	701,000	673,000	99,600	14.2%	14.8%
Global total	7,795,482,000	2,518,834,000	644,260,000	8.3%	25.6%

Source: Todd M. Johnson and Gina A. Zurlo (eds), *World Christian Database* (Leiden/Boston: Brill), accessed January 2020.

Insiders, however, see it differently. They see leadership initiative and action as important. Inflexibility is thought to stifle the work of the Holy Spirit, and so allowing God to dynamically interact with leaders and members in a non-institutional way is seen as positive. Fluidity is then seen as a price worth paying in order to achieve these other goals. At the same time, although the majority of Pentecostal and Charismatic churches hold to similar theologies on core issues, some depart from the general consensus on key points of doctrine while still understanding themselves to be Pentecostals.

Australia and New Zealand currently have a slightly different mix of Pentecostal and Charismatic churches, but they share many similarities with the churches in the rest of Oceania, especially with respect to their formation. Using the Australian descriptors, the most prominent movements are the Australian Christian Churches, formerly Assemblies of God of Australia; Foursquare Gospel Church; Acts Global Church, formerly Apostolic Church of Australia; C3 Church; CRC International; International Network of Churches, formerly Christian Outreach Centre; Life Church International; Potters House; and International Pentecostal Holiness Church.

Irrespective of the contrasting origins of the various Pentecostal and Charismatic movements in Oceania, a common factor is the passion they exhibit to see people come into a living experience with Christ – and to report that information. This has produced a rate of growth well above that of any comparable movement. As a result, Pentecostal churches have come to exert increasing influence in many situations across Oceania.

The most obvious expression of this in the 2018–19 period was the appointment, and then election, of Scott Morrison, an unapologetic member of a Pentecostal church, as prime minister of Australia. However, at least 15 years prior to that, the secular media in Australia – which tend to be both sceptical and critical of Christians and Christianity – had started to notice an unexpected phenomenon. Church life, which they had assumed was in its death throes (or at least predominantly for old people), was

Changes in Pentecostals/Charismatics in Oceania, 1970–2020, growth rate, % per year

Region	Total population	Christian population	Pentecostals/Charismatic population
Oceania	1.54%	0.83%	5.66%
Australia/New Zealand	1.32%	0.22%	5.58%
Melanesia	2.36%	2.47%	5.83%
Micronesia	1.57%	1.51%	4.87%
Polynesia	1.08%	1.04%	4.52%
Global total	1.50%	1.45%	4.95%

Source: Todd M. Johnson and Gina A. Zurlo (eds), *World Christian Database* (Leiden/Boston: Brill), accessed January 2020.

actually growing strongly in some quarters. To their surprise, they found large congregations full of enthusiastic and committed young people. They discovered that the answer to their puzzlement was tied in with the term 'Pentecostal', which many journalists had not heard before. Similarly, journalists were surprised in 2002 when John Howard, then Australia's prime minister, chose to officially open Hillsong Church's new auditorium in Sydney rather than rush to Canberra to attend to affairs of state just a week after many Australians were killed in a bombing in Bali, Indonesia. Many examples could be given as well from other countries in Oceania, where Pentecostal churches and movements similarly have become large and influential.

Gifts of the Holy Spirit

Until the surge in growth in Pentecostal churches in Australia and New Zealand in the 1970s and 1980s, it was common, almost expected, that Sunday morning services would include the public use of the gifts of prophecy and tongues and interpretation, as outlined in 1 Corinthians 12. Both the congregation and those in leadership took the opportunity to exercise these gifts at appropriate times in the services. However, as churches have grown, with many Pentecostal churches now having more than 500 in attendance at any one service, the use of these gifts has tended to be redirected. It is now more typical to see the gift of prophecy or word of knowledge operate from the platform by the pastoral team or ministry guests, or else in small-group environments.

Regarding gifts of the Spirit used in PNG, in my 31 years of ministry there I rarely saw or heard of operation of the gifts of tongues and interpretation in public environments. In a nation of 8.5 million people that has over 800 local languages, a person speaking in an unknown language would have limited impact. Words of prophecy and words of knowledge were reasonably rare. However, the word of wisdom was often seen in life generally, as Christian leaders brought God's wisdom into situations around them, both inside and outside the church. This had significant impact in their communal societies, which depended on wisdom for orderly living, especially in the new situations the communities were facing as they were becoming part of the modern world.

Healing is another significant feature of Pentecostal church life. In the past 110 years, some people in Pentecostal and Charismatic circles have decided to trust only God for their healing rather than to seek treatment made available through medical science. However, the majority of Pentecostal and Charismatic Christians in Oceania would agree that, first of all, God provided the natural healing that our bodies are so well equipped for, and, additionally, God has provided the insights of medical science to assist with healing. They would similarly agree that only God can be the source of supernatural healing (Exodus 4: 7). In the New Testament, healing is expressed through laying hands on the sick (Mark 16: 18), gifts of healing (1 Corinthians 12: 9) and anointing with oil and prayer by the church elders (James 5: 14).

Nevertheless, the end result of the contrasting Western and animistic worldviews from which people of Oceania approach healing could be described using two comparative statements. 'Fewer miracles, more impact' could be used in relation to those of Western backgrounds. Typically, such people need assistance to get past their secular worldview in order to reach out to God in faith for supernatural healing. However, when a healing does take place for them, it results in significant impact, as they see evidence of God at work right within their own situation. By contrast, for those coming from spirit world-oriented animistic backgrounds, miracles from the supernatural have been a familiar part of life, through a range of spirit-world practitioners. For them, reaching out to a supernatural God in faith for healing does not seem strange. However, 'more miracles, less impact' would be the descriptor in such situations, as the impact from the actual healing would need additional follow-up to help the person being prayed for to understand the difference in healing from God compared with their previously known spirit-world sources. When this follow-up is not implemented effectively, 'less impact' is the result, as God is relegated to the role of 'just another power source'.

Melanesian Charismatic Case Study

An illuminating case study revealing both the impact and the complexity of Charismatic Christianity in Melanesia features a movement in the Solomon Islands that bridged to PNG. As documented by Alison Griffiths in *Fire in the Islands! The Acts of the Holy Spirit in the Solomons* (Wheaton: H. Shaw Publishers, 1977), a Holy Spirit renewal movement occurred within the South Seas Evangelical Church in the Solomon Islands (SSECSI) in the early 1970s. Because SSECSI leaders had connections with PNG, the Evangelical Alliance of PNG (EAPNG), the umbrella organisation of which many Evangelical and Pentecostal denominations were members, made the courageous decision to invite SSECSI to send some of their leaders to tour EAPNG member churches. As they toured, they shared their experiences and advocated that others seek the same for themselves. Among the Pentecostal movements, the result of their visit was mostly mutual encouragement. In the Evangelical churches, on the other hand, it opened a new dimension. Here were people who had believed and acted like them in the past, but who were now advocating a new experience of the Holy Spirit. The result was a spiritual transformation in many locations, bringing new dimensions to church life. However, these new experiences were not shaped by prior Pentecostal teaching or by having access to that teaching as it developed. This is an important factor in the story, because in PNG there was limited knowledge of the Old Testament at that stage, and also limited knowledge of the New Testament teaching on the Holy Spirit due to their Evangelical background. The complete Old Testament was not released in the most readily understood PNG national language, Neo-Melanesian Pidgin, until 1989, while most local-language translations of the Bible had included only the New Testament. This meant that the breadth of God's antipathy to other gods and spirit-world beliefs and practices as documented in the Old Testament was not well understood. By contrast, as Melanesians, the local people had extensive knowledge relating to the operation of traditional spirits, especially the way spirits and supernatural powers could be manipulated by rituals.

Furthermore, there was an underlying belief in cargoism, the possibility of producing imported material goods by using newly revealed rituals. When these were fully developed, they became new religious movements known as cargo cults. This imbalance in available knowledge led to some harmful extremes, including the ritual killing of a Christian by the leader of one of these new cults and institutionalised immoral sexual practices in another church. In each case the members and leaders believed that these practices were part of their new cargo cult rituals. Later, corrective teaching was introduced by church leaders and missionaries, and EAPNG conducted a one-week 'Seminar on Revivals' for pastors and missionaries. A booklet of the teaching sessions was subsequently published as *Tok Welkam long Holi Spirit* ('Welcome, Holy Spirit'), which went through a number of printings. Revival movements that have been guided well, both internally and externally, have brought a new and positive dimension to Charismatic Christianity in Melanesia. When not guided well, their long-term fruitfulness has been limited.

Currently, it is quite common to see short-term mission teams and ministries from affluent nations in Oceania conducting ministry in island nations such as PNG, Fiji or Vanuatu. The openness yet complexity of the situation as illustrated in the above case study needs to be understood by those engaging in such ministries. Otherwise, while they aim to see 'more miracles and more impact', there can sometimes be unintended negative consequences.

As the Charismatic movement started to impact many Evangelical and mainline churches in the Western nations of Australia and New Zealand, the Pentecostals learned some very important things from its development. The most important – and, at the same time, the most difficult to learn – was that Pentecostals themselves do not hold any patent on the

Holy Spirit, or any exclusive blueprint for the operation of the Holy Spirit. It appeared that God was working in a new way through the Charismatic experience of individuals, churches and movements, and Pentecostals had to learn to understand and appreciate that.

While Charismatic influence seems to have operated in waves over the years, their long-term positive influence has been significant. During the late twentieth and early twenty-first centuries, individual Charismatic Christians and leaders and churches who have held their ground and pointed others to an experience of the Holy Spirit have exercised significant influence. In addition, visionary leaders in Australia and New Zealand created ministries especially to serve the Charismatic movement, with a Bible college in each nation specifically founded for this purpose, namely Tabor College in Australia and Faith Bible College in New Zealand.

The long-term impact of the Charismatic movement within the Roman Catholic Church in Oceania is to be applauded, due to the increase in spiritual fervour that have influenced both laity and clergy. Some Roman Catholic clergy have stimulated and allowed for Charismatic influence among their parishioners, even though they have not had a Charismatic experience themselves. Decisions of the Second Vatican Council (1962–5) facilitated the emergence of the Charismatic movement within the Catholic Church. Catholics were allowed to access the Bible in their own languages and were also allowed to have contact with Christians of other backgrounds. These two policy changes introduced a 'chicken and egg' process – developing hunger and openness for spiritual growth while simultaneously providing the opportunity to find out about the Charismatic experience from others around them.

Immigration in Australia and New Zealand

In 1901, the Australian government implemented its 'White Australia' policy. It allowed for immigration of people from overseas, but only people who were designated 'white' by race and ethnicity. This opened the door for extensive British immigration and also, after the Second World War, for immigration from countries like Italy and eastern European nations. This policy was overturned by legislation in 1966. However, this White Australia policy resulted in a melting-pot model of migrant integration, as migrants were expected to fully integrate by speaking English and becoming part of Australian culture.

This policy had an interesting impact on AGA that has not always been recognised. Because that melting-pot integration model was part of Australian culture, it was inadvertently and invisibly applied to the church. As such, many Australian Christians assumed that because church attendance was not restricted by race or creed, as long as churches had a policy of welcoming strangers, there was no need to establish churches specifically for these new migrants, serving them in their own languages and cultures. Seeing this as an opportunity being missed, AGUSA sent Italian-speaking missionaries to Australia to establish Italian-language churches to take advantage of the evangelistic opportunity of this migration phenomenon.

When the White Australia policy was changed, migrants from other nations, especially in Asia and the Pacific, were able to migrate to Australia. However, the 'open door but no external initiative' approach of the former era continued in most churches. Although Vietnamese boat people began arriving in Australia in the late 1970s, the first intentional AGA attempt to plant a Vietnamese-language church to minister to them in their own cultural context was not until 1994, in Brisbane. When migrants who have adapted to Australian society attend and get involved in AGA churches, this is seen as a justification of the informal, culturally informed approach, with the term 'multicultural' being the self-definition applied by those churches. Despite the multi-ethnic nature of the attendees, however, the actual operation of the church often remains monocultural. This is an important distinction.

By contrast, the response of migrants from nations with large Christian populations, such as Pacific Island nations, has been to start their own ethnically based churches, often operating in their home languages. Consequently, scattered across Australia's state capital cities are many Fijian, Tongan, Sāmoan and Korean churches, to mention just a few. Until recently, many of these churches, although becoming registered as AGA churches, have not had significant interaction with AGA as a movement.

The New Zealand experience with immigration, on the other hand, has been quite different. The Treaty of Waitangi between the original British colonial settlers and the Māori peoples in 1840 set the stage for a greater awareness of cultural differences in New Zealand as a nation. Furthermore, not burdened with anything like the White Australia policy, New Zealand allowed immigration from many other countries, particularly Pacific Island nations. This has allowed New Zealand as a nation, including Pentecostal churches within New Zealand, to have a 'mosaic' approach to cultural diversity. Individual culture groups of migrants are allowed more freedom and identity. One result has been that the Sāmoan Assemblies of God-oriented churches were able to operate as a movement within a movement for many years, eventually becoming an autonomous Assemblies of God movement operating outside the Assemblies of God New Zealand.

Ongoing Opportunities and Challenges

Reference has already been made to the size and strength of the Pentecostal and Charismatic movements in Oceania. As such, responsibility rests on their shoulders to engage with some of the challenging ministry situations in their contexts. One of these is ministry to the First Peoples of Australia and New Zealand, where issues of recognition, land, identity and spirituality require significant levels of knowledge and sensitivity. Another is ministry to major immigrant communities now living in the nations of Oceania, such as Indians in Fiji, Chinese traders in Pacific nations, or migrants of other religious backgrounds in Australia and New Zealand.

Pentecostal churches often use church structures that afford significant levels of church autonomy. When used well, this can provide focused and well informed ministry in their local situations, along with freedom for the leaders to seek God for vision and strategy for that context. However, when autonomy is unmitigated, without accountability to the overall Christian community, it can lead to problems as liberty becomes licence.

Another strength–weakness continuum is worth noting, namely the active, sometimes almost hyperactive, approach of Pentecostals. This can be summed up by the cliché 'implementation is the Pentecostal feasibility study'. The strategic flexibility implied in this statement is a great strength, when guided by counsel and caution. On many occasions, however, counsel and caution have been disregarded as statements indicating a lack of faith. This has led to some unwise actions, resulting in unnecessary challenges for churches and ministries.

Since the early days of Pentecostal movements, cross-cultural international missions have been a hallmark. As time went on, these fledgling endeavours were enhanced by cultural understanding of how best to facilitate ministry in each particular context. This resonated well with Pentecostal churches in the past and resulted in the development of strong movements in numerous nations in Oceania and beyond. However, the modern situation has brought new challenges. The ability to travel easily, to transfer funds effortlessly and to communicate internationally at little cost has meant that often things are carried out in the name of missions that are not consistent with the original ideals. When combined with a 'can do' attitude, this can result in many other aspects of service that Pentecostals see as significant, 'just because we can'. This is a trend that calls for review, especially when 30% of the world's population do not have culturally appropriate access to the gospel.

Due to the 'redemption and lift' that occurs as people come to a dynamic conversion experience and are discipled well in a Pentecostal or Charismatic church, over time they find themselves better off materially than they were, or even than their contemporaries currently are. Knowing how to use their newfound resources for their own and their family's wellbeing, as well as for the sake of the kingdom of God, is an ongoing challenge. However, it is appropriate to observe that Pentecostals and Charismatics seem better able to handle this than do others, even though it remains a challenge. This is because, first of all, God's blessing in this way is not such a surprise to them and, second, they recognise the blessing as a gift from God that they hold in trust.

Conclusion

With such diversity as represented in the 23 nations of Oceania, this essay has used a series of cameos, themes and individual stories to give a picture of Pentecostal and Charismatic Christianity in the region. Similar cameos could be drawn from the experiences of Pentecostals and Charismatics in many other parts of Oceania. When writing, as a Pentecostal, a compressed account of the people and events of Pentecostal and Charismatic Christianity in Oceania, there is an inherent danger. It can seem that human beings are in focus rather than the person and work of the Holy Spirit, by whose design and enabling the events occurred. From a Pentecostal perspective, we can conclude that by the design and enabling of the Holy Spirit, the Pentecostal and Charismatic movement in Oceania has grown in numbers and in influence, playing its part in fulfilling God's purposes in Oceania.

Bibliography

Austin, Denise, Jacqueline Grey and Paul W. Lewis, *Asia Pacific Pentecostalism* (Leiden: Brill, 2019).

Chant, Barry, *Heart of Fire: The Story of Australian Pentecostalism*, 2nd edn (Unley Park: House of Tabor, 1984).

Forbes, George, *A Church on Fire: The Story of the Assemblies of God of Papua New Guinea* (Mitcham: Mission Mobilisers International, 2001).

Hovey, Kevin G., *Before All Else Fails, Read the Instructions: A Manual for Cross Cultural Christians*, 2nd edn (Brisbane: Harvest Publications, 1995).

Whiteman, Darrell L., 'Melanesian Religions: An Overview', in Ennio Mantovani (ed.), *An Introduction to Melanesian Religions*, Point Series No. 6 (Goroka: Melanesian Institute, 1984), 87–121.

Pacific Conference of Churches

Feleterika Nokise

A distinctive feature of church life in this region has been the Pacific Conference of Churches, which for the past 60 years has been the focus of ecumenical collaboration among the widely scattered Protestant churches of the Pacific Islands. Two inter-related developments, both occurring during the post-Second World War period, were to have a profound impact on the Protestant churches' response to the emerging challenge of ecumenism in the Pacific. First, the establishment of the World Council of Churches (WCC) in 1948 introduced a new dimension to the theological thinking of the Pacific churches. Given the fact that the mainline churches within the Reformed tradition all joined this new global ecclesiastical body, churches in the Pacific naturally became part of this exciting new spiritual venture. And although it was not until 1961 that the Pacific churches were to take concrete action to reflect this new spirit of ecumenical cooperation and partnership, the framework and content of their theological thinking had already been broadened by the advent of the ecumenical movement.

The second key development was the attainment by Sāmoa of independence in 1962. This had a domino effect on other island countries that were trying to shake off the shackles of colonialism. It was therefore not an accident that the Protestant churches of the Pacific had their first collective encounter with ecumenism at the beginning of the 1960s. This period was heralded by the WCC as 'the age of change'. The fact that a number of island churches gathered for the first time in Sāmoa in 1961 could be interpreted as a direct consequence of the winds of change that were sweeping through the world and the universal church at the time. This period was a defining moment for the Pacific, not only on the ecclesiastical front, but also in the political arena.

In retrospect, the Pacific region responded to the tides of change that emanated from global organisations such as the United Nations and from the WCC. This was an acknowledgement by Pacific leaders that they were not unaffected by global changes. On the one hand, it signalled a tacit acceptance on their part that, as a region, they had become a part of the global family. On the other hand, the regional embrace of ecumenism was a clear message from the churches that they were prepared to work together toward visible expressions of the unity they possessed as God's gift to the church. Therefore, by design rather than by coincidence, the leaders and representatives of Protestant churches who attended the inaugural ecumenical gathering in Sāmoa discovered with much excitement the aura of a new spirituality once again invading their shores.

Although the Pacific churches are latecomers in terms of active participation in this fellowship of churches, they are not excluded from being part of what happened prior to 1961. This history is part and parcel of Pacific churches' identity as carriers of ecumenism. The willingness of its church leaders to have their churches join the ecumenical movement during the 1960s and the 1970s was made possible by an awareness that such a history provided the impetus to be involved, as well as the platform to declare their interest in such a quest.

Founding of the Pacific Conference of Churches

The inaugural ecumenical meeting of Pacific churches at Malua in 1961 was their first-ever collective response to issues affecting their life and work. That it was also a response to the trend encouraged by the WCC and the International Missionary Council after the 1948 WCC Amsterdam Assembly for churches to organise into regional bodies does not in any way deny the uniqueness and merit of the Pacific ecumenical movement. This latter point is aptly summed up by one of the founding fathers of ecumenism in the Pacific, the late Revd Dr Sione 'Amanaki Havea: 'This was the first ecumenical step taken for Christian churches and mission to break through theological, social and national levels which had existed in the Pacific region for more than 150 years.... The Malua Conference of 1961 was the first of its kind held predominantly for the Pacific churches.' The Solomon Islander the Revd Leslie Boseto, long-time champion of 'grassroots ecumenism' in the Pacific, expressed a similar sentiment: 'That conference [Malua in 1961] was the foundation stone of ecumenism for the Indigenous people of our Pacific countries.'

Given the novelty of the Malua gathering and the excitement it generated, ideals and faith statements dominated the countless resolutions it passed. Underpinning all the discussions and decisions was the recognition of one overarching theme: 'To Stay Together, To Grow Together, To Do Mission Together'. This, however, posed a major challenge for the Pacific churches in terms of what was needed to portray a visible unity in their relationship. How could unity be realised in a concrete form within the diversity of the churches? It is a tribute to the wisdom of the Pacific ecumenical pioneers that they perceived the only possible solution in terms of the churches themselves actually doing something together. This realisation provided the impetus for the plans to establish two regional organisations.

The births of the Pacific Conference of Churches (whose inaugural Assembly was held in May 1966 at Lifou, New Caledonia) and the Pacific Theological College (formally established in Suva, Fiji, in 1966 after the Lifou Assembly, with its first intake of students in 1968) were the first fruits of the 1961 meeting. These developments heralded the formal beginning of ecumenical activities in the Pacific region. The two institutions were the physical manifestation of the Pacific church leaders' faith in their capacity to pursue and promote ecumenism. In the years that followed, these two regional ecumenical organisations became the flag bearers of the Pacific churches in their search for unity. With the WCC closely mentoring and supporting development programmes and projects based on issues it had identified, and urging the churches to promote them, and with overseas church partners and donors rallying to the call for much-needed resources and general assistance, these two organisations blossomed.

The Flourishing of Ecumenism

The period from 1961 to 1990 is generally acknowledged as the booming era of ecumenical activities among Pacific Protestant churches. Their efforts were all the more creditable in view of the kinds of issues these churches had to address. The most notable of these were nuclear testing (by the French in French Polynesia and the Americans in Micronesia) and struggles for political and church autonomy. Reasserting who they were as Pacific peoples at both the local and regional levels were challenges not for the fainthearted. From a theological perspective, the future of their spiritual heritage and faith pilgrimage was on the line.

The determination of Pacific churches to meet these challenges is to be applauded. It was no small feat. It was the manner in which they did this that suggested that perhaps the spirit of ecumenism was already embedded in their cultural understanding and practices of communal living, and this enabled ecumenism to thrive in its infancy years. Regional gatherings afforded opportunities for the churches to discover that each was already blessed with the essential ingredients of what ecumenical cooperation required.

There was unprecedented support from all the member churches of the Pacific Conference of Churches (PCC). Financial obligations in the form of annual contributions or subscriptions were not only met but were given on time. Leaders – meaning presidents, bishops, moderators and chairmen of the churches – made efforts to attend meetings. Churches sent the appropriate personnel to numerous regional workshops and consultations offered by the PCC. Students from almost all the churches were sent annually to study together at their regional ecumenical theological college, the Pacific Theological College (PTC) in Fiji.

Newly emerging church scholars with higher degrees were seconded by the churches for teaching responsibilities at PTC. Movements, encounters and dialogue among people of different ecclesiastical traditions and cultural heritages intensified, resulting in the gaining of new perspectives, awareness, information and knowledge and a healthy appreciation of each other's uniqueness and limitations. Ecumenism was in a healthy state. All these interactions and inter-relationships had the overall effect of fostering and nurturing the need to support, share and journey together as churches. More importantly, the churches began to listen to each other's concerns and uphold the importance of seeking to discern together what 'unity in diversity' or 'diversity in unity' meant.

Of the many factors contributing to the emerging spirit of optimism that characterised the mood and activities of these first few decades of Pacific ecumenism, perhaps the most profound was the presence of leaders who were visionary and committed to the search for unity: leaders like the Revd Dr Sione 'Amanaki Havea from the Free Wesleyan Church of Tonga; the Revd Setareki Tuilovoni from the Methodist Church of Fiji; the Revd Vavae Toma from the Congregational Christian Church of Sāmoa; Bishop Leonard Alufurai from the Anglican Church in the Solomon Islands; Bishop Patelesio Finau from the Catholic Diocese of Tonga; Bishop Leslie Boseto from the United Church of the Solomon Islands; the Revd Lopeti Taufa from the Free Wesleyan Church of Tonga; Bishop Jabez Bryce from the Anglican Diocese of Polynesia; and many others. There were also outstanding women who represented not only the women but the rank and file of the lay people: Mrs Fetaui Mata'afa from Sāmoa and Mrs Lorine Tevi from Fiji, to mention but two. In the ensuing years, young and energetic ministers of the churches were appointed to strategic positions in the PCC secretariat, the PTC faculty and, from the mid-1970s, the South Pacific Association of Theological Schools (SPATS).

The emergence of new ecumenical leaders of our churches over the years is a direct result of two parallel developments: first, increasing numbers of church workers attending regional workshops, consultations and meetings under the auspices and leadership of the PCC; and secondly, large numbers of ministers who studied and graduated from PTC.

Ecumenism under Threat

These developments, however, belie an emerging problem that threatened to derail the vision of cooperation among the churches. The threat was perceived primarily on two levels. First, despite efforts by the three ecumenical regional organisations to deliver their respective mandates, the support and cooperation of the churches began to decline from the mid-1990s. Financial commitment was found wanting from many

churches. Fewer church leaders attended regional meetings and consultations. At times, the wrong people were sent to represent the churches.
Fewer students were sent to study at PTC. Perhaps the mandates for the
ecumenical organisations had become outdated. Perhaps the needs of the
churches were not acknowledged in the programmes and projects that
were pursued.

Secondly, the organisations functioned as autonomous entities, with
little evidence of concrete cooperation among them in relation to programmes and sharing of resources. The member churches were finding it
increasingly difficult to financially support and maintain these organisations given their own weak economies and the demands of their own local
church needs. It came as no surprise, therefore, that when the churches
entered the twenty-first century the call for a renewed form of cooperation
among the churches began to gain momentum.

Pacific churches had a long-standing expectation that the Pacific Conference of Churches, the Pacific Theological College and the South Pacific
Association of Theological Schools, despite their different mandates,
would achieve some form of cooperation. Their functional purposes seem
to complement each other. They serve basically the same clientele. Their
administrative headquarters are all located in Suva, Fiji. Regrettably,
however, cooperation was never formalised. What emerged was a kind of
ad hoc arrangement whereby there was cross-representation of leaders on
the respective decision-making bodies of these organisations.

These councils and executives are policy-making bodies devoid of
any effectiveness insofar as programmatic planning is concerned. The
possibility of a common strategy, action and usage of resources never
materialised. The possibility of an integrated and interactive approach to
the programmatic and relational work of the organisations suffered the
same fate. There has been no in-depth or profound discussion on how the
work of one relates to or impacts the work of the others. No theological
discussion has taken place to ascertain the ecumenical relevance of the
common issues being faced.

What emerged was the tendency of each to regard a certain area of
concerns as their prerogative. This contributed to the stagnation of constructive ecumenical activity in the region. Unpleasant as this might be,
it is nothing compared with the 'doom and gloom' ecumenism will suffer
in the region if these organisations are allowed to continue as separate
entities devoid of any sense of the structural and programmatic changes
needed to address the issues facing the Pacific churches today. There is no
option but to cooperate, but this cannot happen if perceptions concerning
why change is necessary are not embraced. The churches will continue to
suffer from the pitfalls of ecumenical institutional stagnation if they do

not heed the call to search for a new understanding of a healthy ecumenical reality.

Looking to the Future

The case for a renewed form of ecumenical cooperation between the PCC, PTC and SPATS is compelling. They serve more or less the same churches. Their personnel are members of each other's governing bodies. They encounter problems of the same nature in terms of issues that the churches have identified as urgent and the ongoing problem of financial sustainability. They all court the goodwill and support of the same overseas partners and donors. These commonalities warrant the need not only for constructive discernment of alternatives but also an acceptance that maintaining the status quo will have serious debilitating effects on the ecumenical movement in the region. A non-change approach will lead to a marginalisation of one from the other as well as from the regional and global community. Renewal of cooperation, however, is easier said than done. Fundamental to its becoming a reality is the existence of a spiritual openness, an intellectual openness, a political will and the ability of parties concerned to engage in the kind of comprehensive planning that complementarity requires. Pacific ecumenical bodies are already blessed by the fact that they are held together by mutual ties of one kind or another. This can only enhance the strong cohesiveness embedded in their current make-up. Evidence of a renewed form of ecumenical cooperation is the existence of collective action to promote mutual interests.

Perhaps the time has come for all three ecumenical bodies to seriously consider some essential structural changes. One of these could be the establishment of an Ecumenical Council as a governing body to oversee and coordinate their work. This possibility would be a major exercise in ecclesiastical integration, in constitutional debate and in the associated logistics. But the task is not as daunting as it might at first appear. The ingredients and the tools for such a reconfiguration are available and have been alluded to already.

The tendency for each to regard their individual council as an autonomous entity has contributed to the lack of effective cooperation. Their priority has been safeguarding their own survival rather than ecumenical cooperation and development. The current council structures have outlived their usefulness. Their effectiveness in nurturing and fostering ecumenism in the region has waned in recent years. Many of their decisions, made after careful consideration of constitutional clauses, are undermined and ignored by their own members. Some policies fail to consider the economic and socio-political realities of the member churches, including the churches' struggles to make ends meet.

The Ecumenical Council would serve as the only official regional forum. Its members would be empowered to establish norms and rules for the achievement of objectives and the acceleration of ecumenical awareness and growth. Policies would be coordinated, especially those designed to overcome the problem of mobilising sufficient capital and investment to finance development programmes. A single budget with appropriate allocations would benefit the member churches, with one annual contribution from them for all ecumenical work. A network of effective communication would emerge. An increase in the volume of communication, frequency of face-to-face meetings and number of interactions would encourage cooperation. In addition, better and more effective relationships with overseas partners and donors would increase their knowledge of our efforts to foster unity among ourselves, accept the cost of ownership and free ourselves from the bondage of depending on their financial support. Our ecumenical voice would not only be heard: it would be an authentic and relevant voice.

Then there is a delicate question regarding the catholicity of the church. Are Pacific churches willing to take up the challenge of relating to other faith communities and new churches that have emerged as a result of the rise of neo-Pentecostalism in the Pacific? Churches of the Pacific have a real need to be open to other expressions of Christianity. They have not always been sensitive to the problems and needs of their people, nor sufficiently humble and open to what other expressions of Christianity can contribute. As Christians, as churches, we should be enquiring together as to God's purpose in a multicultural world characterised by a diversity of faiths. The need for ecumenism and mission as reconciliation and learning from and with others is essential for our churches in the Pacific today.

Bibliography

Ernst, Manfred (ed.), *Globalization and the Re-shaping of Christianity in the Pacific Islands* (Suva: Pacific Theological College, 2006).

Ernst, Manfred and Lydia Johnson (eds), *Navigating Troubled Waters: The Ecumenical Movement in the Pacific Islands since the 1980s* (Suva: Pacific Theological College, 2017).

Havea, Sione 'Amanaki, 'Christianity in the Pacific Context', in *South Pacific Theology: Papers from the Consultation on Pacific Theology, Papua New Guinea, January 1986* (Oxford: Regnum Books, 1987), 11–15.

Vaai, Upolu Lumā and Aisake Casimira (eds), *Relational Hermeneutics: Decolonising the Mindset and the Pacific Itulagi* (Suva: University of the South Pacific and Pacific Theological College, 2017).

Key Themes

Faith and Culture

Upolu Lumā Vaai

This chapter is premised on the idea that, in Oceania, eco-relationality offers a suitable space for faith and culture to talk to each other, something we in Oceania call *talanoa* (talk that allows transformative conversational space). In the understanding of Christians in the region, this *talanoa* is made possible by the Spirit of Life, who allows space for our faith to be relational and transforming while at the same time making culture dynamic and fluid. What this means is that Oceanic communities could be able to delve deeper into their faith, specifically Trinitarian faith, if approached from the Indigenous cultural perspective of eco-relationality. The need therefore is to shift from the 'Oceania Turn' spearheaded by Epeli Hauofa that has dominated regional development in the last 30 years to a 'Relational Turn'. This turn invites a deeper and critical look at not only 'colonialism from outside' but, more importantly, at 'colonialism from within'.

This turn to an Oceanic eco-relational worldview promotes a paradigm shift from eco-theology, which has dominated Eurocentric Christianity, to an eco-relational theology grounded on the relational 'life-centred' values of the Triune God revealed in Jesus Christ and creatively manifested through the Spirit 'in' the relational cultural *itulagi* (side of the heaven) of the communities of Oceania. Putting life at the centre of the faith-and-culture conversation as well as Oceanic theologies is critical if the Oceanic churches are to contribute effectively to regional development and stability, especially within a region marred by imperialism, global warming and climate injustices, poor health, poverty, unstable governments, environmental destruction through mining and illegal logging, overfishing, systemic and domestic violence, nuclear threats, militarisation, the suppression of minorities, the erasure of Indigenous cultures and languages, and the legalisation of land grabbing.

The *Oikos* Triplets

Recently a collective call was heard from the Oceanic churches for a renewal of their story of faith. Facilitated by both the Pacific Conference of Churches (PCC) and the Pacific Theological College (PTC), the regional ecumenical institution of the Oceanic churches, the push to change the story is timely and critical. The push for a new story is not just about deconstructing and critiquing the old but rather also about creating a new one and whether the new carries the wisdom, values and needs of the Oceanic communities as these determine the sustainability of a new story. It is also this push for a new story that has brought together PCC leaders to create a platform called the Pacific Ecumenical Council to assist with the vision. In the midst of divisions forced upon an already disfigured region by current global political and economic developments, the Oceanic churches are coming together in full strength to offer an alternative story.

This call for a renewed story is in response to a Eurocentric narrative adopted by many Oceanic churches and embedded in their theologies and mission, in which the *oikos* triplets of ecology, economy and *oikoumene* are forcibly removed from their original eco-relational *aiga* (extended household) and cut off from their mutual connections. Like the 'stolen generation' of Australia, ecology was stolen and became a servant to a Eurocentric scientific household, where it was forcibly reduced to mere 'nature' to be exploited. Economy was removed and became a servant to globalisation, where its role of 'managing a home' was modified to serve a neo-liberal system that manages resources for just a few elites. And *oikoumene* was stolen by the church and made a servant to its human-centric theologies, where it was re-engineered to favour Christianity over all other religions. This deliberate dismembering of the *oikos* triplets from their common roots forcibly altered their identities, roles and purposes. Therefore, in the new Oceanic story we cannot do justice to one of the three unless we include the others. Economy without ecology is aggressively capitalist. *Oikoumene* without ecology is brutally human-centric. And economy without *oikoumene* is cruelly secular.

The churches in Oceania in their new story aim to reunite the *oikos* triplets in order for faith to be holistic and encompassing. This follows the direction proposed by the Pacific Church Leaders' Meeting, both in 2017 and 2018, to frame the new story in the light of 'relational ecumenism'. Relational ecumenism is really about reclaiming the eco-relational connection of the *oikos* triplets that was already present in the Oceanic Indigenous relationalities as well as in the Christian doctrine of the Trinity. The PTC in its contextualisation and ecumenical focus, together with the various influential publications it has recently produced, including some of its programmes such as 'Reweaving the Ecological Mat', spearheaded by its Institute of Mission and Research, aims to achieve this.

At the heart of the eco-relational connection is relationality grounded on the relational Trinitarian story of the 'life-giving' economy of God. On this understanding, through Christ in the Spirit, God relates to us by becoming an integral part of the eco-relational *aiga* in the form of a human being. Also, through Christ in the Spirit, we are invited to share in the abundance of God, who not only 'gives life' but is also the life of the *aiga*. We need to rescue God from a very hierarchical human-centric tendency of mainstream theology. The Oceanic Indigenous communities are more attuned to God as Spirit. It is the Spirit of Life that is at the centre of God's eco-relational connection. Without the Spirit, God's eco-relational connection through Jesus Christ would have been impossible. It is in this work of the Spirit of Life that the Oceanic people believe that the whole of creation is sacred and eco-relational, after the image of God, who is also eco-relational. This eco-relational resurgence and vision of renewal beg for the re-centring of the role of the Spirit of Life in creation. Through the Spirit, God is able to 'live within' the scarcity of life in the *aiga* in order for this *aiga* to 'live within' the abundance of life in God. The most relational way for God to give and affirm life for us is to be 'with us'. On this understanding, wherever and whenever eco-relationality is manifested in the people, land, ocean and sky, God is there, in our multiple eco-relationalities.

Eco-relational Structure of Oceanic Life

For many years, the church created theologies to justify a restructuring of life to suit its human-centric mission. For example, Western theologies and political agendas promote the idea that ecology refers only to the 'natural environment'. In other words, God and human beings exist 'outside' of ecology. This view not only promotes a human-centric approach to creation, it also deliberately severs the Trinitarian conception that all of life is ecological and interconnected.

From an Oceanic relational perspective, the eco-relational *aiga* is not human-centric. All of life in the *aiga* is eco-relational. Eco-theology focuses on how God relates to ecology. Eco-relational theology emphasises the multidimensional mutual relating. We need to set ecology free from the violence of Eurocentric scientific objectification. We need to begin to treat it as family, part of our life-giving organs. Environmental violence does not go down well with most Oceanic Indigenous communities because, in their eco-relational worldview, there is a deep spiritual and emotional connection between the earth and the people. The Fijians refer to this as *tamata ni vavua, vanua ni tamata*, meaning 'the people are the land and the land is the people'. Because relationality was in the beginning through the Spirit of God, this connection was meant to be there. Oceanic Indigenous terms such as *vanua, fenua, fanua* and *aba* have dual meanings connoting both land and people. In order for life to be central, everything in the *aiga* must be perceived as an intimate part of the whole. In this intimacy the people and the earth can exist only 'in relation to the other'. Genesis 2: 7

talks about our 'earth genealogy', in which we are delivered out of the womb of the earth by a midwife God. The land was already there, giving birth to humans with the aid of God. Hence the earth is more than just a piece of dirt or water. It is family!

The Trinitarian Eco-relational Self

The Oceanic eco-relational view of the self is that it is relational and multi-dimensional. In Fiji, Tonga, Sāmoa, Tahiti, New Zealand and Hawaii, for example, *tagata*, *tamata*, *taata* and *kanaka* (each meaning 'person') can be defined only in relation to the earth. The Kanaki/New Caledonia philosopher Jean-Marie Tjibaou once claimed that an Oceanic person is never a principle of individualisation but rather a body of relationship. For example, in Sāmoa the word for soil (*eleele*) is the same as the word for human blood. The word for the earth (*palapala*) is also the same word for human blood. *Ua tafe le palapala* (blood is spilled) means that the earth loses life whenever there is bloodshed. The word for placenta (*fanua*) that holds the unborn baby in the womb of a mother is the same as the word for land and community. The word for the rocks/stones (*fatu*) is the same as the word for the human heart. The word for roots of a tree (*a'a*) is the same word for human genealogy. The word for tongue (*laulaufaiva*), which literally means 'to distribute a catch', connotes a system of distribution of resources rather than a system of digestion. When the newborn's umbilical cord is severed, a ritual is performed to bury this in the ground to reconnect the newborn to the land of the ancestors. This deep connection of humans and the earth is termed by one of Oceania's leading philosophers, Tui Atua, as *fatumanava*, meaning 'the earth in the human heart' and connoting that the human being cannot be treated in isolation from the whole nor be endorsed as ruler of the whole. We can somehow claim that 'it is mine', but we can never claim 'it is me', because what I have 'in me' belongs to someone else. The human being is Trinitarian only in relation to the whole – God, others, earth. To un-relate ourselves from the whole is to un-relate ourselves from the Trinity.

In other words, we human beings are ecological through and through. We are the 'walking land'. There is no disconnection of the earth and the people or a disconnection of life. All of life is a fraternity – ecologically, economically and ecumenically structured. In this respect, when one is affected, all are affected. When one suffers, all suffer. Because God's Story is ecologically rooted through Christ in the Spirit, God suffers from the suffering of the earth. The cross of Jesus Christ presents a radical approach, in which we are called to dare to term the suffering of the innocent earth and vulnerable people as our own suffering. The cross is the framework for our mission to be in deep solidarity with the crucified earth.

The Trinitarian Eco-relational Water

Vai or *wai* (water) is structured relationally. In this structure, despite the fact that these dimensions are distinct, *vai auli* (freshwater) cannot be separated from its *punāvai* (water source) or its *lotoivai* (waterbed or riverbed). They all make up what is called *tino ole vai* (water bodies). The eco-relational structure of water is that all water bodies must not be compartmentalised. The reason is that water is perceived as a whole, with a body, a mind and a life of its own. In this eco-relational structure, water is not spoken of but is spoken to. Because water is seen as a living being, many of our Indigenous belief stories (usually profiled as untrue myths by colonisers) highlight that our forebears used to 'speak to' water. This eco-relational communication means that we need to shift from the idea that 'water is life' (which frames water only in relation to humans) to 'water lives'. Because we are made of water, we therefore live because water lives.

This makes more meaningful Jesus's reference to himself as the *vaiola* (living water). Jesus told the Samaritan woman 'when you drink the water I give you it becomes a gushing fountain of the Holy Spirit, springing up and flooding you with endless life' (John 4: 14); the phrase 'springing up' comes from the Greek verb *hallomenou*, meaning 'jumping' or 'leaping', a verb used only for living beings. It makes sense therefore to Oceanic communities that this text means that we should never confine our lives with physicality. Fullness of life is when we are conscious of the Spirit living in us. Spirituality is when we have a conscious recognition of what has always been there, but we have denied it because we are stuck in the physicality of life. To be spiritually conscious, we need to (re)find our earth roots, such as water.

By acknowledging that water lives and breathes, animated by the Spirit, we acknowledge that any elimination of one aspect or dimension from its life is a spiritual offence. Because all of creation is made up of *vai*, ranging from trees to mountains and even human beings, rearranging its structure will have huge consequences on the whole of creation. Today, bottled-water companies in Oceania think that extracting freshwater has no effects on the riverbed and water channels. Likewise, mining companies think that extracting minerals and soil from the riverbed as is done in many parts of Oceania, particularly Fiji and Hawaii, has no effect on freshwater. In these actions, water is deliberately restructured and rearranged in the name of economic profit, resulting in the dismembering and dissecting of water from its Trinitarian eco-relational structure.

The Trinitarian Eco-relational *Moana*

The *moana* (ocean) also has a Trinitarian eco-relational structure. Its dynamism, fluidity and embrace are symbolic of the embrace of the

Trinity. The former Anglican Diocesan Bishop of Polynesia, Archbishop Winston Halapua, in his '*moana* theology' has been speaking about this Trinitarian nature of the *moana* for quite some time.

We human beings are also made of oceanic materials. Teresia Teaiwa from Kiribati once said that 'we sweat and cry salt, so we know that the ocean is really in our blood' (quoted in Hau'ofa, *We Are the Ocean*, p. 41). Epeli Hau'ofa, from Tonga, coined a well known phrase: 'We are the Ocean, the Ocean is Us'. This underpinning philosophy is now adopted by the Pacific Island Forum and other development agents to frame their development frameworks, such as the 'Blue Pacific'. This raises the question of whether our own Indigenous concepts and wisdom are appropriated through a politics of simulation to accommodate an economic agenda to satisfy the neo-liberal narrative at the expense of the multiple dimensions of life.

One of the Sāmoan words for the human head is *atigisami* (seashell), which encases human thoughts and wisdom. It means therefore that wisdom has an ocean dynamic. For example, *tofa loloto* (wisdom of the deep) is wisdom that is not confined to the shallow and predictable. Like the ocean, it is wisdom that is able to deal with the unpredictability of a situation. *Tofa fetuunai* (flexible wisdom) is wisdom that is dynamic and fluid like the ocean.

Hence the ocean is not just a mass of blue liquid. The ocean bed includes the *matāpuna* (nostrils and breathing sources) for all marine creatures. Some governments in Oceania, such as in Papua New Guinea and in Tonga, have now made it legal for transnational mining corporations to conduct the world's first deep-sea mining exploration in the waters of Oceania. Because the ocean currents flow, the consequences of sea-bed mining are catastrophic compared with land mining, even though this is also destroying many parts of the region. Hence mining one part of the *moana* will affect all. It will have enormous impact on island communities who depend solely on the ocean for their everyday livelihood.

The ocean is supposed to be a gift for all. When we fish, people are encroaching on the domain that is not human. Therefore, humans have to show respect by taking only that which is necessary and beneficial to the whole community. The first fish caught is usually given away, either to the elderly or to those in need, to continue the flow of the ocean on land.

The Trinitarian Eco-relational Work Ethic

When the European colonisers came to the Pacific, they saw the islanders' ways of life as unproductive and immediately labelled islanders as 'lazy' and 'backward'. As a result, the 'lazy Pacific' stereotype found its way into the English textbooks and education system. While this is true to some extent, especially in relation to the dependency attitude many countries and people of Oceania now develop in relation to foreign aid and ways of thinking, this lazy profiling overlooks a very important fact. That is, the islanders' eco-relational work ethic does not fit into the colonisers' industrialised capitalist work ethic of 'growth'.

Two responses to this stereotype can be offered. First, on a Trinitarian understanding, allowing space and room for the other Person to exist is fundamental to the divine life of love. In Oceania, 'less work' each day does not necessarily mean laziness. Rather, it is a relational way to respect the spiritual connectedness of the whole. Less work offers space and room for the land or the ocean to breathe and recuperate. It is an ethics based on the 'less yet more' philosophy of life. That is, having 'less' does not necessarily mean 'decrease' or 'loss' in profit or production as promoted by the neo-liberal capitalist idea of 'growth'. In the neo-liberal capitalist mindset, growth is always perceived within the framework of having more – more profit, more money, more production. In this economic model, having more profit, money and properties means more power. And the dominant powers wanted us to believe that there is no alternative. Economy has always been determined by power and has been the driver of centralising power in the hands of a few, which is why this philosophy of growth is the new holocaust, more grave and deadly than any natural disaster or disease.

Because we see growth in this 'more is better' framework, we refuse to 'live within our means' and to recognise the sustenance of multiple relationships in the *aiga*. In the Oceanic eco-relational ethic, our ancestors believed that overworking the land or overfishing the ocean has consequences harmful to the harmony of the whole. And economy is never about power; it is about sharing and productivity for the sake of the other. Because life is central, 'more' is achieved only through the ability to have 'less'. 'Less' is not the opposite of 'more'. Rather, 'less' is the means to achieve 'more'. This is a 'less yet more' paradox of life that St Paul alluded to in 1 Corinthians and Philippians. The lessening of Godself on the cross is for the purpose of relating, connecting and bonding to what is not God. That relating does not in any way compromise what is 'more' in God, such as divinity and power; rather, it is the very thing that affirms it. It is a way of life that promotes the 'we are' over the 'we have'. Unfortunately, this 'less yet more' Trinitarian way of life that Oceanic people used to practise is now replaced by the 'more is better' development paradigm made popular by the neo-liberal economic system.

Secondly, because of their understanding of the Trinitarian eco-relational structure, many Indigenous communities do not rush into exploiting the earth. The 'lazy Pacific' stereotype sends the message that foreigners, as well as many Oceanic people themselves, misunderstand the dynamics of relationships and the protocols involved. While all of life is sacred because of the inner presence of the Spirit of God, human beings can use or consume something only after the relational protocols are followed. Usually, Indigenous people perform rituals, for example to ask the earth for both permission and pardon that the life of a tree would be lost that day to serve a human need. When a tree is cut, the Sāmoan word that is often used is *oia*, with its root in the word *oi*, meaning to cry in pain. In other words, whenever a tree is cut or something from the earth is killed or extracted, there is groaning and cry of pain. St Paul in Romans 8 compares this painful groaning of creation to the labour pains of a mother who gives birth.

Rituals are performed to respect the dynamics of eco-relationalities. They are meant to heal and mend what is fractured and removed from the revolving circle of life. They are meant to protect the sacredness of the earth from our consumption culture and to remind us that a slow, gentle attitude toward the earth does not really mean 'laziness' but rather a relational way of respecting and honouring the dignity of a life that is not ours.

The church for many centuries has demonised this 'deep connection' that the many Indigenous communities have with the earth. Anything that has to do with acknowledging the sacredness of life and the spiritual nature of all things, the church turns around and labels as either super-stition or heresy. These were and are still used as weapons by the church to control the gospel to suit dominant and mainstream religious and economic agendas. Recently an alternative voice of the church emerged. Pope Francis calls this kind of deep connection to the earth, often promoted by Indigenous communities, 'integral ecology' that allows us to see the earth as family. We employ a respectful relational approach to the earth because it is family, part of the Trinitarian household. Pope Francis has compared our common home to a sister with whom we share our life, or to a beautiful mother who opens her arms to embrace us. Because we treat the earth as a relationship and as a living being who lives because of the Spirit, this should give us a fundamental reason why this gentle, loving and respectful attitude toward the earth should be a way of life.

How can the church promote in its theology this gentle attitude toward the earth yet at the same time affirm progress and development? If the Persons of the Trinity relate to each other in what the Cappadocian Fathers called the 'revolving circle of glory', in which one respects and honours the other in the circle of divine life through gentle, compassionate love and sensitivity, how can we change the mission of the church to include this emotional attitude toward the earth?

Eco-responsibilities and Life-taking

Our close ecological, economic and ecumenical connection with the earth and with each other should give us a new and radical way of solidarity. Rediscovering the *aiga* eco-relational language and ethics should awaken compassion for the earth. It should give us courage to evaluate our consumer economic attitudes toward the earth and other human beings. It should give us the nerve to move from surface advocacy programmes into what Joerg Rieger calls 'deep solidarity' with the earth by speaking against the self-centred sin of 'living beyond our means' that often takes life away, not only from others to consolidate our own, but also from the earth.

Life in the eco-relational *aiga* revolves around equity in the sharing and distribution of resources, caring for the neighbour and giving to those in need. Poverty occurs because of our own hunger for power and privilege, for which we often claim political and religious justification, as well as allowing it a system and context in which to prosper. Therefore, poverty is not just an economic issue. From a relational perspective, it is also ecological and ecumenical. It occurs because today we no longer live relationally in the light of the Trinity. 'Scarcity of life' is a sign that we have abandoned the ecological and ecumenical 'life-giving' principles to serve another god, a tendency that often starts by denying God's life-giving story.

Colonisation is responsible for this scarcity of life. Colonisation can be understood in terms of the word 'colon', which in both Greek and Latin means 'a digestive system'. Colonialism is when 'one' person, community or organisation desires to solidify a digestive system that consumes more power, more money, more wealth and more resources at the expense of the many, including taking life away from earth. More and more we become a community that worships and serves Caesar, the 'life-taking' god of the market empire, rather than the 'life-giving' God of Jesus Christ. With the notion of 'life-taking' directly or indirectly shaping every part of our developmental consciousness, we who follow this market god no longer feel grief, love or suffering. Because of this we no longer mourn the severe distortions caused by the commodification of gifts from God such as our land, ocean, rivers, animals and trees.

Today we no longer feel that 'life-taking' is a sin because it is structured not only physically with the help of policies and legal frameworks but also psychologically. Pope Francis reminds us that we ourselves are dust of the earth, that our very bodies are made up of her elements, that we breathe her air and receive life and refreshment from her waters.

In the current climate-change discourse, we in Oceania like to think and argue that our small island communities contribute little or none of the gas emission which, scientists claim, is the major cause of climate change. As a result, we like to blame rich corporations and big countries for our sinking islands and extreme exposure to sea-level rise and unpredictable weather patterns. However, Oceania must also acknowledge that we are major contributors to climate change in other ways. Our local governments are the very people who pass laws and develop policies that allow rich multinational corporations to conduct deforestation, land and deep-sea mining, and resource extraction. Our local landowners are the very ones who do not think of the ecological consequences when a business deal is wrapped with a huge financial benefit. We in our daily lives wage war on the earth through the continual use of plastics. When we lose remembrance, especially the memory of a deep relational connection and the acknowledgement of everything as 'living', we lose what it means to 'live within our means'. The PCC in its 2018 General Assembly condemned the extraction culture that is unquestionably growing in some parts of Oceania and on which the majority of local communities depend. Thus, the Assembly provided a timely and much-needed prophetic voice to inform our people of the moral dimensions of their economic life according to God's 'life-centred' values.

Eco-relational Mission of Oceanic Churches

Our close ecological, economic and ecumenical connection with the earth should also prompt us to rethink our approach to stewardship. From a Trinitarian eco-relational perspective, our mindsets need to shift from the stewardship idea of 'caring for' creation that has dominated Eurocentric eco-theology into 'living with' creation. In the eco-relational faith, relating precedes caring. Honest and empathetic stewarding means that once we (re)find that intimate emotional and spiritual connection through 'living with' the earth, the 'caring for' should follow. Stewardship is about 'deep connection' that is always spiritual in nature. To 'be there' and to 'be caring' for the earth should start with the resolve to 'be with'. We can honestly love and care for the earth only if we are deeply connected to it.

The inter-relation of faith and culture in Oceania calls for a number of steps to be taken in relation to the contemporary ecological crisis. These include: (1) the creation of a platform where faith and culture meet, which promotes an everyday spirituality that the Oceanic people can own, firmly grounded as it is on their eco-relational faith and life-centred values; (2) the promotion of an eco-relational faith perspective by a fresh analysis that should provide critical reflection on development and regional stability as well as an analysis of the social and ecological ills of the past and present; (3) the creation of a critical reflection on the painful stories of suffering and suppression of life under colonial rule and representations; and (4) the rescue of the *oikos* triplets by creating a sustainable model that reinforces the importance of Oceanic relational values and approaches. Hence there would be the achievement of ecological solidarity, a holistic economic model that is life-giving, and a broader ecumenical narrative to include other religious faiths.

Whenever and wherever life is denied, the church should be the first respondent. There are two dimensions to such a response. On the one hand, the church responds as a *sili'aga* (wisdom custodian) with a relational consciousness that provides fresh theological incentives and ethical guidance directly from the heart of the 'life-giving' gospel of God for the eco-relational *aiga*. The aim is to offer a 'right direction' or 'right orientation' for life. On the other hand, the church responds as the *lima ma vae* (hands and feet) of the gospel in relation to issues of social justice. Because there is no unity without justice, the church finds its identity through the overturning of power structures and corruptive practices, both internal and external, that promote the oppression of people, a self-obsessed digesting culture, and an ecological violence. These two dimensions should be integral parts of its life and mission, as well as its theological education. But to do this, the church must first liberate itself from a narrow, imperial human-centric theology that has hindered its mission and its holistic view of life.

Conclusion

This chapter has demonstrated how the question of faith and culture in Oceania revolves around ecology. All of life is eco-relational and Trinitarian by structure and by the Spirit of Life resembles God. From God, to humanity, to the earth and to communities, all of life is an assemblage of divine relationality. This relational structure defines how we relate to all, including the earth. It is in the eco-relational structure of life that faith and culture meet and engage in *talanoa*. Because 'life' is at the centre of God's story through Christ in the Spirit, it should also be at the centre of the Oceanic churches' new story. In such a story, we need a holistic framing of the *oikos* triplets of ecology, economy and *oikoumene*. Because of the interconnectedness of life in the eco-relational *aiga*, both ecumenism and economy have ecological implications. Therefore, reclaiming the mutual relationship of these three is critical to the new story, a story that is joyfully Christian and truly Oceanic. In such a story, the Oceanic churches should never shy away from critically addressing anything that rearranges God's eco-relational creation to meet human-centric agendas.

Bibliography

Ama'amalele, Tofaeono, *Eco-Theology: Aiga – The Household of Life* (Erlangen: Erlanger Verlag fur Mission und Okumene, 2000).

Hau'ofa, Epeli, *We Are the Ocean: Selected Works* (Honolulu: University of Hawaii, 2008).

Pope Francis, *Encyclical Letter, Laudato Si' of the Holy Father Francis on Care for our Common Home* (Strathfield: St Paul's Publications, 2015).

Vaai, Upolu Lumā, '*E itiiti a lega mea* – Less Yet More! A Pacific Relational Development Paradigm of Life', in Upolu Lumā Vaai and Aisake Casimira (eds), *Relational Hermeneutics: Decolonising the Mindset and the Pacific Itulagi* (Suva: University of the South Pacific and Pacific Theological College, 2017), 215–31.

Vaai, Upolu Lumā and Unaisi Nabobo-Baba (eds), *The Relational Self: Decolonising Personhood in the Pacific* (Suva: University of the South Pacific and Pacific Theological College, 2017).

Worship and Spirituality

Tau'alofa Anga'aelangi and Tanya Riches

Oceanian worship and spirituality are shaped by the experience of the sea. Over the centuries, since European missionaries brought Christianity, this region has made a great contribution to global liturgical practice. Oceania is culturally diverse and geographically expansive, crossing the eastern and western hemispheres. It includes the islands of Melanesia, Micronesia, Polynesia, New Zealand and the vast continent of Australia. The many diverse Indigenous cultures are still present within the region's spirituality and worship, along with Western or European influences as well as many others now present via migration.

On the islands of Oceania, our way of life, culture and values continue to be strongly influenced by the navigations of our ancestors through the deep oceans. For some groups, relocating from the ocean meant a shift in identity and lifestyle – from being seafarers to becoming a people deeply connected to the land. Therefore, their worship and spirituality reflect the bridging transformation of Oceanic people from the sea to land into the future.

Christian spirituality has become deeply embedded in its context via song-sharing rituals. This practice exists across Oceania's islands and reaches even to its deserts. The sharing of musical worship is particularly significant in the region's cities, via the influence of 'Pasifika' peoples (a term connecting the Pacific Island homelands to the diaspora in New Zealand and Australia). Pasifika theology has had a strong influence upon all Western Christian spirituality, but particularly on Charismatic/ Pentecostal worship. Similarly, across the region, dance plays a significant role in telling and retelling the stories and celebrating culture. In the Aboriginal context, visual art is a unique way of communicating spirituality; images often depict the land and its relationship with all living creatures, including humanity, and God. Such creative expressions draw land and ocean into Christian liturgy in uniquely Oceanian ways.

The Pacific Way of Life

Across the South Pacific Ocean, worship and spirituality are a way of life, bound up with participation in the community. Despite the diversity found in the traditions across Pacific communities, a commonality in their myths, legends, values and beliefs reflects an understanding of the interconnectedness of all creation. Worship and spirituality are central to the Pacific way of life because they incorporate the mystery at the heart of reality and the act of living that is continuously transformative.

In Oceania, in pre-missionary times, people lived with their own cosmologies. Every island community held on to myths about the creation of the world, gods and deities, landmarks and astronomy. The community came together in worship, finding the reality of God within their natural environment and using that environment as a space in which to worship. In this context, no temples or church buildings were required. In Melanesian culture, speech and the act of healing played a crucial part in worship. In Fiji, the *kava* is a significant ceremony that represents an act of worship involving welcome, healing, forgiveness and new life. Shamanistic practitioners entered into a trance state in which direct contact with the supernatural was believed to be possible. Worship in Melanesia featured the practice of performing rites while using nature to connect to something greater than the physical world. These pre-missionary forms of worship laid great emphasis on seeking to participate in the community. At the same time, human interconnection did not mean abandoning the rest of the world. Instead, it set a premium on harmony with the entire created order. This harmonious relationship with creation continues to play an important role.

Therefore, spirituality is central to worship because it is the mystery that manifests the interconnectedness of all things. Here, *mana* is a term that describes sacredness or mystery and is almost equivalent in terminology to spirituality. It is a matter of solidarity, a sense of communion with the whole of creation, the embodiment of the life of a people, their history, stories of creation, myths, legends and culture. It evokes a world of understanding and does not restrict itself to the sacred but also embraces the profane – the ordinariness of life.

Contextuality has played a critical role, influencing worship and spirituality in Oceania. Indeed, it has significantly impacted the way the gospel is understood at a grassroots level. This was crystallised in Amanaki Havea's presentation to a World Council of Churches meeting in 1986 when he described Pacific theology as 'coconut theology' and a 'theology of celebration'. He insisted on the need for Christians in Oceania to develop theology in relation to their own context rather than foreign concepts. He proposed that there was a need for the gospel to put down roots in the local soil and exist in the local climate. He pled for a theology that would be seen through Pacific eyes and heard with Pacific ears. Instead of appearing foreign, it should become Indigenous and contextualised. Havea illustrated his point by suggesting that if Jesus had grown up and lived in the Pacific, he might have said, 'I am the coconut of life' rather than 'I am the bread of life'.

Another important note struck by Havea was his proposal that Pacific theology be understood as a theology of celebration. It is a matter of community coming together in an inclusive way, recalling the caring and sharing experienced before the advent of Western individualism. A theology of celebration evokes the manifestation of the presence of God, which was greatly evident in the Pacific Islands before the Good News came in written forms. Pacific theology arises out of the celebrations, the focus on community over individualism, the sharing and caring for one another, the deep sense of hospitality that has manifested God's presence throughout Oceania.

Contextual theology also has shaped the practice of worship by drawing on grassroots cultural celebrations. In this way, the gospel is embodied in an organic way. It takes its cue from what local ears and eyes have heard and seen. Celebrations in Oceania are not reserved specifically for a particular time in the Christian liturgical calendar. The note of celebration runs through the entirety of the worship of the Christian community. A delicate interplay is present between the communal and the individual. To celebrate is to gather in community to celebrate the individual. In contrast, individuals celebrate their presence with the whole assembly.

Pacific Worship Styles

Worship styles in Oceania are shaped by the celebration of creation, the gift of hospitality in all its forms, and the gift of life. It is widely understood that there is a relationship between the land, ocean, water and sky. A shared understanding of the sacredness of land is reflected in the language used to describe it – in Tonga, *fonua*; in Aotearoa New Zealand, *tangata whenua*; in Kiribati, *kainga*; in Sāmoa, *fanua*. In Oceania, creation and all of the earth's living beings are not considered inferior species to humanity. We see ourselves as equal to creation in the sense that we are in a reciprocal relationship. We take care of creation because we see her as a gift from the divine. We care for the earth as we care for our mothers and as we do for our family, because it is alive and is a part of us. Indeed, anything that springs from the earth is seen as a contribution to the reciprocal relationship between humans and the created order in which they are set.

In Tonga and other parts of Oceania, we have our own calendar for the harvesting of local crops. A worship service always celebrates this high point of the year. The local clergy or lay leaders often lead the celebration service. The liturgy mostly focuses on a prayer of thanksgiving praise and blessing. Thanksgiving is to give thanks to God for the gift of fertilised land, and we continue to praise God for being the giver and gardener who has taken care of us. The prayer of blessing is for the relationship we have with the land in our present day and in the future still to come. This expression of spirituality reflects our appreciation of the one we worship who provides for us. Spirituality for us, then, is an expression of appreciation, giving thanks and praise to God for hospitality and providing for us in the past, the present and the future. Various ceremonies celebrate gifts, but notably two gifts: hospitality and life.

Our celebration of hospitality provides a language of spirituality. This style of worship means that our language for God differs from that of the dominant culture of literature. The celebration of the gift of hospitality in Oceania is reflected through our service of hosting those who gather. We do this in sharing a meal or hosting a feast, entertaining the guests with dancing and singing, and providing them with our very best. In Tuvaluan culture, hospitality is a part of the traditional entertainment of the *fatele*, a song and dance that unites people to demonstrate the welcome the community is offering to their guests. Dancing and singing have played a pivotal part in the diverse cultures of Oceania. Hospitality in Oceania is interwoven with entertainment, celebrations and abundant supplies of food. Since the food, music, dancing and community are all recognised as gifts from God, the community's generosity and offering are an act of faith, for we are assured there is enough for ourselves and our neighbours. At the same time, our spirituality demonstrates the gift of hospitality is to be expressed in different ways. Indeed, the sharing of food shows that Gods' gifts are not to be possessed but rather to be distributed.

The gift of life is so precious to us in Oceania that we make it a priority to celebrate milestones that mark the different stages of life. For this reason, the Rotuman culture celebrates the role of parenthood for the first few months after the birth of a child. The mother of the newborn stays put and is served for many months by her husband and family. The next few stages of the individual's life continue to be celebrated with the community and family. For instance, baptism, birthdays and the first menstruation experience for teenage girls are all marked by the family hosting a feast. In the Cook Islands, most young boys grow their hair until their eighth birthday, when their family will hold a haircutting ceremony. Today, we continue to celebrate the gift of life with community as part of sustaining and nurturing each other. Death also is celebrated as a spiritual homecoming. Our celebration of the different stages of life is a manifestation of our spirituality and worship. Our spirituality is complex, but it needs to be expressed, and this is embodied in the celebration of appreciating, thanking and praising God for the breath of life given to us through the creation.

Our spirituality is not limited to those who practise the same faith as ourselves. Instead, it begins with recognising that we are part of the order of creation, so when we worship, we are part of the community with all living things. The worship styles mentioned above reflect an inclusiveness, gathering at an open table, bringing people together rather than leaving them in isolation. This style of worship has influenced the diasporic communities. For instance, some churches in Australia and New Zealand have begun to recognise that the worship and spirituality of Indigenous Oceanic people has much to offer to the life of the church. In fact, worship with creation for many churches is still seen as a part of the liturgical calendar. However, those of us from Oceania know this celebration as an ontological practice. In the same way, we celebrate the gift of life by being communal rather than being individual. The language we use in our worship and spirituality is strongly connected with the music, art and dancing of our traditional culture.

New Zealand

New Zealand's spirituality draws on its diverse population, but particularly its Māori, Pākehā, Pasifika and other migrant groups. The first Roman Catholic services were conducted by Dominican chaplain Fr Paul Antoine Léonard de Villefeix while travelling on the ship *Saint Jean Baptiste*. In addition to celebrating Mass near Whatuwhiwhi in Doubtless Bay on Christmas Day in 1769, he led prayers for the sick and conducted burials. The British cleric Revd Samuel Marsden first established an Anglican presence with the Church Mission Society in 1814. This was under the permission and protection of Ngā Puhi chief Ruatara. The esteem for Marsden's successes in New Zealand contrasted with the disdain for his presence and ministry in Australia, where he is even today known as 'the flogging parson' for his reputedly brutal treatment of the convicts (although the historicity of these events is now disputed). Anglican missionaries played a significant role in the creation of the Treaty of Waitangi, New Zealand's founding document. In most Anglican services, the traditional liturgy was followed by readings from the Book of Common Prayer, or, in Māori circles, its equivalent, Te Rawiri. The Charismatic movement had a significant influence on the Anglican Church in New Zealand from 1966. This was reflected in the prayerbook *A New Zealand Prayer Book / He Karakia Mihinare O Aotearoa*, published in 1988.

Scottish settlers brought Presbyterianism in 1840. Since then, however, the Presbyterian church has grown into an ethnically diverse church centred in Aotearoa New Zealand. Similarly, the Reformed Church was initially constituted by Dutch settlers; however, it has since incorporated Māori, Pasifika and other immigrant cultural influences.

The official songbook, *Sing to the Lord*, was printed in 2013. It contains various musical arrangements of the biblical psalms and a wide variety of hymns. The Reformed movement in New Zealand emphasises corporate confession of sin and assurance of pardon as a distinct worship practice. In addition, there are various notable other New Zealand Pentecostal churches and para-church movements, many of which have a current or had a previous focus upon worship practice, including the Assemblies of God and Worship Central. Their gatherings and conferences have been highly influential in forming shared practices that also greatly influenced Australia.

The Māori recognised many gods and spiritual influences within their culture and its ceremonies. However, from the late 1820s, Māori transformed their religious and political lives, as they made Christianity their own. These contextualisation movements have made significant headway in most denominations. Māori prophetic religious movements often centred on the loss of Māori land and culture. For example, Pai Mārire (goodness and peace) emerged during the wars and in disillusionment with missionaries. The Māori King Movement provided moral authority for resistance against the state. Te Kooti Arikirangi Te Tūruki founded the Ringatū (raised hand) movement. At the same time, he was imprisoned on the Chatham Islands and became particularly popular in the Bay of Plenty. Māori farmer Tahupōtiki Wiremu Rātana united many dispossessed Māori tribes to challenge the New Zealand prime minister and British Crown to honour the Treaty of Waitangi. The Rātana Church allied with the Labour Party, an alliance that lasted until the 1990s. Māori worship and spirituality today are practised both on ancestral lands and also in cities among the urban diaspora.

The Torres Strait

The Torres Strait is a particularly Christianised area of Australia with its own unique culture, languages and rituals. Regarding worship and spirituality, Torres Strait Islanders are united by connection to the *Tagai*, which represents the stories that provide the foundation for the region's spiritual beliefs. These stories focus on the stars, telling of the seafaring ancestors, and placing everything in the cosmos. However, the region's annual Coming of the Light ceremony is an important event commemorating the arrival of the Bible on the shores of the Torres Strait. Initial missionaries were Anglican; the Revd Samuel MacFarlane, a member of the London Missionary Society, arrived in 1841 and was received by the Warrior Clan Elder Dabad, on the island of Erub. Each annual celebration includes a re-enactment of MacFarlane's landing, with hymn singing, feasting and *ailan dans* (island dance) that strengthen community and family ties. This acceptance of both the missionaries and the Christian faith caused profound changes. Today, however, various other denominations of Christianity have also influenced worship practice.

The Australian Mainland

Worship and spirituality on the Australian mainland today are shaped by a decline in church attendance, the rise of post-war migration from overseas and within Australia, the emergence of Indigenous faith communities and leadership, and new movements in contemporary and Charismatic worship.

Despite its origin in England and its role in the British Empire, the Anglican Church in Australia has been influential in shaping the nation's identity, spiritual values and beliefs. The first Anglican worship service held on Australian soil took place in 1788, at Sydney Cove. It was led by Richard Johnson, a chaplain from the Church of England. For six decades during the twentieth century, the Anglican Church remained the largest Christian denomination in Australia. It concentrated on replicating the Church of England as its parent church, duplicating its ecclesial structure, hymn books, Book of Common Prayer and eucharistic formularies. However, *An Australian Prayer Book* was published in 1978 after prolonged revisions. An alternative, *A Prayer Book for Australia*, was published in 1995. The influence of the Anglican Church is still deeply instilled in many parts of Australian culture and society. A significant institution is that of the Anglo-Catholic or high church wing of the Anglican Church, with its origins in the nineteenth-century Oxford Movement. Its influence is seen in Australia in the unique architectural designs of church buildings and cathedrals informed by this tradition. Its use of symbolism, music, ceremonies, eucharistic vestments, furnishings and fittings have influenced several mainstream denominations and faith communities regarding liturgy and clerical dress. In contrast, Evangelicalism is more influential in the Sydney diocese, with its worship borrowing from international as well as local free liturgy traditions. Indigenous leaders have noted that the Australian church continues to struggle to develop a worship and spirituality that is born out of its own grassroots rather than one that has evolved from the tradition following the First Fleet.

With a substantial minority Irish presence from the outset of the colony, Roman Catholic Christianity was initially suppressed and prevented from gathering for worship in Australia. On 15 May 1803, Fr James Dixon (who had been conditionally emancipated) was permitted to celebrate Mass, purportedly wearing vestments made from curtains and with a chalice made of tin. However, the governor again prohibited worship after the Irish-led 1804 Castle Hill rebellion. Fr Jeremiah O'Flynn, an Irish Cistercian monk, was subsequently appointed Prefect Apostolic of New Holland. He performed priestly duties secretly before being arrested and deported back to London. In response, two further priests, John Joseph Therry and Philip Connolly, travelled to the colony in 1820. Finally, Governor Lachlan Macquarie laid the foundation stone for the first building, St Mary's Cathedral, on 29 October 1821 in Sydney. Worship practices in the early years were influenced by the Benedictine, Ignatian and Josephite orders. During the gold rush, the Jesuits were extremely active in mission in the Outback and in building what are now some of the country's most elite educational institutions. The Catholic Church's institutional history, however, has been overshadowed by its participation in the Stolen Generation, where children were removed from their parents, as well as largely unaddressed clergy abuse.

Pope John Paul II's historic address in 1986 in Alice Springs, Australia, glossed over much of this history. Still, it continued a push towards inculturation in the Catholic Church. The event took place on the Caterpillar Dreaming, with the Pope welcomed by Arrente elders. As he completed his speech, he took a large gum branch, reached into a clay coolamon (carrying vessel, which later would be used in the Alice Springs church for baptisms) and blessed the people with water. At this moment, an electrical storm thundered out. Various other significant events have been hosted in Australia, including the twenty-third World Youth Day in 2008 led by Pope Benedict XVI and with more than a million attendees. A year earlier, the Journey of the Cross and Icon Pilgrimage travelled around the dioceses of Australia with a 3.8-metre cross and statue of the Virgin Mary, engaging Catholic parishes and concluding with the global youth event. There are also various Australian Catholics who worship according to Chaldean, Maronite, Melkite and Ukrainian rites.

The Uniting Church in Australia (UCA) was founded in 1977 as an amalgamation of Methodist, Congregationalist and many Presbyterian congregations. This church is liturgically varied and uses both contemporary and traditional hymns from both *The Australian Hymn Book* and *Together in Song*. Additionally, they draw upon various international influences, such as the Jesus Movement, through to more conventional Reformed services. Liturgical dress in the UCA is generally understated and is optional for ministers and other leaders of worship. When the liturgical dress is worn, it most commonly consists of a white alb and a stole (for ministers and deacons) or scarf (for lay preachers). The colour of the scarf or stole is often related to the events of the liturgical calendar. The church has various guidelines for inclusion in language and practice that seeks to incorporate various ages and cultures, as well as to recognise neurodiversity, gender and sexuality.

The Orthodox Divine Liturgy was celebrated in Sydney first in 1820, by the priest-monk Kioysii at Kirribilli Point during a Russian Antarctic expedition. The foundation stones of the first Greek Orthodox church were laid in 1898 in Sydney's Surrey Hills. The Orthodox community grew slowly through the 1920s via migration from Greece, Russia, Serbia and Romania. However, it was not until the mid-nineteenth century that mass migration of workers led to a steep increase in participation, worshipping in both English and their languages of origin. Therefore, in January 1970, the Holy Synod of the Ecumenical Patriarchate decided for practical reasons that New Zealand should be separated from the Greek Orthodox Archdiocese of Australia. The Standing Conference of Canonical Orthodox Churches in Australia was founded in 1979 under the leadership of Archbishop Stylianos (Harkianakis). It sought to promote cooperation among the Orthodox jurisdictions in Australia, under the permanent chairmanship of the representative of the Ecumenical Patriarchate; however, the Episcopal Assembly of Oceania unofficially superseded this group. A significant occasion for the Orthodox was the historic official visit of His All Holiness Ecumenical Patriarch Bartholomew in November 1996. Another notable event was the Olympic Games in 2000 with the participation of a 200-member Millennium Choir of the Archdiocese, which, together with the Children's Choir drawn from the Orthodox schools in Sydney, made a deep impression.

Seventh-day Adventists arrived in Australia largely from the USA. Melbourne was the site of the first Adventist congregation, formed on 10 January 1886 with 29 members. Other regional denominational influences include the Churches of Christ and Restorationist movements, as well as Pentecostalism (for more detail see below) and various innovative missional church worship gathering forms (also often called emerging, alternative or fresh expressions in more traditional denominations).

Australian Reconciliation Movement

Since the colonisation of Australia, Indigenous Australians have had contact with missionaries. This relationship has been a complex one. In some instances, the missions became instruments of government policy, engaging in practices that forcibly separated Aboriginal children from their families to maximise control over the children's education into Christian ways and beliefs. In this way, missions contributed to the suppression of Aboriginal cultural practices and languages. However, not all missions were agents of government policies. Some respected Aboriginal ways of life and the importance of ceremonial and cultural practice.

Today, however, there is an increasing awareness that liturgy and spiritual experience must be viewed through the prism of the developing reconciliation of Australia's First and Second Peoples. This form of reconciliation conversation has been particularly influential within the Uniting Church in Australia. It is enshrined in the preamble to the constitution, with an apology tabled and a framework laid out. In this context, there are a number of facets to this prism; the First Peoples of Australia have made suggestions for the Second People to learn and commit to a new covenant of reconciliation and work for the future generation of Australia. The first facet is to recognise the spirituality of the First Peoples, to acknowledge and respect their sense of the interconnectedness of land, culture and language. The second is to stand in solidarity and seek justice with the First Peoples. Words are not enough; there is a need for justice to be done. This involves non-Indigenous Australians coming to terms with painful aspects of their history and understanding how much they have to learn from their fellow citizens who are Aboriginal and Torres Strait Islanders. Worship and spirituality can open up creative spaces that permit uncomfortable questions about God and call for action as a result. This environment includes the possibility of new relationships being created. However, this requires a mutual partnership where First and Second Peoples walk alongside each other. This becomes a quest for mainstream denominations to reflect upon their own traditions and their influence on the development of Australian identity post-settlement.

Aboriginal-led worship movements include Hermannsburg SA's Central Australian Aboriginal Women's Choir, which was started by Lutheran missionaries and is now led by choirmaster Morris Stuart. He is African in heritage but grew up in Guyana in the Caribbean. More than 50 Baroque hymns have been translated into languages like Western Arrarnta and Pitjantjatjara. Additionally, singalong movements throughout the continent incorporated more recently authored Christian choruses. Anthropologists, including Ronald and Catherine Berndt, noted the Northern Territory's Adjustment Movement as significant. This 1979 revival on Elcho Island resulted in the Yolngu Elders publicly revealing their sacred objects and recommending a new way forward that incorporated both Aboriginal lore and non-Aboriginal law. Elders declared they would be 'Christian in a Yolngu world and Yolngu in a Christian world'. Within this revival movement, there were various creative innovations of baptism, marriage and other Yolngu rituals. Another significant contemporary movement is the Grasstree Gathering, pioneered by Jean Phillips, which gathers various senior Aboriginal Christian leaders, including Graham Paulson, Ray Minniecon and Neville Naden. This movement is facilitated by Waka Waka Christian Brooke Prentis.

Many Aboriginal people draw Christian and Dreaming spiritualities together. This can make particularly significant contributions in addressing the trauma of communities. For example, Miriam Rose Ungunmerr's *didarri* practices incorporate inner, deep listening and quiet, still awareness. This word means a deep spring. It recognises a type of waiting and responsive listening required for life on the Australian land. In this way, water is vital for all cultures in Oceania.

Charismatic/Pentecostal Worship

The influence of Oceanian Pentecostalism upon worship and spirituality globally is profound. Similarly, musical worship was vital in the history of the region. From the 1800s, the region's missionaries sought to develop Indigenous song-sharing rituals using congregational hymns (such as 'Onward Christian Soldiers') to spread the evangelistic message. Some argue that the Charismatic/Pentecostal movement initially drew on these regional Oceanian understandings of *mana* (sacredness), applying it to the music of the church as 'anointed'. Still today, songs spread important prophetic messages for the church. Popular theologies note God's power as transmitted via these song forms.

During the 1970s and 1980s, New Zealand's Scripture in Song movement was a significant influence on the Charismatic movement. Many of these songs were verbatim biblical passages. Some well known choruses include 'Therefore the Redeemed of the Lord', 'Highest Place', 'I Exalt Thee' and 'You are Exalted, oh God'. The migration of several influential New Zealander pastors to plant churches transported this focus to musical worship to Australia. In the 1980s and 1990s, the C3 movement played an important role in writing music for Christian youth. Various musical collaborations included the para-church ministry Youth Alive, which hosted evangelistic rallies and produced rock music via tapes and CDs. Similarly, Planetshakers initially began as a conference contextualising Christianity for youth but quickly transformed into a multi-site church. Many other Pentecostal groups have created and shared songs for congregational worship.

Of all church music producers in Australia, however, Hillsong is undoubtedly the best-known. Its worship is now so recognisable that it is effectively a genre of music in its own right. Hillsong Church was founded in Sydney in 1983 by married couple Brian and Bobbie Houston, who had immigrated from New Zealand. Initially, the church was called Hills Christian Life Centre, with its globally distributed, live recorded musical worship published under the name of Hillsong. However, the music became so popular that the church adopted the name of its publishing house. Inaugurated in 1986, the annual Hillsong Conference is Australia's largest Christian gathering, with up to 30,000 people meeting to worship together.

Hillsong's praise and worship albums have achieved both Australian and international mainstream success. Many of these records hit both secular and Christian charts, and in 2018 *What a Beautiful Name* won three Dove Awards and a Grammy. However, this music has increasing cultural and linguistic diversity; for example, in 2012 *The Global Project* featured several of their most popular songs translated into nine languages. Many different musical artists and worship leaders participate in the annual Hillsong Church (Hillsong Live) albums, with their popularity often resulting in global fame. For example, Geoff Bullock, Darlene Zschech, Taya Smith and Joel Houston are some notable contributors. Extremely popular Hillsongs include 'Shout to the Lord', 'Mighty to Save', 'Oceans' and 'Cornerstone', along with many, many others. The song 'This I Believe (The Creed)' was inspired by the Apostles' Creed. Hillsong's youth bands Hillsong United and Young and Free tour regularly and have success in their own right. The music of Hillsong has been globally influential upon Christianity.

Oceanian Pentecostalism is diverse and increasingly influential in other regions of the world where new congregations have been planted. Similarly, various international forms of Pentecostalism are influential in Oceania, including Korean, Nigerian, South African and Brazilian. As these movements take hold, they are simultaneously transforming the region's spirituality and adopting local characteristics.

Bibliography

Budden, Chris, 'Acknowledging First Peoples in Christian Worship in Australia', in Stephen Burns and Anita Monro (eds), *Christian Worship in Australia* (Strathfield: St Paul''s Publications, 2009), 59–68.

Habel, Norman C., *Reconciliation: Searching for Australia's Soul* (Adelaide: Griffin Press, 1999).

Havea, Sione Amanaki, 'Christianity in the Pacific Context', in *South Pacific Theology: Papers from the Consultation on Pacific Theology, Papua New Guinea, January 1986* (Oxford: Regnum Books, 1987), 11–15.

Pattel-Gray, Anne, *Through Aboriginal Eyes: The Cry from the Wilderness* (Geneva: WCC, 1991).

Riches, Tanya and Tom Wagner (eds), *The Hillsong Movement Examined: You Call Me Out Upon the Waters* (Cham: Palgrave Macmillan, 2017).

Theology

Nāsili Vaka'uta and Darrell Jackson

Melanesia, Polynesia and Micronesia
Nāsili Vaka'uta

This section attends to theological proposals from Oceanic islanders and those who do theology from Oceanic standpoints. 'Oceania' is used with reference to the geographical sub-regions of Melanesia, Polynesia and Micronesia. It also carries the enlarged vision proposed by the late Tongan sociologist 'Epeli Hau'ofa in his much-celebrated essay 'Our Sea of Islands', in which he calls for a shift from the name 'Pacific Islands' to 'Oceania'. The former, he argues, gives a false impression that promotes a colonial land-based view of the region as tiny islands scattered over a vast ocean – hence, 'islands in the sea'. It also fosters a sense of smallness and peripherality, which in turn consigns the region to the margin and underside of mainstream discourses.

A better view of the region, according to Hau'ofa, should be based on its vast ocean-space, which serves as a common home for its inhabitants. Oceania is big, because Oceania is not 'islands in the sea' but a 'sea of islands'. Out of this sea of islands – with its diverse and rich cultures, languages, worldviews, belief systems and traditions – have sprung forth 'waves of theologies', most of which flow against the currents of Christian orthodoxy and the 'imperial-patriarchal-supremacist' theological perspectives of missionaries who landed on the many shores of Oceania. These waves ripple in various directions and defy any attempt to generalise and/or homogenise.

It is not possible here to provide an exhaustive account. The focus is on key theological moments – moments that address key issues that confront islands and islanders; make significant contributions to theological scholarship; influence the direction of theology in the region; and promote justice, freedom, equality and transformation in Oceania.

The emergence of the volume *South Pacific Theology* in 1987 is arguably the first significant theological moment (*South Pacific Theology: Papers from the Consultation on Pacific Theology, Papua New Guinea, January 1986*, Paramatta and Oxford: World Vision International South Pacific and Regnum Books, 1987). In a sense, this was a jubilee moment in doing theology in Oceania, a practice of freedom. Responding to a 1976 call by the then Governor General of Papua New Guinea, Sir John Guise, and bringing together new theological proposals from the Port Moresby consultation on Pacific theology in 1986, *South Pacific Theology* recognised the need to shift from 'missionary-positioned' theologies (which were for the most part imperial, Western and Eurocentric in orientation) and to look for ideas that were closer to home and relevant. That came with a renewed appreciation of local cultures and native religions, an attempt to recover and reclaim what was condemned by missionaries, an acknowledgement of Oceanic identities and ways of being, and a new sense of freedom to talk about the divine, humanity and nature in a different but familiar manner.

Sione 'Amanaki Havea's proposal for a 'coconut theology' set the tone for a theological mo(ve)ment that rippled across Oceania and beyond. The two main avenues for disseminating works from theologians who joined this movement in subsequent years were the *Pacific Journal of Theology* from SPATS (South Pacific Association of Theological Schools) and the *Melanesian Journal of Theology* from MATS (Melanesian Association of Theological Schools). The 1990s saw more theological activities dealing with identity questions and aspects of island cultures that previous theological conversations had ignored, especially those condemned by missionaries as barbaric.

Charles W. Forman, in his 2005 article 'Finding Our Own Voice: The Reinterpreting of Christianity by Oceanian Theologians', captures well the development and terrain of theologies in the region up to that point (*International Bulletin of Missionary Research*, 29:3 (July 2005), 115–22). Forman draws attention to the fact that theological activities in Oceania were no longer done by outsiders but by islanders. He then discusses the works of four key theologians, namely Havea, Ilaitia Sevati Tuwere, Leslie Boseto and Bishop Patelesio Finau. All were leaders of their respective churches. Their influence paved the way for increased interest in the area, but they never failed to carry out their prophetic duties, especially in speaking out against social injustices and in critiquing dehumanising aspects of their own cultures.

In addition to the above four, Forman also introduced three other islanders who had published works on theological subjects. The first is Lalomilo Kamu, whose work *The Sāmoan Culture and the Christian Gospel* (Apia: Donna Lou Kamu, 1996) criticises both the European missionaries for their negative attitude toward Oceanic cultures and the Sāmoan church for being 'too conciliatory' toward culture. The second, Pothin Wete, brings another perspective as an Indigenous Kanak from New Caledonia. He calls for complete independence from France and describes his work as 'Kanak liberation theology'. The third, Amaamalele Tofaeono, from American Sāmoa, was the first from this region to publish in the area of eco-theology. His work *Eco-theology: Aiga – The Household of Life* (Erlangen: Erlanger Verlag für Mission und Ökumene, 2000) was driven by the global ecological crisis, which to him was worsened by the narrow anthropocentric Christian view of creation. He proposes the Sāmoan concept of *aiga* as an alternative, a concept that deals with creation in its totality.

Following Forman's lead was an article by Neil Darragh, a Catholic priest and theologian from Aotearoa New Zealand, with the title 'Pacific Island Theology' (2007). Darragh's survey explored local theological writings from both Indigenous and non-Indigenous islanders. He groups these works into three categories. Localisation, the first, he defines as the interweaving of overseas forms of the Christian gospel with Pacific cultures. The second, public engagement, encompasses theologians reflecting on the issues of the society. In ecclesiology, the third category, Darragh sees a move from competitive ways of doing theology and church to an emphasis on ecumenical dialogue characterised by respectful collaboration.

Such collaboration led to another key theological moment, marked by the publication of the volume *Weavings: Women Doing Theology in Oceania* (Lydia Johnson and Joan Alleluia Filemoni-Tofaeono (eds), Suva: USP/ SPATS, 2003). Contributors were from various denominations, including Keiti Ann Kanongata'a, a leading female theologian and a Roman Catholic nun. They pushed the boundary of what was then (and still is) a male-dominated movement and presented some important theological milestones. They also raised awareness of issues women experienced, and wove together various strands of liberation theology sprinkled with island flavours. This set the stage for the emphasis on gender justice, which has become one of the key features of the current landscape of theology in Oceania.

The current landscape of theology is shaped largely by issues that are affecting the lives of people in the islands. These issues are multi-dimensional: social, ecological, economic and political as well as ecclesial. Socially, Oceania is marred by the brutal reality of gender-based violence and sexual abuse, especially against women and children. Addressing this issue has been challenging due to cultural taboos and shame. Neither was it traditionally a topic of choice for theological research. This changed when Mercy Maliko, a Sāmoan female public theologian, focused her doctoral research at the University of Otago on domestic violence in Sāmoa. She brought to the fore the fact that nearly half of Sāmoan women have been subject to abuse by intimate partners or parents. She also argued that the growing number of reported cases of domestic violence – along with many other cases that are not reported – should make domestic violence a priority in theological reflection. Maliko created a key theological moment not only in academia but also within the community and church.

On the ecological front, theologians reflect on the ecological vulnerability of the islands of Oceania. These islands are greatly exposed to the effects of climate change, which is real and alarming. The sea is rising and islands are drowning, especially in the cases of Tuvalu and Kiribati. Cyclones come almost annually, leaving many people homeless (especially in the outer islands), destroying Oceania's agricultural assets, food and water supply, and increasingly making the economy more vulnerable. Issues of ecological degradation due to exploitation of resources and pollution are also present. Deforestation is still a reality in many countries, like the Solomon Islands. This ecological challenge serves as the basis for theological reflections by island theologians such as Cliff Bird from the Solomon Islands in his article 'Hermeneutics of Ecology and Its Relationship to the Identity of the *Oikos* in Oceania' (*Pacific Journal of Theology*, series II, 46 (2011), 19–33) and Upolu Lumā Vaai in 'Others Are Enjoying Life From Our Death: Eco-relational Theology and a Methodist Ecological Revolution in Oceania', a paper he presented at the Oxford Institute of Methodist Theological Studies in 2018.

Economically, neo-liberalist ideals have done more harm than good to the region. Oceania is economically dependent, no matter how export-oriented the islands are vis-à-vis the world market. Capitalist visions and neo-liberal policies have swept the region like 'economic tsunamis'; they ebb and flow, they bring and take whatever they can in and out of the region. The worst-case scenario is for islands to 'prostitute' themselves for money, and some have fallen into that trap. Neo-liberalism requires that if you do not have anything to sell, sell yourself! Everything (people, sea, land, air) is a product and must be traded without restrictions in a global market that is driven by greed and unfair distribution of resources. Oceania is crying for economic justice. This is the focus of a paper ('Fale-'o-kāinga: Rethinking Biblical Interpretation Eco-wise') delivered by the present author at the Society of Asian Biblical Studies meeting at the Methodist Theological Seminary, Seoul, South Korea, on 5 July 2018.

Politically, imperialism has never left Oceania's shores. The imperial programme of 'colonial translation' or 'colonial cloning' has altered (in some cases irreversibly and violently) the geographical, cultural, political, educational, linguistic, religious, ecological, economic and psychological landscapes of many countries and peoples. Through that programme, regional and national boundaries in Oceania were redrawn and new borders created. Sāmoa was split into Western and American, each controlled by different empires. Bougainville, which is ethnically part of the Solomon Islands, was given to Papua New Guinea. Those new borders created political tensions and, tragically, people are geographically and ethnically displaced and even murdered. West Papua, in particular, was cut off from Papua New Guinea and given to Indonesia, which created the only land border in the region and led to a genocide that is largely ignored by the global community. Oceania is crying for social and political justice. This is manifested theologically in publications like the volume edited by Mark Brett and Jione Havea, *Colonial Contexts and Postcolonial Theologies: Storyweaving in the Asia-Pacific* (London: Palgrave, 2014). The volume brings together concerns from contributors Oceania-wide about the current political climate and the ongoing effect of imperialism and the ongoing presence of imperial powers and settler colonisers in various islands such as Aotearoa New Zealand.

Ecclesially, church-related issues call for theological attention as well. The church and its dogmatic positions can be suffocating and life-threatening. The way most churches do theologies and interpret the Bible are still very much stuck in the nineteenth century and continue to embrace 'missionary positions' more than anything else. One needs only to browse through the issues of the *Melanesian Journal of Theology* to see the evidence. To borrow Jione Havea's terminology, theologies in Oceanic churches are 'going stale', because the methods of theological analysis have also gone stale. There is a need to adjust our 'theologising posture' to be grounded in real life and in the community of real people. There is also the need to reposition Oceania's theological outlook. The ongoing association of suffering and sin is a case in point. In doing so, churches run the risk of further demonising those who need transformation and healing the most.

Theology in Oceania still has unfinished business and some further miles to walk. There is, for example, lack of theological reflection on the rights of those within the LGBTQI+ community. Sexuality is still very much a topic to be ignored, and churches are not willing to learn and make their decisions based on available information. The predominant view on sexuality is based largely on the Bible and tradition, with no openness to new information and no consideration for those whose identity and experience are different from those of the rest. The volume *Sexuality, Ideology and the Bible: Antipodean Engagements* (Sheffield: Sheffield Phoenix Press, 2015), edited by Robert J. Myles and Caroline Blyth, is a good place to start this conversation, but theologians who are working in the islands of Oceania have to be willing to engage in such conversations in an open and free manner. This is a theological moment that is yet to come, and it is very much needed.

Australia and New Zealand
Darrell Jackson

I am writing this from my home, situated on Darramuragal land, although I work on Wurundjeri land. In acknowledging elders – past, present and emerging – as the traditional owners of these lands, I attempt to bracket my own work here as that of a migrant European theologian, now living in Sydney and working in Melbourne, Australia. The responsible practice of my theological profession in Australia, and my hesitation in commenting on theological education on the eastern side of the Tasman Sea, requires an honest recognition of the many unresolved consequences of European colonisation and the manner in which this has shaped the practice of theology on this Land.

In the above section, Nāsili Vaka'uta prefers to use 'Oceania' rather than the 'Pacific Islands', because the vast ocean space his analysis encompasses is better described as a 'sea of islands' providing a 'common home for its inhabitants'. In contrast, the experience of 'Australia' reverses this order. The common home is instead a vast island, even though most of its twenty-first-century inhabitants dwell on its coastal margins, close to water.

To describe Australia with sole reference to its being a 'nation' obscures the fact that it is a federated commonwealth of six states plus three internal and seven external territories. However, a more ancient territorial claim rests with over 700 tribal groups, representing some 270 language families, commonly acknowledged as the traditional owners of the Land that now comprises 'Australia'.

Most contemporary theologians in Australia are, as Chris Budden suggests, doing 'theology in the face of the claim of Indigenous people … that they knew God before the invaders brought the gospel'. If Australia's Aboriginal and Torres Strait Islander peoples are 'First Peoples', then my theology here is a 'Second People's theology' which I practise as an invader rather than a guest. All of my theology on this land is practised in light of a deeply fractured relationship with its traditional custodians.

Theological education in Australia
Most tertiary theological educators in Australia provide a broad range of theological programmes, the majority of which are designed to equip the individual for pastoral or other ministry service within Australia. This fact alone suggests that 'theology' has been commodified and domesticated for quality-assured delivery by educational institutions. 'Theology' is primarily something to be studied and applied.

Theological study in Australia has been largely the preserve of denominationally sponsored theological colleges. Few Australian universities have offered programmes of theological study, and in some instances are prevented from doing so by a founding Act of Parliament (including the University of Melbourne, for example). The University of Sydney BD was offered only between 1935 and 1960, while the early 1960s saw a number of theological consortia establish partnerships with university departments to offer programmes in theological studies (e.g. the Adelaide College of Divinity offering degrees through Flinders University and the Perth College of Divinity offering degrees through Murdoch University). Theological programmes would eventually also be offered by the Australian Catholic University, Charles Sturt University and the University of Notre Dame Australia, joined for a short period by the University of Newcastle.

From as early as 1891, denominational colleges sensed advantages in forming theological consortia, with the establishment of the Australian College of Theology (ACT) in that year. Initially comprising Anglican colleges, the ACT now includes a range of other denominational colleges. Similar collaboration characterises the Sydney College of Divinity (1983), the Perth College of Divinity (1985) and the former Melbourne College of Divinity. The Melbourne College of Divinity, founded as a theological consortium of colleges in 1910, has subsequently gained the status of 'university of specialisation', operating since 2011 as the University of Divinity. Several theological providers, individual and consortia, have gained self-accredited status, including Moore College, Excelsia, Alphacrucis and the Sydney College of Divinity.

Theological education in Australia has been irrevocably shaped by its exclusion from the government-funded universities. Charles Sherlock's 2009 study of the sector identified 69 providers, offering 6,209 equivalent full-time student loads. Submissions to the Australian Research Council for 2018 show that 11 universities had faculty who were research active in the field of either philosophy and religion or religious studies – the primary reporting categories for theology, Christian history, Christian ethics, practical theology and biblical studies.

Theological study across the sector is supported by the work of the Australian and New Zealand Association of Theological Schools (ANZATS), established in 1968, and its journal, *Colloquium*. Alongside ANZATS are a range of discipline-specific scholarly associations in which theological scholars can participate for mutual benefit, including the disciplines of practical theology, biblical studies, mission studies, Christian history and patristics. A number of these also produce peer-reviewed journals.

Theological education in Aotearoa/New Zealand

Three years after the signing of the Treaty of Waitangi in 1840, Anglicans among the British colonisers of New Zealand established St John's

Theological College in Auckland. In 1877, Presbyterians opened the Theological Hall in Dunedin. Its successor, Knox College, was opened in 1909. Roman Catholic seminarians were educated in Auckland from 1850 to 1869, at Mount St Mary's College, Hawkes Bay, from 1889, and at Holy Cross College, Mosgiel, from 1900. In 1998 a partnership between these colleges led to the Good Shepherd College – Te Hepara Pai – offering theological and clerical education within the Roman Catholic tradition. For Baptists, theological education was first offered in 1926, through the New Zealand Baptist Theological College, later Carey College. By 1934 the Assemblies of God church was operating theological colleges in Auckland, Hamilton, Wellington and Christchurch. The largest non-denominational provider, Laidlaw College, was established in 1922 in Auckland as the Bible Training Institute. In 1952 the Presbyterian Church tabled proposals for a Māori Synod and Theological College and Te Wananga a Rangi has offered theological education and ministry preparation since 1953.

In 1968, the Methodist Trinity College and Anglican St John's College set up the Joint Board of Theological Studies. Despite the subsequent stalling of denominational union, a review of the colleges in 1984 urged steps toward degree studies. A partnership with the Baptists subsequently constituted the Auckland Consortium for Theological Education (ACTE) in 1985. The ACTE offered the BTheol through Melbourne College of Divinity from 1988 but in 1990 switched to teaching an alternative BTheol through Auckland University, with master's and doctoral studies following shortly thereafter.

Broader associations and partnerships furnish various levels of support, including collaborative approaches to curriculum development and support, accreditation, quality assurance and faculty development, including, for example, the New Zealand Association of Theological Schools and the Christian Theological and Ministries Education Society, with 18 member colleges and two associate colleges. The Australian College of Theology continues to accredit programmes for Laidlaw College.

The 1960 Parry report into New Zealand's university education recognised the strength of the argument for introducing Religious Studies into the university curriculum, but progress to this end was slow and inconsistent. By 1969 the universities of Otago and Canterbury had made a beginning, and Massey and Victoria universities were exploring options. By 1971, the University of Auckland was actively exploring the possibility of a department and faculty of theology.

Massey University introduced Religious Studies in 1970, funded by interested churches. Victoria University, in Wellington, has hosted a Religious Studies Programme since 1971, growing to eight faculty members by 2008, though there had been shrinkage in the sector by 2019. The University of Otago established a lectureship in the phenomenology of religion in 1966 and currently offers the only university-based theology programme in New Zealand, via a partnership with five theological colleges. The University of Canterbury began offering Religious Studies, located within the Philosophy Department, in 1965 and an MA degree was first offered there in 1971. A review of the work of ACTE saw it replaced with a School of Theology at the University of Auckland in 2002. The University now offers degrees in the broader field of Religious and Theological Studies, located in the Arts Faculty. In 2020 Auckland University of Technology was accrediting doctoral programmes for four theological colleges.

In advancing an argument for theological education in the university, supporters point to the dialogical and rhetorical competencies that are often closely associated with the discipline. The contribution of articulate and dialogically competent theologians to the government's bio-ethics public hearings in 2005 as well as to the shaping of assessment criteria developed by the New Zealand Qualification Authority in the early 1990s are illustrations of the value of theological study in the university. These various contributions found resonance within the broader academic community.

Australian theology

The dominant conservative Evangelicalism of Sydney's Anglican diocese drew upon British Evangelicalism. It was hostile to the construction of anything that might be described as 'Australian theology', preferring a theological analysis of human culture allied with social and historical research. Writing in 2017, Vice Chancellor of the University of Divinity, Professor Peter Sherlock, referred to a 1977 article in which Richard Campbell argued that Christian theology in Australia has been derivative of European and North American theologies. Theology might have taken root in Australia, but it was not at that point an Australian theology.

Successively, Indigenous, contextual and postcolonial scholars have assumed that the derivative nature of theology in Australia is a necessary starting point for their scholarly critique and engagement and that this serves as a stimulus to developing an authentically Australian theology. Postcolonial theologians critiqued 'Eurocentric' Protestant and Roman Catholic theologies for obscuring the Australian context, in which Aboriginal peoples were present. Such approaches were implicitly critical of conservative Evangelical theologians at colleges such as Moore College in Sydney. A more radical theological vision appears in the proposal that Australian theology can emerge only in the context of invasion and dispossession, against a demand for justice, and an acknowledgement of the Aboriginal land upon which theological debate and dialogue take place. The intended or unintended consequences of contextual theology continue to exercise some theologians in Australia. The geographical distance of Australia from countries of immigrant origin and centres of perceived theological authority gives rise to a concern that an overly contextual Australian theology will be at the expense of international disconnection. Over the closing decades of the twentieth century and the early decades of the twenty-first century, Protestant and Roman Catholic scholars have wrestled with the extent to which an Australian contextual theology must learn from overly domesticated or 'cosy' contextualisations. Contextual theology, in emphasising discontinuity with derivative forms of theology, remains authentically Christian theology to the extent that it can explore and articulate appropriate continuities with other forms of Christian testimony.

Sherlock's 2017 Marshall Lecture is an unapologetic call for a theology that 'engages seriously with its Australian context', one of many such calls in recent decades. Delineating the contours of what an appropriately contextual Australian theology will address is likely to occupy the attention of theologians and biblical scholars over coming decades. What is offered here is an initial review of contextual factors that will require careful attention by 'Second People' theologians if such theology is to have any relevance on the lands of the Darramuragal or the Wurundjeri people, for example.

'Land' is central to any contextual form of theology in Australia. Theologians sensitive to context are largely convinced that the issue of land cannot be ignored. This cannot be disassociated from calls that the theological curriculum should engage climate change, justice for Indigenous Australians and migration. Solely Eurocentric approaches to such issues in Australia will prove wholly inadequate to the complex inter-relationship these issues pose for Indigenous and non-Indigenous scholars alike.

Proposals that an Australian theology will work with notions of 'new' and 'ordinariness' sit alongside the fact of pre-European aboriginal mythologies that persist among Aboriginal and Torres Strait Islander peoples in contemporary Australia. The prior faith and spirituality of Indigenous Australians is proving increasingly to be a vital resource for theological imagination in Australia. An Australian theology requires deep immersion in the memories of forced displacement from land by European settlers, immersion that resists the tendency to suppress memories and which makes pilgrimage to the sites of resistance and suffering situated on land that is sacred to Indigenous Australians.

Aotearoa/New Zealand theology
Theological education and formation have encountered transition and transformation over the last decade. By 2015, Anglicans and Presbyterians were offering ministry training that required the prior study of theology at a university or theological college. The Presbyterian Knox College, for example, became a School of Ministry in 1997 when the University of Otago assumed responsibility for delivering theology. It has since been renamed the Knox Centre for Ministry and Leadership; its ministry formation programme requires a two-year internship for candidates who already hold a theological degree from elsewhere, typically from the University of Otago.

The University of Otago's Centre for Theology and Public Issues, established in 2016 by academics from the Theology Programme, became the first research centre in New Zealand to examine political, social and economic issues from a theological perspective. With this move, theological educators took steps to actively resist the political and intellectual pressure that sought to consign theology to the merely private and religious domains. Theologians began to imagine a God who was effective in the New Zealand context, transforming local practice and stimulating the imagination of not merely professional theologians but also multiple stakeholders in the community, especially where such imagination was held communally.

In a sympathetic assessment of trends in theological education and religious studies in 2019, Geoff Troughton suggested that the healthy student enrolment numbers were a response to courses that advocated thematic and non-partisan approaches to the study of religion and theology in the specific context of New Zealand. Over the same period, colleges such as St John's have been pioneering responses to the bicultural nature of New Zealand society. The implications of the Waitangi Treaty for theological education can be seen in St John's decision to introduce a new curriculum in 2006, replacing the dominant Western theological curriculum and pedagogy with one that honoured Māori as the Indigenous people of the land. The monocultural ethos has been replaced by one in which three colleges act as a triumvirate, representing equally Māori, Polynesian and Pākehā (European). Through its model of theological education, St John's has demonstrated commitment to confronting otherness, respecting diversity and exploring togetherness.

The appeal of such moves is wider than simply the immediate benefit of a richer theological curriculum, for they also contribute to the wider debates about the degree to which New Zealand is a secular nation. More recently, perceptive commentators on religions and secularity in New Zealand have noted the emergence of a bicultural society (Māori–Pākehā) in which sacred and secular inter-penetrate in accounts of history and public policy. While some theological schools will doubtless continue to struggle with the implications of such views, the New Zealand scholar of gospel and culture Harold Turner was honest about the potential for epistemological affinities between Māori and Christian cosmologies, for example. Complementing Turner's brief reflections upon the influence that a study of land and place might have upon an understanding of Christianity in New Zealand, it seems likely that a theology which takes Aotearoa/New Zealand as its starting point, rather than its destination, will remain attentive to the material, to the body, to space, the ocean, geographical location, geophysical fragility, hybridity and the notion of borderland spaces. Consequently, an authentic theology from Aotearoa/New Zealand will, of necessity, be hermeneutical and inter-disciplinary in nature and, ultimately, bicultural.

Indigenous First People's theologies

Observations about the overwhelmingly British character of Evangelical theology in Australia during the 1980s would probably correlate closely with the European or North American heritage of most individual theologians then teaching in Australia's theological schools and colleges. Today, their voices are still the numerically dominant voices in the conversation (including the modest contribution here!).

However, Australia's theological institutions are now employing a small, though growing, number of theologians from Oceania and Asia, with some institutions exploring how to engage with, resource and employ Indigenous theologians. There are certain reluctances to doing so. Earlier in this essay I noted a resistance to Australian forms of theology, and I suggest here that embracing the utility of pre-European (taken to imply 'pre-Christian') theologies, cosmologies or 'dreaming' will likely be resisted with equal or greater passion. More importantly, there is the frequently unacknowledged reality that embracing their utility will be painful for non-Indigenous theologians as they are critiqued and challenged by their encounter with the trauma of Indigenous experience and the distinct expressions of Indigenous spirituality.

Happily, the nature and quality of theological reflection of theologians from Oceania and Asia, working in Australia, is proving to be a vital resource for decolonising Eurocentric theologies and theological activity. They draw attention to the delusion that 'Western' theology is universal in character. They remind us that European theology has always been a local theology, albeit vested with the appearance of universality. Eurocentric theologians fail to see these limitations and become conscious of them only when non-Western theologians point out the difficulties faced by European migrants trying to contextualise on a land in which they are not Indigenous.

Contextual, liberation and postcolonial modes of reading and theologising have been, and remain, hugely significant for current and emerging Indigenous theologians in constructing Indigenous forms of Australian theology. In 2017, the Melbourne-based University of Divinity and Whitley College entered a partnership with the NAIITS Indigenous Learning Community to offer taught and research programmes accessible to Indigenous students taught and supervised by Indigenous faculty. Founded in 2001, NAIITS (formerly the North American Institute for Indigenous Theological Studies) has institutional partners in Canada, Australia and the USA, through which it awards a range of degree programmes. The first Australian Indigenous students to graduate from courses taught within the terms of the partnership did so in 2019. In the same year, the first NAIITS doctoral students were enrolled in the University of Divinity's PhD programme in the expectation that Indigenous Australian PhD students would soon enrol and begin the advanced research and study of Indigenous theology necessary for long-term sustainability in the sector.

Even as the search continues for Australian theologies, the achievements of this particular partnership point toward the multiplication of truly Indigenous forms of Australian theology emerging over coming decades. This, and other theological initiatives like it, will better equip theological institutes in Australia to transition from offering theology in Australia to offering authentic and coherent qualifications in Australian theology.

Bibliography

Brett, Mark and Jione Havea (eds), *Colonial Contexts and Postcolonial Theologies: Storyweaving in the Asia-Pacific* (New York: Palgrave, 2014).

Budden, Chris, *Following Jesus in Invaded Space: Doing Theology on Aboriginal Land* (Cambridge: James Clarke, 2011).

Havea, Jione, *Postcolonial Voices from Downunder: Indigenous Matters, Confronting Readings* (Eugene: Pickwick Publications, 2017).

Myles, Robert and Caroline Blyth (eds), *Sexuality, Ideology and the Bible: Antipodean Engagements* (Sheffield: Sheffield Phoenix Press, 2015).

Sherlock, Peter, *Why Australia Needs Theology*, The Barry Marshall Lecture (Melbourne: Trinity College Theological School, 2017).

Social and Political Context

Aisake Casimira

Since the turn of the century, the Oceania region has shifted in the trajectory of its political and economic development. While still shaped by the interests of major world powers, the region is not so much subject to issues of security as it is subject to political and economic interests, notably those of China. In addition, Fiji, with its 'look north' policy and its diplomatic realignment, has challenged the hegemony of Australia and New Zealand through development, trade and military power.

This analysis contextualises the interplay of geopolitical interests and the re-emergence of self-determination among the Pacific Island states. It examines these influences in a region within a 'context of insecurity' and undergoing transition, and concludes with an urgent moral challenge to its religious communities, especially the churches and their mission mandates.

A Congested Geopolitical Context

After decades of neglect following the Cold War, the Pacific Islands once again became a region of interest at the turn of the twenty-first century. There are two reasons for this change: the 'war on terror' placing a spotlight on security strategy in the Pacific, and China's rise (and, to an extent, Russia's rise) in geopolitical influence. By 2013, the potential threat China posed to both Australia and the USA demanded *realpolitik* and open admission of direct competition.

In a 2013 report produced for the Pacific Islands Forum (PIF), a review team led by Sir Mekere Morauta (Prime Minister of Papua New Guinea from 1999 to 2002) highlighted the lack of political ownership in the PIF's 2004 Pacific Plan and the fact that it did not result in the regionalism that was intended. The team instead recommended a broader framework that would promote countries' collective efforts and institute a deeper form of regionalism than one simply delimited by specific outcomes. The report was also a response to the brooding discontent of the island states against the powers of the status quo and to their growing desire to control their own fates. Against this backdrop, more Pacific Island states sought to explore their own alternative regional frameworks.

However, the 2013 institution of the Pacific Islands Development Forum (PIDF) — formerly the Friends of Fiji Forum — disrupted what was hoped to be a turning point in reshaping Pacific regionalism. Comprising 11 Pacific Island states (sans Australia and New Zealand), the PIDF was established to pursue sustainable development while voicing discontent over the excessive influence of Australia and New Zealand in PIF policy-making, at the expense of the smaller island states. Such undue influence was perceived as a deterrent to opposition voices; with Australia and New Zealand providing a significant portion of the Forum Secretariat's income and aid donors admitted as members, many island voices had become reluctant to speak out.

Fiji's trepidation about external interventions (especially by Australia and New Zealand) in its national affairs and its initial suspensions from the PIF and from the Commonwealth served as motivation for the formation of the PIDF. This also influenced its 'look north' policy – a reference to Asia, but more specifically China – which drives the PIDF's foreign policy strategy and has reshaped diplomacy in the region. This policy communicated that small states would not simply be passive re-cipients of development aid from benevolent donors, nor would island states be denied a voice at the table in international development and climate change strategies. Fiji's initiatives have intensified the reshaping of regional alliances and diplomatic relations, giving rise to a new Pacific diplomacy occasioned not simply by Fiji's efforts but in addition by the geopolitical weight of China, the disquiet over regionalism and these combined effects upon the traditional powers in the region.

Thus, China's rise in Pacific influence has been aided by the ineffective-ness of PIF's 2004 Pacific Plan, the ensuing disaffection of Pacific Island states, and Fiji's 'look north' policy enshrined in the PIDF. Although China had already been involved in Pacific Island trade and development since the 1980s, it was preoccupied with Taiwanese containment among Pacific Island countries. However, the 'war on terror' following the September 2011 terrorist attacks in the USA, along with the political crises in the Solomon Islands, Fiji and Bougainville, led to a shift in China's role in the region. With China increasing its stake in the Pacific, the resulting competition in the region could undermine the fragile governing capaci-ties of Pacific Island states. Despite Fiji's increased influence, geopolitical manoeuvring might instead align Fiji to one of the major powers. Thus, Fiji is compelled to establish political expediency amid the jockeying powers.

By the time PIF leaders met in Tuvalu in August 2019, the Pacific region had been geopolitically mapped, akin to the colonial political exercises of the eighteenth and nineteenth centuries. And just as it did then, this mapping exercise ignored the Pacific Islands' priorities, which today include climate change, development, democracy building and societal security. The US refashioned the Indo-Pacific into a geopolitical map that stretched from the west coast of the USA to the east coast of Africa, a reconfiguration welcomed by its allies. China authored the Maritime Silk Road, an extension of its Belt and Road initiative, while Australia rolled out the Pacific Step-Up, brushing aside issues of climate change and re-settlement. In the meantime, Indonesia, an emerging power in Southeast Asia, launched its Pacific Elevation without addressing its blatant human rights abuses in West Papua.

In 2017, the PIF Secretariat adopted the Blue Pacific, a conceptual framework for Pacific regionalism, as its own version of regional mapping. This was intended to be the Pacific Islands' political and economic leverage against the major powers in the region. However, despite laudable efforts behind the framework, such leverage will not be strong enough to resist the superpowers' geopolitical interests in the Pacific Island region. Its success will depend on Pacific Island leaders asserting their priorities in this new geopolitical map with respect to the priorities of the major powers over land and sea resources and trade and security preferences. The framework will be shaped by how well the citizens it represents exercise their capacity for sound policy analysis and to pursue a 'different story of development' in the Pacific.

With the advent of the COVID-19 pandemic in 2020, self-determination in Pacific diplomacy and trade policy hangs in the balance. Despite the World Bank providing large-scale infrastructure aid to Fiji, Papua New Guinea, Tonga and other island nations, the rise in unemployment, suicides and gender-based violence begs the question of whether the COVID-19 response package would be better served by having Pacific nations propose their own model of development. While improving health services is important, enhancing resilience is far more sustainable.

But what is the role of civil institutions, such as churches, in this geopolitical scheme? One important element is the absence of a counter-narrative to the dominant perspectives on development, governance, security and climate change. A counter-narrative to global powers' neo-liberal trajectories is imperative, and while churches are best placed to help drive it, they will need to liberate themselves from dependency and to engage with their national and regional contexts far more confidently than they currently do.

A Context of Insecurity

Since the 1980s, the Pacific has erupted in ethnic and political violence, beginning with the first military coup in Fiji in 1987. Such conflicts have also erupted in places like Papua New Guinea, Kanaky (New Caledonia), Tonga and Māòhi Nui (French Polynesia). West Papua (occupied and annexed by Indonesia since 1969 through dubious means) continues to be exploited for its natural resources, and its people are subjected to serious human rights abuses by the Indonesian state and its enforcement agencies.

This account is not to suggest that political violence and inter-ethnic and tribal conflicts in the island nations were absent prior to independence. It is simply to indicate that political independence has not been a panacea. The wholesale adoption of institutional structures by newly independent democratic states was a fairly smooth transition for some, but for others it has been fraught with political disruptions and conflict, leading to the rise of post-independence violence.

Many of the conflicts in the Pacific since the late 1990s have been caused by unequal distribution of benefits from resources in the areas of mining, logging, fishing and economic development. Urban drift and the associated high levels of unemployment have the potential to create further social and political grievances and to threaten political stability. While these issues do not portend an irreversible slide into chaos, it is also true that this 'context of insecurity' offers geopolitical advantages to more powerful forces and governments.

Development Aid as Security
At the turn of the twenty-first century, the ethnic crisis in the Solomon Islands (colloquially, 'The Tension') became for Australia what Iraq was to the USA. A new foreign policy emerged, underpinned by the view that the world powers were united against the terrorism of the embittered, weaker actors and, thus, strategic partnerships were necessary to provide development aid. Such partnerships are often accompanied by military interventions, on the pretext of creating a more 'civilised world' where freedom and democracy are hallmarks.

However, such regional military interventions have instead heightened instability since the collapse of communism and the triumphal march of global capitalism. Developments in the Asia-Pacific region, such as the increase of US military support to the Philippines government and the Bali terrorist bombing, have reinforced this conclusion. These events impact how regional issues such as poverty, HIV and AIDS, sea-level rise, nuclear testing and pro-independence struggles are perceived. For example, the Australian government's portrayal of refugees from Asia and the Middle East in the early 2000s as threats to sovereignty has been instrumentalised by politicians for elections, anti-immigration policies, the war in Iraq and defence spending.

'Security' can be employed to create a sense of danger associated with 'others' and thus lead to policies that manufacture an artificial 'us' against a phantom threat. While interventions might lead to increased human security, they can mean different kinds of risks to certain groups. The

Pacific has seen such things as a rise of non-communicable diseases (NCDs) in most Pacific Island states; the curtailing of freedom of speech in Tonga; nuclear test compensation for Māòhi Nui, Fiji, Kiribati and the Marshall Islands; and sea-level rise in Kiribati and Tuvalu due to climate change. In this regard, security, understood as resourcing mechanisms against crime and international terrorism, needs to be part of the framework discussion. This framework is fundamental to any long-lasting solution and it must include investments in education, health, poverty alleviation and the search for a sustainable and effective developmental model.

Unfortunately, this definition of 'security' is precluded by donors' development agendas and their security interests. This is problematic in that basic human needs and rights are regarded as 'security' issues only when they directly affect the interests of developed countries. The Australian military intervention in the Solomon Islands in the early 2000s and Indonesia's provision of law enforcement training to the Melanesian Spearhead Group (MSG) are responses consistent with this view of Pacific issues as security problems. The latter feeds into the growing social agitation in the face of Indonesia's brutal suppression of the West Papua people.

While the foreign policies of donor countries – Australia, New Zealand, China and Indonesia in particular – purport to be for the security of the Pacific region, it is likely that these policies protect their own geopolitical interests. By casting Melanesian countries as the 'arc of instability' and the Solomon Islands as a 'failed state', donor countries may establish justifications for military interventions solely based on island states harbouring terrorists and drug traffickers. However, this perspective, framed only in the interests of world powers' peace and security, not only overlooks the endemic instability of island nations but also risks their marginalisation as quiet neighbours of incidental concern.

One cannot overlook the opportunities in security spending, notably in developmental priorities such as education and sanitation. However, with Overseas Development Assistance (ODA) requiring that Pacific Island countries show how these expenditures will address the security concerns of donor countries, it is not assured that such spending will not bolster arms sales and bureaucratic bribes. ODA aid that was redefined to include peacekeeping operations and military assistance has been reframed to serve donor countries' geopolitical military and economic interests. Aid from China, Australia, the USA, Russia and Indonesia has become highly politicised and their anti-terrorism policies open the gates for military spending. The danger is that any human rights protest – such as that of people's movements, trade unions and civil society organisations (CSOs) – can be targeted by anti-terrorism legislation. Since 2006, Fiji has moved to minimise such resistance by revising its labour laws to weaken the unions and by making it more difficult to obtain permits for public protest marches. Where anti-terrorism policies hold sway, it seems that the poor become the enemy.

Neo-liberalism and Consumerism

The economies of most Pacific Island Countries (PIC) are partly monetised and partly based on subsistence. However, with the introduction of neo-liberal capitalism worldwide in the mid-1980s and 'structural adjustment policy' packages, such economies have been plunged into poverty due to mandated privatisation and austerity.

Such policies were reinforced by regional trade agreements – the Pacific Island Countries Trade Agreement and the Pacific Agreement on Closer Economic Relations Plus – that were detriments to the development of PIC societies. While this development benefited a few, it resulted in social alienation (mainly among young people) and scepticism toward political institutions. These trends in essence stem from the era of Reaganism and Thatcherism in the 1980s and its 'no alternative' mantra, which helped dismantle many social welfare systems instituted after the Second World War. What is fundamental in this neo-liberal process is the marginalisation of environmental and community concerns, sacrificing Indigenous values for a market-driven, positivist ideal. What has historically been driving imperialist and colonial endeavours has, in the nineteenth and twentieth centuries, driven capitalism and free enterprise.

Throughout history, distinctive human communities have developed intricate systems and norms of wealth creation and distribution – governing principles and ethics that on the one hand conserve and sustain and on the other provide for development. However, under the neo-liberal banner, these autochthonous worldviews are undermined, deemed irrelevant to 'development' understood as 'more and more growth'. International financial institutions, academia (religious and secular), and even civil society organisations either ignore the deleterious effects of neo-liberalism or they simply adopt a defeatist position and settle for mere stopgaps.

This obsession with 'more' has been shown to foster greater insecurity and inequality. As a result, the influence of richer countries is expanding rapidly, with regional powers like Australia and New Zealand accused of employing bullying tactics through the Pacific Islands Forum Secretariat. Resource extraction by Asian countries such as China, Indonesia and Malaysia and its impact on the environment and island communities is a growing concern, with an open season on regional fish stocks, forests, and land and seabed mining. Such ecological and social changes paint the environment as nothing more than a resource to meet human needs.

With these social shifts, poverty is a major concern in the Pacific, with figures up 30% in countries such as Fiji in its 2013–14 survey. Despite private and public research on poverty and development, most studies mainly affirm the worsening poverty situations in the Pacific, suggesting remedies involving more resource extraction (land mining and lately seabed mining), agriculture, housing, forestry and fisheries, income generation projects and small-business schemes. Unless the fundamentals of development are critiqued and changed, the solutions might turn out to be problems themselves.

Public health in most island countries is another grave concern. In 2010, non-communicable diseases were reported to be the leading cause of death in the region (8 out of every 10) and the biggest drain on national budgets. In large part, this situation stems from the dramatic changes in the diets and eating habits of Pacific peoples, changes that are a consequence of current developmental theory, policy and practice, driven largely by neo-liberal capitalism.

Governance and Development

Democratic governance was adopted by the countries in the region upon independence from the colonial powers. Tonga, Sāmoa and Fiji (until the mid-2000s) adopted varying amalgamations of democratic systems and traditional cultural forms of governance, such as the chiefly system in Fiji, the *matai* system in Sāmoa and the monarchy and nobles in Tonga. However, today the island nations struggle to conceptualise democracy within cultures where communal rights have a higher value than individual rights. Such transitions came with serious and protracted problems. Fiji, Papua New Guinea, Tonga and the Solomon Islands are still wrestling with the contrasts between democracy and their traditional cultures. A case study of Fiji's struggle with democracy published in 2008 revealed the inadequacies of a one-size-fits-all approach to democratic governance for all countries in the Pacific. In addition, flawed leadership has led to corruption and a waste of public resources, whether in the misuse of public money or the immoral behaviour of politicians and church and community leaders. Remedies are needed for these perceived weak governing institutions and political leadership cultures. For the long term, cultivating a sense of civic responsibility and a political leadership culture is key. Moreover, investing in children and youth and in nation-building efforts needs to be a priority for governments, churches and CSOs.

The rapid transition from communally oriented societies to cash economies has also contributed to the decay of traditional social structures. Urbanisation has begun to dismantle social structures across the Pacific. Slum-like settlements have been spreading in places like Suva, Port

Moresby, Tarawa, Funafuti and Papeete since the early 2000s, overwhelming public services. Malnourishment, something Pacific Island societies once proudly claimed as unknown in this part of the world, is spreading rapidly in some urban areas.

Given this dramatic social and political change, one remedy is often said to be 'good governance'. While the press for institutional reforms nearly always follows military or other forms of intervention, the proponents of such interventions need to be mindful of unintended consequences that lead to the reinvention of governments' roles and functions.

Under the impact of neo-liberal capitalism since the 1980s, governments are behaving like the chief executive officers of multinational companies, ensuring a habitat for global investment rather than promoting human dignity and the rights of their citizens. They are primarily concerned with delivering maximum services at minimum costs, favouring incentives for investors rather than those of the general populace, incentives that should include an equitable distribution of wealth, income and natural resources, full employment, and access to housing, health and education. Development problems in the Pacific are in part due to lower standards of public administration.

However, like all discourses of development, the 'good governance' narrative can mask a host of related issues. It is inconceivable that a country like Papua New Guinea or the Solomon Islands can look like Australia, when these countries, which have been independent for only 30 years or so, have never had the same levels of investment. The problem is not that corrupt politicians capture aid but that donor countries give aid to whoever has power. In addition, shocking discrepancies exist between the amounts of development aid from donors and the trillions of dollars that go from developing and least-developed countries to donor countries and, in many cases, to foreign corporations.

Developed countries often misunderstand what makes Pacific societies work. Implementations of governance imposed from outside are often assumed to be the best remedy, irrespective of cultural contexts and historical narratives. In turn, developing countries are required to mould themselves in the image of developed countries, with little or no regard to other models of development and governance. In fact, many of these institutions of governance, established as requirements of neo-liberal economics, have done little to change poverty, infant mortality and illiteracy rates in several countries.

Human Rights and Self-determination

Political and civil rights abuses are increasing in Pacific Island states. From the reported abuse and torture of dissidents during the Fiji coup of 2006 to the Papua New Guinea government's use of force against university students in 2016, some governments have been reacting to human rights advancement with the curtailing of the right to free expression and the diminution of workers' rights to collective bargaining. Recently, the United Nations has moved to recognise climate change-induced resettlement as a human right, an impending reality that has great import for Pacific societies. In response, much investment is being poured into democracy and human rights education and advocacy, particularly that of women and children.

Rates of violence against women (and children) in the Pacific Islands are among the highest in the world relative to the population. According to a study by UNIFEM (United Nations Development Fund for Women) in 2010, the rate of gender-based violence is as high as 85% in some countries, with regional studies showing that in Fiji 80% of women go through some form of violence in the home. In some respects, the churches in the Pacific have begun to address this issue. The Fiji churches started a video campaign in 2018, denouncing violence against women and affirming their dignity, while in late 2019 the Catholic Archbishop of Suva issued a response against the misuse of Scripture regarding the submissiveness of women. Other examples include the United Church in Papua New Guinea's programme on gender theology and male advocacy, the Anglican Diocese of Polynesia's House of Sarah and Safe Church initiatives, the Methodist Church in Fiji's advocacy work on the issue and the programme initiated by the United Church of the Solomon Islands to address gender-based violence in its schools. Culture, religion and men are often cited as the sources of violence against women and children.

The struggle for political self-determination continues in some Pacific Island nations, with Kanaky, Māòhi Nui, Rapa Nui (Easter Island) and West Papua still under colonial rule. Prior to and after the decade of the 1980s, the political self-determination struggles at times involved violence and loss of life, as in Māòhi Nui and Kanaky. These national struggles were also the strategic focus of protests by the anti-nuclear and independence efforts coordinated by the Pacific Concerns Resource Centre, the secretariat of the Nuclear Free and Independent Pacific movement, from the late 1960s to the late 1990s. In these struggles, the Pacific churches, through the Pacific Conference of Churches secretariat, were instrumental in organising protests and supporting these movements, drawing on regional and international network links with the World Council of Churches and other global church associations.

In 2015, the United Liberation Movement for West Papua (ULMWP), a representative movement for West Papuan independence, was granted observer status with the Melanesian Spearhead Group (MSG). However, by 2020 the ULMWP's application for full membership in the MSG had still not been addressed. In the meantime, the nations of Vanuatu, the Marshall Islands, the Solomon Islands, Tonga, Palau and Nauru took Indonesia's human rights abuses in West Papua to the 2016 United Nations General Assembly, asking the United Nations to send a fact-finding mission to West Papua to investigate Indonesia's human abuses. This 'Group of 6', as they have come to be known, is in fact an alternative strategy to the failure of the MSG to substantively address the full membership application of the ULMWP.

In many respects, the human rights instruments instituted by the United Nations are indispensable to Pacific societies' political and social development, their political self-determination and their struggle for social justice. At the same time, the churches and civil society must be vigilant against a 'human rights culture' that is largely driven by neo-liberalism. Neo-liberal claims about the human person as purely utilitarian and individualistic are disastrous for democratic maturity, social development and cohesion, and cultural sustainability.

In debates over public service, labour law reforms, and the privatisation of 'the commons', discussion of the common good ignores discussions about collective commitment, obligations and restraint. Such is the effect of hyper-individualism upon more community-oriented cultures and 'commons' living. Choice is the leading concept of the neo-liberal age of supermarkets, the internet and advertisements, providing quick answers to people's 'wants'. However, this wealth of choices obscures the questions of purpose, questions such as 'What is the meaning of life?' The question, then, becomes, 'What would Pacific communities lose if one "global culture" dominates all others, if their distinctive voices are lost in the conversations about meaning and purpose?' People learn to be human not by adhering to an abstract code of human conduct but, rather, through their cultural, religious and social norms, obligations, commitments and social relationships.

The neo-liberal market has undermined Pacific peoples' ability to talk of public goods – the things that they do not buy or own but share – such as trust, reciprocity, respect and public services such as parks, libraries and cultural centres. The challenge for the churches and civil society is to disassociate their human rights discourse from the neo-liberal market mentality, so that human rights become 'covenantal' rather than 'transactional' and human security is not reduced to mere consumerism.

Climate Change and Resettlement
The systematic destruction of the environment in the region, of water and land, continues unabated. If logging and over-fishing continue at the

present levels, the Pacific Islands will have to prepare for a future with two of the major traditional resources (fish and forestry) exhausted. That some of the low-lying atolls in the region are going to disappear is not a matter of if but of when.

Environmental degradation is in part a consequence of choice and in part a consequence of the growing consumerism in Pacific societies, what Pope Francis calls a modern 'throwaway' culture. It is estimated that Sāmoa, for example, generates around 0.4 kg of waste per person every day, estimated at a daily 90,000 kg. In Honiara, Solomon Islands, the total solid waste generated per person per day is estimated to be 0.75–1.0 kg, a combined 80 tonnes of waste per day. To varying degrees, similar scenarios exist across the Pacific Islands. Plastics are the biggest polluter of the Pacific Ocean, reportedly at approximately 7 million tonnes in weight and covering an area the size of Texas in the USA and up to nine feet deep. Any solution depends on a major shift in economic models that factors in cleanup costs.

Climate change will drastically affect local sources of livelihoods such as food and water, along with their security. In particular, key future impacts are related to extended periods of drought in some areas and, on the other hand, soil degradation and loss of fertility as a result of increased precipitation in other areas, both of which will negatively impact agriculture and food security. Scientific studies state that in the absence of adaptation, a high island such as Fiji could experience damage costing up to US$52 million per year by 2050.

Fisheries, which contribute significantly to GDP and the livelihoods of the rural poor in many of the Pacific Islands, are likely to be significantly impacted by climate change. For example, more intense tropical cyclones and rises in sea level will negatively impact inshore fisheries and food supplies, especially in rural areas. In addition, rising sea levels and the increased frequency and severity of cyclones will force the resettlement of populations, with a 2050 estimate, in the worst-case scenario, of 600,000 Pacific Islanders facing resettlement associated with climate change across the region.

Climate change also threatens to obliterate many life forms upon which the natural and human ecosystems depend for survival and continuity of existence. It is not unreasonable to expect that within 50 years, 25% of animal and plant species will vanish due to the effects of climate change. Yet it is also the unchecked intrusions of human beings, often driven by greed for wealth and power, that threaten the delicate balance that sustains the natural environment. Churches and the ecumenical movement, as a collective voice of a moral impetus, cannot afford to deny the gravity of the present ecological crisis.

Churches and Civil Society

Churches and civil society comprise the most fundamental sustaining force in the Pacific region. In this regard, and particularly in relation to the ecumenical movement in the Pacific, there is an urgent need to strengthen their role in the analysis and framing of the above issues, as well as to counter the linear and one-dimensional view that underpins geopolitical interventions and the neo-liberal capitalist ethic of how life ought to be lived in the Pacific.

With an unprecedented generation of wealth, a wide range of choices available to those able to choose, and relative ease of travel between island nations, the region's full embrace of neo-liberal capitalism and its ethic since the mid-1980s has led to the recent growth in regional economies. Yet, despite these outward signs of 'progress', Pacific governments, churches and societal organisations share the impetus to craft a counter-narrative. With neo-liberalism fundamentally reshaping the ethics of Pacific communities toward efficiency, therapy and productivity, a counter-narrative is required to defend the poor, whose sources of income are exploited for the benefit of others.

These issues highlight a deepening disquiet that churches and the ecumenical movement in the Pacific must face. If governments are more concerned with the rights of the large national and international investors and businesses, who will ensure that the rights of the marginalised are safeguarded? Present political campaigns appeal to people's fear and insecurity but ask citizens to accept 'the way things are'. This is further compounded by the use of catchphrases such as 'failed states' or 'weak democracies', whereby Pacific societies are convinced that they must implement neo-liberal reforms because of their small economies of scale and geographical isolation and, more importantly, because there is simply 'no alternative'.

The 'managerial state' that guides political and economic life is not interested in substantive moral discourse about what kind of Pacific societies people seek to collectively create. Until recently, Pacific communities were aided in the shift to modernity and postmodernity, because they could rely on the stability of a permanent job, a marriage for life and a place of identity. Such virtues constitute continuity and 'the familiar' – that which gives people the strength to cope with the unfamiliar. However, these 'stabilities' are increasingly difficult to find today. Employment is increasingly part time or short term and contractual. Across the region, marriages are dissolving, perhaps influenced in part by the endless advertisements that say that one is only as good as one's next purchase. The consequence for Pacific Islanders is a devaluing of parental responsibilities and a destabilising of extended family households.

While Pacific communities might be adaptive, they are not made for constant and relentless change. When their world becomes larger than their villages or settlements, ethics becomes problematic. The residual effect is that empathy diminishes as society moves away from members of the family to the world at large. As people's sense of involvement in the lives of others has been in inverse proportion to the distance separating them, the media have effectively abolished distance. This has brought images of suffering and despair into Pacific people's immediate experience. Consequently, people's sense of compassion runs far ahead of their capacity to act and, as a result, their moral sense is simultaneously activated and frustrated. It is fair to say that such uncertainty has negatively impacted people's ability to empathise – and perhaps, in turn, to cooperate.

These moral concerns compel churches to seek a new way of engaging with their people's struggles for meaning and purpose. While post-modernity eschews a 'big narrative', it is apparent that a narrative is needed for self-belief and renewal. People in the Pacific need a moral vision and a counter-narrative that situates the source of action and responsibility within themselves. The construction of such a vision will, of necessity, include the key values of human dignity, justice, compassion, hope and peace. If churches fail to understand the causes of alienation and conflict in the region, if they fail to understand the insidious effects of geopolitical and neo-liberal forces, then, despite any advances in development, they risk becoming passive in the face of a flood of violence in the coming century.

Conclusion

Pacific governments, churches and traditional institutions play an important role in addressing the challenges outlined above. Churches, with their faith traditions, have a shared narrative that can counter the narratives communicated by the violence, dependency, injustice, environmental expediency and political oppression perpetuated by neo-liberalism. Just as the Pacific churches constructed an ecumenical narrative to counter colonialism in the early years, they must now, out of necessity and as a demand of their faith, provide a vision of hope for their people while contesting the neo-liberal worldview. Biblical theology anchors humanity in the image of God. Secure in this knowledge, as individuals and communities, people of the Pacific have the power to choose, act and take responsibility for their destiny, and so must the Pacific churches and their ecumenical movement.

The community spirit incorporated into Pacific Christianity is a strong asset for churches, who can work together on common issues to foster a Pacific-Christian identity. However, ecumenical renewal is by no means straightforward. Educational programmes on ecumenism must address the current theological conservatism and doctrinal differences that threaten the delicate theological, social and political equilibrium of their people. In the long term, efforts to substantively renew the ecumenical movement at national and regional levels will need a renewed vision based on the churches' shared, contextualised Christian faith. As social institutions charged with the mission mandate to advocate God's kingdom that is at once 'here and not yet', the Pacific churches must articulate the silent cries of those among their people who today suffer from need, hunger, disease, powerlessness and lack of freedom, independence and self-determination. Giving voice to the voiceless, since the days of the prophets and Jesus, has been an essential task of the churches' faith traditions and one of their most majestic virtues.

Bibliography

Anisi, Anna and Manfred Ernst, 'The Historical Development of Christianity in Oceania', in Lamin Sanneh and Michael McClymond (eds), *The Wiley Blackwell Companion to World Christianity* (Oxford: Wiley-Blackwell, 2016), 588–604.

Ernst, Manfred (ed.), *Globalization and the Re-shaping of Christianity in the Pacific Islands* (Suva: Pacific Theological College, 2006).

McDougall, Derek, 'China and Oceania', in Andreas Holtz, Matthias Kowasch and Oliver Hasenkamp (eds), *A Region in Transition: Politics and Power in the Pacific Island Countries*, (Saarbrücken: Saarland University Press [Presses Universitaires de la Sarre], 2016), 169–84.

O'Keefe, Michael, 'The Strategic Context of the New Pacific Diplomacy', in Greg Fry and Sandra Tarte (eds), *The New Pacific Diplomacy* (Canberra: Australian National University Press, 2015), 125–36.

Tarte, Sandra, 'Regionalism and Changing Regional Order in the Pacific Islands', *Asia and the Pacific Policy Studies*, 1:2 (May 2014), 312–27.

Mission and Evangelism

Faafetai Aiava

It is seldom possible to discuss mission or evangelism in Oceania without some reference to history. This is due partly to the difficulty of disassociating Christianity from the images of foreign missionaries carrying Bibles unto our shores and partly because both terms were instrumental in the infamous agenda to convert and civilise the 'heathen' from their 'savage' ways. However, in assessing the general flow of mission and evangelism in Oceania, the initial focus here is continuity. It is not an attempt to sweep painful memories under the carpet, but an attempt to reposition some of the Oceanic perceptions of mission and evangelism in a way that is fluid. For reasons of clarity, mission and evangelism in the ensuing discussion will be treated synonymously as 'mission'. This is based on the premise that when the one is purged of its debilitating baggage and perceived in a new light, so is the other. As discussed later, the dichotomous treatment of both is not only problematic, but it also presupposes a gap that ought to be bridged.

Decolonising or Re-wombing Mission?
In Oceanic cultures, it is commonly understood that a person's unique mission in life or, in its broadest sense, in the universe begins in the womb. If we take this to be the genesis of mission, then it is the womb and not the colon that ought to underpin our thoughts about mission. The painstaking truth about past mission activity is that it contains many instances of local cultures being consumed by that of foreigners.

The expected and perhaps reactionary response from local contemporary thinkers would be to take a decolonising route, one that somewhat frees Indigenous cultures from the colon of the dominant culture. Such efforts can be seen in the influx of literature from Oceanic academics rallying to contextualise, indigenise, accommodate and appropriate the social-religious-political systems of the West. Be that as it may, the question must be asked whether these efforts – some more than others – have really transcended 'colon talk' or if perpetrators and victims are merely sharing the same platform.

I propose that decolonising mission is not enough and, to some degree, not sustainable. Whether the conversation is initiated by the colonised or the coloniser, it still succumbs to a dualistic tension. The next step in my eyes would be to re-organ-ise our thinking around the womb. The Oceanic terms *vanua, fanua, fenua, fonua* and *whenua* – which simultaneously translate as womb, placenta and land – tell of a more holistic mission governed by connections (human and land) and not control. Such connection was affirmed in Aotearoa (New Zealand) when the Whanganui River was the first to be rendered the same rights as a person on 20 March 2017. This precedent was put in place after the Indigenous Māori community successfully argued that the river is their ancestor. Similar sentiments are shared by the First Peoples of Australia, who believe that land does not belong to people but the other way round. Needless to say, these worldviews and Indigenous reference points have been largely ignored in past mission dialogue.

The proposal for the re-wombing of mission is about taking the decolonising discourse to new heights, by appealing to a platform in which what is practised in the name of mission is not dictated by power or defined by power struggles but is nurtured through relationships. Through this lens, mission will be discussed not so much as a combative operation to conquer sin and death (characteristic of decolonising) but a mission of love carried out freely for the formation, sustenance and renewal of life. By using this as their theological basis, Oceanic Christians are enabled to critique the 'mission talk' that has been shaped by the 'colon' and similar thinking patterns that have been institutionalised as 'God talk' (*theos-logos*). It could also provide a good opportunity to review those theologies of mission that function within a dichotomous framework where God and the world coexist in unending conflict.

An Oceanic Theology of Mission

The propagated return to the symbol of the womb is both particular to Oceania and universal. This is deliberate. I am equally convinced that despite its familiarity and widespread appeal, the symbol can never be completely emptied of its theological worth. This is of course if we are willing to accept the biblical notion that all life begins with God (Psalms 19: 1, 95: 4–5, 104: 24–5; Job 12: 10; John 1: 3; Romans 1: 20).

In the context of mission, this shared life in the Creator and between all living creatures has been more or less an appendage to the more institutionalised drive for unity. If one considers the ecumenical conviction that mission and unity belong together in a postcolonial context, the next and perhaps more pressing question would be, 'What does mission without life look like?'

This question alludes to a theological reconstruction of mission that moves from having unity as its sole purpose to one that is driven toward life and its flourishing. This return to the life-giving and life-affirming dimension of mission and its fight against the prevailing atrocities that deny life promotes mission as being rooted in God's own life. The gravest concern about practising mission under the banner of unity is that it attributes, and subsequently reduces, the temporal dimension of mission to the altruistic efforts of humans striving for social, political and economic justice, as if God were uninterested. Among many other implications, it can lead Christians to a misplaced sense of superiority over and above other creatures. The practical repercussions – aside from its obvious neglect of the land, which has been largely subjected to the united activities of humans – is that a predominantly anthropocentric view of mission results in the church palming off its responsibilities.

Nonetheless, it would be unwise to dismiss the unitive goals of mission as laid out in the Nicene teachings of the church as 'One, Holy, Catholic and Apostolic' or Jesus's divine mandate that 'they may all be one' (John 17: 21). The real perpetrator on trial here is not unity but uniformity. Given the suspicion that mission has functioned for so long in a colon fashion, the militarisation of oneness into uniformity is not surprising. From the Oceanic perspective of a divine womb (*vanua, fanua, fenua, fonua, whenua*), unity is already assumed, based on our intimate knowledge of land as mother and the inner workings of the mother–child relationship. In these contexts, it is life formed through shared relations and resources that acts as point of origin and ultimate goal.

More importantly, the notion of the other is never lost. The distinct heartbeats functioning within an expectant mother's body are exemplary of the way that life, from its inception, is diverse and other-oriented. Though the mother is the sole provider and the child in the womb is dependent, there is no theological anomaly. There is no better way to learn about our mission in life than in the other-oriented activities of its author. This is not to be confused with the dependency syndrome that human societies impose on one another – that is, societies who perceive God as ruling over life from a distance. From a more Oceanic perspective, God, like a pregnant mother who sacrifices her own desires and becomes vulnerable for the sake of the child, is revealed as an immanent God, in whose body life is never isolated.

In the eyes of an Oceanic faith, the workings of mission are to be administered through trust and not dependence. This resonates with another recurring malpractice of Christian mission. It is not so much the tendency to equate its tasks with God's, once again stemming from a misplaced sense of superiority, but in the way that 'parental rights' to the gospel are claimed metaphorically. According to this view, 'the other' is like an orphan who cannot be trusted and, therefore, must be adopted by the gospel. This process ends up condemning our God-given cultures as though they could not also point us to the God of the gospel but instead to an inferior parent of 'pagan' origin.

This competitive sibling rivalry was common not only in the initial encounters between Oceanic peoples and overseas missionaries but also in the arrangements made between the various mission bodies deciding who goes where in relation to the Pacific Islands. To put it bluntly, such an approach to mission is life-denying. It does not take God's labour of love seriously when the distinctness of the other is collapsed in the name of mission. It treats diversity as a pain that should be avoided and not as something that is inevitable in mission as it is in birthing. Seeing mission in this light gives us a deeper understanding of the event of Easter and its role in the giving and renewing of life. The challenge for mission, therefore, is to establish connections of life in all its diversity. To begin with the premise that all life has been redeemed through God's labour promises an alternative approach to non-believers as well as a renewed basis for interfaith dialogue.

If mission both in Oceania and globally intends to enter a stage of rebirth, a good starting point would be with God's life as revealed in Scripture. If the Latin root of the word 'mission' is anything to go by, it is God who ultimately performs the 'sending' and it is in being 'sent' that the church was brought to life. The convoluted understanding that the church has its own mission apart from God is ill-founded. It presupposes a mechanistic view of mission much like the transmission of a vehicle responsible for the transfer (trans-mission) of power from the engine to its axle. Within this process, the church is elevated into an intermediary position of power between God and the rest of creation. This ultimately puts the latter at risk of being drip-fed the transformative power of the gospel by the former.

Missions that continue to function within this mechanistic mode of trans-mission in Oceania have duly run their course. Although all theology is subject to human error and finitude, being co-(m)missioned by the Triune God offers a more holistic vantage point. Such an outlook fosters a relationship of cooperative and interdependent living as opposed to a life of self-preservation and independence.

While the institutional church has undoubtedly made enormous strides in terms of mission in Oceania, it tends to overlook the plain fact that the Great Commissioning was uttered to ordinary Galileans (Matthew 28: 16–20). Like the sharing of food, blood and even emotions emanating from the symbol of the womb, church mission at its very core is about regular people mutually putting our trust in God and the co-birthing effort to point others to that reality.

The Present Climate of Mission

The future of mission in Oceania is by no means stagnant. Today there is still a strong mission presence through the form of sponsorship programmes and funding incentives that have been instrumental in the advancement of local churches and theological colleges. Again, the main concern of this undertaking is not about condemning the achievements of mission but rather encouraging positive and constructive continuity.

Corresponding with an earlier point about the temporal dimension of mission, it has become commonplace today to speak of mission in a language similar to that of economic development. Talk of growth is accompanied by figures and statistics pointing to infrastructure, property, membership numbers and the like. This prioritising of the economic ignores the power dynamic integral to partnerships founded on a supply-and-demand basis. In reality, it is the funding partner that determines the terms of the 'relationship' and ultimately how the recipient partner ought to comply.

As in the trans-mission paradigm, power (economic) is routed toward but never fully rooted in the recipient communities. Consequently, a culture of dependency is established and reinforced. Local and aspiring church leaders are either overlooked or crippled in terms of making their ministries more contextually relevant. Meanwhile, mission boards maintain a sense of satisfaction as the numerical data reflect growth in terms of productivity, rather than in the gifts of the Spirit manifested in people. From a co-(m)missioning perspective, all resources (spiritual and material) are communal gifts to be shared by all. Thus, similar to the point made about treating mission and evangelism inseparably, development should not be limited to the economic but should be about enhancing the holistic dimensions of life for all. Unfortunately, Oceania has been exposed to the twin extremes of reducing mission to the social, economic and political sphere and of confining mission to strictly evangelism or the saving of souls. There is need for a more holistic framework that resonates more deeply with the Christian understanding of an abundant life (John 10: 10) and the Oceanic worldview that the body and soul exist in relationship and not tension.

This is not to say that local missions led by Oceanic Christians are immune from the dominant trends. In fact, it is becoming increasingly apparent that Oceanic churches have been more interested in self-preservation and membership growth in the last half century than they have in grassroots ministries or outreach. This has transpired in many ways, but I will underline two. First, mission has been riddled with financial constraints, due partly to the centralisation of funds and partly because the funds required for the daily operation of churches have been safeguarded by bureaucratic structures. Secondly, the newly gained independence of many Oceanic churches brought with it an emphasis on ecclesial maintenance instead of spiritual vitality. Therefore, what some in Oceania label as sheep-stealing – whereby new religious movements have been accused of coercing mainline Christians to 'convert' – others have described as a mass exodus, in which the financial obligations of mainline churches have left members with no other choice but to seek alternatives.

Regardless of where the mistrust originated or how it intensified, a renewed theology of mission could prove both helpful and timely. Without transforming our mindsets, Christians will continue to approach mission with an economic consciousness that lends itself to capitalistic strategies and policies. What this means in terms of the distribution and management of resources is that we end up privileging between the needy and the less needy, forgetting that in human history and in the economy of salvation, God made no such choice. Moreover, Christians will continue to speak of the *oikos* (household, the whole creation) as belonging to humans, much like mission has been treated as a directive from the church and not to it. If, therefore, Christians are serious about reviving our joint vocation to participate in God's life of undiscriminating love, we must learn to recognise that any kind of 'development' done in the name of mission must take its cues from God's salvific acts.

Remaining Challenges of Mission

The wide possibilities stemming from the alternative theology proposed earlier and the growing climate of mistrust are juxtaposed for a reason. Given the fact that the visible and fallible church still awaits its fulfilment in God, this constant tension is as necessary as it is healthy. Similar to the inseparability of the cross and the Easter event, holding the two together can help Christians, even if only by accident, to meet the challenges that remain.

The cliché that Oceanic churches have turned from their sending capacity to their seating capacity has created a continual problem for mission as well as the ecumenical movement in the region. It is not that churches have become selfish or inward-looking, but rather they have lost touch with their divine commissioning. While self-preservation is crucial for mission to function, Christians ought to be reminded that mission cannot be divorced from the labour of love that took place in God.

This inward turn has come with further implications for mission – namely, the neglect of responsibility to denounce evil in the world. In other words, the avoidance of pain has led to complacency in relation to evangelism and contentment in relation to economic stability. One needs only to attend select meetings of the different mission committees built into

Oceanic churches to see how far up the agenda financial interaction with international partners has gone compared with helping communities in need. As a result, the survival and flourishing of the church are prioritised at the expense of those who are denied the fullness of life. The peculiar placement of Oceanic churches in more prestigious positions is telling not only of the systemic shaping of our perceptions but also of the increasing number of Christians following economic trends. This tunnel vision implies a great need for Oceanic Christians to disentangle themselves from the processes that rely heavily on others to tell us where to look and what to see.

A major issue for the churches today is their susceptibility to the trends of neo-liberal capitalism. Economics increasingly governs every sphere of life, and it is not easy for the churches to resist this hegemony. Politics and the market economy are shaping thinking and governing action within the churches of the Pacific today. The plight of the ecumenical mission in Oceania continues to be destabilised by capitalistic tendencies. This is but one among a surplus of underlying issues common today. Suffice it to say that the image of a canoe 'navigating troubled waters' is a very fitting description of both ecumenism and Christian mission in general.

This leads us back to the increasing number of new religious groups that one might assume were additional passengers in the aforementioned canoe, yet, in reality, are treated as synonymous with the rough seas. While the discrimination extends also to the newer faiths established in Oceania, this discussion is limited for reasons of space to the tensions between the mainline churches and the newer Christian denominations, including those classified as breakaway churches. It is also worth noting that the root causes and the underlying factors of this tension are too vast to mention here. This essay hypothesises that much of it boils down to the way that the various Christian churches have willingly or unconsciously subscribed to the illusions of security, control and piety.

Regarding security, mainline churches have become comfortable in positions of dominance due to the fact that multiple generations of nominal Christians simply have been born into the church. This is further secured by village and familial ties. On the contrary, newer churches offering more by way of economic stability preach on the perils of church offerings (characteristic of mainline churches), while ironically displaying material wealth as a divine reward to the faithful.

Regarding control, mainline churches have become so fervent in their prioritisation of structures, policies and academic competence that matters of mission and even worship have been severely constrained. When coupled with a culture of silence, youths are sidelined as being unimportant and lay Christians are left feeling somewhat subordinated. The flipside is that newer churches claiming a pneumatological rebirth practise mission with a sense of command over the Spirit, as though God moves in some churches more than others.

In relation to the third illusion, of piety, leaders of mainline churches have been heavily criticised for preaching the gospel while living far from it. At the other end, 'born-again Christians' have accused members of mainline churches of living a less than holy life. Like the sibling rivalry mentioned above, this back-and-forth continues to the point that the Bible is exploited by the particularities of each and mission is no longer a joint vocation but a race for conversion.

I refer to all three as illusions because they are elusive to Oceanic Christians, regardless of what we might think. Theologically speaking, a faith that is secured in God manifests itself in the world through both worship and how we relate to the other. This faith, when it is consistent with the divine example, can be embodied only through relationships; otherwise, it is empty. Piety, therefore, is not an entitlement of churches to be used as a yardstick but a gift of God to the faithful. The greatest difficulty in getting the various Christian denominations to work together is that their mission efforts continue to be undermined by colon thinking. The underpinning ideology that one church has all the answers or is superior to another is both digestive and life-denying. This is why determining who is at fault is just as harmful as subordinating God into a particular this or that. What is most detrimental about colonising God is that our subsequent treatment of the other completes the cycle. Mission will continue to operate as a subordinate arm of the church, as opposed to churches participating in God's mission. Capitalism will continue to direct our attention to the numbers, breeding further mistrust and competitiveness. Any attempt to homogenise the diverse groups would lead to further backlash, and the cycle of exclusion continues.

A theology of liberation is pivotal to the reshaping of Christianity in Oceania. Additionally, Christians must be mindful that any liberating effort must first come out of God's life of relationality. This liberating act did not materialise through any human resolve or merit but rather through God's relentless desire for communion. By going beyond the distinctive feature of Latin American Liberation theology, where theological reflection is considered secondary to praxis, I add that any praxis in which we engage as a church should first seek its cues and ultimate goal in God's liberating acts. This is not to condemn the anthropocentric dimension of mission but rather to stimulate it further by grounding it radically deeper in God's mission.

One of the obvious difficulties in sounding a theology of liberation in Oceania is finding common concerns, as the needs of each island nation are as unique as the injustices they face. In relation to the land, however, a resounding convergence can be found. As mentioned earlier regarding the revered status of land in Oceania, it continues to be treated by Christian mission as non-living and an expendable resource. This has much to do with mission following the trends of economic development. Rallying for an eco-relational turn, the current principal of the Pacific Theological College in Fiji, Upolu Lumā Vaai, launched for the first time an Earth Justice Advocacy programme in the College. Going beyond the ecclesial norm of praying for the environment or simply raising community awareness on our ecological responsibilities, this programme serves more as a sobering reminder to Oceanic Christians that God was never isolated from our sacred cosmologies and the intimate bonds we once shared with the land.

This likely explains why the literature on mission and evangelism in Oceania lacks any in-depth discussions of why the land and the environment are (theologically) integral to Christian mission. At most, the impacts of climate change are discussed within the context of food security. Within this dynamic, liberation remains servant to the living just as much as the climate supposedly exists in the service of humans. More importantly, this dynamic ignores the voices of the doubly oppressed rendered as 'non-living'. The point being made here is that the ecological efforts of Oceanic Christians ought to stem from a deep-seated conviction that the *oikos* is the theatre of God's self-communication manifested in the richness of our surroundings and contexts. This relational understanding is what I believe differentiates Christian mission from that of social activists.

But this lament is not aimed only at the capitalistic societies or the foreign missionaries that condemned our cosmic parentage. It is also a challenge to its Indigenous communities that still understand and uphold the sacredness of the land through rituals. The continued burying of umbilical cords of newborns in ancestral soils, the constant recital of our common origin with the land, and the flora recipes carefully preserved by traditional healers are living testimonies that our mission toward 'the other' transcends human beings. This worldview of land as part and parcel of the Oceanic self comes with an ironic challenge. That is, when we neglect our ecological responsibilities, we also renounce our identity as people of Oceania.

This paradigm shift toward seeing human life as interwoven with that of the cosmic community is the philosophical background to a project that started in 2017. The Pacific Theological College, in partnership with the Pacific Conference of Churches and the Oceania Centre for Arts of the University of the South Pacific, embarked on a regional strategy titled 'Reweaving the Ecological Mat' (REM). It is a 'self-determination strategy' aimed at addressing the challenges arising from the ecological crisis in the region. Changes in lifestyle, spurred on by consumerism and the 'more and more' ethic of development, not only cause environmental destruction and, hence, exacerbate climatic changes, but also increasingly produce unhealthy populations, a result of an increasing reliance on processed food. The statistics on population health, poverty, depleting fish stocks and over-logging are indicators of this ecological crisis. The Pacific is no paradise, but neither should it be seen as having no existing frameworks, based on Indigenous and religious knowledge and spirituality, that are relevant to these challenges. The pace and content of 'Western'-type development over the past 40–50 years and its consequential impacts on economic, political and social life in the Pacific contributed much to the challenges within and among the Pacific Island states. At the core of this ecological crisis is the loss of vision and understanding of the delicate interdependence of life, a vision that once guided and ensured the survival of Pacific Island generations for centuries. The 'ecological crisis' refers to the progressive disruption and rupture of these relationships, and where once Pacific communities practised conservation methods, in their own unique ways, on their forests, lands, rivers and marine resources, today these are mere commodities.

The REM strategy is driven by the idea that the region can determine its own future, based on its religious and Indigenous texts, its worldviews and the experiences and lessons of current realities. For most Pacific societies, particularly the Indigenous communities, the ecology means much more than the natural environment. It is about the myriad intricate relationships of people, land, forest, rivers and sea, and the norms that govern, connect and link them into a web of sustaining life and meaning. It is about the framework, norms and values that guide this intricate web of relationships. Much of this framework relates to how communities are to relate to their natural environment and the governing norms on the use of land, forest, rivers and sea resources. In most Pacific Indigenous communities, there is always in existence an interdependent view of humans' place in creation and their reliance on the natural environment for sustenance, and conversely on their responsibility to protect and conserve.

This strategy affirms that to address the challenges of the ecological crisis, the region needs to look at these through the perspective of their two main sources – Indigenous and religious texts – as interpretive keys of their experiences of development today. The inherited concept of development and its assumptions, for example, need to be examined with respect to the question 'What is development from the perspective of the Pacific's diverse Indigenous and religious texts, and their worldviews?' The basic idea is that the region needs to build its own house of development ideals and indicators, and these might be different from what the 'Western' world considers to be the ideals and indicators of development.

Put simply, the project is one of 'com-(m)issioning' instead of 'trans-missioning'. It is not necessarily aimed at 'conversion', although relevant in a re-immersive sense, but rather at reweaving relationships. If the 'womb' image (rather than the 'colon' image) is central to understanding mission in Oceania today, then such a project, in philosophical and practical terms, is mission from the 'womb'. There is a movement among the conservation-ists to recognise the relevance of Indigenous and Christian spirituality in their work, and the thrust is also upheld by academics working in univer-sities within the region.

Conclusion

This essay has focused heavily on the problems inherent in past and present missions rather than elaborating solutions. This lopsidedness can be explained by the chosen precautionary approach, which focuses on changing the mindset, as opposed to a reactionary one, which revolves around damage control. From this perspective, the problems in mission are treated more as opportunities for reciprocal learning instead of failures that require total overhaul. By employing the Oceanic and universal symbol of the womb, this essay is essentially appealing for a mission rebirth. This can be seen in the various attempts not only to harmonise the joys and pains of mission work, but also to change the platform of discussion from decolonising (stagnant) to a more relational landscape (fluid). Whether or not re-wombing mission is the most appropriate next step in Oceania cannot be answered with any certainty. But this does not mean one cannot entertain the possibilities. For instance, what would be the impact of mission beginning in a space of mutuality and interdepend-ence instead of in a site of struggle? What happens when mission is rooted in God's relational self-communication rather than following the routes of economic trends? What would happen when distinct mission bodies privilege connection and not control? How would mission be transformed by the notion of a shared commissioning and not a transmission of authority? How would mission pan out beyond the framework of visible unity but in a framework of life that values the rich knowledge systems of Indigenous communities and the essential contributions of non-humans? Only time will tell.

Bibliography

Ernst, Manfred, *The Winds of Change: Rapidly Growing Religious Groups in the Pacific Islands* (Suva: Pacific Theological College, 1994).

Ernst, Manfred (ed.), *Globalization and the Re-shaping of Christianity in the Pacific Islands* (Suva: Pacific Theological College, 2006).

Ernst, Manfred and Lydia Johnson (eds), *Navigating Troubled Waters: The Ecumenical Movement in the Pacific Islands since the 1980s* (Suva: Pacific Theological College, 2017).

Garrett, John, *To Live among the Stars: Christian Origins in Oceania* (Geneva: WCC; and Suva: Institute of Pacific Studies, USP, 1982).

Morissey, John and Richard Keelan, *The Call to be Just: An Introduction to the Social Teaching of the Catholic Church* (Samabula: Society of St Columban Leader Press, no date).

Gender

Victoria Kavafolau

Gender and Christianity is a theme not often discussed in church pulpits, public spaces or social gatherings in Oceania. The aim of this essay is to consider gender relations as understood in the Oceania context and observe the impacts of Christianity on the understanding of gender in the twenty-first century, as well as the impact of changing understandings of gender on Christianity.

The Pacific Islands

The introduction of Christianity and its propagation throughout the Pacific by Christian missionaries brought about economic, cultural and spiritual transformations. Such transformations were influenced by colonialism and the gradual spread of Western civilisation. In a context not yet exposed to the growth of modernity and the dispersion of Christianity, Pacific Island nations were oblivious to the rapid development of the surrounding continents. Nevertheless, the approach of globalisation meant a revolutionary shift in Pacific history marked by the conversion of most island nations and the economic development of the provinces. Christianity greatly influenced the Pacific way of life, and one area where it had an immense impact is in regard to the perception of gender.

Gender is not a well favoured concept in popular discourse in the Pacific. To speak of gender is to address specifically male and female roles and responsibilities. The language of man and woman is much more readily accepted than the language of gender. To speak of gender is to understand the role and characteristics of man and woman in a wider context. Gender is understood beyond the biological, involving many aspects of the perception of a person, place or thing. Gender is not necessarily applied to persons but is defined by social relations, cultural practices and traditional observances.

Both conservative and progressive approaches to gender can be found in the Pacific region. The conservative understanding of gender tends to stress a biological view of people as male and female, while the progressive understanding of gender takes account of sexual identities beyond those of male and female and is alert to the concerns of the LGBTQ+ community. The conservative approach to gender is generally upheld by Christian churches in Oceania, with the exception of the Uniting Church in Australia and the Methodist Church in New Zealand. The prevailing view is that gender is God-given, not humanly or socially synthesised. This does not negate the love of God for all people, regardless of gender identity. The minority progressive view of gender takes a more open-minded attitude. It is influenced by awareness that identities other than male and female are gradually becoming socially accepted and might eventually become the norm for society and state. It seeks to accept all identities, whether male, female or other. This approach is influential in secular countries such as Australia and New Zealand and is beginning to emerge in Fiji.

Gender roles and relationships

Gender roles in the Pacific Island context are governed by the culture and tradition of a society. Patriarchal societies and social hierarchies are social constructions that determine the responsibilities and positions of both men and women. Such roles determine acceptable domestic behaviour, social conduct and social status for both sexes. In general, traditional gender roles dictate that men are the acceptable candidates for leadership roles in both domestic and public sectors. Women are perceived as domestic and in certain cultures, such as the Solomon Islands, are expected to be docile and subservient.

A common misapprehension of 'gender' in the Pacific Island context is that it is shorthand for women's rights and feminism. However, when properly understood, consideration of gender relations rests on an understanding that gender is inclusive of both men and women. Recent trends in development theory have shifted the emphasis from women to gender so that the roles of men are brought into the discussion, for to talk of gender is to address the roles of men and women. To talk of the roles of men and women is to dialogue on their responsibilities not only in domestic spaces but in public spheres also. What many Pacific Islanders find uncomfortable is specifically discoursing on the subject of gender equality. Pacific culture and tradition govern gender roles. Any attempt to modify the structures that set the specific roles of men and women is highly disfavoured.

Before the twenty-first century, gender was not a prominent theme for discussion in any Oceanic context. This is chiefly because cultural and traditional norms have established the roles of men and women and these came to be considered the customary way of life for the community. It was the rise of feminism in the Pacific that highlighted the need for gender equality. Scholars began to assess the roles and status of women in the Pacific in light of the feminist wave emerging in the 1970s. The first major issue to be tackled was the social issue of gender-based violence, specifically domestic violence. Often, the norms of social construction on gender within a Pacific Island society resulted in the marginalisation of women and children. These social constructions are often enforced by those who are higher up in the social hierarchy. Addressing gender relations and promoting gender equality are seen as means of liberation, particularly for women who have been sidelined as insignificant.

Gender imbalance is evident in both the public and the private sectors. From the workplace in government and parliament to leadership roles in the churches and local communities, the role of women is limited since they are still considered to be restricted to domestic roles and responsibilities. A significant contributing factor to gender imbalance is male violence. Women still live in fear of men in their communities. The Fiji Women's Crisis Centre reported that in January and February 2020 alone, 154 cases of abuse, including rape and child sexual abuse, were recorded. Of those, 102 cases involved domestic violence. In 2019, a total of 833 cases of abuse was recorded. Papua New Guinea too suffers from high rates of domestic violence and gang rape.

Despite the high incidence of gender-based violence, the status of women differs significantly in Melanesia compared with Polynesia and Micronesia. Women in Melanesia, but specifically the New Guinea Highlands, are seen as inferior to men, and it was normal for women to be dominated. Labour was strictly determined by sex so that men laboured in hunting, heavy gardening and warfare while women engaged in domestic chores. The prevalent marginalisation of Melanesian women was due to their bodily fluids. Women were considered to be polluted and capable of polluting men with their menstrual blood. In the Western Highlands, women lived separately from men and were considered to be intrinsically unclean, such that they should be avoided.

Polynesians observe a social hierarchy or systematic ranking in their societies. This is reflected in the perception of women in Polynesia and some parts of Micronesia. Although they hold certain similarities in roles to Melanesia, distinct approaches to the status of women are evident. In Polynesia, women are able to acquire significant status or high rank in a society in which rank takes precedence over gender. Polynesian women of chiefly descent can take on chiefly roles. Tahitian women play active roles in decision-making about the economy and public matters. Although not considered equal, Tahitian men and women express a balanced approach in relation to each other. The Sāmoan *taupou* (daughter of a high chief) and high-ranking women were governed under different rules from those that applied to the female commoners. For example, they were required not to involve themselves in any sexual relationship, whereas the female commoners were exempt from this rule. The Tongan *fahu* (father's eldest sister) and the *mehikitanga* (father's sister) are examples of roles that accorded an exalted status to women in Tongan society. The *fahu* and the *mehikitanga* are treated with the utmost respect in all family gatherings and social occasions, among both chiefs and commoners. In Micronesia, a high-ranking position is also ascribed to women of chiefly descent. However, this does not necessarily mean that they acquire authority to exercise power in public affairs.

Regardless of the opportunity for women to acquire high-ranking positions in society, responsibilities and labour are still determined by the sexes. Similarly with Melanesia, women are expected to handle domestic housework and are responsible for the upbringing of the children. Responsibilities are strictly domestic. Men are expected to provide crops and food for the family; they handle civil and public decision-making and are considered the superior sex in society at large.

Gender and Christianity

The emergence of Christianity in the region brought about cultural and spiritual reforms. Gone are the days of Indigenous religions practising idolatry to nature and material objects. Since the arrival of the Christian missionaries, it is the God of Israel who has been the focus of worship. As Christianity developed and progressed in the Pacific Islands, cultural observances, traditional practices and religious beliefs gradually conformed to biblical teaching. Scriptural ethics and morals became the fundamental principles that governed the Pacific way of life.

Christianity is now the dominant religion in Oceania. This means that the Christian churches have immense power to promote and encourage social development and human dignity. They take an ecumenical approach to addressing pastoral tasks and practical agendas in the churches and local communities. One of the prominent Christian organisations in Oceania is the Pacific Conference of Churches (PCC), which has more than 30 Christian denominations in its membership. The PCC operates on three core frameworks, promoting ecumenism, stewardship and self-determination. Interestingly, women and gender issues are maintained as an imperative constituent of all three core frameworks.

Christianity has certainly had an impact on gender issues in the twenty-first century. First, Christianity acknowledges the dignity and significance of all people as created by God and seeks to liberate especially women and children from the oppression of social and cultural structures. Traditionally, Pacific Island communities deemed their cultural and social systems to be absolute. However, since the arrival of Christianity, the Bible became the absolute authority. This brought a new perspective on gender, since the Bible teaches that God created humanity in God's image or likeness to be male and female, thus establishing that male and female are not differentiated in God's eyes as both reflect the *imago Dei* (image of God). An example of cultural conformity to Scriptural ethics is the agenda pursued by the Papua New Guinea Church Partnership Programme (CPP). The CPP acknowledges the marginalisation of women and children in most Lowlands and Highlands communities and tribes. With the aid of seven partner churches in Papua New Guinea, its mission is to promote equal gender relations and ameliorate human development across their region. Theology is their primary tool for tackling such social issues.

Secondly, to an extent, the impact of Christianity on gender has resulted in the gradual diminution of patriarchal power in Pacific societies. With the dispersion of gender equality awareness across the Pacific during the early twenty-first century, Christianity influenced the liberation of women from the domination of men in Pacific countries. Tonga, for example, is known for its social hierarchy and patriarchal orientation. However, women are increasingly held in high regard, whether it be among commoners or in the monarchy. Women participate in decision-making in both domestic and public sectors. They are accorded great status and dignity and, although not encouraged in equality with men, are still honoured as significant in society.

Thirdly, the development of Christianity in the twenty-first century has seen more women in leadership roles – in government and parliament, but particularly roles in the clergy and in theological education. In the Pacific Island context, women are still widely regarded as being confined to domestic roles. Nonetheless, women have broadened their roles in society and have taken on responsibilities beyond the home. In the past 10 years, Pacific Christian churches such as the Fiji Methodist Church, the Free Wesleyan Church of Tonga and the United Church of the Solomon Islands have ordained more women as ministers. Theological education has seen women on the rise as lecturers and they have contributed immensely to shaping Pacific theology. Where this was not enforced in the twentieth century, since 2000 there has been a turning point for gender relations in Oceania.

Fourthly, Christianity has developed throughout the past 20 years and has enhanced cultural and traditional practices as aligned with the will of God. Christianity did not seek to abolish Pacific culture and tradition but to adapt the message of the gospel to the Pacific way of life (although this approach brought with it colonisation and globalisation). As a result, the culture and traditions of the Pacific region are very much preserved to this day. However, perceptions of gender are enlightened by Christianity to enable people to acknowledge that women and men are equal in the eyes of God. They differ in biological structure and God-given responsibilities but are assigned the same likeness and promised the same blessing.

Finally, the greatest impact of Christianity on gender is ascribed to the utilisation of biblical teaching to counter gender-based violence and abuse. An example of this is a research project led by Sāmoan theologian Mercy Ah Siu-Maliko, the Church Responses to Gender-Based Violence Against Women in Sāmoa. Siu-Maliko and her team provided Bible case studies to deepen understanding of the issue of violence against women and adopted faith-based approaches as a response to violence against women. Similar approaches are employed by Cliff Bird of the Solomon Islands, who aims to promote gender equality throughout Oceania by identifying 15 biblical-theological perspectives on human dignity. The Bible is widely recognised as the basis for moral and ethical conduct in the Christian Pacific. Given its absolute authority for ethical living and cultural reformation, it is a highly influential text when it comes to addressing issues of gender-based violence.

In addition, gender-relations courses have been introduced to Pacific theological education and have been crafted into curricula for theological seminaries. In a region where gender has traditionally been defined through sex-specific labour roles, the slow shift of theological education to address contemporary issues is a revolutionary effort of the Christian denominations in the Pacific to unshackle people from oppressive social and cultural norms. The South Pacific Association of Theological Schools (SPATS) has incorporated the themes of domestic violence and gender equality into theological curricula. With the contribution of UnitingWorld, a Gender Equality Theology curriculum was produced and presented to the SPATS Commission and the Pacific Church Leaders' Meeting. Due to language and interpretation barriers, this course has been titled *Human Equality and Dignity in the Divine Economy* and caters to level 4–5 Certificate degree. This development in Pacific theological education is the latest move toward redefining gender in light of Christianity's influence during the twenty-first century.

Gender relations have caught the attention of Christian denominations, fundamentally because many of their members are affected by gender injustice. With social justice issues on the rise, such as gender inequality and gender-based violence, Christian churches are aware of and are taking measures to tackle such issues. So, with the ecumenical agenda of the Pacific Council of Churches, the approach of church ministries and Christian theology in this century is employing a contemporary issue-based approach in addressing a sensitive matter. Foremost among issues of current concern are women/gender relations and children/youth issues. Gender is one of the rising themes in the Pacific today that is slowly coming to dominate theological discussions and have an impact on social development.

With 95% of Pacific Islanders being Christians, significant responsibility falls upon the Christian community to mould the ethical and moral principles of Pacific peoples. To introduce the discourse of gender in a patriarchal society supported by social structural norms embedded for hundreds of years is no small task. Nonetheless, churches are active today challenging traditions that place women in a lesser and unfavourable position at home, at church and in the community. Thus, Christianity is an authoritative apparatus for change and reformation. In this century, Pacific Island communities have seen social change and cultural adjustment in relation to gender, and Christianity has been a major contributor to this revolutionary change.

New Zealand

No country is free from gender-relation issues. Whether it be social or domestic, religious or secular, public or political, gender inequality can be identified in all sectors. New Zealand as a secular state is highly rated as an advocate for gender equality. It is secular not in the sense that secularism dominates the public sphere to the extent that religion is prohibited but in the sense that the public sphere is religiously plural and there is no state church. Advocating gender equality does not necessarily mean that total equality of men and women has been achieved. In fact, the rates of domestic violence and gender inequality in the workplace are quite high. As a multicultural and multireligious nation, although very accepting of gender equality, there are barriers that express major imbalances in the treatment of women and how gender is perceived in its secular society. Where the Pacific Islands tend to uphold a conservative approach to gender, New Zealand can be found to be accommodating both conservative and progressive approaches.

Gender Equal NZ conducted a survey in 2019 that revealed that 80% of respondents believed that gender equality should be a fundamental human right. The fact that 20% disagreed demonstrates that the society accommodates different views on questions of gender. The survey examined gender relations in New Zealand and highlighted that male and female gender roles should not be assigned according to sex. Responsibilities in the home and in the workplace should not be limited to individuals based on their gender. This survey presents the general understanding of New Zealanders on gender equality. These, however, are only perceptions on the subject of gender equality, and the question remains how far convictions about gender equality have found practical expression. Thirty per cent of New Zealanders believe that gender equality has been achieved, which only goes to prove that awareness on gender issues is lacking. The major issues that require adequate measures to tackle and resolve are the rise of family violence and gender inequality in society and in the workplace.

Regardless, women in New Zealand are recognised in prominent leadership roles across the public and private sectors. Work and employment are not assigned according to gender. Women are climbing the social hierarchy quite significantly and are contributing to the economy, to social development and, most importantly, to political life. Prime Minister Jacinda Ardern is a chief example of this. However, that gender inequality is still present in the workplace is demonstrated by the gender wage gap. It is also exposed by high levels of domestic violence. Statistics from the Ministry of Social Development's 'It's Not OK' campaign show that 76% of family violence occurrences never reach the police. The year 2019 recorded the most victims (12 women) killed by intimate partner violence since 2009. One in three women experience sexual harassment at some point in their lifetime. These realities capture the status of women in society.

In church environments, women occupy leadership roles in the clergy and are not discouraged from seeking ordination. In the 1990s, the issue of gender and Christianity in New Zealand was approached theologically by enquiring about the identity of women in God. This arose out of a feminist agenda and the push for the identity of women to be acknowledged in both secular and religious spaces. Although historically there had not been much dialogue from Christian churches in New Zealand on gender issues, groups such as the Salvation Army Women Ministries, the Association of Anglican Women and the Methodist Women's Fellowship contributed to liberating women from domestic and economic oppression. To an extent, by providing workshops, theological education and pastoral care, they began to tackle the factors contributing to the marginalisation of women.

Australia

Australia is also considered a secular state. The 2016 census revealed that Christianity is the dominant religion in Australia, representing 86% of religious Australians. This statistic begs the question of the influence of Christianity as regards gender in Australia and how understanding of gender has developed over the twenty-first century.

Gender relations in Australia differ greatly from those of the Pacific Islands. Where gender relations in the islands demonstrate a clear division of labour by sex both socially and culturally, gender relations in Australia employ a more laid-back approach insofar as women are not as oppressed as their counterparts in the Pacific Islands. Similarly to New Zealand, gender is addressed, for the most part, by the progressive approach. The Australian Human Rights Commission published statistics in 2018 on factors that reveal the existence of gender inequality in Australian communities. Such factors include sexual harassment of women (in domestic and workplace environments, among others) and imbalanced treatment of women compared with men.

When it comes to roles and responsibilities, in both the domestic and public sectors there is a unisex approach to sharing and exercising those roles. Men work to provide for the family but so do women. Women maintain household responsibilities but so do men. However, this unisex practice of sharing roles and responsibilities depends to a degree on ethnic backgrounds. In a multicultural society, the norms of Western civilisation cannot be forced upon conservatives who remain steadfast in upholding their respective cultural and traditional practices. The impression of gender relations in the mainstream of Australian society can sometimes disguise the fact that there are sectors where very different dynamics apply. As Australia is a multicultural and multireligious state, unequal treatment of women can be observed in the workplace, and in domestic spaces there are always cases of abuse.

As a secular state with Christianity as the predominant faith, gender questions have occasioned a major tug of war between the state and religion. A prime example of this is the acceptance of same-sex marriage by the Uniting Church in Australia. December 2017 marked state acceptance of same-sex marriage in Australia. Nine months later, the Uniting Church in Australia's Additional Marriage Liturgy (2018) publication was issued, clearly allowing same-sex marriage. It aimed to provide for the diversity of the church membership yet at the same time to uphold fundamental beliefs concerning marriage. This resulted in much debate over the biblical integrity and theological implications of such a decision from one of the three main Christian denominations.

There is no question that homosexuality and the rise of the LGBTQ+ community in the Pacific opens a whole new discussion on issues of gender. The Christian community in Australia struggles to address the subject of homosexuality. The Uniting Church was first to address the matter, and the outcome of that conversation was to accept same-sex marriage out of inclusion of its members and under the concept of advocating unity in diversity. The Catholic Church in Australia refuses to acknowledge any form of marriage other than the lifelong union of a man and a woman. The majority of the Anglican churches in Australia are conservative in outlook and have been opposing same-sex marriage, as they maintain it is contrary to biblical teaching and dogma. On the other hand, secular society has no problem accepting homosexuality, as demonstrated by the annual Pride Parade of Mardi Gras.

Christian churches in the Pacific clearly define gender on a biological understanding – that is, strictly man and woman. Christian conservatives in Australia also strongly uphold this definition of gender. However, the shift of twenty-first century understanding of gender identifies individualities as more than male and female by including gender identities such as lesbian, gay, bisexual, transgender and queer. With the major Christian denominations deeply rooted in biblical teachings specifically on man and woman, it is a challenge for the LGBTQ+ community to find any theological justifications for their definition of gender. The contribution of Christian conservatives to the understanding of gender is adamantly to maintain its biological definition as it is presented at birth so as not to complicate God's creation of humankind.

The Christian community in Australia strongly advocates women's rights and acknowledges the benefits they bring to both the clergy and the public sector. This suggests that Australia might have a greater role in relation to the Pacific Islands, bringing about awareness not only of gender equality but also seeking to liberate women and children from social and cultural oppression. Such outreach has been successfully executed by UnitingWorld and Uniting Justice, programmes of the Uniting Church in Australia, with target goals to change mindsets and to encourage leadership roles.

The most common contribution from Australia and New Zealand to gender relations in the Pacific Region is centralised in challenging and combating social norms and structures that bring about gender inequality. Christianity in Australia portrays a contrasting image on the understanding of gender to that which prevails in the Pacific Islands. With parallel situations, it is safe to say the perception of gender in the churches of Australia and New Zealand is due to the multicultural and multireligious societies in which they find themselves. Not only that, but secularism and globalisation also contribute to how gender is defined in both countries in the twenty-first century.

The Uniting Church in Australia has been active throughout the Pacific during the twenty-first century promoting a Gender Equality Theology (GET) programme. In the Pacific, the term 'gender equality' is perceived as a Western ideology aimed at devaluing male responsibilities, dissolving cultural and traditional norms on male and female roles, and encouraging women to become superior. There is a need to raise consciousness and provide training on issues of gender equality and women's rights. This has been the goal of GET training sessions and workshops facilitated throughout the Pacific region by UnitingWorld, Pacific Women (an organisation committed to developing opportunities for Pacific women), the Pacific Council of Churches, Papua New Guinea Church Partnership Programme, Ma'a Fafine mo Fāmili (a Tongan NGO promoting women's rights and safety in the family), United Nations Development Programme in the Pacific and many more NGOs and church congregations. These programmes seek to balance gender relations in Oceania so as to protect men and women from social oppression and abuse.

Conclusion

Throughout the vast region of Oceania, gender is perceived, expressed and comprehended differently in different contexts. With the advance of the twenty-first century and the increase of attention being devoted to gender-based issues, it has become imperative for the Christian community to engage with such issues in light of biblical teaching about God's intention for men and women.

In a culturally embedded region, balancing gender relations in Oceania faces challenges such as patriarchal societies and social constructions that are deeply rooted in tradition. Nonetheless, the contribution of Christianity to gender is immense in relieving both men and women from harmful cultural practices, unjust social norms and gender-based violence. Gender relations in Oceania demonstrate the strict roles that have traditionally been assigned according to sex. Such determination of labour by sex results in women being perceived to be inferior to men. This in turn leads to gender inequality, gender-based violence and social oppression on the basis of gender. Observing the role of Christianity in this region in the twenty-first century allows us to conclude that it plays a vital role in overcoming gender injustice by exposing the God-intended right and dignity of both male and female. The fundamental impact of Christianity on gender relations in Oceania has been to effect a gradual shift in gender relations toward gender equality. Gender in the Pacific has seized the attention of Christianity, calling forth reformation and revival of both men and women from cultural classification of gender to faith-based reflection on gender.

Bibliography

Asia Development Bank, *Solomon Islands Country Gender Assessment* (Mandaluyong: Asia Development Bank, 2015).

Biersack, Aletta, Margaret Jolly and Martha Macintyre, *Gender Violence and Human Rights: Seeking Justice in Fiji, Papua New Guinea and Vanuatu* (Canberra: ANU Press, 2016).

Kotoisuva, Edwina, 'Domestic Violence – A View from the Fiji Women's Crisis Centre', *Pacific Journal of Theology*, series II, 30 (2003), 41–5.

Macintyre, Martha and Ceridwen Spark (eds), *Transformations of Gender in Melanesia* (Canberra: ANU Press, 2017).

Siu-Maliko, Mercy Ah, Melanie Beres, Caroline Blyth, Ramona Boodoosingh, Tess Patterson and David Tombs, *Church Responses to Gender-Based Violence Against Women in Sāmoa* (Auckland: New Zealand Institute for Pacific Research, 2016).

Religious Freedom

Jacqueline Ryle

The introduction of Christianity into Oceania is widely viewed as a success story for Christian mission, since within 200 years most of the peoples of Oceania had taken on the *lotu* (Christian faith). Much of the mission endeavour was conducted by thousands of Pacific Islanders, under the leadership of small groups of missionaries from Europe, North America, South America, Australia and New Zealand. Pacific Islander theologians emphasise that their ancestors' strong beliefs in a divine presence and in the afterlife made them very open to Christian faith and produced a remarkable strength of belief. At the same time, missionaries imported historical denominational conflicts and antagonisms to their mission fields and Pacific Islanders incorporated these faith identities and divisions into historical and existing local power dynamics, resulting in some places in bitter conflict and battles. In many cases such divisions have been passed on through the generations to the present day, though in Fiji, Tonga and Kiribati these conflicts and antagonisms have largely disappeared. Prejudices within new churches against mainline churches, such as the Catholic Church, cause new rifts and divisions.

Christianity's strong historical roots and contemporary foundational place in nations across Oceania is borne out in population statistics. According to the 2019 US State Department Freedom of Religion Report, most Pacific Island states, except Fiji, have a Christian population of more than 90%. Kiribati, with a Christian population of 99%, 57% of whom are Catholics, tops the statistics. In addition to the presence of historic mainline churches, the numbers of localised syncretic new religions and movements are increasing, and the list of globalising Pentecostal and fundamentalist churches across the region is ever-expanding.

These developments, responses to the increasing pace of societal and sociocultural change, come at the cost of historic mainline church membership. Growing numbers, especially of young people, are drawn by the vibrant worship style and contemporary music of Protestant Pentecostal and Evangelical churches and groups that link to transnational globalising networks. This increasing diversity of competing churches challenges the previously taken-for-granted position of historic mainline, especially

Protestant, churches, which, in general, have been unable to find solutions to stem the loss of members.

While offering individuals alternative faith options based on choice rather than an inherited faith based on family and clan allegiance, joining new churches often leads to domestic disputes, domestic violence, and dissent and division within families, clans, villages and communities. The traditional role of religion as a source of communal coherence and solidarity is displaced by fragmenting dynamics that are both a symptom of and a contributing factor to a weakening of communality in favour of individualism.

Rights, Freedoms and Obligations

Freedom of religion was drafted as part of the United Nations Universal Declaration of Human Rights (UDHR) in 1948. Article 18 of the UDHR states,

> Everyone has the right to freedom of thought, conscience and religion: this right includes the freedom to change his religion or belief, and the freedom alone or in community with others and in public or private, to manifest his belief in teaching, practice, worship and observance.

Discussions in Pacific Island nations that draw on the UDHR to promulgate rights-based issues, such as women's rights and the rights of sexual-minority persons, are often dismissed as imposing Western values on Pacific Island traditions, cultures and religion. Yet the UDHR document was a highly international one, drafted by representatives of an extremely broad range of countries, cutting across continents – and initially not supported by the UK or the USA. Most Pacific Island constitutions draw on this document and on the later International Covenant on Civil and Political Rights from 1966.

At the same time, the freedoms outlined in these documents are not easily translatable to Pacific Island contexts. In Pacific Island cultures a person is never an individual in the Western sense but always relationally constituted, embedded within closely interwoven clan and communal relationships and obligations. Discussions on freedom of religion in Oceania need therefore to be contextualised in relation to local, historically situated sociocultural and religious complexities. These include traditional values of consensus, harmony and homogeneity in community life; widespread patriarchal dominance in gender and family relations; women's generally limited access to decision-making; traditional leadership by chiefs or male elders in church allegiance and practice; and pervasive communal pressure to conform to given norms and practices, such as belonging to a given denomination, attending church every Sunday or paying levies.

Membership of historic mainline churches is based on the interweaving of church-, faith- and communally-based cultural practices and obligations. Adherence to new fundamentalist or Pentecostal churches usually requires adherents to eschew communal cultural practices and, often, to break with family and cultural commitments. This adds to tensions between those who belong to old and to new churches. These tensions in turn lead to increased religious intolerance and can result in the banishment of individuals or minority religious groups from villages.

Pacific Island Constitutions

The interweaving of religion, tradition and politics in Pacific Island cultures makes these interdependent elements almost indistinguishable from each other. The Fijian religio-cultural structure of *vanua, lotu, matanitu* (belonging to the land and tradition, Christian faith, and government), known as the Three Pillars of Fijian society, was transposed to parts of Papua New Guinea by Fijian missionaries, and similar constructs exist in other Pacific Island countries. The centrality of these interweavings is displayed by the prominent place that Christianity holds in almost all Pacific Island national constitutions. In different ways these constitutions acknowledge God and the blessings given by God, recognise the centrality of Christianity in the past, present and future, and affirm community responsibilities and duties as well as individual human rights.

In his research paper for the Fiji Constitutional Review Process in 1995, the late Revd Paula Niukula, former president of the Methodist Church in Fiji, argued against the call by the then Methodist Church leadership in Fiji to declare Fiji a Christian state. He noted five different ways in which Oceanic constitutions reflect the *relations* between religion and the state. Some Preambles, such as those of Sāmoa and Tonga, affirm faith in God. Others, such as Vanuatu's, acknowledge a place for Christianity, often in relation to custom and tradition. Others again, such as that of the Solomon Islands, refer more generally to God's guidance and blessing on the nation.

Tonga's constitution from 1875 predates any human rights legislation. And, except for the most recent Pacific Island nation, Palau, which became independent in 1994, all Pacific Island constitutions were drawn up between 1962 and 1980, during decolonisation. Sāmoa became the first independent Pacific Island nation, in 1962; Vanuatu gained independence in 1980. All constitutions include a Bill of Rights, based on the UDHR, that includes freedom of belief and expression. Several constitutions note duties and community values as well as individual human rights. The Tongan constitution is the only one that has a Sunday observance clause. Niukula noted that despite the prominence of Christianity in all constitutions in Oceania at that time, none stated that Christianity should be the state religion. This, however, is no longer the case, as in 2017 Sāmoa became a Christian state in the *de jure* sense. The original wording of Article 1 of the Sāmoan constitution was 'Sāmoa is founded on God'. This wording expressed a religious conception that could include all religious groups. The amended Article 1 now reads 'Sāmoa is a Christian nation founded of God the Father, the Son and the Holy Spirit'. This conception of God is indisputably Christian. The rationale for adopting the change was to embed Christianity within the body of the constitution, so that it is legally binding, as the wording in a preamble is not legally binding. Another reason given for the change was to protect Sāmoa from religious tensions in the future – from within and from outside influences, with reference given to violent religious wars elsewhere. Although official statistics are lacking, there are very small numbers of Hindus, Buddhists, Muslims and Jews in Sāmoa, mainly in the capital, Apia. While Sāmoa is now legally a Christian state, the rights of the individual to freedom of religion, as outlined in Article 11, remain unchanged. At the same time, observers note that the constitutional change could result in denominational rivalry for religious influence in Sāmoan politics.

Papua New Guinea (PNG) is in line to become the second officially Christian state in Oceania. On 18 August 2020 the National Executive Council approved a proposal to 'clearly declare Christianity as the Official State Religion in the Constitution…. Other religions will be allowed to practice their faith in the country but with respect to the [*sic*] Christianity as the Official State Religion', Prime Minister James Marabe is quoted as saying on the Department of the Prime Minister and Executive Council's website, noting that PNG's non-Christian population is 4%. The approval of this constitutional change will, he said, secure the long-term peace and safety of PNG. He added, 'Should the Constitution of PNG protect the freedom of religion by limiting it to Christianity, potential religious bigotry that could give rise to civil war, chaos and instability will be averted'.

So, similar to the Sāmoan rationale for declaring the country a *de jure* Christian state, PNG cites the violence of religious wars elsewhere, with specific reference to the Middle East. Churches and civil society organisations have opposed the move, saying it threatens freedom of religion. Indeed, declaring PNG a Christian state opens up the question, as also with regard to Sāmoa, of which denomination will be the determining one in a Christian state.

A heated debate that broke out in the PNG media in November and December 2013 concerning the controversial actions of the speaker of the PNG national parliament, Theodore Zurenuoc, a fundamentalist Christian, illustrates this point. Zurenuoc started removing from Parliament House traditional carvings he deemed idolatrous, in a personal project to spiritually cleanse the house of what he considered demonic forces contained in the material objects. Zurenuoc's acts sparked a fiery debate in PNG's two national newspapers and on social media.

The preamble to the constitution of PNG declares that the country is founded on two basic principles, 'our cultural heritage and our Christianity'. However, this interweaving of culture and Christianity pertains only to the historic mainline churches. These churches are theologically in dialogue with people and culture, and interwoven with traditions, past and present. Fundamentalist and Pentecostal churches, on the other hand, are interconnected to global Christian communities. These churches generally classify that which is pre-Christian as demonic, to be battled against in 'spiritual warfare' and conquered by the 'superior' power of Christianity. The understanding is strongly dualistic and Pauline in its sharp division between pre-conversion darkness and the light of Christianity. All things traditional and all acts associated with tradition and the past are linked with darkness and sin. The language employed is militant, and actions against this darkness are considered 'spiritual warfare'.

On the one side of the PNG debate, then, were Christians of fundamentalist and Pentecostal backgrounds who saw Zurenuoc as doing God's will through spiritual warfare, exorcising dangerous and destructive forces from the parliament building. On the other were Christians from mainline churches, and others, who saw Zurenuoc as committing cultural sacrilege by destroying invaluable cultural heritage. These contesting representations demonstrate the highly complex field of Christianities in PNG that is mirrored in other Pacific Island societies.

Fiji – A Secular State

Perhaps the country in the region where issues of religious freedom have come into clearest focus is Fiji, with its multi-ethnic and multi-religious composition and turbulent post-independence coup history. In 2013 Fiji's then military government adopted by decree a new constitution that declared Fiji a secular state. This added another dimension to Fiji's complex religious, ethnic and political landscape. Fiji is a meeting point of contested, entangled and often unclear representations of culture, tradition, religion, freedom of religion and secularism, and is therefore of particular interest in discussions on freedom of religion in Oceania in the twenty-first century.

In 2020, according to UN estimations, the population of Fiji was 896,445. Although the most recent census was in 2017, the most recent available statistics on religious affiliation are from the 2007 census. At that time, the population was just over 837,000. Religious affiliation in Fiji has always run almost entirely along ethnic lines. In 2007, 57% of the population was *iTaukei* (Indigenous Fijian) and almost all were Christian; 37% were Indo-Fijian, most of whom were Hindu. According to the census, 64.5% of the population was Christian, 27.9% Hindu and 6.3% Muslim. The Methodist Church counted 34.6% of the population, the Roman Catholic Church 9.1%.

The constitution made *de jure* what had been *de facto* since independence from the UK in 1970: Fiji has always been a secular state, and freedom of religion had always been guaranteed by former governments, though not formerly written into the constitutions. Yet from the mid-1980s ethnic tensions between the two main ethnic groups led a vocal minority of militant ethno-nationalist groups, mainly from certain quarters of the Methodist Church, to advocate for Fiji being declared a Christian state. Two military coups in 1987 and a civilian coup in 2000, directed against the Indo-Fijian community, were actively supported by the Methodist Church in Fiji. A fourth coup, in 2006, led by the current Prime Minister, Voreqe Bainimarama – ostensibly a 'clean-up' coup to root out corruption – resulted in the forming of a military government that was in place until the elections of 2014.

While the declaration of Fiji as a secular state was a response to the threat of Fiji being declared a Christian state, the manner of its making and its adoption by decree were highly contentious. The 2013 constitution replaced a 2012 draft constitution that had been broadly accepted throughout the country. It was the result of an extensive and in-depth review process, led by an overseas constitutional expert, consulting all levels of society, including civil society organisations, religious bodies and individuals. However, when the draft constitution was about to be released to the public, the military government intervened. All copies were burned at the printer's and, giving no time for more than symbolic civic consultation, the government made its own amendments and then adopted by decree the 2013 constitution, with its secular-state declaration.

The shock and dismay this effected throughout society meant that the 2013 constitution is viewed by many Fijians as having been 'thrust down our throats'. The lack of consultation and lack of explanation then and since of what the term 'secular state' – an entirely new term in Fiji society – means and entails is problematic. And to a large part of the population it will always be associated with the manner in which the 2013 constitution was adopted.

Yet to the Indo-Fijian communities of Fiji's many different Indian religions, the declaration of Fiji as a secular state was a watershed moment. They felt a greater sense of legal protection than they had before. Having experienced stones being thrown on the roofs of houses during prayers and temples being looted and burned, a priest from the Arja Samaj Hindu organisation in Fiji commented, '[There's] assurance that [should] anyone should disturb you in your prayers, you … have recourse to the law … that the law should protect you … [should there be] any … misbehaviour against any religion.' His point was echoed by the national president of Fiji's largest Hindu organisation, Sanatan Dharm Pratinidhi Sabha Fiji. 'That was the sunrise for us', he said. 'We were very happy … that now there will be less burning of temples' (interviews with author, July 2019).

Fiji's Christians, on the other hand, were deeply concerned. Many lay Christians felt they had lost the freedom to be Christians. Many were under the impression that Fiji had always been a Christian state and that this had now been taken from them. To many Christians it appeared that God had been removed from the constitution and from society. To Christian theologians and church leaders, such as Roman Catholic Archbishop Dr Loy Chong, newly installed in 2013 with the episcopal motto 'To be church in the world', there was concern at the interpretation of the wording of the constitution and how this might be used to limit the freedom of the prophetic role of churches in society.

While the separation of church and state in the constitution is in keeping with Roman Catholic teaching, Clause 1:4(2) of the constitution, that 'religion is personal', is problematic, according to Archbishop Chong, and could be used to silence the prophetic voice of the church. Between 2009 and 2013 the Methodist Church in Fiji had been prohibited by the government from holding its annual conference. Fiji thus had already experienced the infringement of freedom of religion. 'They [said] "you can have your religion but it can have nothing to do with society" – which denies the public character [of faith]' (Chong, interview with author, 2014).

Fiji's 2013 constitution departs in significant ways from the country's previous constitutions and from all other Pacific Island constitutions in that it does not mention Christianity and, though peoples, cultures, traditions and languages are mentioned, there is no mention of religion in the Preamble. The concerns of Christians in the country were well expressed by Archbishop Chong when he stated,

> The constitution should reflect the values that a country holds. And a lot of our values are embedded in religious institutions. A constitution is supposed to protect values, what we hold to be important. When a constitution does not reflect [our] values it's almost contradictory to what we hold in our hearts. (Interview with author, February 2014)

These are concerns not only of the Catholic Church in Fiji; they are shared by all church leaders, who are anxious about the ramifications that the 2013 constitution might have for freedom of religion in the country. Lack of consultation and lack of open, clear and nuanced societal debate on the declaration of Fiji as a secular state means that concern voiced about the secular state is often interpreted as support for a Christian state.

However, Archbishop Chong has made it clear that 'We do not want a theocracy. We never said we want a Christian state. However, we are concerned about whether a secularist state wants to reduce faith to a purely individualistic matter.' The vision of the church is 'a secular state that is respectful of religious beliefs present in society' (Dr Peter Loy Chong, Archbishop of Suva, *Agenzia Fides*, 11 December 2013).

Faith-based Education and the State

Another issue of contention between churches and the Fiji government derives from the Ministry of Education's introduction of the so-called Open Merit Recruitment System of Selection (OMRSS) for head teacher and teaching appointments at primary and high schools. Rendering redundant memorandums of understanding between the education boards of different faiths and the Ministry that had been in place for decades, the OMRSS gives the Ministry of Education sole control of all recruitment. Faith-based organisations have consistently requested of the Ministry that school principals or head teachers should be members of the faith of the school to which they are appointed, so that they are able to support the ethos of that school. Yet to many people involved in faith-based education, the Ministry appears to be following a strategy of replacing teachers and heads of faith-based schools with appointees of other faiths.

This absence of consultation with faith-based organisations gives a clear sense that this is a strategic diluting of religious influence as part of a policy of tighter government control of society. It also fails to recognise the significant historical contribution made to education in Fiji by different religions, as well as their continuing contribution, and is considered an infringement of freedom of religion as guaranteed in Article 22(4) of the constitution. This states that 'Every religious community or denomination, and every cultural or social community, has the right to establish, maintain and manage places of education whether or not it receives financial assistance from the State, provided that the educational institution maintains any standard prescribed by law.' The Catholic Church alone runs 44 primary schools, 19 secondary schools and Corpus Christi Teacher's College, and has 1,000 registered Catholic teachers. In early 2019, when tensions between churches and the government were at their highest, Archbishop Loy Chong threatened to close all Catholic schools.

As the elected chair of the multifaith committee set up by the faith organisations, among the requests made by Archbishop Chong to the Ministry of Education were that the choice of head teacher be based not only on excellent performance but also on the ability to uphold and foster the ethos of the school; that appointments of school heads be made in consultation with the school management committee; that a representative of the faith-based organisation be a member of the recruiting panel for school heads; that a percentage of the teachers belong to the faith of the school; and that the agreement between the Education Ministry and faith-based organisations and communities on the above issues be documented as part of the Education Act to ensure the stability and security of faith-based schools.

A high-profile court case between the Seventh-day Adventist Church in Fiji and the Fijian government concerns the Adventist Church's challenge to the Ministry of Education's appointment of a Catholic head teacher to one of its high schools. The Seventh-day Adventist Church won its case in November 2019. The Fijian government appealed and at the time of writing the appeal had not yet been heard. By far the majority of Fiji's schools are faith-based, so the outcome of this court case has great significance for churches and religious organisations.

The faith-based school appointments issue clearly demonstrates that while declaring Fiji a secular state in 2013 was ostensibly a move to guarantee freedom of religion, the current government – under the same leadership as the military government in 2013 – seems more intent on controlling religion, systematically weakening it, and replacing it with increasing levels of secularisation and government control. Many observers see this as part of a wider strategy by the government of crushing Indigenous Fijian sociocultural structures based on the tripartite conceptual understanding of *vanua* (belonging to the land and people), *lotu* (church) and *matanitu* (governance) in order to radically reshape Fiji into a modern, Western-style nation-state.

Australia and New Zealand

Provision for religious freedom in Australia and New Zealand is shaped primarily by Western traditions. The religious freedom clause in the federal constitution in Australia is based on the First Amendment to the US constitution. It states,

> The Commonwealth shall not make any law for establishing any religion, or for imposing any religious observance, or for prohibiting the free exercise of any religion, and no religious test shall be required as a qualification for any office or public trust under the Commonwealth.

Australia clearly understands itself to be a secular country with separation of church and state and no state religion. Legislation at the state and territory level provides for freedom of religion, though Tasmania is the only state with a constitution that specifically provides citizens with the right to profess and practise their religion. Most states and territories do, however, have legislation that prohibits discrimination on the basis of a person's religion.

Recent debate has centred around the freedom of individuals and institutions to express religiously held views on sexuality, marriage and family life that would otherwise be regarded as discriminatory. The lack of a comprehensive Bill of Rights means that this is contested terrain, as demonstrated in 2019 by the sacking of Sāmoan Australian rugby player Israel Folau for his controversial posting on social media: 'Drunks, Homosexuals, Adulterers, Liars, Fornicators, Thieves, Atheists, Idolators: Hell Awaits You. Repent! Only Jesus Saves.' Folau took Rugby Australia to court, arguing that the termination of his contract was a case of religious discrimination. The dispute, the first of its kind in Australian legal history, was settled out of court. The case highlights what may be considered a fine line between freedom of religion and freedom of expression, and discriminatory, derogatory speech directed against individuals or communities. At the time of writing, a Religious Freedom Bill was being prepared, particularly with a view to protecting the rights of employees to express their religious convictions in the course of their professional lives.

While Australia's ethos in relation to religion is generally easy-going and tolerant, it also has shrill political voices of religious intolerance at the political level, as is experienced across the world today. High-profile events in recent years such as the Melbourne and Sydney Islamist terrorist attacks in 2017, the 2019 Christchurch terror attacks by an Australian white supremacist, and the trial of Roman Catholic Cardinal Pell in Melbourne in 2019 on charges of child abuse have highlighted tensions between the growing secularism of Australian society and religion. The Islamist terror attacks led on the one hand to anti-Muslim sentiments and reactions against Muslims on social media and in public spaces. On the other they led to many expressions of solidarity and empathy from non-Muslims toward Muslims, including the physical protection of Muslims travelling on public transport. The contemporary rise in anti-Semitism, harassment and attacks on Jewish people, recorded in almost all societies across the world, is also a reality in Australia.

New Zealand, too, is a secular society and observes freedom of religion. The 1990 Bill of Rights Act states, 'Everyone has the right to freedom of thought, conscience, religion, and belief, including the right to adopt and hold opinions without interference.' The government does not require the licensing or registration of religious groups, but if a religious group desires to collect money for any charitable purpose – including the advancement of its religion – and obtain tax benefits, it must register with the Department of Internal Affairs. Christians are free to profess and advocate their beliefs, including through forming political parties, with two currently registered political parties having a Christian basis. At the same time, New Zealand is one of the most secular countries in the world, with 49% of the population professing to have no religion. A 2018 Commonwealth report found that of its 53 member nations, New Zealand is the country with the greatest religious freedom.

This ethos came into global view in the aftermath of the 15 March 2019 Christchurch terror attacks by an Australian white supremacist at two mosques, in which 51 Muslims lost their lives and 49 were injured. The shock and sadness experienced throughout the nation and the ways in which New Zealanders responded with empathy and care were relayed across the world. The images of Prime Minister Jacinda Ardern, her hair respectfully covered by a scarf, embracing grieving Muslim women sent out strong messages of multiculturalism, religious respect, inclusivity and love of neighbour. In a further gesture of solidarity with the Muslim community, the New Zealand government invited a Muslim imam to intone the Quranic bismillah in praise of Allah at the opening of the parliamentary session on 19 March, days after the massacre. Other powerful messages of solidarity were expressed in performances of the *haka* throughout the country. The Christchurch attacks brought New Zealanders together in an outpouring of grief and sorrow at the tragedy that had been wrought by an outsider on their land. The moment also opened up for discussions at all levels of society the structural inequalities, tensions and insidious violence of everyday prejudice against minority groups, the casual racism and legacy of New Zealand's colonial past that lie, often unnoticed by the privileged, under the surface of society, as in all other societies across the world.

Fiji lost three members of the country's small Muslim community in the Christchurch attacks. Interfaith vigils were held at the main mosque in Suva, at the Anglican Cathedral and at the University of the South Pacific campus. Beneath the sense of sharing in the tragedy and loss of a close neighbour and member of the Pacific *vuvale* (family) were other feelings of unease at the knowledge that religious violence of such proportions had now come so close to home. And, as in New Zealand, it brought up similar discussions of how easily prejudice and racism simmer under the surface and, especially, circulate in social media postings.

Conclusion

This essay has shown that the concept of freedom of religion is not easily translatable to Pacific Island cultures. Just as in Pacific Island cultures a person is never an individual in the Western sense but always relationally constituted, embedded within closely interwoven clan and communal relationships and obligations, so it is with freedom of religion. On the one hand, it is written into constitutions based on the UDHR. On the other, it is embedded in complex fields of contested and contesting representations of Christianity, culture, tradition, politics and secularism. Discussions on freedom of religion in Oceania need therefore to be contextualised in relation to local, historically situated sociocultural and religious complexities. And these local complexities are in turn inextricably inter-connected with wider regional and global processes, past and present.

Bibliography

Fer, Yannick, 'Religion, Pluralism, and Conflicts in the Pacific Islands', in Andrew R. Murphy (ed.), *The Blackwell Companion to Religion and Violence* (Chichester: Blackwell, 2011), 461–72.

Niukula, Paula, 'Religion and the State', in B. V. Lal and T. R. Vakatora (eds), *Fiji in Transition: Research Papers of the Fiji Constitution Review Commission, Vol. 1* (Suva: School of Social and Economic Development, University of the South Pacific, 1997), 53–79.

Ryle, Jacqueline, *My God, My Land: Interwoven Paths of Christianity and Tradition in Fiji* (Farnham: Ashgate, 2010).

Ryle, Jacqueline, 'Roots of Land and Church: The Christian State Debate in Fiji', *International Journal for the Study of the Christian Church*, 5: 1 (2005), 58–78.

Tomlinson, Matt and Debra McDougall, 'Introduction – Christian Politics in Oceania', in Matt Tomlinson and Debra McDougall (eds), *Christian Politics in Oceania* (New York: Berghahn Books, 2013), 1–21.

Inter-religious Relations

Elizabeth Krishna and Tessa Mackenzie

Despite scant examples of a large-scale religious plurality in Oceania, some island nations, such as the Solomon Islands, Tuvalu and Papua New Guinea (PNG), are able to model inter-religious coexistence, albeit in small, contextualised circumstances. This essay briefly profiles such cases but focuses on religious plurality as it is demonstrated in Fiji and in Australia, the countries with the greatest religious diversity within this region.

Island Nations

The population of the Solomon Islands is predominantly Christian. Islam, brought to the islands from the 1980s and 1990s, was popular among youths in the early years but became most visible during the conflicts that raged around the turn of the millennium. There is a minority group of Buddhists as well. Due to the minimal presence of Islam and Buddhism – there are no mosques or Buddhist temples – worship is held in leaders' homes. The Bahá'í Faith is also present as a minority, with an established centre for meetings.

Despite the lack of official relationship between faiths, cultural relationships exist between individual members from different religions. During the ISIS encroachment in some parts of the world, there was an increase of young people in the region joining Islam; however, it did not result in confrontation between Muslims and Christians, this ostensible detente reflecting a deep-rooted respect for freedom of religion in the Solomon Islands.

Religions in Tuvalu include Christianity, the Bahá'í Faith and one Muslim family. Both Islam and Bahá'í are registered religious organisations and have permanent places of worship. Christians enjoy a relatively peaceful coexistence with non-Christians.

Papua New Guinea features Christianity as a majority religion, together with the Bahá'í Faith and small communities of Muslims, Hindus, Jews and Buddhists. Christianity, Islam, the Bahá'í Faith and Jehovah's Witnesses are registered religious organisations and each has permanent places of worship. Though PNG is regarded as a Christian nation, there is no hostility to non-Christians.

Religions in Fiji

Fiji was ruled by the British government during the colonial period and gained independence in 1970. Constitutionally, the prime minister of Fiji is the head of government and the president is the head of state. Fiji as a nation has undergone major challenges of conflicts, natural disasters and traumas since gaining independence. The coups of 1987, 2000 and 2006 have left psychological scars on many people, after much violence, corruption, mass exodus, ethnic and religious divisions, discrimination, violation of human rights and insecurity among the population. Unfortunately, for the majority of the population, a thorough healing process for those experiences of trauma has never been carried out. These multiple unfavourable events have continuously divided its society and have also severely impacted its economy.

After the arrival of Christianity more than 200 years ago, only small, unacknowledged vestiges remain of primitive religious practices and customs of the Indigenous population embedded in the traditional culture of Fiji. Today, most Indigenous Fijians are Christians. The indenture system brought in by the British colonial government in 1879 introduced Hinduism, Islam and a minority of Sikhs into Fiji. The colonial masters from the very beginning enforced and encouraged segregation between the Indigenous Fijians and Indo-Fijians. However, over the last 50 years there has been greater assimilation, mainly at the village and grassroots levels, in workplaces and in sporting, social and religious celebrations. The religious, socio-economic and political divide remains as an underlying cause of friction among the people.

Fiji is also home for Rotumans, Tongans, Sāmoans, Europeans, Chinese, Koreans, Filipinos, Japanese, Tuvaluans, Sri Lankans, Indians from India, Solomon Islanders, Papua New Guineans, Africans and some other, smaller ethnic groups. Some are in the country on employment contracts. Many Chinese, Filipinos and Koreans have become Fijian citizens.

There was, to a great extent, cultural and religious peace in Fiji before 1987, but since the events of 1987, ethnic and religious divisions have been experienced and continue to widen, though in some of the rural settlements the relationship is better than it is in towns and cities. During the time of the first coup in 1987, some temples (especially Hindu temples), mosques and churches were desecrated and destroyed, and sacred literature was burned. This was a clear sign of religious intolerance, disrespect and lack of understanding and knowledge of one's own religious teachings, which in the case of Fiji would also implicate those calling for the country to be declared a Christian state. Some Hindu temples continue to be desecrated and vandalised. New Pentecostal churches and new Hindu sects continue to emerge.

In the recent past, Fiji has become a highly diverse nation in terms of culture and religion. The upheavals of the past, natural disasters, unemployment and non-renewal of land leases have also brought about internal migration, with densely populated towns and cities. This has also contributed toward social breakdown, increased crime rates, housing issues, and inflation in rental and property prices in cities and towns. The more diverse existence of religions and cultures in the present day can also become a possible cause of more conflicts in the future. On the other hand, this same diversity of religion/culture/ethnicity also makes Fiji a unique and enriching place to live.

In the Fijian context, religion and culture are treasured and provide identity for most of the population. Religion and culture can be both a powerful dividing tool in the hands of opportunists and an equally powerful means of enriching and unifying the people toward peaceful and harmonious existence. This dynamic, however, provides opportunities for common grounds of understanding and healing, thus enabling better understanding, trust, tolerance and acceptance of the differences and relations within the population. Such an opportunity was taken up by a few people in the wake of religious upheaval during the 1987 coup to bring about better understanding and reconciliation among the population. These few began to meet and discuss what was happening and discover ways to address the situation. This was the informal beginning of Interfaith Search Fiji (ISF).

Before 1987, there was a relatively stable tolerance between the three main religions in Fiji: Christianity, Hinduism and Islam. At that time there was a more pronounced division between the three main ethnic groups, of whom the *iTaukei* (Indigenous Fijians) were mainly Methodist Christians. During the 1960s and 1970s the advent of Evangelical groups from America took place alongside the move to political independence from Britain. These new Christians brought an emphasis on evangelisation and condemnation of 'idol worshippers'. People being converted from Hinduism were made to burn all items of religious significance, including things that were of spiritual and cultural significance.

The formal process and formation of ISF was undertaken in the 1990s. It was established to build respect and understanding between people of different religious traditions in Fiji. In its early years, ISF was nationwide in effect and gained publicity. The foundation and focus of ISF activities are sourced from the Holy Scriptures and every activity begins with a silent prayer to show respect for each other's religion. Additionally, ISF allows only vegetarian meals and refreshments in all its activities to allow respect and inclusiveness, as vegetarian food is accepted by people of all religions.

In 2000, when politicians were held captive by the then coup leaders, silent prayer was held daily for an hour in the Anglican Cathedral, attended by many people of different religious traditions. Regular inter-religious prayer was held weekly in the same venue for some years. Multifaith prayer sessions have been organised by ISF at times of national or worldwide crisis and before national elections in Fiji. ISF had also organised many workshops in the four regions of Fiji on inter-religious dialogue, together with numerous panel discussions on topics that affect the population across the board It had also facilitated inter-religious workshops for young people from different religious backgrounds. Such panel discussions and workshops have been especially effective in engaging more Christian denominations for the organisation, despite failing to attract participation in other methods.

ISF has also worked together with non-governmental organisations to respond to calls for submissions from the United Nations office based in Fiji. The organisation has formulated Prayer for Fiji and Prayer before Meals, which is used in all ISF activities and has also been used at some national events. ISF upon request has also formulated prayer for the Department of Police and the Judicial Department, used before commencement of their meetings. It has also published books and pamphlets and has shared scripture quotations on a given topic or theme and its practical application in the lives of the followers of respective faith denominations. Within this monthly scripture-sharing, feasts of the faith denominations celebrated in that particular month are also shared, with their significance and rituals.

In the Fiji context, festive celebrations such as Christmas celebrated by Christians, Deep-a-wali (Diwali) celebrated by Hindus and Eid celebrated by Muslims are occasions when people of different faith denominations come together and visit each other during the celebrations. Rugby is one sport which also unites Fijians, despite ethnic and religious differences. Meanwhile, the current government, which came into power via a military coup in 2006, has constituted Fiji as a secular state. It has also determined that all people are identified as 'Fijians' and the Indigenous population as 'iTaukei'.

Since the institution of the ISF, engaging many of the Christian denominations in interfaith activities has been an ongoing challenge. The dominant Christian denomination, the Methodist Church, and the dominant Muslim denomination, the Fiji Muslim League, left ISF in the early years of its inception and, despite many efforts, neither has returned as an official member. On one occasion, during a time of heightened political tension, the Methodist Church used nationwide broadcasts to ban its members from attending ISF events.

Another challenge today is to find ways to interest people in inter-religious dialogue, given the lack of interest among young people. There are still obstacles in understanding Christian teaching condemning idol worship as evil. Many of the religious leaders do not have much interest in interfaith dialogue. Thus, taken together, securing funds to support such initiatives proves to be a big challenge.

Religions in Australia

Beginning in 2017, Religions for Peace Australia (RfP), a multifaith network committed to social and religious wellbeing in the country, prepared a report detailing the progress of interfaith/worldview engagement. Entitled *Audit of Multifaith/Interfaith Groups and Institutions and Their Activities Across Australia: From the Grassroots to International Engagement*, it examined the inter-religious dynamics of an Australian secular society that is dramatically changing over time. In the past two decades, the country has both become more secular and more religiously diverse, with Islam overtaking Buddhism in the past five years as the largest non-Christian religion in Australia.

These changes have profound implications for Australia's civil society and politics. For example, international developments since the 11 September 2001 attacks on the USA have elevated issues of faith and worldviews in the public spotlight. As such issues have been politicised by individuals and parties within the country, there is clear need for a social cohesion policy that bridges the religious groups and secular humanist traditions in a multiculturalist frame. And while it might be reductionistic to imagine such a goal entailed in a singular policy, the effort to articulate a twenty-first-century Australian multiculturalism would help initiate and sustain engagement between groups.

The audit revealed that interfaith engagement, rather than directly spearheaded by the government, was instead advanced by volunteers, part-time workers (mostly appointed by religious bodies such as the Catholic Church and local government councils) and a small group of academics. In other words, such interfaith engagement has been initiated by government policy and programme development to the degree that warrants a response to situations involving religions, such as religiously inspired terrorism and inquiries by the Royal Commission into Child Sexual Abuse. Rather, the report illuminated the work of organisations such as the National Council of Churches of Australia, which were engaging in intrafaith discussions for the purposes of healing historical rifts, and organisations such as the Jewish, Christian, and Muslim Association, which began in Melbourne in 2003 and which has been conducting interfaith relations on a national level. Despite the lack of a coordinated national policy of social cohesion on religious plurality, efforts on behalf of the state to achieve such dialogue must be noted. For instance, the Faith Communities Council of Victoria was formed as a multifaith, government-funded body. Its creation stemmed from the efforts of several religious groups, academics, multifaith networks and individuals as a practical emanation from the Parliament of the World's Religions in 2009.

Churches also have agencies of their own involved in ecumenical efforts, especially since the 11 September attacks. The Australian Catholic Council for Ecumenism and Interreligious Relations Commission (of the Catholic Church) and Pax Christi (part of a global Catholic peace movement formed in 1970) are such church groups. The Uniting Church in Australia devotes an entire section on its website, called 'Relations to Other Faiths', to interfaith efforts. Moreover, national interfaith efforts by Buddhists exist through the Federation of Australian Buddhist Councils and by Hindus through the Sathya Sai Organization. Other notable small religious groups involved in interfaith engagement include the Bahá'í, Brahma Kumaris and Quakers.

In 2017, the Queensland government established a multifaith board with the impetus coming from Dr Brian Adams, director of Griffith University's Centre for Interfaith and Cultural Dialogue, and other multifaith advocates. Such multifaith advisory boards join religious leaders with state governments to help forge social cohesion; however, such foundations have proven to be unreliable. Even fewer states – only New South Wales and Victoria – have multifaith police advisory boards where faith leaders meet with state police. Tasmania and Queensland have shown models of informal police and faith leader networks. The VictPol Multifaith Council, established in 2005, has been an exemplary model for Victoria for community policing. The initiative has attracted international attention and has been extremely useful at times of crisis such as the foiled attack on Federation Square and St Paul's Cathedral in December 2016.

Multifaith engagement among youths currently exists in several territories, through existing networks and educational programmes. Such groups include the Youth Multifaith Network, run in conjunction with Victoria police, and a group supported by the Brahma Kumaris and the Church of Jesus Christ of Latter-day Saints. In addition, the Centre for Interfaith and Cultural Dialogue based at Griffith University has a popular following among the youth. However, in 2010, Religions for Peace Victoria with Monash University initiated a meeting with religious education academics to look at issues surrounding religious education in Australian primary and secondary schools. While the government was proposing a National Curriculum that included religious affairs, in 2014 the project ran into trouble due to the Commonwealth government's insistence on having an emphasis on the Judaeo-Christian tradition. At the same time, volunteers of Buddhist, Bahá'í, Hindu, Jewish, Muslim, Sikh and Christian traditions were teaching Special Religious Instruction classes, the curriculum regulated by the Religions for Peace Victoria branch. However, due to government policy that restricted the teaching of these classes to lunchtimes or after school, these programmes are few in number.

Despite such obstacles and the cobbled nature of historical interfaith efforts in Australia, several national groups continue to engage in multifaith/interfaith/worldview understandings, such as the Australian Partnership of Religious Organizations and the United Religions Initiative. However, Religions for Peace Australia is the most active group in the country; in 2014, RfP Australia became affiliated with the Canberra Interfaith Forum and the Multifaith Association of South Australia. A year later RfP commenced linking with Griffith University's Centre for Interfaith and Cultural Dialogue, and in 2017 with the Centre for Muslim States and Societies at the University of Western Australia.

Conclusion

While interfaith work is done at various levels across Oceania, in a modern world of multi-religious and multi-ethnic tensions, there is room for significant improvement, with an onus on governments to take a leading role in supporting and addressing such ethnic and religious conflicts. In the Fijian context, such improvements can begin with inter-religious/interfaith dialogue. Churches in the country need to be more open to other religions and to be engaged together in working for the good of the nation and the people as a whole. Meanwhile, in Australia, efforts toward interfaith engagement need to cohere under an encompassing framework, addressing diverse worldviews not just within the country but among trading partners in Oceania. Despite fledgling groups doing their part, due to the commitments of churches and individuals, a lack of policy implementation has resulted in Australia lagging behind comparable nations that have more developed multifaith programmes and policies – for example, in their primary and secondary schools. Funds poured into counterterrorism resulting from an overreaction to inter-religious tension might be better used to fund the development and maintenance of Australia's social cohesion within and beyond its borders.

Bibliography

Australian Multicultural Council, *Interfaith and Social Cohesion in Australia: Looking to the Future*, The Australian Multicultural Council's Report to the Australian Government, June 2014 (Canberra: Australian Government, Department of Social Services, 2014).

Bushell, Stephen, *Fiji's Faiths: Who We Are and What We Believe* (Suva: Interfaith Search, 1990).

Halafoff, Anna, *Interfaith Youth in Australia: A Critical Reflection on Religious Diversity, Literacy and Identity* (Leiden: Brill, 2018).

Halafoff, Anna, *The Multifaith Movement: Global Risks and Cosmopolitan Solutions* (Dordrecht: Springer, 2013).

Research for this essay was via written interviews with the students of Pacific Theological College from the Solomon Islands, Tuvalu and Papua New Guinea. This essay also drew on work by Dr Brian J. Adams, director of the Center for Interfaith and Cultural Dialogue, Griffith University, Queensland, Australia; Dr Susan Ennis and Emeritus Professor Desmond Cahill, OAM; and Religions for Peace Australia's *Audit of Multifaith/Interfaith Groups and Institutions and Their Activities Across Australia: From the Grassroots to International Engagement.*

Integrity of Creation

Cliff Bird

In light of recent and current experiences globally, especially the globe-impacting nature and magnitude of the COVID-19 pandemic, integrity of creation is not only a very timely topic but also a critically important one. In the midst of the human pain, suffering and deaths caused by the pandemic, many around the world see the silver linings. Social media posts, popular articles as well as scholarly works highlight how Earth starts to breathe and live again as a direct result of lockdowns, grounded flights and the besieged air and sea travel industries, diminished industrial and manufacturing operations, and reduced sea-based trade, to name but a few. Of the multiple learnings that have come about, without a doubt one stands out: namely, that human activities and interferences with and intrusions into creation's natural processes and vitality are shown to be responsible for the rapid degradation of Earth and Earth's rhythms and systems.

The COVID-19 pandemic, perhaps more as a tangential consequence, has brought back the issue of the integrity of creation to the foreground of human consciousness and deliberations, especially with the rhetoric to break free from one kind of being world and to move toward a new kind of being world. 'Being world' is an appropriate phrase because we can and do make and unmake this one world. Only a few historical moments throughout the centuries could be said to bear on creation's integrity, and without a doubt the COVID-19 pandemic is one such historical moment. In the context of Oceania, integrity of creation must, as a matter of ethical responsibility and necessity, be seen as a continuum that bridges the past and present and that points to possible futures.

Oceania: Contextual Platform

Given that this volume focuses on Oceania, it is necessary to begin from an understanding of this term. The descriptor 'Oceania' is increasingly used in the place of 'Pacific'. In keeping with this trend, 'Oceania' is used throughout this book, and for justifiable reasons. Firstly, the descriptor 'Pacific' carries with it, and is burdened with, colonial overtones and baggage and, therefore, needs to be discontinued in favour of 'Oceania'. The late Epeli Hau'ofa's *A New Oceania: Rediscovering Our Sea of Islands*

(1993) is both pioneering and exemplary of this perspective. Secondly, 'Oceania' is more fitting given that oceans and seas are the more dominant features of the island nations, not so much 'land'. And thirdly, there is the need to shift global perspectives of, gaze upon, and narratives of the islands from romanticised or demonised notions to pragmatic and more-true-to-context notions.

It is necessary at the outset to highlight some challenges that come with the topic of this essay. The first are the manifold diversities that exist in the countries lumped under Oceania, a label that covers the many differently sized island countries that are commonly referred to as the South Pacific as well as, according to the United Nations' definition, Australia and New Zealand. Cultures, views, experiences and practices of Christianity across the region are not uniform. This has given rise to the use of the plural 'Christianities' in Oceania. The second is the degree of ambiguity that surrounds the term 'integrity' and the phrase 'integrity of creation.' What exactly do these renderings mean? Who and what defines integrity and integrity of creation? Is integrity intrinsic to creation or is it imposed on creation by some extrinsic valuer or valuation system and method? A commendable degree of clarity has emerged from the scholarly work carried out ecumenically under the umbrella of the World Council of Churches since the closing decade of the twentieth century. The question with regard to this essay is whether that emerging clarity resonates with Christianity in Oceania. A related question has to do with integrity of creation in pre-Christian Oceania. This leads to the third challenge: a retrospective discussion and application of a late-twentieth-century theological thought-conversation to Christianity in Oceania, let alone in pre-Christian Oceania, is subject to historiographical pitfalls. This is especially so when the Christianity or Christianities that intruded upon Oceania was or were focused primarily on salvation rather than on creation.

Absence of Creation Theology in the Missionary Project

This historiographical challenge quite logically is linked to a very important yet perhaps less talked-about issue, namely continuity and discontinuity of pre-Christian creation views and narratives in Christianity in Oceania. Did the coming of Christianity mean a clean break from previously held beliefs, simply discontinuing all the preceding traditional religious and traditional cultural worldviews? Or did Christianity open up to these pre-Christian notions, resulting in a continuity of these in one form or other and to one degree or other in Christianity in Oceania today? The position taken in this essay is that both continuity and discontinuity of pre-Christian creation views and narratives exist in present-day Christianity in Oceania. However, as will be discussed shortly, continuity of these aspects remained as the unofficial and unwritten elements of church life and practice, becoming formally recognised and affirmed more as a resurgence and reclaiming of pre-Christian worldviews only when contextual theology became commonplace in theological education and institutions in Oceania.

Both written works and oral traditions recall that the primary goal of the missionary project and ensuing activities in Oceania was for the salvation of the heathens through the gospel of Jesus Christ. First, this goal followed from the great spiritual awakenings in Europe in the eighteenth century, when emphasis was on conversion and salvation of wayward and sinful human beings. The call by missionaries to abandon traditional religions and cultures and to convert to and embrace Christianity echoed throughout the islands of Oceania. The Christian God was presented in terms of power encounters and complete distinction from the gods of traditional religions – the former as novel light and the latter as utter darkness. Consequently, and secondly, with very few exceptions, pioneer missionaries did not have creation and its integrity on their theological and missiological radar. As such, it featured very minimally, if at all, in their missionary and evangelistic zeal. On the contrary, there was desacralisation and demonisation of deeply embedded relationships and religious or spiritual attachments Indigenous peoples had with elements of/in creation. Thirdly, throughout most of Oceania, colonisation, Christianity and the early workings of global trade came together. The logical outcome of this triadic constellation was a utilitarian and instrumentalist presentation and understanding of Christianity in relation to creation and its integrity. Moreover, it formed and established a multifaceted dualism, including dualism between the material and spiritual – the former as the domain of darkness and death, and the latter of light and life. This understanding of Christianity implied that creation and its constituents, especially those with utilitarian and instrumental value for people, were there for the benefit and advancement of human communities.

Salvation Theology versus Creation Theology?

The problem of an anthropocentric, utilitarian and dualistic conception of creation predates Christianity and goes back to its Judaic precedents and roots as embedded in the Hebrew scriptures that form an integral part of the Christian Bible, particularly so in the apocalyptic literature. The Greek metaphysical view of creation, which prevailed in the inter-testamental period and in the early centuries of the first millennium, cemented this conception of creation in Christianity from its inception. Whether the biblical texts themselves or particular readings and interpretations of the texts are at the problem's core continues to be an issue of dynamic debate.

On the one hand, the forms of Christianity that arrived in Oceania were couched in the particular Judaeo-Christian tradition that elevates human beings above all other creatures and glorifies human salvation and salvation history at the expense of creation and its integrity. There can be little argument that the most dominant feature of such Christianity was the core message that in both the Old Testament and New Testament, it was/is the drama of salvation — and God's involvement in its unfolding and fulfilment – that is the central and endearing truth. In this Judaeo-Christian panoramic narrative, creation was/is merely the backdrop to and stage upon which the great drama of salvation was and is played out. In other words, in this Christianity that was introduced into Oceania, creation was played down and salvation played up all the way. Creation was made to play second fiddle to the mighty salvific acts of God in the course of history – what a well known missionary to Oceania, Alan Tippett, describes as 'the great spiritual salvation of mankind' in his *Solomon Islands Christianity* (1967). In truth, for the longer part of the history of Christianity in Oceania, this theology of salvation has predominated, which in the view of the author is a partner in bed with the neo-liberal economic model that pushes for endless growth at the cost of creation, its constituents and integrity.

On the other hand, and from alternative readings and interpretations of the scriptures, creation was/is neither merely a backdrop to or simply a stage for drama, nor just a passive character in the great salvation mega-story. In this view, creation is not an object with only utilitarian and instrumental value but a subject in its own right, and an active agent in the great story of salvation – or, more precisely, stories of salvation. This alternative understanding presents creation and salvation as intertwined, in which case there is no dualism between history-culture and nature, or between redemption and creation. Highly commendable, such alternative approaches to engaging Judaeo-Christian biblical texts and traditions is one that is gaining strength and acceptance with works by the Earth Bible Project and by authors such as Theodore Hiebert (*The Yahwist's Landscape: Nature and Religion in Early Israel*, 2008) and Oceanic academic Jione Havea (*Jonah: An Earth Bible Commentary*, 2020). In retrospect, and sadly, the Christianity that penetrated Oceania hardly featured this kind of biblical-theological grounding, and for the better half of its short history, it was this lack that characterised Christianity in Oceania in a major way. It is to this second approach that the remainder of this essay is committed.

Reinterpretation of Christianity in Oceania

A major turning point for Christianity in Oceania, particularly in relation to creation theology in general, began in earnest in the late 1960s and early 1970s. Two noteworthy developments happened across Oceania from that time. First, on the regional front, came nationalistic movements toward political independence. Although these were political movements in the main, discussions and conversations touched on cultures and elements connecting people to creation, including the relationality of people and their identities to the land and sea and their constituents, and the connectedness of the people's spirituality to creation through worship, totemism, and daily livelihood activities and interactions. In other words, these political movements afforded Oceanic peoples, academics and theologians the opportunities for initial political and theological discourse in context. Secondly, and closely connected to the first, was the rise of contextual theology, particularly in the Two-Thirds World. In fact, the biggest breakthrough for theology in Oceania as well as for the developing world in general was in terms of the broadening of sources in which theology might recognise 'context' in addition to the Bible and Christian traditions. Use and acceptance of 'contextualisation' of theology was official by the early 1970s, and contextual theology, with the primary use of and reliance on cultures, traditional religion and symbolic systems, took off in Oceania. In hindsight, this global theological development, coupled with nationalistic aspirations across Oceania, provided the *kairos* moment for a resurgence of creation spiritualities, which were belittled and unfriended by the forms of Christianity that had earlier intruded on our 'Sea of Islands'. In effect, therefore, what began from that point in time was a reinterpretation of Christianity by theologians across Oceania – a reinterpretation that breathed new life and vitality into a predominant and pervasive version of Christianity that was rich in soteriological knowledge and drive and yet that was, at the same time, bankrupt in its creation theology.

In light of the foregoing, when articulating the integrity of creation in Christianity in Oceania, the point of reference has to be the refashioned and reinterpreted Christianity from the late 1960s and early 1970s to the present time. Two factors underpin this position. Firstly, what happened from this period reconnected with the pre-Christian creation spiritualities, and, secondly, if integrity of creation were defined primarily by creation's intrinsic value – which it should be – then to speak of such integrity of creation in Christianity in Oceania prior to the 1970s is without historical support and therefore superfluous. In the Oceanic context, integrity of creation is not just about one element or one aspect of/in creation. It is about the totality, the interconnectedness – the relationality – of creation's every constituent and their places, purposes and functions in relation to the overall scheme of things. From an Oceanic perspective, the following are key and intertwining strands of the integrity of creation in Christianity.

(1) *Oceanic peoples' view of the world*. Two important aspects of Oceanic worldviews are important to highlight. First, the deep sense of inter-connectedness or relationality of all life means that there is neither a culture/nature dualism nor a redemption/creation dichotomy. Secondly, it is a generally articulated and accepted position that (Indigenous) Oceanic peoples have always been quite religious, well before the intrusion of the various expressions of Christianity into the islands. In this light, the ways in which Oceanic ancestors and forebears lived in creation through their immediate environments were very much influenced and shaped by views and experiences they held of their immediate world.

(2) *Life and livelihoods; wellbeing and wholeness*. At its core, creation for Oceanic peoples is about livelihoods, wellbeing and wholeness of life. For the majority of people, daily livelihood and experience are based on the inter-relatedness of land, sea and atmosphere. As such, subsistence existence is still the mainstay of life and livelihoods. The Oceanic ecumeni-cal position is that such subsistence is not merely for physical sustenance; it is deeply relational and theological. God is pro-life and God's Spirit or Breath is the source of life. It follows, therefore, that life support systems, networks, processes and arrangements – including primarily the land, sea and atmosphere – are manifestations of the life-giving and life-affirming relationships within creation itself. Human wellbeing, wholeness and flourishing, therefore, are not just a matter of fact but a deeply theological-existential purpose and undertaking. Oceanic peoples share in the life of God through the Spirit and through the life-giving and life-supporting elements in creation. As such, the wellbeing, wholeness and flourishing of this shared life is enhanced or hindered within the context of creation that is most immediate and tangible to them. Creation care means caring for life in its entirety and moving toward fullness of life both in the here and now and into the future.

(3) *Primacy and interconnectedness of life*. Since the reinterpretation of Christianity in Oceania from the late 1960s and early 1970s, the centrality of life has been a key theological theme, expressed in one way or other over time, such as: most fundamental value; protection and celebration of Life; life-centredness; ecology of life; primacy of life; and many more. The life of which Pacific theologians speak is not compartmentalised but is one complete whole, including yet at the same time transcending biological life. This is obvious from the languages of the Pacific in which life is im-mediately and directly connected with breath and spirit. It is also life in relationships and inter-relationships with and between people, between people and their immediate environments, and between people and the divine. Along the kataphatic (or cataphatic) tradition – which uses positive ('God is…') language to describe the divine – primacy and fullness of life

in traditional Oceanic thought that continues into Christianity could be stated as the human desire for wellbeing and fulfilment in every aspect of life, be it health, success, fecundity, respect, honour or egalitarianism. Along the apophatic (negative or 'God is not...') tradition, it could be stated as the absence of forces that stand in destructive tension with life, such as sickness, conflict, infecundity, poverty, dishonour or death.

(4) *Life is interconnected or relational.* The land–sea–atmosphere web of life has readability characteristics that have enabled Oceanic people to live in meaningful relationships with one another and with their immediate environments over centuries. Life is spoken of and experienced as one integrated, whole existence where the physical, spiritual, sacred and secular dovetail. Many Oceanic theologians and academics speak of the interconnectedness of the rhythms and processes of the land with those of the ocean and the moon in the sky, and of how human life is intricately interwoven with these rhythms and processes. They speak of how the oceans and seas connect the islands of Oceania rather than separate them. Underlying all of this is the assurance that fullness of life is possible only within the interconnectedness of all life in creation. As pioneer theologian and regional-global ecumenist Revd Sir Leslie Boseto evocatively expresses it, human existence and survival can never be separated from the land and sea and atmosphere, and this life is rooted both in God and in creation.

(5) *Home and belonging.* Oceanic peoples have always had a deep sense of attachment to place, to home. For instance, the Indigenous Māori people in Aotearoa New Zealand cherish the tradition of the *Papatūānuku* (Mother Earth, origin or source of life, being home) and Australian Aborigines the tradition of *Ngarranggarni* or *Tjukula* or *Jukurrpa* (Dreamtime) to speak of connectedness to place, among other religio-cultural significances. Even now with migration, Oceanic peoples continue to have a strong sense of belonging to their motherland and to their particular 'place' in it. This sense of at-homeness is rooted in the religio-cultural belief of land as the ground of being – metaphorically as Mother – and ritualised through the act of burying a child's life-source (placenta) and umbilical cord in the ground, a sacred ritual of connecting the child and mother with Earth. Home is a microcosm of the encompassing nature of life in its wholeness and inter-relatedness and is well captured in the pan-Oceanic parlance that combines fland–sea–atmosphere, for example *vanua* in Fiji, *fenua* in Māòhi Nui, *fanua* in Sāmoa, *fonua* in Tonga, *whenua* in New Zealand (Māori) and *hanua* and *auhenua* in parts of Melanesia. Home is about ever-widening human relationships – with family and community and wider society. Home is about economic wellbeing and sufficiency. Home is about living responsibly and caringly with all that supports and upholds life – the immediate environment, which is the most tangible part of

creation of which Oceanic peoples are an integral part. This sense of being at home is underpinned by a growing revival and reclaiming of a deep creation spirituality that combines the totality of life. As a consequence of the COVID-19 pandemic, there is growing and widening call for this holistic creation spirituality to be the driver for a new vision and direction for Oceanic peoples.

(6) *Family-communal identity*. Oceanic peoples' identities are closely connected to and shaped by their immediate environments. In Oceania, the identity of a person is formed not in isolation from community but in association with and involvement in it, as well as in interacting with one's environment. In a similar way, identity and formation of human communities are not only connected within themselves but also intimately interconnected to and shaped by the totality of the land–sea–atmosphere community. This deep sense of familial and communal identity that is attached to creation is embodied in place names and totems of tribes and communities. These are a reflection of the phenomenological and sacred relationalities that communities and tribes have with their immediate environment. Oceanic theologians have written about the Trinity as Community of Persons. God as Creator continually creates and recreates. Incarnational Christology implies that the pre-existent Christ becomes enfleshed in material reality. Spirit – Source of Life – continues to breathe new life into the community of creation.

(7) Mana *and salvation*. Among other articulations, theologians in Oceania see the environment, and creation in general, also in terms of *mana* and salvation. *Mana* is a widely debated concept in Oceania and beyond, particularly by both theologians and anthropologists. The point of contention is whether the term should be understood as a noun or as a stative verb, or possibly as both. The debate is as interesting as it is academic, perpetuated mostly by non-Oceanic peoples who try to find a European verbal equivalent to *mana*. For Oceanic peoples, *mana* is an ideal and state of being (mainly related to the spirits and ancestors), an activity (as it affected human beings) and a process (as it involves the rhythms and seasons of the land–sea–atmosphere web of life). As such, for Oceanic creation spirituality, *mana* is not an either/or but a both/and category. Thus, from the Oceanic religio-cultural epistemology, the land–sea–atmosphere complex – in other words, creation – is the most immediate and tangible form and symbol of the grace or *mana* of God for Oceanic peoples.

It is from this understanding of *mana* that an Oceanic perspective and understanding of salvation must emanate, for without *mana* there is no salvation – salvation that is tangible and earthy, present and yet unfolding, intricately connected with and derived from the immediacy and tangible-ness of creation. In Oceania one cannot speak of salvation without speaking also of the land–sea–atmosphere web of life. In this way salvation in Oceania could be described in terms of gaining or regaining the ultimate fullness of life. Thus, on the one hand, salvation constitutes and reflects the human desire for wellbeing and fulfilment in every aspect of life, be it health, success, fertility, respect or honour. On the other hand, salvation is seen as the absence of forces that stand in destructive tension with life, such as sickness, death, infertility, poverty or dishonour – the life-denying and life-negating forces. Obviously, this understanding and experience of salvation is intricately connected with the tangibleness of creation – the salvific benefits and values of the land–sea–atmosphere life-community.

In the first place, this understanding and experience of salvation differs from the traditional and common understanding discussed earlier in this essay, in which it is completely detached from creation and even presented as an escape from creation. Relatedly, and in the second place, it has direct implications for creation care. However, creation care is more than stewardship, for stewardship, if it is not properly understood, can still be interpreted in terms of human beings' position over and above all other non-human creatures. Stewardship that primarily affirms and respects the integrity of creation – creation's intrinsic value and creation as subject in its own right – and appreciates its utility or instrumental value only secondarily is a creation theology worth cherishing and propagating.

Currents of Resistance, Winds of Destruction

An essay on 'Integrity of Creation in Christianity in Oceania' cannot and must not ignore the counteracting forces. These are forces that ignore and deny that creation is endowed with intrinsic integrity, and forces that are bent on the destruction of creation through the unbridled exploitation of Earth's constituents as mere resources of production. While human beings through their subsistence activities do some harm to the immediate environments, the extractive industries on the land and in the sea are the biggest culprits. Right now, seabed mining is a source of deep concern in many countries in the region.

As highlighted earlier, the Christianity that intruded upon Oceania was bankrupt as far as creation theology was concerned. Also highlighted earlier was the turning point through a reinterpretation of Christianity by Oceanic theologians who, by reviving religio-cultural worldviews, developed and articulated theologies on creation. Even so, theologies and doctrines that focus on the salvation of humanity, exemplified by popular phrases such as 'salvation of souls' or 'souls to Jesus', are symptomatic of the persistency of such creation-bankrupt theologies. This goes to show that while significant shifts and transformations in theological thinking and perspectives have occurred, this rather narrow and limited theological orientation, which stresses the salvation of souls, persists still. The need to mainstream contextual theologies that advance the integrity of creation is as urgent as it is an imperative. The challenges to achieving this are large and many. Even so, the encouraging news is that in the midst of the suffering, pain and loss which the COVID-19 pandemic has caused, and is still causing, an awakening across Oceania is directing the regional gaze and attention to the integrity and centrality of creation – particularly in view of its own in-built and intrinsic resilience, which have resurged.

Academics, including theologians, have long argued that the neo-liberal model of economic development is primarily responsible for much of the degradation of creation and its integrity. At its inception, and as a composite offshoot of the industrial revolution and scientific enlightenment, capitalism desacralised and commoditised creation's most tangible features. This model – which is propelled by its obsession with endless growth, based primarily on non-renewable resource extraction and exploitation – is not compatible with but rather destructive to the wellbeing of creation, most immediately Earth, our one common home. Such a model thrives on sucking up the resources of the earth, cutting down trees, polluting water, pumping industrial waste into the atmosphere, ploughing up wetlands and mining in ecologically sensitive spaces. To one extent or another, across Oceania these and other impacts have been seen and experienced in various ways. For Oceania, the most disconcerting and worrying problem of this model of development is anthropogenic climate change and its various impacts in the region. Oceanic people obviously live on the shoreline in consecutive moments of the present, with climate change entering the local history, and are feeling the effects of climate change and global warming with increasing intensity and destructiveness in the islands: rising sea levels, eroding shorelines, seepage of seawater into groundwater tables, more frequent king tides, salinisation of coastal farm land, falling trees and palms, relocation of homes, and the associated sense of socio-cultural, spiritual and psychological dislocation. Recent scientific research highlights the threats of climate change in Oceania to be temperature rise, sea-level rise and more storminess.

Serious questions and issues arise from the scenario described above. First, what does integrity of creation mean when the shorelines of small, low-lying atoll countries of Oceania are eroding; seas encroaching onto residential areas, resulting in relocations; water tables becoming increasing salinised; and coconut palms, a staple crop in these places, continuously falling into the sea under rising tides? Secondly, what does integrity of creation mean when countries and those most immediately responsible for anthropogenic climate change and its impacts continue to refuse to take responsibility and make the necessary systems and lifestyle changes?

Visioning Possible New Futures

At the end of 2018, the Pacific Theological College and the Pacific Conference of Churches initiated the project 'Changing the Story'. This major project was launched in March 2019 during a regional ecumenical conference: 'Reweaving the Ecological Mat Conference: Pacific Churches Act on Ecological and Development Issues'. This project was a response to serious concerns raised by church leaders in Oceania on the environmentally destructive practices and tendencies of the neo-liberal economic paradigm, and the inappropriate measures of wellbeing that it espouses and advances, which are not only foreign but also clearly exclusive of almost every aspect that is essential in speaking about wellbeing in Oceania. A very important component of this project, of which the author is team leader, is to develop a user-friendly methodology which communities and churches in Oceania can use in revaluing their land–sea–atmosphere environments and, therefore, be empowered against greedy and unscrupulous so-called developers.

Crucial to this project is Reweaving the Ecological Mat, a research project on rethinking and changing the story of development in Oceania. Reweaving the Ecological Mat is grounded in critical theological thinking, revisiting the wisdom and values of traditional religion and cultures, and critiquing the prevailing neo-liberal economic paradigm. The outcome of this project is the publication *Ecological Framework for Development* (2020). The Pacific Theological College, in conjunction with other higher institutions of learning, have sent out an invitation, 'Call for Vision', for people to express their post-COVID-19 vision for Oceania. Multiple people have responded positively, and the book *From the Deep: Pasifiki Voices for a New Story* (2020) is the product of this call. Both of these projects, and their outcomes, are about articulating, charting and envisioning possible new futures for Oceania. Integral to both projects and publications is creation, especially as it is seen, talked about and experienced in the context of our Sea of Islands.

What these two projects and the resultant publications show is that Christianity in Oceania is bursting into new life and venturing into once-taboo areas for theological engagement and action. In particular, the drive to shift development perspectives and practice by working to change the current model through 'going back to creation' is quite pioneering. Even more novel is the engagement with theology, religious scriptures and traditional spiritualities in such trailblazing work. The commitment to making sure that economic development does not undermine the very foundation of its existence and operations is paramount in envisioning possible new futures for Oceania. This means, first and foremost, affirming and respecting the integrity of creation. From what is happening now across the region, there is a bright future for reclaiming the integrity of creation in Oceania. Affirming and respecting this integrity of creation on the part of human beings is part and parcel of what it all means and takes. *Ecological Framework for Development* provides a list of contextually framed measures of wellbeing, the first of which is the land–sea–atmosphere web of life being in a healthy, generative and supportive state (integrity of ecology). This is creation spirituality driving the agenda for development in Oceania. This is truth for the future of interconnected and holistic life for people in Oceania. It must be lived out in the consciousness that humanity is but one strand in the land–sea–atmosphere web of interconnected life.

Bibliography

Boseto, Leslie, 'Do Not Separate Us from Our Land', *Pacific Journal of Theology*, series II, 13 (1995), 69–72.

Halapua, Winston, *Waves of God's Embrace: Sacred Perspectives from the Ocean* (Norwich: Canterbury Press, 2008).

Hau'ofa, Epeli, *A New Oceania: Rediscovering Our Sea of Islands* (Suva: University of the South Pacific in association with Beake House, 1993).

Tofaeono, Ama'amalele, *Eco-Theology: AIGA – The Household of God. A Perspective from Living Myths and Traditions of Sāmoa* (Erlangen: Erlangen Verlag Fur Mission und Okumene, 2000).

Tuwere, Ilaitia S., *Vanua: Towards a Fijian Theology of Place* (Suva: Institute of Pacific Studies/ University of the South Pacific, 2002).

Indigenous Spirituality

Cruz Karauti-Fox

Tangaroa i te titi, Tangaroa i te tata,
Eueu ki te rangi!
Kia tae atu te tere o Ru ki uta i te enua.

Tangaroa, supreme on high, Tangaroa, supreme below,
Open the sky!
So that Ru may reach the land.

Hundreds of years after its composition, this chant is still used for welcoming dignitaries by Cook Islanders at home and abroad. During the great settlement of the Pacific by Polynesian explorers, Ru, a chief navigator of the South Pacific, found his canoe, *Ngapuariki*, in the midst of a great storm. In encountering the danger and fearing for the safety of his people on board, he incanted this chant to Tangaroa o te Moana (Guardian of the Ocean). At the conclusion of the chant, the sky cleared, the sun shone through and the great waves of the ocean became calm. This enabled the canoe to arrive safely at a newly discovered land, Utataki-Enua-o-Ru-ki-te-Moana (a land searched for and found upon the sea by Ru).

The action of the opening sky, and the surety of one's canoe making it safely to shore, is an ongoing process for Indigenous Pacific people in the twenty-first century. Throughout the impacts of colonialism, diaspora, climate change and technology, and the fight for language, cultural rights and economic sustainability, Indigenous Pacific spirituality is no different in its expression to that of the clearing sky – the primary focus of Indigenous Pacific spirituality being that the *vaka vaerua* (spiritual canoe of the Pacific people) grounds itself on shore, enabling safety, life, wellbeing and growth.

This essay will offer a definition of Indigenous Pacific spirituality, identify the continuing impact of Christianity on the Indigenous spirituality of the Pacific and the impact of Indigenous Pacific spirituality on Christianity in the modern context. In conclusion it will discuss an ongoing paradigm of relationship between Christianity and Indigenous Pacific spirituality, noting the latter's fundamental importance to the Indigenous peoples of the Pacific.

Moana: Defining Pacific Indigenous Spirituality

Moana is an ancient Polynesian word to describe the ocean. In its meta-phorical imagery, the Indigenous spiritualities of the Pacific are as wide and variant as trying to describe the fullness of the ever-changing *moana*. Considering its mystery and depth, one must also take into account the diversity of this spirituality so as to avoid too much abstraction and generalisation in reaching a definition. Western categories have their limitations in this sphere. To gain a true understanding of the spirituality of the *moana*, one must be connected to the milieu and have epistemo-logical connectivity with the environment from which Pacific people draw their spirituality. Though extremities of diversity may exist, through the use of *moana* one can nonetheless gain an understanding of the connected-ness through which the Indigenous Pacific context engages. This *moana* network implies a connectedness not only of geography but also of the genealogical, linguistic, ethnological, epistemological, anthropological and spiritual milieus of Indigenous Pacific peoples.

Like mathematician Hermann Minkowski's notion of spacetime as the union of space and time, the *moana* is the means of union between space and time for the Indigenous peoples of the Pacific. In a similar way, it can be argued that the *moana* shares the same sacramentality as the Catholic belief in the full union of creation through the *Mystici Corporis Christi* by means of transubstantiation. Similar to the holy elements of Jesus's body and blood, the *moana* is what connects us to all of creation and that which is beyond ourselves as Pacific people.

Tangaroa, the great traditional deity of the *moana*, is omnipotent, as seen in Ru's chant acknowledging 'Tangaroa supreme on high, Tangaroa supreme below'. In such a belief, *moana* is not only the physical means of connectivity but also the metaphysical means for those who interact with it, and those who believe in the connectivity of *moana*.

Here, it is important to note that the relationships of Indigenous Pacific spirituality function around *kairos* (opportunity time) and not *chronos* (clock time). The proverb *Kia whakatōmuri te haere whakamua* ('I walk into the future focusing on the past') is also indicative of transcending time. The past, the present and the future are inter-relative. Life itself is a con-tinuous cosmic process.

Every Indigenous Pacific person has a sense of the presence of the divine being. This belief in *Atua/atua* (God/gods) has been apparent since the beginning of creation, as told through traditional song and chant, and today is nourished by the written scriptures of Christian origin. Pre-Christian understandings of God/gods can be seen in the belief of Pacific peoples in Io (Supreme God), Oro (god of war), Tangaroa (god of the sea), Rangi (sky father), Papa (earth mother), Tawhirimatea (god of the wind),

Tane (god of the forest) and Rongo (god of peace). Belief in these pre-Christian deities can be found in differing forms around the Pacific, both as supreme creators and as personifications of the natural world. They spiritualise the environment and interconnect it with human life.

The continuous relationship between *Atua* (God), *tangata* (people) and *whenua* (land) can be seen as the fundamental matrix of Māori spirituality. In this holistic understanding of being, *Atua*, *tangata* and *whenua* are directly inter-related. There is no hierarchical dependency or lineality, but *Atua*, *tangata* and *whenua* remain in a continuous mutual dialogue. *Atua* is understood as the Supreme Being and Creator of all things. *Tangata* is generally understood as humanity as well as people's corporate identities and tribal and family groups. And *whenua* is understood as the land and its geographical features. Land is very important to Māori, as it is from the soil that the first human was created. Without the land and its resources, humans cease to exist. Māori call themselves *Tangata Whenua* (people of the land). Such a label reiterates their deep connectedness with land. Without God, both people and land cease to exist.

Through the notions of *mauri* (life force), *whakapapa* (genealogy), *mana* (spiritual power), *tapu* (sacredness), *manaakitanga* (hospitality) and *aroha* (love), a panentheistic reality of Māori spirituality can be identified. *Mauri* is the life force or ethos of all created matter. By means of *whakapapa*, *mauri* is present in every particle of matter. *Mana* is the 'spiritual authority and power' of created matter as given by God, and *tapu* is the sacramental state or being of matter when placed under the authority of God. Another important feature of Pacific spirituality is *manaakitanga*, a means of provision and charity toward others, which, in its totality, is an expression of *aroha* between beings. Healthy spiritual balance is maintained when *manaakitanga* and *aroha* are practised.

Through these concepts the relationship with *Atua* is manifested in all of created matter. While *whenua* (land) is used as the fundamental relationship for identity for New Zealand Māori, throughout Polynesia, this fundamental relationship for identity can be identified more clearly in the *moana* (ocean). *Moana* as a word and concept is not unique to one specific Polynesian context but encompasses all of the Pacific nations. In replacing *whenua* with *moana*, the same principles of relationship are still apparent for the environment and its sacramentality. The concepts of *whakapapa*, *mauri*, *mana*, *tapu*, *manaakitanga* and *aroha* still function in the same way, but through relationship with *moana* rather than *whenua*.

Incoming Tide: Christian Colonial Influence

Wherever one travels in the Pacific, the influence of Christianity can be seen, heard and felt throughout the whole *moana* environment. The impact of Christianity on *Atua/atua* (God/gods), *tangata* (people) and *moana* (ocean) has been significant since the arrival and influence of Christian missionaries in the late eighteenth and early nineteenth centuries.

It can be argued that European missionaries invaded Indigenous cultures of the Pacific. Their primary task was initially to replace the Indigenous context and belief systems with their own Eurocentric identities and understandings. Christian theology, education, the influence of written language, missionary ideas of civilisation and the perpetuation of *sola scriptura* continue to support ideologies such as colonialism, monotheistic dominance, Gnosticism and Augustinian interpretations of morality, and dominion over the environment. This continuous process exercises both negative and positive influences on the matrix of the *Atua/atua–tangata–moana* understanding of Indigenous Pacific spirituality. Christian theology and written language still pervade the Indigenous contexts of the Pacific, particularly through the Western education that is offered by church and government schools throughout the region.

A significant linguistic move made by the missionaries was their decision to use the term *atua* to name the Christian God. In written language they used the capitalised form, *Atua*, to distinguish it from lesser *atua* or deities. Therefore, the differentiation of the monotheistic *Atua* (God) from *atua* (god) proved significant for the Indigenous spirituality of the Pacific. This orthographic convention had a great influence on the belief in the polytheistic deities of the Pacific, causing many of the stories and beliefs around these deities to be lost. As a result of the conversion of much of the Pacific to Christianity, the monotheistic *Atua* is enshrined in many national anthems and coats of arms of Pacific nations. Tonga's and Sāmoa's national mottos, *Koe Otua mo Tonga ko hoku tofia* ('From God and Tonga I descend') and *Fa'avae i le Atua Sāmoa* ('Sāmoa is founded on God'), and the first lines of the national anthems of New Zealand and the Cook Islands, *E Ihowa Atua* ('O God Jehova') and *Te Atua mou e* ('For you O God'), demonstrate that all now identify with the centrality of the monotheistic *Atua*.

The concepts of original sin and belief in Jesus Christ as the sole mode of salvation for the individual have significantly influenced many Pacific people today and shaped their spirituality. From their introduction in the Pacific up until the present, these concepts continue to clash with Indigenous spirituality. The focus on individual sin and individual salvation contrasts with the collective understanding of existence as practised by many Polynesian cultures. The practice of individual confession and having a personal relationship with Jesus Christ are ideas that have perpetuated individuality in contrast to the collective understanding of relationship and identity as demonstrated in the Moana model of spirituality.

Written language was not introduced to the Pacific until the arrival of Christianity. In Christian belief, it is fundamental for God to be known through the written word. The paramountcy of knowing the written word has dominated Pacific peoples to the extent that this extreme importance of being literate has caused traditional practices of language communication to become obsolete. Because of this, there has been a drastic deterioration of traditional songs, chants, dances and visual art forms, which originally conveyed Indigenous understandings of *Atua*. Hence, these traditional practices are no longer a primary means of spiritual expression and communication.

The overt patriarchy found in Christian language, theology and practice creates many negative influences on culture and the practice of spirituality throughout the Indigenous Pacific. This patriarchal ideology exists in stark contrast to many Indigenous Pacific views of matriarchy, and many traditional means of leadership, such as *Ariki Tepaeru* (female leader) roles in society, became subservient roles due to patriarchal ideologies. The Christian God, known as Father and Son, perpetuates and supports this dominant patriarchal ideology, especially in religious institutions whose leaders were expected to be male.

The impact of biblical authority continues to be perpetuated in contemporary Pacific contexts. God as *Atua* is known through the written word as a source of direction in all Pacific countries. In the Kingdom of Tonga, the Cook Islands, Tokelau and Sāmoa, laws limit people's activities on Sundays. This includes the closure of shops, businesses and government agencies. Such law enforcement reflects a national commitment to adhere to the commandment to keep the Sabbath holy as required by Exodus 20: 8.

Christian understandings of morality influenced by biblical authority – and as perpetuated in Gnostic and Augustinian ideologies of sin that denigrate the body, condemn sexual desire, urge sexual abstinence and tolerate sexual activity only for procreative intentions – still pervade much of Pacific society today. The culturally acceptable dress of the individual is generally expected to be modest, covering the majority of a person's body. This is to discourage sexual arousal. Homosexuality and the act of sodomy are criminal offences in many Pacific countries, such as the Cook Islands and Sāmoa, and many Pacific Island families still frown upon sexual relationships outside marriage.

The idea of dominion over creation as expressed in the Genesis narrative and the individualistic understanding of salvation in the Western Christian message has affected Pacific peoples' interactions with their *moana* environment. The hierarchical view of creation and the position of humanity as overlords, fuelled by individualistic gain, consumerism and economic growth, have had a detrimental impact on the Pacific peoples, who are subjected to the exploitation of natural resources in activities such as deep-sea drilling and the dumping of rubbish. In this understanding of Christianity, the relationship to *moana* is one of hierarchy and dominion, and not necessarily a relationship of dialogue, mutual benefit and positive communal relationship.

Part of the impact of missionary Christianity in the Pacific has been to replace Indigenous belief systems with Eurocentric identities and understandings. This process of replacement, identified as colonisation, is still witnessed today through the continuing loss of Indigenous language and culture. For the majority of the Pacific, colonialism and Christianity are so intertwined that even in the twenty-first century it is hard to separate them in government, church and cultural contexts. Hence the Christian/colonial influence is now embedded in the formation and existence of the Indigenous Pacific. If this were removed, the contemporary Indigenous identity would become unrecognisable. The monarchical structure of the Kingdom of Tonga, the official church advisory group of Christian churches in the Cook Islands, and even the official public holidays of Christmas and Easter in New Zealand are all examples of this highly co-dependent existence.

Turning Tide: Inculturation

Notwithstanding the disturbance it has brought to Indigenous Pacific spirituality, the message of the gospel is celebrated and its positive impact is influential throughout the Pacific. The love of God, the peace offered by the gospel message and the wonder of the divine mystery totally permeate Pacific identity. When consideration is given to the positive impacts of Christianity in the Pacific, it can be observed that Indigenous spirituality has shaped the expression, practice and existence of Christianity. This impact can be seen through the expressions of theology, traditional practices, the yearning for Indigenous reconciliation with the effects of the colonial past, Christian education, written language and understandings of Christian morality.

The monotheistic God of Christianity transcends time and space and allows a relationship to remain even when separation occurs. This is especially important for those of the Pacific diaspora. With dislocation from *tangata* (people) and *moana* (ocean), *Atua* (God) is a phenomenon that continues relatability with *whakapapa* (genealogy), *tapu* (sacredness), *mana* (spiritual power), *manaakitanga* (hospitality), *aroha* (love), cultural beliefs and connection to home. God-the-Moana is incarnated in the person of Jesus Christ. Through this idea, Christ has taken on a uniquely Pacific persona. In the imagery of Christ-the-Moana, for Pacific people, God in Christ becomes more tangible and relatable in the Pacific context. Like the *moana*, God is omnipotent, ever moving, ever changing and the sustainer of life, not only for fish and whales and sea urchins, but for the people who found new lands by venturing out upon the vast ocean, the ancestors of present-day Pacific people. The *moana* is our great means of connectedness. It connects us to the past, beyond ourselves and to others who live far away. Likewise, through the *moana*, in Christ, *Atua, tangata* and *moana* transcend both time and space.

The traditional practices of prayer and worship are fundamental in the life of Indigenous communities. They begin meetings and are central to special occasions such as weddings, birthdays and funeral rites. Many of these prayers are strongly influenced by Christianity and thus have taken on their own Christo-Indigenous forms, whether within established Christian churches or syncretistic Christian religious forms of belief. Because of the impact of Christianity on the ancestors of present-day Pacific people, many traditional rites of prayer and worship were dismissed, obliterated and forgotten. The Christian prayer as influenced by the Bible and practices of the church became the main expression of spiritual connectedness to the divine. *Karakia* (prayer and worship) are fundamental in *tangihanga* (mourning processes) in New Zealand Māori contexts. *Karakia* enable a safe passage of the deceased in the afterlife and comfort the bereaved living. Therefore, the majority of Māori expect to have a minister of a Christian denomination officiate these *karakia*. In such instances, Christian ministers must adapt to the cultural situation in which they find themselves, so as to respond in a culturally and spiritually acceptable manner to the Indigenous context. Prayers such as the commendation and committal from the Christian funerary tradition give mourners comfort in what Māori deem to be the spiritual return of the spirit to *Hawaiki*, the spiritual home of the Māori.

The Christian churches have an immense role to play in the decolonisation of the cultures, languages and beliefs of Indigenous Pacific people as well as in redressing the injustices of the colonial past. The establishment and autonomy of Indigenous churches such as Tikanga Māori and Tikanga Pasifika within the Anglican Church in Aotearoa New Zealand and Polynesia is central to its structure and way of being. The Treaty of Waitangi signed in 1840 between Māori chiefs and the British Crown, and thus regarded as the founding document of New Zealand, is used as a foundation on which the churches can address many social justice issues, including the returning of land unjustly taken from Māori during the height of the colonial era.

In the education sector, Indigenous Christian schools are well established and flourishing. Within these schools, in contrast to traditional Western modes of learning, curricula on Indigenous language, culture and values are prioritised. Schools such as Hato Paora, Te Aute and Hukarere colleges in New Zealand and Nukutere College in Rarotonga celebrate and practise a uniquely Indigenous expression of Christianity.

Indigenous Pacific theologies impact our current view of Christianity throughout the Pacific. Decolonising methodologies and theologies such as Theomoana, Coconut Theology and Māori Systematic Theology play an important role. The work of Indigenous Pacific scholars such as Jenny Te Paa Daniel, Nāsili Vaka'uta, Winston Halapua, Mosese Ma'alio, Sione Amanaki Havea, Henare Tate and Māori Marsden continue to influence theological thought and Indigenous understanding of and toward Christianity.

Contributing to the decolonisation of Christianity and theology is the fundamental use of Pacific languages in biblical and church contexts. The creation of new liturgies and revised translations of the Bible is ongoing. The Bible Society New Zealand's revision of Te Paipera Tapu (The Holy Bible) into modern Te Reo Māori (Māori language) is a commitment in the Society's Māori Bible Kaituitui Initiative. The ongoing creation of new liturgies in the establishment of Te Pihopatanga o Aotearoa's Tangihanga Liturgical Committee is leading to the creation and composition of uniquely Māori Christian funeral liturgies.

Many churches throughout the Pacific still hold fast to a biblical fundamentalist view of theology and practices concerning sex and relationships. The influence of traditional Indigenous understandings of morality and culture has deeply contributed to ongoing discussions concerning strict colonial ideas of sex, marriage and perceptions of sin. Some churches acknowledge and accept same-sex relationships to the point of changing their canonical laws for the blessing, and even marriage, of same-sex partners in their churches. Such a move has been instigated in the changing of formularies in the Anglican Church in Aotearoa New Zealand and Polynesia. In 2018, its General Synod passed a motion whereby bishops could allow the blessing of same-sex relationships in their dioceses. This discussion was significantly influenced by the Indigenous Māori members of the church, who, through the traditions of their elders, saw these blessing ceremonies as a means of regaining *mana* (spiritual power) and *tapu* (sacredness), affirming the sanctity of human relationships.

Talanoa (Discussion)

In looking at the examples of these tides, a great wave of relationship between Christianity and Indigenous Pacific spirituality continues in the twenty-first century. In the impacts of both Christianity and Indigenous spirituality on each other, it can be seen that Indigenous spirituality of the Pacific creates a strong foundation for itself in Christianity, and Christianity creates a strong foundation for itself in the Indigenous spirituality of the Pacific. In its fullness of functionality, this continuous active process of adaptability and foundation-building is the product of an ongoing paradigm of dynamic relationship. It is a great *talanoa* (discussion).

Talanoa is a Polynesian word that generally translates as 'talk' or 'discuss'. The action of *talanoa* is a process that requires dialogue between parties. In a *talanoa* environment, participants and their speech are respected. In a Tongan understanding, *talanoa* requires *ofa* (love), *mafana* (warmth), *malie* (pleasure) and *faka'apa'apa* (respect).

This great *talanoa* is fundamental for Pacific people. The Christian-Indigenous paradigm of relationship provides safety in a world of uncertainty, life in a milieu dominated by Western attitudes and growth in an understanding of wellbeing pertinent to all aspects of Pacific people. Like Ru's canoe, this paradigm of relationship is a means to make sure that the *vaka vaerua* (spiritual canoe of Pacific peoples) makes it to shore, ensuring safety, wellbeing and growth. The benefit of this *talanoa* can be seen in its adaptability but also in the steadfastness of *Atua*, the implications surrounding care for creation and the notion of transcendent connectedness with *moana*.

Despite the missionaries' colonialistic influence on traditional beliefs of *atua* throughout the Pacific, *Atua* is still acknowledged in the Trinitarian God. The importance of the Trinitarian God is demonstrated through the faith and religious alliance that Indigenous Pacific people hold. *Atua* can be seen in the idea of the *Imago Dei*. Through the *Imago Dei*, the relationship between *Atua* and *tangata* (people) is strengthened by means of acknowledging an individual's divine characteristics. Consequently, by the influence of this *Atua/tangata* relationship a major impact on people's interactions with themselves and one another occurs, which in the Christian understanding culminates in positive attitudes. By such attitudes, *manaakitanga* (hospitality) and *aroha* (love) prevail. This is seen in the civil obedience observed by the majority throughout the Pacific region.

In this *talanoa*, the belief that *Atua* is omnipotent and never changing in a world so influenced by change has great benefits for Pacific people. Pacific people's lives are littered with change, from Western and advancing technological influence to fluctuating weather patterns, tsunamis, earthquakes and rising sea levels. The notion that *Atua* does not change, as expressed in the omnipotent God of Christian scripture, brings peace and stability to the lives of Pacific peoples. This is expressed in the great faith in God demonstrated by people's dedication to Christian churches throughout the entire region.

Kaitiakitanga (guardianship) is an Indigenous Māori term that incorporates the valued concepts of *mauri* (life force), *tapu* (sacredness), *mana* (spiritual power), *manaakitanga* and *aroha* in relation to the natural environment. In acknowledging the *mauri* of all parts of creation, the divinity of creation is acknowledged. By means of this acknowledgement of creation, there is an acknowledgement between divinity and the inanimate, the animate, the physical and the metaphysical, as discussed in the holistic function of the Moana model of spirituality. Here, a deeper spiritual relationship between people and the whole natural environment occurs. When a spiritual connectedness with the natural environment is acknowledged, the result is ongoing intentional care of the natural environment.

Through this acknowledgement and consequential care, the concept of *tapu* is practised by way of restricting certain parts of the natural environment. This is enacted through the use of *rahui* (restriction). In such enforcements of *tapu*, *mana* is respected, thus allowing *manaakitanga* and *aroha* to permeate at the centre of this relationship. This strengthens the relationship between *moana* and *tangata*, which has a positive impact on both. When the safety and wellbeing of the natural environment is prioritised, people are ensured the same safety, wellbeing and growth.

This ongoing *talanoa* provides a connection for Pacific people to their culture, heritage, land and other people, in a relationship that transcends both time and space. Because of its sacramental aspects and spiritual transcendence, Christianity inter-relates with the *moana* context in the same way that the *moana* inter-relates with Christianity, as seen through the Moana model of spirituality. In people's interactions and connection with Christianity, not only do they connect to the Trinitarian God, but they connect to *moana*, God's creation, and *tangata*, both the living and the departed. Through the same paradigm of relationship, connecting with *moana* therefore connects one with *Atua* and *tangata*, the church triumphant and militant, ancestors, but also living culture and language. In the same paradigm of relationship, in connecting with *tangata*, culture, language and church, one also connects with *moana*, the natural environment, and *Atua*.

For Indigenous people of the Pacific diaspora in particular, this means of relationship is vital to their wellbeing and identity. Due to the diaspora, many find themselves dislocated from their cultural contexts and ancestral geography. But through this *talanoa* between Christianity and Indigenous Pacific spirituality, these individuals can find vitality in relationships such as prayer, church or connecting to the local environment by which they themselves live.

Conclusion

In this essay we have looked at a definition of Indigenous Pacific spirituality, where, through a Moana model of spirituality, *Atua* (God), *tangata* (people) and *moana* (ocean) exist in a relationship of mutual interdependency. In such a model, relationship refers not only to the physical but also to the metaphysical means of connectivity for those who interact with it and those who believe.

This essay has discussed the continuous incoming tide of Christianity and the impact on Indigenous spirituality of Christian theology, education, written language, missionary ideas of civilisation and the perpetuation of biblical authority. These influences support ideologies such as colonialism, monotheistic dominance, Augustinian interpretations of morality and dominion over the environment. It has also discussed the changing tide of Christianity's inculturation in Pacific spirituality. This is seen in Indigenous expressions of theology, adoption of traditional practices, yearning for Indigenous reconciliation from impacts of the colonial past, the development of Christian education, the use of Indigenous language in Christian contexts and the influence of Indigenous interpretations of morality on Christianity.

In looking at the motions of these tides, it has been argued that a great wave of relationship continues in the twenty-first century – a great *talanoa* (discussion). This *talanoa* is one of adaptability, survival, and inter-generational and inter-chronological transcendency, and it surpasses space. This *talanoa* pervades Pacific society in many ways, and by doing so enables safety, wellbeing and growth for the people who engage with it. In the imagery of the Polynesian explorer Ru, this *talanoa* between Christianity and Indigenous Pacific spirituality is the clearing sky which enables the *vaka vaerua* (spiritual canoe of Pacific people) to reach the shore.

Bibliography

Ferris-Leary, Helen Erana, *An Analytical Perspective on Moana Research and the Case of Tongan Faiva* (Auckland: University of Auckland, 2013).

Halapua, Winston, 'Moana Methodology: A Way of Promoting Dynamic Leadership' (presented at Talanoa Oceania 2008 and available online at https://sites.google.com/a/nomoa.com/talanoa/Home/papers-presentations/halapua--moana; accessed 15 June 2020).

Marsden, Māori, 'God, Man and Universe: A Māori View', in Michael King (ed.), *Te Ao Hurihuri: Aspects of Māoritanga* (Auckland: Reed, 1992), 117–37.

Tate, Henare, *Towards Some Foundations of a Systematic Māori Theology: He tirohanga anganui ki ētahi kaupapa hōhonu mō te whakapono Māori* (Auckland: University of Auckland, 2010).

Walker, Ranginui, *Ka Whawhai Tonu Mātou: Struggle Without End* (Auckland: Penguin, 1990).

Migration and Diaspora

Andrew Williams

Migration and mobility are inherent features of the peoples of the South Pacific. From Polynesian migration throughout the islands of the region during the pre-European historical period to the labour migrations in comparatively recent decades, mobility remains a central component of the lives of many Pacific Islanders. Yet, while Islander populations are highly mobile in terms of employment and education, substantial bonds of kinship and relationships to village and land remain. The networks and linkages that characterise diasporic mobilities are integral to the Pacific peoples, and much of the welfare of the ordinary people of Oceania depends on informal movement along ancient routes drawn in blood-lines invisible to the enforcers of the laws of confinement and regulated mobility. The transmission of the gospel in Oceania was largely under-taken by the movement of Pacific Islanders themselves. The movement of people in the Pacific can be traced from island group to island group as locals took upon themselves the task of evangelising the region. In almost every island group, mission and church growth are intertwined with the voluntary migrations of several thousand Pacific Islanders, usually under the guidance of small groups of white missionaries. The spread of Christianity has been largely by the contacts of Islanders with Islanders in everyday life.

A Geography of the Sea

This volume is about people of the sea. For the people who inhabit the thousands of islands in Oceania – many so small that the cartographer finds it difficult to represent them on a map of the Pacific Basin – the sea is the essence of history and geography. Whether as a route or as a barrier, as a source of sustenance or a destructive force, the sea has been and remains critical to geopolitics, social organisation and economic development. If one works in the island countries of Oceania, the answers to many critical questions require reference to this ever-present, all-pervasive, constantly moving sea.

At the heart of any assessment of mobility, identity and development in Oceania is a perspective on an island world, and its inhabitants, that is predicated on a particular geography. It is a geography that invokes the image of a 'sea of islands' rather than the more conventional approach that identifies and differentiates between numerous, fragmented, isolated microstates scattered across a vast ocean. In this alternative geography, the sea is incorporated at the outset into the definition of place; it is not considered to be simply a barrier separating one cluster of small, fragmented land masses from another. Oceania is a large world, full of places in which to make homes, where generations of seafaring peoples who habitually roamed the seas continue to travel vast distances in order to enlarge the range of options they have for economic and social development.

Just as the ancestors of today's Pacific Islanders undertook the longest sea crossings for successful settlement ever made before the seventeenth century, a second diaspora of Pacific peoples over the past 40 years has proved to be one of the most interesting in modern times in terms of motivations, complexity, and economic and social consequences. International migration in Oceania since the 1950s has resulted in an unusual, if not unique, creation of transnational social and economic relationships at family levels that in some respects transcend the state as the primary socio-economic grouping for whole peoples.

The early patterns of inter-island mobility, such as that between Tonga, Sāmoa and Fiji, continued and expanded once Europeans entered the Pacific and colonised all but Tonga. The colonial era afforded opportunities for movement within and beyond the Pacific, initially for men working on European and American vessels in the late nineteenth century. By the mid-nineteenth century a labour trade had emerged in which Islanders, mainly from what had become known as Melanesia, spread across the Pacific to work on plantations and into Queensland, Australia, to work in the sugar cane fields. Other Islanders found their way to port towns like Auckland in New Zealand and Sydney in Australia, and settled there as the earliest Pacific migrants. Some of this movement was voluntary as people sought new ways to access the goods and money that were rapidly transforming their home economies, while some was part of the notorious 'blackbirding' in which people were taken against their will. Movement between the islands also involved Islander missionaries, from the late nineteenth century to mid-twentieth century, with the mainly east–west flow of these missionaries reversing the direction of the initial migrations into the Pacific.

The Pacific was the last region of the world to be affected by European and American imperialism and, after the Second World War, it was also the last region to undergo the often difficult process of decolonisation. This began in 1962, when Western Sāmoa (now Sāmoa) gained independence, and continued throughout the 1970s and 1980s, although even today some of the islands are not fully independent. It was during this post-war era that people began to migrate from the Pacific in significant numbers, and this movement was influenced by the colonial history of the islands. The USA and New Zealand opened pathways for migration for Islanders with whom they had colonial ties, whereas other nations with colonies in the Pacific, such as the UK, Germany and Australia, did not follow suit. In the case of French colonies there was significantly more movement of French settlers into these countries than of Islanders to France. To some extent this influenced the predominance of migration from the regions known as Polynesia and Micronesia, with far less movement from the region known as Melanesia in the Western Pacific.

Destinations: New Zealand, Australia, North America

To begin to understand how Pacific Islander migration to various countries has impacted the migrants' own Christian faith activities and patterns, the host societies and churches, and the home churches in the Islands, it is necessary to sketch a brief outline of recent diasporic movements to better understand how people have come to relocate. From this we can then trace some patterns in church behaviour.

New Zealand's role in the Pacific during the colonial era has shaped its history of migration, as have frequent changes in immigration policies over the years. In the post-war era New Zealand gave citizenship to people from the Cook Islands and Niue, which it had formally annexed at the beginning of the twentieth century, and Tokelau, which it had administered since 1926. The Cook Islands and Niue are now self-governing territories in free association with New Zealand, while Tokelau remains a non-self-governing country. Each of these countries continues to have close ties to New Zealand. Many people have used their citizenship to migrate, so that the populations remaining in the islands are now considerably smaller than the migrant and overseas-born populations living in New Zealand.

In contrast, Western Sāmoans did not gain citizenship rights in New Zealand. Sāmoa was split into Western Sāmoa and American Sāmoa during the colonial era, and, after a period of German rule, New Zealand administered Western Sāmoa on behalf of the League of Nations and then the United Nations from 1918 until 1962, when it gained independence. Nevertheless, many Sāmoans have migrated to New Zealand. A Sāmoan quota was established in 1970, permitting 1,100 Sāmoans to immigrate each year. Another shift in policy in 2002 introduced the Pacific Access Category, which allows 250 migrants annually from Tonga, 75 from Kiribati and 75 from Tuvalu, and, since 2003, a further 250 migrants from Fiji. In late 2006 New Zealand again shifted its migration policies toward the Pacific and reopened access for seasonal agricultural workers, including those from Melanesia, first through the Seasonal Work Permit policy, then most recently the Recognised Seasonal Employer scheme, specifically aimed at eligible Pacific Island Forum member nations and offering 5,000 places per year.

In addition to the Pacific Islanders who have entered New Zealand under these various policies and schemes, others have settled in New Zealand as illegal immigrants, or 'overstayers'. This became a contentious issue in the 1970s, and although the New Zealand government responded with heavy-handed tactics for removing those who could be found, it also held amnesties that enabled many to gain permanent residence and remain in the country. Today, the many pathways that have led Pacific Islanders to New Zealand have resulted in a 'Pasifika' population in which Sāmoans are the largest group, followed by Cook Islanders, Tongans, Niueans, Fijians and Tokelauans.

Australia tended to discourage migration from the Pacific through its 'White Australia' policy, in force from 1901 to 1973, and placed an emphasis on skilled migration. Nevertheless, there has been significant migration into Australia from the Pacific by various means, particularly the Trans-Tasman Travel Arrangement, which allowed Australians and New Zealanders to move easily between the two countries to visit, live and work. Many New Zealanders have taken advantage of this arrangement to move to Australia, as have many Pacific Islanders, who first became citizens of New Zealand. In Australia today, the largest group of Pacific immigrants is from Fiji, mainly Indo-Fijians who have entered as skilled migrants, followed by Sāmoans, Tongans and Cook Islanders.

As in the case of New Zealand, the history of Pacific migration into the USA has been shaped by its colonial ties and ongoing political associations. The USA controlled American Sāmoa from 1900, and since 1951 these islands have been an unincorporated territory of the USA, granting American Sāmoans the status of US nationals and giving them free entry to the USA, but fewer rights than US citizens. The USA also grants free access to citizens of the Federated States of Micronesia, the Republic of the Marshall Islands and the Republic of Belau (Palau), known collectively as the Compact States since the Compact of Free Association in 1986. In addition, Guam, which has been a US territory since 1898, has the 1950 Organic Act of Guam, which gives its inhabitants US citizenship.

Other Islanders, particularly Tongans and Sāmoans, have migrated to the USA by various means, such as 'step migration' through American Sāmoa and Hawai'i. Many others had their moves to the USA facilitated by membership in the Church of Jesus Christ of Latter-day Saints, and they have settled around Mormon centres in Utah and Hawai'i. Some Pacific Islanders also have been able to migrate through the Green Card lottery system. Today, Sāmoans are the largest Pacific population in the USA, followed by Micronesians, Tongans and Fijians.

These strong links were first established by the early migrants, who, for the most part, settled permanently in their new homes. From the start, many expressed an intention to return home, but relatively few have done so, at least not permanently, and second and third generations of these populations are now established in the destination countries. Temporary migration has also taken place, particularly to New Zealand, where, as we have seen, various short-term labour schemes have been introduced. In recent years the opportunities for temporary migration have been expanding, as people with different skills – teachers, rugby players, soldiers, health workers and so on – look globally for opportunities for mobility. Pacific Islanders now live and work in places such as the Gulf States, the Middle East and Japan. This movement of skilled workers and professionals adds to the concerns about 'brain drain' that are often expressed in relation to longer-term migrants.

It has been suggested that there are three determining factors in a Pacific Islander's life: faith, family and finances. While the motivation for migration might be driven largely by family and financial considerations, there is no doubt that the place of faith continues as a primary source of meaning for most Pacific Islanders. Even where there are small communities of people, they begin to find each other and to gather together, and before long that gathering includes a religious element. In most Pacific Islander gatherings there will always be an acknowledgement of God. We see this in, for example, family celebrations like birthdays, graduations and weddings, but also in many other situations – like the Pacific rugby teams that pray and sing hymns before taking the field for a match.

So people begin to find each other in one location, often through family connections, and a church community is formed. Such groups, while dealing with their new cultural context, often work even harder to maintain their remembered cultural understandings. For this reason, the language and customs of the migrant group sometimes can be more 'traditional' than one might find if visiting the home country, as they have been locked in at the time of migration, whereas the home country might be evolving at some points. At the same time, there will be changes to adapt to the new environment – different food and consumer goods, for example. In this way the diasporic community 'falls between the cracks' – it is not fully integrated into the church life of the host community, but it is already starting to do things differently from the home community, while wanting to hold as closely as possible to that remembered culture.

At the same time, the migrant communities enliven the 'receiving' churches. They often bring more vitality and passion to church life than would otherwise be found in a Western context. They also tend to have a different age profile – Western congregations tend to be ageing and declining in numbers, while Pacific Islander congregations are multi-generational and function as an extended community, particularly for times of celebration.

Whether they move away from the islands temporarily or permanently, few Pacific migrants do not maintain ties with their homelands, and there is an ongoing flow of people, money, goods and ideas between those at home and overseas, and across the diaspora. Within the Pacific context, both positive and negative outcomes of transnationalism must be considered. Given the strong adherence of most Pacific migrants to churches with close ties to their counterparts in the islands, it would be impossible to discuss Pacific transnationalism without acknowledging religion and gender differences in relation to two highly significant themes: remitting patterns (where it is acknowledged that women are the most frequent and reliable remitters) and the challenge facing the second generation of migrants.

Remittances

A range of factors – including limited domestic resources, small land masses and geographical isolation, declining commodity prices, limited opportunities to generate income, environmental problems, government policies that create obstacles to change and the rising expectations of the population – have all been cited as factors in the creation of a reliance on remittances and foreign aid in order for the small island countries to remain economically viable. This gives rise to a discussion on the issue of dependency, generating considerable debate about the role of remittances in the home country. A key argument is that remittances are used primarily for consumption and therefore act as a disincentive to investment and local production, hindering development and creating a dependent relationship between those at home and the migrants.

The issue of remittances is a key concern for understanding the Pacific diaspora. The money that migrants send not only critically supports families but also can progressively rework gender relations, support education and the acquisition of professional skills, and facilitate local community development through new health clinics, water systems, places of worship and sports facilities. Remittances might also, though, undermine local labour markets, fuel price increases, create new status hierarchies and generate patterns of economic dependence.

In the broader context of migration, maximising the benefits of international migration is crucial, because it is highly valued throughout the region for social and economic reasons. As long as considerable economic challenges face island states, as their population growth rates remain above world averages, as development prospects are few, as the possibility of declining aid becomes more apparent and as expectations rise, the ability to migrate will be crucial.

The question of remittances is also central to understanding the connection between churches both 'home' and 'away'. Churches that have been established in a new country will have divided loyalties. They will feel an obligation to the new country – and perhaps now belong within a new denominational structure with its own rules and regulations about giving and supporting wider church activities – but because of family obligations and kinship connections will also feel responsibility for the wellbeing of the church at home in the Islands. In Pacific cultures of reciprocal hospitality and gift-giving, certain demands are felt deeply when one is asked to support a cause (particularly when it comes with the spiritual overtones of supporting a church programme). In this way, many diasporic churches, while belonging to a denomination in the new country, feel obliged to support the work of their 'home' church when asked. Sometimes such asking takes the form of a visit by an individual or group raising funds for a particular church project back home and perceiving that the diasporic community will be wealthier and more able to support the cause than residents of the Island nation. Of course, this assumption is not always correct, and families are sometimes put in severe financial hardship in their new land because of the continual demands to support a church-sponsored fund-raiser. This can lead to resentment and division in the diasporic community over which projects to support and disagreement about how close the ties with the home church/denomination should be.

Ministers and church members who return to the Islands to participate in church conferences and meetings are expected to bring gifts, including money, on such occasions. Diasporic communities might find a home within a new denomination in their new country that provides them with a structure, perhaps a building (which might otherwise be under-utilised) for worship and church activities, but the need to maintain cultural and family links – which, as we have seen, includes close ties to a church – means that there will continue to be traffic back and forth between the people of these communities. There is also a rise in divisions in the church between those who want to be linked only with the home church/denomination, those who want to be linked only with the church/denomination in their new country, those who want the best of both worlds, and those who opt for a complete break and either join a church with no ties back home or establish a completely new church/denomination which can then relate on its own terms with communities in the country of origin.

A discussion of the issue of remittances leads directly into another critical issue for diasporic communities – the place of the second (and subsequent) generations of migrants. Tonga is a case in point and will be used to exemplify the situation of the entire region. Although children of migrants have been relatively successful, many would readily admit that they do not send remittances to Tonga, partly because they feel they have no family there whom they feel obliged to support, but also because the demands of participating in their local Tongan community are high. Many second-generation Tongans in the diaspora do not feel responsible for supporting Tonga's economy and they resent the burden such support has placed on their parents' generation – and, more tellingly, often believe that while Tonga welcomes their financial contribution it does not accept them as truly 'Tongan'. The reluctance of second-generation Tongans to shoulder the burden their parents have borne raises some serious questions about Tonga's future economic situation that are only just beginning to be considered.

Closely tied to the issue of what uses are made of remittances is the question of why remittances are sent, and it is simplistic to assume that they are just altruistic gifts to kin and country. Remittances are also sent for personal investment, to maintain land rights, and to prepare for re-tirement, although in the latter case few elderly Tongans do in fact return to Tonga, because their children and grandchildren are based overseas. If we look at these migrants' reasons for remitting, it is obvious that few members of the second generation overseas are likely to have similar motives, so why would they remit?

Second-generation Migrants

Transnational ties differ markedly between the first and second genera-tions. Points of contact weaken substantially in the transition from the first to second generation of immigrant populations. For example, evidence suggests that immigrants develop strong links with their countries of origin through community development work in the home villages. However, second-generation youth do not necessarily feel obliged to take part in the village association; the migrants' children do not feel they owe anything to the village. The strong emotional ties between migrants and their native land are not easily replicated in the second generation. Most research concludes that transnationalism declines with the second genera-tion and usually finds that, overall, only a tiny proportion (2.4%) have visited their parents' country of origin and remitted at least once a year.

Nonetheless, many Tongan second-generation younger people feel a strong connection with the village of their parents/grandparents and accept that they have a role to play in supporting the home village, perhaps because of the opportunities and privilege they enjoy in a more developed country. At the same time, and allowing for this caveat, many of these young people are not fluent Tongan speakers, and therefore some of their cultural understandings are more developed by their association with their second-generation peers in their new country, where they may now be seen as a sub-cultural group within the new land.

Second-generation Tongans face a great deal of pressure to conform to the 'Tongan' way of behaving (*anga fakatonga*). If they eventually 'settle down' and move into mainstream jobs and domesticity, is this any guarantee that they will suddenly establish ties to Tonga and begin sending remittances? Will other young people, struggling against the poverty their families have faced since they migrated, find a way to help support Tonga's economy? Even those who have 'made it' in their host nation might be unwilling to provide the level of financial support their parents gave to Tonga, since this would mean sacrificing some of the material and other benefits of their success. There are complex issues here, including the resentment of many young people of their parents' funnelling of family income to churches and Tonga, and the pressure placed on them to be evidence of the success of the migration process. Migration was not just about helping kin in Tonga, but to increase the opportunities for migrants' children, and where those children have been able to achieve some upward social mobility, they need to demonstrate this through their lifestyles. Further complicating the picture is the reality that participation in the local community can also absorb considerable resources.

Tongans are not in exile, as were groups first identified as diasporic (such as Jews). However, conditions in Tonga, such as land shortage, unemployment and low wages, combined with the increasing cost of living in Tonga and the perceived opportunities for material and educational advancement in Western nations, create a situation that makes emigration imperative for many Tongans.

Much of the discussion on Tongan migration focuses on its impact in Tonga or on the economic aspects of migration, particularly the practice of sending remittances. However, new studies of diasporic Tongans all agree that the most important resource networks for Tongan immigrants are the church and the extended family. For Pacific Islanders in Australia, these resource networks have contributed to social harmony and welfare support within the community, while also allowing Islanders to retain their traditional cultural values and languages. However, these networks are weakening and certainly have not prevented many Tongan immigrants experiencing a range of problems, such as isolation from the wider community, unemployment, inadequate housing, marriage breakdown, domestic violence and alcohol abuse. In addition, the extent to which 'traditional cultural values and languages' are retained is highly variable between and within Islander populations. The issue of whether traditional culture is being retained, lost or adapted is, of course, inseparable from the issue of cultural identity.

The Role of the Church

In Australia, the relatively small and highly dispersed population of Pacific Islanders retains a sense of community primarily through its churches. For example, there are Tongan congregations of the Uniting Church, the Wesleyan Methodist Church, the Catholic Church, the Church of Tonga, the Tokaikolo Fellowship and the Maama Fo'ou. Most of these churches have several congregations in different areas of the main capital cities and some are also found in rural areas.

The proliferation of churches is partly the result of the population's dispersal combined with factionalism, but it also indicates the importance of the church as a social institution for Pacific Islanders. Since they first began to settle in Australia in the 1960s, Pacific Islanders have established their own church congregations, often travelling considerable distances to attend. It is not unusual for some parishioners to travel more than an hour's drive to participate. Ministers in Pacific Islander churches are accorded great respect and wield a considerable amount of power, and the differences between the congregations are determined as much by the inclinations of individual ministers as by differing religious practices.

Considerable rivalry exists between the churches, with some vying to be seen as more 'traditional' in cultural terms and others claiming that their more Western approach better assists the settlement process. The Uniting Church in Australia straddles the traditional and the modern, holding services in both English and Pacific Islander languages and combining both Islander and Australian elements in its activities. These churches are of particular interest because they are actively involved in the process of cultural reconstruction and demand a great deal of their members' time and other resources.

Parishioners usually attend both morning and afternoon services on Sundays, often having a break for tea and food in the church hall during the middle of the day. Children attend Sunday school and join the adults in the service. Both services sometimes stretch for more than two hours. In addition, there is often a Wednesday evening service, Bible study and choir practice each week, and young people attend the youth group on Friday evenings. About once a month the Sunday-school children perform items in church, and every two months a special youth service is held. The minister and some core church members are active in the community, helping newcomers find accommodation and employment, assisting with financing education, and at times conducting their own language lessons for young people who have not learned their mother tongue. The minister of the church is central to all of these activities, as well as assisting the courts and welfare authorities to help with interpreting and visiting Islanders in prison, among numerous other pastoral duties.

This church also holds seminars, camps and discussions with invited speakers, during all of which participants self-consciously reaffirm, contest and refashion aspects of 'the proper/Islander way'. The church places a strong focus on young people, explicitly to address the problems they face in the context of migration, and the youth programme is well attended. This focus on youth is common to many of the Islander churches. The various Islander churches are not simply places of worship. They provide social opportunities, mediate between immigrants and their new society, and are sites for the reaffirmation and reconstitution of cultural identity.

Conclusion

The evidence suggests that the Pacific Islander diasporic churches will continue to flourish for some time to come. Evidence from other migrant communities further suggests that though there might be a waning of interest among the second generation in their cultural roots (loss of language, other cultural practices), it is sometimes the third or fourth generation that wants to reclaim a sense of identity through an understanding of cultural origins (including language learning). Diasporic churches function not only as worshipping congregations but also as cultural centres, keeping alive language and customs from the home community. At the same time, those customs must adapt to the new environment, and so while some aspects of the culture remain static, other parts evolve and shift to meet the challenges.

One of the great missionary insights of the last 50 years has been that mission happens 'from everywhere to everywhere'. If that is true, then the church must rethink what it means to be a receiver of those who were formerly thought of in the category of needing to be evangelised, or 'saved'. The Uniting Church in Australia declared in its Basis of Union in 1977 that it 'believes that Christians in Australia are called to bear witness to a unity of faith and life in Christ which transcends cultural and economic, national and racial boundaries'. In 1985 it declared itself to be a multicultural church, observing that 'the fact that our membership comprises people of many races, cultures and languages is a reminder that the church is both product and agent of mission'. We live in an age of increasing mobility of people and yet at the same time a moment of increasing need for hospitality for those who find themselves displaced or dislocated, for whatever reason, from their cultural roots. In welcoming the stranger, the church must continue to know itself as both 'product and agent' of mission in this day and age.

Bibliography

Cruz, Gemma Tulud, *An Intercultural Theology of Migration: Pilgrims in the Wilderness* (Leiden: Brill, 2010).

Cruz, Gemma Tulud, *Toward a Theology of Migration: Social Justice and Religious Experience* (New York: Palgrave Macmillan, 2014).

Fer, Yannick, 'Polynesian Protestantism: From Local Church to Evangelical Networks', *Archives de Sciences Sociales des Religions*, 157 (2012), 47–66.

Gomes, Catherine and Brenda S. A. Yeoh, *Transnational Migrations in the Asia-Pacific: Transformative Experiences in the Age of Digital Media* (London: Rowman & Littlefield, 2018).

Petrou, Kristie, *If Everyone Returned, the Island Would Sink: Urbanisation and Migration in Vanuatu* (New York: Berghahn, 2020).

Conclusion

The Future of Christianity in Oceania

Katalina Tahaafe-Williams

Contemporary church historians and religious commentators wisely resist the presumption that current trajectories discerned in global Christianity are blueprints for its future possibilities. Likewise, this concluding chapter simply seeks to engage some key themes highlighted in the preceding essays that might be significant for the future of Christianity in Oceania. The fact is, two decades into the twenty-first century, Christianity can still claim religious dominance in Oceania, with over 90% of the total Pacific Islands populations and over 50% of the region's more religiously diverse and secularising centres of New Zealand and Australia. Given this reality it is hard to imagine Christianity ceasing to be a significant presence in the region, at least in the foreseeable future. This is not to claim that Christianity's future in Oceania is guaranteed, nor is it a statement about the form and shape in which it might exist. This is a hopeful moment for re-imagining the future story of Christianity in Oceania – for re-visioning the kind of Christian presence Christ is calling his church to be in the vast liquid continent as it moves forward.

While the historic mainline churches still hold the numerical upper hand, there is no denying that the rapid growth of Pentecostal-Charismatic religiosity is reshaping the Christian landscape in Oceania. Much of the newer Christian presence and activities in the region are shaped by a form of Pentecostal-Charismatic Christianity particular to the USA. Given that country's major role as a driving force of globalisation and the spread of modern capitalism, it is no surprise that the success of the new religious groups is attributed to their capacity to adapt to globalising processes. Indeed, some would assert that, in the same way that historic missions were constant companions of the colonial enterprise, so the new churches are utilising tools of globalisation to strengthen and spread their message.

The viability of churches and their activities in the region inevitably frames concerns for Oceania's Christian future. Currently, signs of Christian energy and vitality point to the newer religious groups. Sadly, images of declining presence characterise the historic mainline churches. At a global level, the differences between the two types of church are often articulated in terms of one subscribing to a gospel of prosperity at the expense of the theology of the cross, while the other is seen as prioritising a social gospel over and above a concern for the saving of souls. In Oceania, however, the line differentiating the two is not so easily defined. Both exhibit common characteristics made manifest in their adherence to a certain form of theological conservatism and an uncritical acceptance of the so-called neo-liberal market culture. An additional common characteristic pertains to their evident ease with biblical notions of the supernatural, dreams and prophecies. A closer look, however, reveals the Pentecostal paradox, whereby it rejects Pacific traditional values yet embraces religious practices consistent with supernatural elements found in Pacific traditional religions.

Although it would be premature to settle for the demise of denominationalism, the absence of responses from mainline churches to the rapid social and religious changes taking place in the region is remarkable. Among Pacific theologians, including authors in this volume, is a deep concern about the church's diminishing capacity to assume what is seen as its legitimate role in countering oppressive social influences in the region and to claim its voice in the public space. This is especially so when the state is seen to be lagging in its duty to serve and protect its citizens. Despite political undercurrents about religion's proper role in secular matters, the church's public role in the Pacific Islands is normative and represents a blurring of the line between church and state unique to the region. It is in fact a testimony to the rootedness of Christianity in South Pacific societies and cultures, though in this instance both church and state are evidently caught up in the neo-liberal capitalistic wave sweeping through Oceania. This might explain the Pacific churches' apparent lack of interest in social analysis and the lack of theological challenge to the major changes seen in the region. Certainly, there are signs of progressive theological activity in the mainline churches, but this is largely limited to interests in cultural contextualisation rather than critiques of current socio-economic realities. The present volume highlights the concern that Pacific churches reposition their theological outlook or risk being so far removed from reality as to be irrelevant to the daily lives of Pacific Islanders.

The Australian and New Zealand Christian landscapes are facing similar religious changes and sweeping globalisation accompanied by secularism. Ironically, here the separation between church and state is unambiguous, but mainline churches in the two 'big islands' are less constrained in publicly voicing socio-economic concerns. While they are not as tied to the mission mindset of the nineteenth and twentieth centuries, their efforts to develop distinctly Australian and New Zealand theologies have been hindered somewhat by an underlying nostalgic attachment to European theologies. Against all odds, the persistence of Indigenous theological and spiritual activities in both countries has inspired commitment in mainline churches to develop theologies distinct to their respective contexts. Integral to such efforts is the recognition that both are invaded spaces – which fact must be meaningfully addressed in the emerging theologies.

Contrary to the rather gloomy trends associated with mainline churches in Oceania, demographic evidence shows that the Roman Catholic Church has doubled in size within the last 50 years. Important implications here include an affirmation of the Catholic Church's exceptional capacity for a viable future and for providing a significant mainline alternative to the growing challenges of the new religious movements. A concerning challenge of note is the erosion of traditional social structures, particularly the breaking down in extended familial/kinship ties and communal culture, which have been essential for regional stability and cohesion.

Questions of Christian vitality and energy also revolve around issues of worship and spirituality. Undoubtedly the use of modern music and technology in Pentecostal-Charismatic worship has played an important role in developing the strong presence of new religious groups in Oceania. It is notable that Indigenous music and dance were already well established in the region as integral to traditional cultural rituals and ceremonies, which the early missionaries exploited for spreading the gospel message through hymns and choral music and which mainline churches have maintained to the present. More recently, new religious groups found the same fertile musical soil and borrowed the example of early missionaries, but this time utilising popular musical techniques and modern technologies.

The volume highlights the centrality of creation to spirituality and worship in Oceania, emphasising the interconnectedness of all things and the harmonious relationship between human beings and all of nature. A communal cultural orientation is fundamental to how Pacific Islanders understand God's gift of life and is experienced in the rich Oceanian spirituality of thanksgiving, celebration and hospitality. Additional aspects of the history of European colonisation, modern migration and the revival of Indigenous self-consciousness in New Zealand and Australia also inform and shape worship and spirituality in the region. Of increasing importance is the inclusion of the push for reconciliation between Indigenous and non-Indigenous peoples in liturgical and spiritual expressions. Specifically, in Australia awareness is growing that worship and spirituality need to be understood in terms of the developing reconciliation between Australia's First and Second Peoples.

At the core of Oceania's spirituality is a vision for the reconciliation of all things, of all creation, and fundamentally no stronger statement can be made for the integrity of creation. Pacific eco-theologians and climate-change activists continue to debate the meaning of the integrity of creation for the liquid continent, whose populations contribute the least to anthropogenic climate change, and for those countries most immediately responsible for it. Here the role of Pacific churches in providing theological responses and action that inspire a shift in current development perspectives and practices to more creation-sensitive models is critical. Put another way, an Oceanian spirituality characterised by the interconnectedness of all things and the reconciliation of all creation is paramount for driving an Oceanian development agenda that truly respects the integrity of creation.

The emphasis on the interconnectedness of all things is strongly evident in the dynamics between Indigenous spirituality and Christianity in the region. Juxtaposing historical influences of colonialism, monotheistic tendencies, Augustinian moral orientations and Judaeo-Christian notions of environmental domination is the Talanoa Paradigm, which reasserts the Pacific Indigenous spirituality of interdependency, relationship and dialogue. The Talanoa Paradigm promotes adaptability, intergenerational relations and survival as vital for the wellbeing and sustainability of Pacific Christians. Again, the reconciling impulses characteristic of Oceanian spirituality are affirmed by the eco-relational structure of life at the interface between faith and culture. Eco-relationality frames a holistic vision for the future of Oceanian Christianity in terms of the so-called '*oikos* triplets' of ecology, economy and *oikoumene*. The future of Christianity in the liquid continent is seen as profoundly diminished when the ecological implications of economic systems and ecumenical relations are not considered seriously. The point is made that eco-relationality demands mutual relationships between the environment, the economy and ecumenism, with the capacity to challenge anthropocentric agendas promoted at the expense of the rest of God's creation.

Of course, the vitality and future possibilities of Christianity in the region cannot be a serious consideration without the presence and involvement of women and youth. Charting the future story of Oceanian Christianity without the voices and participation of women and youth ought to be unimaginable. In Pacific churches that are still quite hierarchical and predominantly patriarchal, these are fundamental ongoing concerns for Christianity. The dynamics of gender roles and notions of masculinity and femininity in the region are quite complex given the huge impact in Pacific cultures of the early Christian missionaries and the influences of the newer religious movements. Recent Christian activities focusing on gender equality have been welcomed as making a distinction between cultural versus faith-based understandings of gender. The complexities mentioned signal the necessity of seeking resolutions to gender imbalances in the region via contextual means and agencies, and, by extension, the same approach applies to the whole question of human sexuality. Culturally appropriate approaches are necessary precisely because solutions that are contextually sensitive, relevant and sustainable are critical for the participation of women and youth in the future story of Oceanian Christianity.

A major agenda in imagining future possibilities for Christianity in Oceania must be theological education. Clearly, the cry within the region for the churches' increased theological capacity to engage with socio-economic trends and changes is loud and clear. Equipping Christian leaders and ministry agents in social-analysis, administrative, finance and management skills must be prioritised in theological education and ministry formation. Limiting such priorities to spiritual matters undermines Christianity's viability in Oceania for the twenty-first century. Further, increased capacity in theological education and ministerial formation presupposes improvements with regard to gender equality and relations.

Continuing attention to inter-religious relations and dialogue is called for, given the evidence of increasing religious diversity, particularly in Australia and New Zealand, due to inward migration. Growing the Oceanian churches' capacity for multi-religious cohesion is especially important as a potential counter to the concerning rise in religious fundamentalism currently seen in the Pentecostal-Charismatic and Orthodox traditions. Similarly, the ongoing challenge to Christian unity also calls for increased attention. Historical mainline churches need to re-vision an ecumenical future for Oceania that is more inclusive and can make the connections with the newer religious groups and other world faiths as their presence become more visible. There are promising signs of younger generations of theologians and ecumenists from several traditions, including the Orthodox and Pentecostal-Charismatic, actively seeking this broader ecumenism. Interestingly, visible within the Pentecostal-Charismatic groups are moves for more open and wider dialogue, clearly implying that not all in that tradition are apolitical or anti-intellectual. As conventional expressions of ecumenism fade, the model being pioneered by the Global Christian Forum, which brings together Christians from a broad range of traditions, including Pentecostal-Charismatic, Orthodox, Roman Catholic and Protestant, holds significant potential in the Oceania context. Exciting and creative possibilities for Christianity in Oceania are surely in store if concerted efforts are focused on finding and adopting new ways for dialogue and cooperation beyond denominational bounds.

Such aspirations for the future of Christianity in Oceania have resource implications. Over the years, however, entrenched dependency on external donors has disabled Pacific churches from building their capacity for self-sufficiency. It has weakened their positions and abilities to participate in countering socio-economic trends detrimental to regional cohesion and wellbeing and is an added hindrance with regard to generating the political will to effect changes that are necessary. A growing consensus among religious commentators suggests that strong, visionary and informed leadership with deep spiritual integrity is essential as a first step for positive change. Such leadership would have the courage and boldness to recognise the resources and agencies present in the region and to mobilise and utilise them in strategic planning and action. Such leadership would also have the insight and wisdom to draw on traditional structures and practices well tested in the history of the region, such as kinship bonds and the communal culture of giving, for charting the future story for Oceanian Christianity. Such leadership will welcome and embrace initiatives for well rounded, well informed theological education and ministerial formation as indispensable for ministry and mission in the twenty-first century. These are the necessary steps in the right direction toward self-sufficiency, sustainability and release from paralysing dependency.

Perhaps this is also the space in which to negotiate with the Pacific migrant churches and diasporic communities abroad about how the extensive resources they represent – not just in remittances, which is vast in itself, but also in the myriad areas of life – can be better utilised in re-visioning the future of Oceanian Christianity. Australia and New Zealand as the two big islands of the liquid continent are also invested in this negotiation, given their significant demographic impacts on the current Christian landscape in Oceania and in its projected future. Undoubtedly, a key challenge to be faced in both islands is secularism. Just over a decade ago, Tom Frame predicted that, by 2030, Australian churches that lack credible and attractive alternative offerings to popular culture will disappear and that first to go will be the 'left-leaning cause-driven liberal Protestant churches that lack doctrinal rigour and are preoccupied with the promotion of social justice and cultural inclusion' (*Losing My Religion*, p. 299). If asked, he might well have assigned the same fate to the sister islands across the Tasman Sea. Might this be the fate of Christianity in Oceania? Granted, much can change in a decade, but the demographic evidence presented in the present volume cannot be easily dismissed. As Philip Jenkins reminded the world almost two decades ago,

> Christianity is never as weak as it appears nor as strong as it appears. And whether we look backward or forward in history, we can see that time and again Christianity demonstrates a breathtaking ability to transform weakness into strength. (Philip Jenkins, *The Next Christendom: The Coming of Global Christianity*, p. 220)

Insofar as charting, re-visioning and imagining possible new futures for Christianity in Oceania go, this volume of the Edinburgh Companions to Global Christianity provides rich pickings for articulating a future story of Oceanian Christianity that is, as Upolu Lumā Vaai proposes in his essay, 'joyfully Christian and truly Oceanic'. For myself, I would imagine a future Oceanian Christianity that holds together firmly and unapologetically doctrinal rigour, spiritual depth and social responsibility as defining characteristics of Christian presence in the region. Surely, in these troubled times overshadowed by more than the global pandemic, followers of Jesus in the twenty-first century are more than ever obliged to foster an informed faith that can be a buffer against a globalising neo-liberal individualistic culture that saturates our every waking moment with what Karl Marx would call 'soulless' noise. Would that not be the kind of Christian presence in Oceania that is worth aspiring to?

Bibliography

Ernst, Manfred (ed.), *Globalization and the Re-shaping of Christianity in the Pacific Islands* (Suva: Pacific Theological College, 2006).

Ernst, Manfred, *Winds of Change: Rapidly Growing Religious Groups in the Pacific Islands* (Suva: Pacific Theological College, 1994).

Ernst, Manfred and Lydia Johnson (eds), *Navigating Troubled Waters: The Ecumenical Movement in the Pacific Islands since the 1980s* (Suva: Pacific Theological College, 2017).

Frame, Tom, *Losing My Religion: Unbelief in Australia* (Sydney: UNSW Press, 2009).

Jenkins, Philip, *The Next Christendom: The Coming of Global Christianity* (Oxford: Oxford University Press, 2002).

Appendices

Christianity by Country

The table that begins overleaf provides a quick-reference, country-by-country listing for Christianity and its major traditions for all the countries that appear in this volume. These statistics are found in the *World Christian Database* (see Methodology and Sources) and all figures relate to 1970 and 2020. Small numbers are left unrounded to distinguish known small populations from zero but do not represent precise estimates.

The columns are as follows:

- Country (name of country in English)
- Region in which country is located
- Total population of country (United Nations estimate, 1970, 2020) and total numbers and percentage of population in each tradition
- Percentage mean annual growth rate, 1970–2020.

The last page of the table presents regional totals.

Country	Region	Tradition	1970 Population	%	2020 Population	%	Growth rate (%), 1970–2020
American Samoa	Polynesia	Total population	27,300	100.0%	55,800	100.0%	1.4%
		Christians	27,000	99.0%	54,400	97.5%	1.4%
		Anglicans	100	0.4%	60	0.1%	−1.0%
		Independents	2,600	9.6%	21,500	38.5%	4.3%
		Protestants	18,500	67.8%	41,900	75.1%	1.6%
		Catholics	5,000	18.3%	16,000	28.7%	2.4%
		Evangelicals	2,500	9.1%	15,400	27.6%	3.7%
		Pentecostals/ Charismatics	1,600	5.8%	23,500	42.1%	5.5%
Australia	Australia/ New Zealand	Total population	12,843,000	100.0%	25,398,000	100.0%	1.4%
		Christians	11,945,000	93.0%	13,744,000	54.1%	0.3%
		Anglicans	3,777,000	29.4%	3,488,000	13.8%	−0.2%
		Independents	343,000	2.7%	800,000	3.1%	1.7%
		Orthodox	328,000	2.6%	1,100,000	4.3%	2.5%
		Protestants	1,899,000	14.8%	2,372,000	9.3%	0.4%
		Catholics	3,038,000	23.7%	5,900,000	23.2%	1.3%
		Evangelicals	2,516,000	19.6%	2,553,000	10.1%	0.0%
		Pentecostals/ Charismatics	102,000	0.8%	1,550,000	6.1%	5.6%
Cook Islands	Polynesia	Total population	21,400	100.0%	17,500	100.0%	−0.4%
		Christians	21,300	99.3%	16,800	96.1%	−0.5%
		Anglicans	100	0.5%	90	0.5%	−0.2%
		Independents	1,300	6.0%	3,000	17.1%	1.7%
		Protestants	16,100	75.4%	10,700	61.1%	−0.8%
		Catholics	2,300	10.6%	4,900	28.0%	1.6%
		Evangelicals	740	3.5%	1,100	6.3%	0.8%
		Pentecostals/ Charismatics	130	0.6%	3,000	17.1%	6.5%
Fiji	Melanesia	Total population	521,000	100.0%	925,000	100.0%	1.2%
		Christians	263,000	50.5%	598,000	64.6%	1.7%
		Anglicans	6,500	1.2%	7,300	1.0%	0.7%
		Independents	4,700	0.9%	114,000	12.3%	6.6%
		Protestants	187,000	36.0%	408,000	43.9%	1.6%
		Catholics	43,500	8.4%	115,000	12.4%	2.0%
		Evangelicals	47,500	9.1%	181,000	19.6%	2.7%
		Pentecostals/ Charismatics	20,800	4.0%	200,000	21.6%	4.6%
French Polynesia	Polynesia	Total population	110,000	100.0%	291,000	100.0%	2.0%
		Christians	106,000	96.1%	272,000	93.7%	1.9%
		Independents	9,700	8.8%	51,800	17.8%	3.4%
		Protestants	47,000	42.5%	104,000	35.8%	1.6%
		Catholics	36,000	32.5%	120,000	41.3%	2.4%
		Evangelicals	2,300	2.1%	8,900	3.1%	2.7%
		Pentecostals/ Charismatics	1,100	1.0%	27,000	9.3%	6.7%

Country	Region	Tradition	1970 Population	%	2020 Population	%	Growth rate (%), 1970–2020
Guam	Micronesia	Total population	83,900	100.0%	169,000	100.0%	1.4%
		Christians	80,700	96.2%	158,000	93.6%	1.4%
		Anglicans	500	0.6%	1,200	0.7%	1.8%
		Independents	1,700	2.0%	8,800	5.2%	3.4%
		Protestants	11,000	13.2%	13,900	8.2%	0.5%
		Catholics	68,000	81.1%	138,000	81.6%	1.4%
		Evangelicals	5,700	6.8%	10,000	5.9%	1.1%
		Pentecostals/ Charismatics	2,700	3.2%	12,000	7.1%	3.0%
Kiribati	Micronesia	Total population	51,200	100.0%	122,000	100.0%	1.8%
		Christians	50,000	97.7%	119,000	96.9%	1.7%
		Independents	50	0.1%	20,300	16.6%	12.8%
		Protestants	24,600	48.1%	47,400	38.7%	1.3%
		Catholics	23,900	46.7%	56,800	46.4%	1.7%
		Evangelicals	2,100	4.2%	5,200	4.2%	1.8%
		Pentecostals/ Charismatics	540	1.1%	10,000	8.2%	6.0%
Marshall Islands	Micronesia	Total population	20,400	100.0%	53,300	100.0%	1.9%
		Christians	19,200	94.1%	50,300	94.4%	1.9%
		Independents	140	0.7%	10,200	19.1%	9.0%
		Protestants	14,500	71.1%	50,000	93.9%	2.5%
		Catholics	2,000	9.8%	5,500	10.3%	2.0%
		Evangelicals	5,100	25.2%	35,600	66.9%	3.9%
		Pentecostals/ Charismatics	4,000	19.6%	37,500	70.4%	4.6%
Micronesia	Micronesia	Total population	61,400	100.0%	108,000	100.0%	1.1%
		Christians	57,600	93.8%	102,000	94.5%	1.1%
		Independents	320	0.5%	9,000	8.4%	6.9%
		Protestants	27,300	44.4%	49,000	45.5%	1.2%
		Catholics	20,000	32.6%	65,000	60.3%	2.4%
		Evangelicals	4,800	7.9%	19,500	18.1%	2.8%
		Pentecostals/ Charismatics	260	0.4%	10,800	10.0%	7.7%
Nauru	Micronesia	Total population	6,500	100.0%	11,200	100.0%	1.1%
		Christians	5,300	82.3%	8,300	74.2%	0.9%
		Anglicans	150	2.3%	450	4.0%	2.2%
		Independents	0	0.0%	830	7.4%	9.2%
		Protestants	2,700	41.6%	5,400	47.7%	1.4%
		Catholics	1,200	18.5%	3,300	29.4%	2.0%
		Evangelicals	120	1.8%	790	7.0%	3.9%
		Pentecostals/ Charismatics	0	0.0%	1,600	14.4%	10.7%

Country	Region	Tradition	1970 Population	%	2020 Population	%	Growth rate (%), 1970–2020
New Caledonia	Melanesia	Total population	105,000	100.0%	287,000	100.0%	2.0%
		Christians	96,300	91.5%	243,000	84.8%	1.9%
		Anglicans	50	0.0%	280	0.1%	3.5%
		Independents	4,000	3.8%	25,000	8.7%	3.7%
		Protestants	17,900	17.0%	43,100	15.0%	1.8%
		Catholics	73,600	69.9%	144,000	50.1%	1.3%
		Evangelicals	3,900	3.7%	19,500	6.8%	3.3%
		Pentecostals/ Charismatics	1,300	1.2%	19,000	6.6%	5.5%
New Zealand	Australia/ New Zealand	Total population	2,818,000	100.0%	4,834,000	100.0%	1.1%
		Christians	2,688,000	95.4%	2,619,000	54.2%	−0.1%
		Anglicans	876,000	31.1%	590,000	12.2%	−0.8%
		Independents	85,900	3.0%	334,000	6.9%	2.8%
		Orthodox	5,500	0.2%	14,800	0.3%	2.0%
		Protestants	837,000	29.7%	710,000	14.7%	−0.3%
		Catholics	426,000	15.1%	543,000	11.2%	0.5%
		Evangelicals	756,000	26.8%	590,000	12.2%	−0.5%
		Pentecostals/ Charismatics	28,200	1.0%	420,000	8.7%	5.5%
Niue	Polynesia	Total population	5,100	100.0%	1,600	100.0%	−2.3%
		Christians	5,100	99.9%	1,600	96.6%	−2.3%
		Anglicans	30	0.6%	40	2.5%	0.6%
		Independents	380	7.4%	460	27.9%	0.4%
		Protestants	3,800	73.2%	860	52.7%	−2.9%
		Catholics	220	4.3%	150	9.2%	−0.8%
		Evangelicals	220	4.3%	50	3.1%	−2.9%
		Pentecostals/ Charismatics	0	0.0%	200	12.3%	6.2%
Northern Mariana Islands	Micronesia	Total population	13,100	100.0%	55,300	100.0%	2.9%
		Christians	12,900	98.0%	43,100	77.9%	2.4%
		Independents	0	0.0%	11,000	19.9%	15.0%
		Protestants	1,100	8.5%	7,300	13.2%	3.8%
		Catholics	11,400	86.8%	41,300	74.6%	2.6%
		Evangelicals	170	1.3%	5,000	9.0%	6.9%
		Pentecostals/ Charismatics	0	0.0%	8,000	14.5%	14.3%
Palau	Micronesia	Total population	11,500	100.0%	22,400	100.0%	1.3%
		Christians	11,300	98.0%	20,600	91.6%	1.2%
		Independents	4,400	38.7%	2,400	10.7%	−1.2%
		Protestants	2,600	22.8%	9,300	41.4%	2.6%
		Catholics	4,000	34.8%	8,200	36.5%	1.4%
		Evangelicals	2,500	21.5%	5,700	25.4%	1.7%
		Pentecostals/ Charismatics	88	0.8%	2,200	9.8%	6.6%

Country	Region	Tradition	1970 Population	%	2020 Population	%	Growth rate (%), 1970–2020
Papua New Guinea	Melanesia	Total population	2,528,000	100.0%	8,756,000	100.0%	2.5%
		Christians	2,390,000	94.6%	8,338,000	95.2%	2.5%
		Anglicans	60,000	2.4%	230,000	2.6%	2.7%
		Independents	21,300	0.8%	440,000	5.0%	6.2%
		Orthodox	200	0.0%	400	0.0%	1.4%
		Protestants	918,000	36.3%	4,050,000	46.3%	3.0%
		Catholics	694,000	27.4%	2,300,000	26.3%	2.4%
		Evangelicals	370,000	14.6%	2,300,000	26.3%	3.7%
		Pentecostals/ Charismatics	109,000	4.3%	1,950,000	22.3%	5.9%
Samoa	Polynesia	Total population	143,000	100.0%	200,000	100.0%	0.7%
		Christians	141,000	98.7%	198,000	98.8%	0.7%
		Anglicans	350	0.2%	340	0.2%	−0.1%
		Independents	20,200	14.1%	84,000	42.0%	2.9%
		Protestants	82,500	57.6%	125,000	62.5%	0.8%
		Catholics	29,800	20.8%	38,000	19.0%	0.5%
		Evangelicals	9,000	6.3%	26,700	13.3%	2.2%
		Pentecostals/ Charismatics	3,900	2.7%	29,500	14.7%	4.1%
Solomon Islands	Melanesia	Total population	160,000	100.0%	647,000	100.0%	2.8%
		Christians	150,000	93.8%	615,000	95.0%	2.9%
		Anglicans	49,000	30.6%	200,000	30.9%	2.9%
		Independents	7,300	4.6%	45,000	7.0%	3.7%
		Protestants	47,300	29.5%	235,000	36.3%	3.3%
		Catholics	30,800	19.2%	132,000	20.4%	3.0%
		Evangelicals	36,000	22.5%	165,000	25.5%	3.1%
		Pentecostals/ Charismatics	4,800	3.0%	105,000	16.2%	6.4%
Tokelau	Polynesia	Total population	1,600	100.0%	1,400	100.0%	−0.4%
		Christians	1,600	96.3%	1,300	94.5%	−0.4%
		Independents	0	0.0%	20	1.5%	6.2%
		Protestants	1,000	63.4%	800	59.0%	−0.5%
		Catholics	400	24.7%	500	36.8%	0.4%
		Evangelicals	56	3.5%	80	5.9%	0.7%
		Pentecostals/ Charismatics	0	0.0%	65	4.8%	3.8%
Tonga	Polynesia	Total population	84,400	100.0%	111,000	100.0%	0.6%
		Christians	83,200	98.7%	106,000	95.7%	0.5%
		Anglicans	800	0.9%	1,800	1.6%	1.6%
		Independents	26,200	31.0%	84,500	76.1%	2.4%
		Protestants	38,700	45.9%	43,800	39.4%	0.2%
		Catholics	14,300	17.0%	14,400	13.0%	0.0%
		Evangelicals	6,700	7.9%	8,500	7.7%	0.5%
		Pentecostals/ Charismatics	4,300	5.0%	14,100	12.7%	2.4%

Country	Region	Tradition	1970		2020		Growth rate (%), 1970–2020
			Population	%	Population	%	
Tuvalu	Polynesia	Total population	7,300	100.0%	11,500	100.0%	0.9%
		Christians	7,200	98.6%	10,900	94.8%	0.8%
		Independents	24	0.3%	920	8.0%	7.6%
		Protestants	7,100	96.9%	9,600	83.9%	0.6%
		Catholics	100	1.4%	100	0.9%	0.0%
		Evangelicals	290	4.0%	580	5.0%	1.4%
		Pentecostals/ Charismatics	7	0.1%	1,900	16.5%	11.7%
Vanuatu	Melanesia	Total population	85,400	100.0%	294,000	100.0%	2.5%
		Christians	78,000	91.3%	275,000	93.5%	2.6%
		Anglicans	10,000	11.7%	36,500	12.4%	2.6%
		Independents	9,100	10.7%	30,200	10.3%	2.4%
		Protestants	37,000	43.3%	189,000	64.4%	3.3%
		Catholics	13,200	15.4%	33,000	11.2%	1.9%
		Evangelicals	15,400	18.0%	111,000	37.8%	4.0%
		Pentecostals/ Charismatics	4,600	5.4%	110,000	37.4%	6.5%
Wallis and Futuna Islands	Polynesia	Total population	8,800	100.0%	11,600	100.0%	0.5%
		Christians	8,700	98.9%	11,200	97.0%	0.5%
		Independents	0	0.0%	60	0.5%	3.6%
		Protestants	0	0.0%	200	1.7%	6.2%
		Catholics	8,400	95.0%	11,000	95.0%	0.5%
		Evangelicals	0	0.0%	40	0.3%	7.7%
		Pentecostals/ Charismatics	0	0.0%	340	2.9%	7.3%

Region	Tradition	1970 Population	%	2015 Population	%	Growth rate (%), 1970–2015
Australia/ New Zealand	Australia/ New Zealand					
		Total population	15,661,000	100.0%	30,233,000	100.0%	1.3%
		Christians	14,633,000	93.4%	16,363,000	54.1%	0.2%
		Anglicans	4,653,000	29.7%	4,078,000	13.5%	−0.3%
		Independents	429,000	2.7%	1,134,000	3.8%	2.0%
		Orthodox	333,000	2.1%	1,115,000	3.7%	2.4%
		Protestants	2,736,000	17.5%	3,082,000	10.2%	0.2%
		Catholics	3,464,000	22.1%	6,443,000	21.3%	1.2%
		Evangelicals	3,272,000	20.9%	3,143,000	10.4%	−0.1%
		Pentecostals/ Charismatics	130,000	0.8%	1,970,000	6.5%	5.6%
Melanesia	Melanesia					
		Total population	3,399,000	100.0%	10,909,000	100.0%	2.4%
		Christians	2,978,000	87.6%	10,069,000	92.3%	2.5%
		Anglicans	126,000	3.7%	474,000	4.4%	2.7%
		Independents	46,400	1.4%	654,000	6.0%	5.4%
		Orthodox	200	0.0%	400	0.0%	1.4%
		Protestants	1,207,000	35.5%	4,925,000	45.1%	2.9%
		Catholics	855,000	25.1%	2,724,000	25.0%	2.3%
		Evangelicals	473,000	13.9%	2,777,000	25.5%	3.6%
		Pentecostals/ Charismatics	140,000	4.1%	2,384,000	21.9%	5.8%
Micronesia	Micronesia					
		Total population	248,000	100.0%	541,000	100.0%	1.6%
		Christians	237,000	95.6%	501,000	92.5%	1.5%
		Anglicans	650	0.3%	1,700	0.3%	1.9%
		Independents	6,600	2.7%	62,500	11.5%	4.6%
		Protestants	83,900	33.8%	182,000	33.7%	1.6%
		Catholics	131,000	52.6%	318,000	58.7%	1.8%
		Evangelicals	20,600	8.3%	81,800	15.1%	2.8%
		Pentecostals/ Charismatics	7,600	3.1%	82,100	15.2%	4.9%
Polynesia	Polynesia					
		Total population	410,000	100.0%	701,000	100.0%	1.1%
		Christians	402,000	98.1%	673,000	95.9%	1.0%
		Anglicans	1,400	0.3%	2,300	0.3%	1.1%
		Independents	60,400	14.7%	246,000	35.1%	2.9%
		Protestants	215,000	52.4%	337,000	48.0%	0.9%
		Catholics	96,500	23.6%	205,000	29.2%	1.5%
		Evangelicals	21,800	5.3%	61,400	8.7%	2.1%
		Pentecostals/ Charismatics	10,900	2.7%	99,600	14.2%	4.5%

Methodology and Sources of Christian and Religious Affiliation

Todd M. Johnson and Gina A. Zurlo

Unless otherwise designated, the demographic figures in this book, both in the colour section and in the tables throughout, are from the *World Christian Database* (Leiden/Boston: Brill). This essay offers a concise explanation of methods and sources related to the database. It is adapted from longer treatments in Todd M. Johnson and Brian J. Grim, *The World's Religions in Figures: An Introduction to International Religious Demography* (Oxford: Wiley-Blackwell, 2013) and Todd M. Johnson and Gina A. Zurlo, *World Christian Encyclopedia*, 3rd edition (Edinburgh: Edinburgh University Press, 2019). The *World Christian Database* (*WCD*) includes detailed information on 45,000 Christian denominations and on religions in every country of the world. Extensive data are available on 234 countries and 13,000 ethno-linguistic peoples, as well as on 5,000 cities and 3,000 provinces. Information is readily available on religious activities, growth rates, religious literature, worker activity and demographics. Sources are evaluated and reviewed on a weekly basis by a professional staff dedicated to expanding and updating the *WCD*, and the database is updated quarterly.

The Right to Profess One's Choice

The starting point of this methodology is the United Nations 1948 Universal Declaration of Human Rights, Article 18:

> Everyone has the right to freedom of thought, conscience and religion; this right includes freedom to change his religion or belief, and freedom, either alone or in community with others and in public or private, to manifest his religion or belief in teaching, practice, worship and observance.

Since its promulgation, this group of phrases has been incorporated into the state constitutions of a large number of countries across the world. This fundamental right also includes the right to claim the religion of one's choice, and the right to be called a follower of that religion and to be enumerated as such. The section on religious freedom in the constitutions of very many nations uses the exact words of the Universal Declaration, and many countries instruct their census personnel to observe this principle. Public declaration must therefore be taken seriously when endeavouring to survey the extent of religious and non-religious affiliation around the world.

Religious Demography

The origins of the field of religious demography lie in the church censuses conducted in most European societies. For many years and in many countries, churches produced the most complete censuses of the population. They achieved this largely by recording baptisms and funerals. These data, however, were seen not as referring to specific religious communities, but rather to the larger homogeneous societies. With the decline of national churches in Europe beginning in the nineteenth and continuing into the twentieth century, governments began tracking births and deaths, eventually replacing churches as the main bodies collecting detailed information on human populations. Although thousands of sources for international religious demography are available, ranging from censuses and demographic surveys to statistics collected and reported by religious groups themselves, little has been done by scholars in religion, sociology, or other disciplines to collect, collate and analyse these data.

Sources

Data for religious demography fall broadly under five major headings:

1. Censuses in which a religious question is asked

In the twentieth century, approximately half the world's countries asked a question related to religion in their official national population censuses. Since 1990, however, this number has been declining as developing countries have dropped the question, deeming it too expensive (in many countries each question in a census costs well over US$1 million), uninteresting or controversial. As a result, some countries that historically included a religion question have not done so in their censuses since 1990. National censuses are the best starting point for the identification of religious adherents, because they generally cover the entire population.

2. Censuses in which an ethnicity or language question is asked

In the absence of a question on religion, another helpful piece of information from a census is ethnicity or language. This is especially true when a particular ethnic group can be equated with a particular religion. For example, over 99% of Somalis are Muslim, so the number of Somalis in, say, Sweden is an indication of a part of the Muslim community there.

Similarly, a question that asks for country of birth can be useful. If the answer is 'Nepal' there is a significant chance that the individual or community is Hindu. In each of these cases the assumption is made (if there is no further information) that the religion of the transplanted ethnic or linguistic community is the same as that in the home country.

3. Surveys and polls

In the absence of census data on religion, large-scale demographic surveys such as MEASURE (Monitoring and Evaluation to Assess and Use Results) and Demographic and Health Surveys (DHS) often include a question about the respondent's religious affiliation. In some instances, demographic surveys by groups such as UNICEF (the United Nations Children's Fund) include a religious affiliation question. Demographic surveys, although less comprehensive than a national census, have several advantages over other types of general population surveys and polls. DHS are highly regarded by demographers and social scientists, and provide valuable nationally representative data on religion. Surveys can also be commissioned in light of a dearth of data on a particular subject and results can be used to search for correlations between different variables.

4. Scholarly monographs

Every year, scholars publish hundreds of monographs on particular religions or religions in particular countries or regions. Such monographs differ from other sources in that they attempt to provide an overall profile of religion in an area or country, bringing to light local sources of quantitative data as well as qualitative information that provides layers of context and background.

5. Religion statistics in yearbooks and handbooks

Religious communities keep track of their members, using everything from simple lists to elaborate membership reports. The most detailed data collection and analysis is undertaken each year by some 45,000 Christian denominations and their 4.7 million constituent churches and congregations of believers. The latter invest over US$1.1 billion annually for a massive, decentralised and largely uncoordinated global census of Christians. In sum, they send out around 10 million printed questionnaires in 3,000 different languages, covering 180 major religious subjects reporting on 2,000 socio-religious variables. This collection of data provides a year-by-year snapshot of the progress or decline of Christianity's diverse movements, offering an enormous body of data from which researchers can track trends and make projections. Statistics collected by religious communities often enable researchers to distinguish between two categories of religionists – practising and non-practising – based on whether or not they take part in the ongoing organised life of the religion.

In addition to the above categories, there are governmental statistical reports, questionnaires and reports from collaborators, field surveys and interviews, correspondence with national informants, unpublished documentation, encyclopaedias, dictionaries and directories of religions, print and web-based contemporary descriptions of religions, and dissertations and theses on religion. The best practices in determining the religious affiliation of any population utilise as many sources as possible.

Affiliation

There are at least two different perspectives on what it means to be a Christian: professing Christians and affiliated Christians. Utilising the United Nations Universal Declaration of Human Rights as a foundation, 'professing Christians' means all those who profess to be Christians in government censuses or public-opinion polls, that is, who declare or identify themselves as Christians, who say 'I am a Christian' or 'We are Christians' when asked the question 'What is your religion?'

However, not all those who profess to be Christians are affiliated to organised churches and denominations. Therefore, 'affiliated Christians' are those known to the churches or known to the clergy (usually by names and addresses) and claimed in their statistics, that is, those enrolled on the churches' books or records, with totals that can be substantiated. This usually means all known baptised Christians and their children, and other adherents; it is sometimes termed the 'total Christian community' (because affiliated Christians are those who are not primarily individual Christians but who primarily belong to the corporate community of Christ), or 'inclusive membership' (because affiliated Christians are church members). This definition of 'Christians' is what the churches usually mean by the term (and thus the *WCD*), and statistics on such affiliated Christians are what the churches themselves collect and publish. In all countries, it may be assumed with confidence that the churches know better than the state how many Christians are affiliated to them. This therefore indicates a second measure of the total Christians that is quite independent of the first (government census figures of professing Christians).

Children

The family is by far the most important instrumentality through which individuals acquire personal, cultural and social self-identification. In consequence, children of church members are more likely to remain members than those whose parents are not church members. Children of ardent and practising Christians usually are, to the extent that their years permit, ardent and practising Christians. However, many churches do not enumerate children under 15 years. One reason is that it has been widely noted that most conversion crises occur in the 13–20-year age group in Christian families or in majority Christian contexts. On this view, therefore, children who have not yet reached 15 cannot reasonably be expected to be practising and believing Christians. The *WCD* takes the opposite view: children and infants also can properly be called Christians, and can actively and regularly (to the extent of their ability) practise the Christian faith. Consequently, where Christian denominations do not count children in their membership rolls, their membership is reported in our adult category. A total community figure is calculated (in the absence of any additional information from the denomination) by adding in the average number of children reported in United Nations statistics for the given country. Thus, the total community figures are comparable from one denomination to the next whether or not they count children in their membership.

Choice of Best Data Available
Religious demography must attempt to be comprehensive. In certain countries where no hard statistical data or reliable surveys are available, researchers have to rely on the informed estimates of experts in the area and subject. Researchers make no detailed attempt at a critique of each nation's censuses and polls or each church's statistical operations. After examining what is available, researchers then select the best data available until such time as better data come into existence. In addition, there are a number of areas of religious life where it is impossible to obtain accurate statistics, usually because of state opposition to particular tradition(s). Thus it will probably never be possible to get exact numbers of, for example, atheists in Indonesia or Bahá'í in Iran. Where such information is necessary, reasonable and somewhat conservative estimates are made.

Reconciling Discrepancies in Survey Data
There are post-survey strategies that help general population surveys better reflect the actual composition of a particular country. For instance, if in a survey of 1,000 people, 60% were women and 40% were men, but we know that women and men are each 50% of the country's total population based on a recent census, then each woman's response on the general population survey would be weighted down by a factor of 500/600 and each man's response would be weighted up by a factor of 500/400. Such adjustments are called weighting.

Other adjustments made to general population surveys may require taking into account that they are meant to be representative of only adult populations. Therefore their results require adjustments, particularly if some religious groups have more children than others in the same country. This requires either a complete roster of members of each household or some other way to estimate the number of children living in the household with the adults. When a complete roster is unavailable, most estimates of religious affiliation of children assume that they have the same religion as their one of their parents (usually assumed by demographers to be the religion of the mother). Differences in fertility rates between religious groups are particularly useful in estimating religious differentials among children. This is because demographic projections include children, who will increase the size of their religious community. It may introduce some bias to the degree that the father's religion is more likely to be the religion of the children than that of the mother.

Example: Coptic Church in Egypt

At times, the results from government censuses and information from religious communities can be strikingly different. For example, in Egypt, where the vast majority of the population is Muslim, government censuses taken every 10 years have shown consistently for the past 100 years that a declining share of the population declare themselves as or profess to be Christians. In the most recent census, some 5% identified as Christian. However, church estimates point to a percentage figure three times larger (15%). This discrepancy may be due to overestimates by the churches or attributed, at least in part, to social pressure on some Christians to record themselves as Muslims. Further, according to news reports, some Egyptian Christians have complained that they are listed on official identity cards as Muslims. It also might be that church reports include Egyptian Christians working as expatriates outside of Egypt, while the census does not, or that the churches simply overestimate their numbers.

Such a lack of clarity is compounded by media reports and even Egyptian government announcements repeatedly claiming that Christians make up 10% or more of the country's approximately 80 million people, despite the fact that the census repeatedly reports only 5%. The highest share of Christians found in an Egyptian census was in 1927 (8.3%). Figures for Egyptian Christians declined in each subsequent census, with Christians seemingly making up 5.7% of the Egyptian population in 1996. The report from the most recent census, conducted in 2006, does not, however, provide data on religious affiliation, but a sample of the 2006 census data is available through the Integrated Public Use Microdata Series, International (IPUMS). They sample the same Christian share (about 5%) as the latest Egyptian Demographic and Health Survey, with a sample size of 16,527 women aged 15–49 years.

According to the Pew Forum's analysis of Global Restrictions on Religion (see www.pewforum.org), Egypt has very high scores for government restrictions on religion as well as high scores for social hostilities involving religion. These factors might lead some Christians to be cautious about revealing their identity. Regardless of the actual number, it is very likely that Christians are declining as a proportion of Egypt's population, even if their absolute numbers are not falling. On the one hand, Christian fertility in Egypt has been lower than Muslim fertility. On the other, it is possible that large numbers of Christians have left the country, although a 2012 study by the Pew Forum on the religious affiliation of migrants around the world has not found evidence of an especially large Egyptian Christian diaspora.

Dates of Statistics

It is important, in changing situations, to know the exact date (year, perhaps also month and sometimes even day) to which particular statistics apply. This methodology compares government statistics on religion with statistics from religious communities themselves; but in doing so, it must be remembered that a government census (or a public-opinion poll) is almost always taken on a single, known day, whereas, by contrast, religious statistics are compiled over a lengthy period – perhaps three, four or even five years from the local grassroots counting of heads to final compilation of totals by a large denomination or church. Denominational totals published in 2020 therefore probably refer to the situation in 2017, 2016 or even 2015.

Counting Pentecostals

Three types of Pentecostals

For the purpose of understanding the diverse global phenomenon of Pentecostalism, it is useful to divide the movement into three kinds, or types. First are denominational Pentecostals, organised into denominations in the early part of the twentieth century. Second are Charismatics, individuals in the mainline denominations (primarily after the mid-twentieth century). Third are Independent Charismatics, those who broke free of denominational Pentecostalism or mainline denominations to form their own networks. A more detailed treatment can be found in Todd M. Johnson and Gina A. Zurlo, *Introducing Spirit-Empowered Christianity: The Global Pentecostal and Charismatic Movement in the 21st Century* (Tulsa, OK: Oral Roberts University Press, 2020).

Pentecostals (Type 1)

Pentecostals are defined as Christians who are members of the explicitly Pentecostal denominations whose major characteristic is a new experience of the energising ministry of the Holy Spirit that most other Christians have considered to be highly unusual. This is interpreted as a rediscovery of the spiritual gifts of New Testament times and their restoration to ordinary Christian life and ministry. Classical Pentecostalism usually is held to have begun in the United States in 1901, although most scholars have moved to a 'multiple origins' theory of the birth of modern Pentecostalism, emphasising early activity outside of the Western World. For a brief period, Pentecostalism expected to remain an interdenominational movement within the existing churches, but from 1909 onwards its members increasingly were ejected from mainline bodies and so forced to begin new organised denominations.

Pentecostal denominations hold the distinctive teachings that all Christians should seek a post-conversion religious experience called baptism in the Holy Spirit and that a Spirit-baptised believer may receive one or more of the supernatural gifts known in the early church: the ability to prophesy; to practise divine healing through prayer; to speak (glossolalia), interpret or sing in tongues; to sing in the Spirit, dance in the Spirit, pray with upraised hands; to receive dreams, visions, words of wisdom, words of knowledge; to discern spirits; and to perform miracles, power encounters, exorcisms (casting out demons), resuscitations, deliverances, or other signs and wonders.

From 1906 onwards, the hallmark of explicitly Pentecostal denominations, by comparison with Holiness/Perfectionist denominations, has been the single addition of speaking in other tongues as the 'initial evidence' of one's having received the baptism of the Holy Spirit, whether or not one subsequently experiences regularly the gift of tongues. Most Pentecostal denominations teach that tongues-speaking is mandatory for all members, but in reality today not all members have practised this gift, either initially or as an ongoing experience. Pentecostals are defined here as all associated with explicitly Pentecostal denominations that identify themselves in explicitly Pentecostal terms, or with other denominations that as a whole are phenomenologically Pentecostal in teaching and practice.

Among Protestants (coded as 'P-') are Pentecostal denominations such as the Assemblies of God. Sub-categories of Oneness, Baptistic, Holiness, Perfectionist and Apostolic were retained from earlier research. Each minor tradition within Pentecostalism is considered to be 100% Pentecostal (all members of Pentecostal denominations are counted as Pentecostals).

Charismatics (Type 2)

Charismatics are defined as Christians affiliated to non-Pentecostal denominations (Anglican, Protestant, Catholic, Orthodox) who receive the experiences above in what has been termed the Charismatic movement. The Charismatic movement's roots go back to early Pentecostalism, but its rapid expansion has been mainly since 1960 (later called the Charismatic renewal). Charismatics usually describe themselves as having been 'renewed in the Spirit' and as experiencing the Spirit's supernatural and miraculous and energising power. They remain within, and form organised renewal groups within, their older mainline non-Pentecostal denominations (instead of leaving to join Pentecostal denominations). They demonstrate any or all of the *charismata pneumatika* (gifts of the Spirit), including signs and wonders (but with glossolalia regarded as optional).

Type 2 recognises the existence of Pentecostal individuals within the Anglican, Roman Catholic, Orthodox and Protestant traditions. These are designated 'Charismatic' and evaluated by country as Catholic Charismatics, Anglican Charismatics and so on, designating renewal within an existing tradition. For example, the beginning of the Charismatic movement in Anglican churches is described by Episcopal priest Dennis Bennett in *Nine O'Clock in the Morning* (Alachua, FL: Bridge-Logos, 1970). Traditions are assessed to determine what percentage of adherents identify themselves as Charismatics, ranging from 0% to 100%. Self-identification percentages for Charismatics were calculated by contacting renewal agencies working within denominations.

Independent Charismatics (Type 3)

While the classification and chronology of the first two types is straightforward, there are thousands of churches and movements that 'resemble' the first two types but do not fit their definitions. These constitute a third type and often predate the first two types. For lack of a better term, these are called 'Independent Charismatics'. Part of the rationale for this term is the fact that they are largely found in the Independent category of the overall taxonomy of Christians. Thus, Type 3 includes Pentecostal or semi-Pentecostal members of the 250-year-old Independent movement of Christians, primarily in the global South, of churches begun without reference to Western Christianity. These Indigenous movements, although not all explicitly Pentecostal, nevertheless have the main features of Pentecostalism. In addition, since Azusa Street, thousands of schismatic or other Independent Charismatic churches have come out of Type 1 Pentecostals and Type 2 Charismatic movements. They consist of Christians who, unrelated to or no longer related to the Pentecostal or Charismatic denominations, have become filled with the Spirit, or empowered by the Spirit and have experienced the Spirit's ministry (although usually without recognising a baptism in the Spirit separate from conversion); who exercise gifts of the Spirit (with much less emphasis on tongues, as optional or even absent or unnecessary) and emphasise signs and wonders, supernatural miracles and power encounters; but also do not identify themselves as either Pentecostals (Type 1) or Charismatics (Type 2). In a number of countries they exhibit Pentecostal and Charismatic phenomena but combine this with rejection of Pentecostal terminology. These believers frequently are identified by their leadership as Independent, Post-denominationalist, Restorationist, Radical, Neo-Apostolic or 'Third Wave.'

Thus, the third type is Independent Charismatics (also known in the literature as neo-Charismatics or neo-Pentecostals), who are not in Protestant Pentecostal denominations (Type 1), nor are they individual Charismatics in the traditional churches (Type 2). Type 3 is the most diverse of the three types and ranges from house churches in China to African Initiated Churches to white-led Charismatic networks in the Western world. It includes Pentecostals who had split off from established Protestant denominations (Type 1) and who were then labelled as Independent. Independent churches formed by Charismatic leaders (Type 2) who founded new congregations and networks are also included. Some Independent Charismatics speak in tongues, but healing and power evangelism are more prominent in this type than in the other two.

Three types together

One difficulty that has plagued all researchers and historians of Pentecostalism is what to call the overarching movement. Some have used 'Pentecostalism' or 'Global Pentecostalism', while others have used 'Charismatic'. Still others have used 'Pentecostal and Charismatic'. David Barrett originally used the lengthy phrase 'the Pentecostal and Charismatic Renewal of the Holy Spirit', which he later shortened to 'Renewal'. He then coined the term 'Renewalist' to refer to all three waves or types. For the purposes of this series, we use the term 'Pentecostals/Charismatics' to refer to all three types.

A demographic overview of Pentecostals/Charismatics (all types) illustrates the complexities of both the spread of the movement across the countries of the world and the striking diversity of the churches themselves. While current ways of understanding Pentecostals, Charismatics and Independent Charismatics reveal a global movement of immense proportions, perspectives on classification, counting and assessment of the movement are likely to continue to evolve. In the meantime, hundreds of millions of Christians across all traditions will continue to participate in the movement – bringing vitality in some denominations and schism in others. They will also promote social transformation in some communities and show little participation in others. What is certain is that, for the foreseeable future, Christianity as a whole will continue to experience the growth pains of this global phenomenon.

Counting Evangelicals

Any effective and comprehensive method for counting Evangelicals must take into consideration denominational affiliation, self-identification and theology. The results of counting Evangelicals are directly related to denominational membership figures. Strictly speaking, denominational affiliation means official membership on a church roll.

Method 1: Individuals in denominations that are 100% Evangelical

The first category of Evangelicals includes individuals who are found in denominations that are coded 100% Evangelical. That is, membership of an Evangelical council (national, regional or global) is assessed for every denomination and those denominations that have Evangelical affiliations are classed as 100% Evangelical. Consequently, 100% of the members of these denominations are considered Evangelical. Using this method alone, the *WCD* estimates there are 200 million Evangelicals in the world. As of 2020, the nine largest 100% Evangelical denominations in the world were all Protestant, and the five largest 100% Evangelical denominations were found in Brazil, Ethiopia, Nigeria and Indonesia, reflecting the global scope of the movement.

Method 2: Individuals who self-identify as Evangelical in non-100% Evangelical denominations

For those denominations not identified as 100% Evangelical, an estimate is made of the percentage (0–99%) of members who self-identify as Evangelical. Self-identification percentages for Evangelicals in non-100% Evangelical denominations are verified by contacting key figures within each denomination, and each estimate is sourced in documentation housed at the Center for the Study of Global Christianity.

Adding together figures from both 100% and partially Evangelical denominations gives a total of 386 million Evangelicals worldwide. Looking at both 100% and non-100% Evangelical denominations reveals that the movement has a significant presence beyond Western Protestantism. Some of the denominations with the most Evangelicals are within Anglicanism in the global South, such as the Anglican Church of Nigeria and the Church of Uganda. Chinese house churches (classified as Independents) taken together constitute the denomination with the third most Evangelicals globally. The United Kingdom (the Church of England) and the United States (the Southern Baptist Convention), however, are still important locations of the movement.

Method 3: Evangelicals not affiliated with any denomination (Unaffiliated Evangelicals)

To date, no studies have addressed directly how many Evangelicals are denominationally unaffiliated. However, two well known realities (in Western Christianity in particular) appear to provide indirect evidence for this undocumented trend. The first is reflected in recent research indicating the unaffiliated are not uniformly non-religious. The Pew Research Center reported that 68% of America's unaffiliated believe in God. It is reasonable to assume that a notable proportion of Christians is among the ranks of the unaffiliated by virtue of Christianity being the largest religion in many of the countries studied. The second reality is the acknowledged fact that unaffiliated Christians often attend and are active in churches, including Evangelical churches, without becoming official members. These unaffiliated Christians profess allegiance and commitment to Christ but do not maintain church affiliation.

Dynamics of Change in Religious Populations

The question of how and why the number of religious adherents changes over time is critical to the study of international religious demography. It is more complex than simply 'counting heads' via births and deaths – a well established area in quantitative sociological studies – but in addition involves the multifaceted areas of religious conversion and migration. The migration of religious people has only in the past few years become a more researched area of demographic study, and issues surrounding religious conversion continue to be under-represented in the field. Data on religion from a wide range of sources – including from the religious communities themselves, as well as governments and scholars – must be employed to understand the total scope of religious affiliation. Given data on a particular religion from two separate points in time, the question can be raised, 'What are the dynamics by which the number of adherents changes over time?' The dynamics of change in religious affiliation can be reduced to three sets of empirical population data that together enable enumeration of the increase or decrease in adherents over time. To measure overall change, these three sets can be defined as follows: (1) births minus deaths; (2) converts to minus converts from; and (3) immigrants minus emigrants. The first variable in each of these three sets (births, converts to, immigrants) measures increase, whereas the second (deaths, converts from, emigrants) measures decrease. All future (and current) projections of religious affiliation, within any subset of the global population (normally a country or region), will account for these dynamics, and the changes themselves are dependent on these dynamics.

Births

The primary mechanism of global religious demographic change is (live) births. Children are almost always counted as having the religion of their parents (as is the law in Norway, for example). In simple terms, if populations that are predominantly Muslim, for example, have more children on average than those that are predominantly Christian or Hindu, then over time (all other things being equal) Muslims will become an increasingly larger percentage of that population. This means that the relative size of a religious population has a close statistical relationship to birth rates.

Deaths

Even as births increase their memberships, religious communities experience constant loss through the deaths of members. Although this often includes tragic, unanticipated deaths of younger members, it most frequently affects the elderly members. Thus, changes in health care and technology can positively impact religious communities if members live longer.

Births minus deaths/total fertility rate

The change over time in any given population is most simply expressed as the number of births into the community minus the number of deaths out of it. Many religious communities around the world experience little else in the dynamics of their growth or decline. Detailed projections rely on a number of estimated measures, including life expectancy, population age structures and the total fertility rate. This means that any attempt to understand the dynamics of religious affiliation must be based firmly on demographic projections of births and deaths.

Converts to

It is a common observation that individuals (or even whole villages or communities) change allegiance from one religion to another (or to no religion at all). Unfortunately, one of the problems in studying conversion is the paucity of information on it. Reliable data on conversions are hard to obtain, for a number of reasons. Although some national censuses ask people about their religion, they do not directly ask whether people have converted to their present faith. A few cross-national surveys do contain questions about religious switching, but even in those surveys it is difficult to assess whether more people leave a religion than enter it. In some countries, legal and social consequences make conversion difficult, and survey respondents might be reluctant to speak honestly about the topic. In particular, Hinduism is for many Hindus (as is Islam for many Muslims) not just a religion but also an ethnic or cultural identity that does not depend on whether a person actively practises the faith. Thus even non-practising or secular Hindus may still consider themselves, and be viewed by their neighbours, as Hindus.

Converts from

Conversion to a new religion, as mentioned above, also involves conversion from a previous one. Thus, a convert to Islam is, at the same time, a convert from another religion. In the twentieth and twenty-first centuries, the most converts from Christianity were and continue to be found largely among those in the Western world who have decided to be agnostics or atheists.

Converts to minus converts from

The net conversion rate in a population is calculated by subtracting the number of 'converts from' from the number of 'converts to'. Conversion to and conversion from will likely continue to play a role in changing religious demographics in the future.

Immigrants

Equally important at the international level is how the movement of people across national borders impacts religious affiliation. Once religious communities are established through immigration they often grow vigorously (for a time) via high birth rates.

Emigrants

In a reversal of nineteenth-century European colonisation of Africa, Asia and parts of the Americas, the late twentieth century witnessed waves of emigration of people from these regions to the Western world. The impact on religious affiliation is significant.

Immigrants minus emigrants

In the twenty-first century, international migration continues to have a significant impact on the religious composition of individual countries. One can try to anticipate the way in which expected immigration and emigration trends will affect a country's population over time. One profound change to be expected is the increase of religious pluralism in almost every country of the world. Increasing religious pluralism is not always welcomed and can be seen as a political, cultural, national or religious threat.

The six dynamics discussed above determine changes in religious demographics. Gains are the result of three positive dynamics: births, conversions to, and immigration. Losses are the result of three negative dynamics: deaths, conversions from, and emigration. The net change in religious demographics is the result of gains minus losses. The balance of dynamics can be reflected in any proportions (for example, mainly births for gains, mainly conversions from for losses) but can also be represented by pairing the gains and losses by type: births versus deaths, converts to versus converts from, and immigrants versus emigrants. In each case, the net change (either positive or negative) will be the difference between the two. This means that any attempt to understand religious affiliation in the past, present or future must be firmly based on demographic dynamics. A proper awareness of these dynamics and their significance is thus vital both for undertaking and for interpreting studies of the future of religion.

Measuring Growth Rates

The rates of growth, increase, decrease or decline of membership in many congregations can readily be measured from their annually reported statistics. This has been done by obtaining the statistics for two different years, where possible five years apart (to minimise the effects of roll-cleaning and other annual irregularities), usually 2000–5 and 2010–15, and working out the average annual growth rate as a percentage. Great care must be taken in such computations to ensure that the statistics used are measuring exactly the same entity (especially geographically) for each of the two years concerned. Growth, as a percentage increase or decrease per year, must be measured by dividing any annual increase by the identical category of total. Thus a church, for example, in a particular country with 500,000 total adherents (including children) in 2010 which grows to 600,000 total adherents (including children) in 2015 shows an increase of 600,000 minus 500,000 = 100,000, which divided by 5 = 20,000 a year, which divided by the mean membership of 550,000 gives an increase rate of 3.64% per year. In practice, the methodology follows a more accurate method by using the 1970 to 2015 figures for each denomination to arrive at average annual growth rates.

There are different ways of measuring the growth of a religious body. First, one can measure either adults only, or total community including children. Secondly, the growth rate of a church or religious grouping can be measured over a single day, or a month, a year, a decade, or 50 years – and all will yield differing results. This survey is concerned primarily to measure long-term rates. A growth rate measured for a specific religious body over a two- or three-year period may not be sustained over a decade.

Projecting Religious Populations

The starting point of future studies is natural growth of the total population of the country or region of interest, using demographic projections as a baseline. Three major areas beyond natural growth are utilised to improve the projections. First, birth and death rates vary among religious communities within a particular country. Secondly, increasing numbers of people are likely to change their religious affiliations in the future. Thirdly, immigration and emigration trends will impact a country's population over time. The highest-quality projections for religious communities are built on cohort-component projections that use differential rates for each religion: age-specific fertility rates by religion, age structure in five-year age-and-sex cohorts by religion, migration rates by religion, and mortality by religion.

Unfortunately, this kind of detail is not yet available for many countries (half of censuses do not ask a question about religion). Fortunately, the process of filling in missing data using demographic and smaller-scale general population surveys is underway, and as these data become available through the Pew–Templeton Global Religious Futures Project, researchers will have access to these data through the *World Religion Database*, where they will be archived in full, with summary results available at the Pew Forum's website. In the meantime, projections cannot solely rely on the cohort-component method. Instead, they use a hybrid projection method. First, the 2020 religious composition of each country is established as the baseline. Then, utilising the United Nations medium variant cohort-component projections of populations for five-year periods up to 2050, future religious shares are modestly adjusted from the 2020 baseline. Adjustments are based on analysis of past differential growth rates of religious groups, factoring in historical patterns of religious switching and possible future attenuation of past trends. Finally, these projections take into account how immigrants might alter the future religious composition of country populations.

Ethno-linguistic People Groups

A problem for social science research is the lack of available survey and polling data in non-Western countries. While the United States and many European countries have a long history of engaging in this kind of research, many often more underdeveloped countries can be difficult to access and/or speak languages difficult for Western researchers. The *WCD*'s method directly addresses this methodological challenge through its additional taxonomy of the world's ethnic groups, which are paired with religious statistics.

A 'peoples' taxonomy must take into account both ethnicity and language. The approach taken in 'Ethnosphere' in Part 8 of the *World Christian Encyclopedia*, 2nd edition (2001) was to match ethnic codes with language codes, which produced over 13,700 distinct ethno-linguistic peoples. Not all combinations of ethnicity and language are possible, but nevertheless every person in the world can be categorised as belonging to an ethno-linguistic people (mutually exclusive). For example, there are ethnic Kazaks who speak Kazak as their mother tongue and ethnic Kazaks who speak Russian as their mother tongue. These, then, are two separate ethno-linguistic peoples.

The work of determining the religious breakdown of ethno-linguistic peoples was begun in the 1970s in Africa, where many Christian churches reported the ethnic breakdown of their congregations. Utilising data gathered by religious bodies and in government censuses, estimates of religious affiliation for all peoples was completed in the mid-1990s and published in the second edition of the *World Christian Encyclopedia*. These data continue to be updated and published in the *World Christian Database* and *World Religion Database*.

Each distinct ethno-linguistic group in a country is assigned varying shares of the 18 categories of religion. For example, the Japanese in Japan are reported as 56% Mahayana Buddhist, 23% various New religionist, 10% agnostic, 3% atheist, 2% Shinto and 1% Christian. Each group is traced throughout the world with the assumption that whatever their religious breakdown is in their home country will be the same abroad. This allows researchers to locate Christian people in predominantly non-Christian countries. For example, the *WCD* reports that Pakistan – a Muslim-majority country – is also home to over 2 million Christians. While Christians are found among Muslim-majority people groups (for example, Punjabi at 4% Christian), they are also present in the country as ex-pats, such as French (65% Christian) and British (70% Christian).

Conclusion

There are a variety of issues related to finding and choosing the best data sources of religious affiliation. Censuses are generally accepted as the most reliable, but there are times when they fail to present the full picture, for example because they omit certain regions of a country or because they do not ask clear or detailed questions about religion. General-population surveys can often fill the gap, but, depending on their quality, they may also have some bias. At times, religious groups may have very different estimates of their sizes than are found by censuses and surveys, but for some types of data, such as denominations of Protestantism, estimates by the groups may be the best information available. Finally, for religions such as Islam, Hinduism, Buddhism and Judaism, subgroup information is routinely missing from censuses and surveys. Estimates for the subgroups of these religions often rely on indirect measures, such as ethnic groups likely to adhere to a particular subgroup or expert analysis of multiple ethnological and anthropological sources. Thus, it is important to take into consideration many different kinds of data in order to arrive at the best estimate of a particular religious population in a country.

Index